KAPLAN) BAR REVIEW

MEE Subjects Outline Materials 2019

Course Companion

Special thanks to: Lauren Allen, Esq., Adam Feren, Esq., Christopher Fromm, Esq., Elizabeth Horowitz, Esq., Steven Marietti, Esq., Adam Maze, Esq., Nicole Pirog, Esq., Mike Power, Esq., Tammi Rice, Esq., Shalom Sands, Esq., Lisa Young, Esq.

Published by Kaplan Publishing, a division of Kaplan, Inc.
750 Third Avenue
New York, NY 10017

10 9 8 7 6 5 4 3 2 1

ISBN: 978-1-5062-5137-0

MASTER TABLE OF CONTENTS

WILLS

Agency

TABLE OF CONTENTS

I. THE NATURE AND SCOPE OF AGENCY

A. In General

1. The law of agency is concerned with how the actions made on behalf of one person consequently create obligations for another person. A variety of considerations can make it beneficial to have another act in one's stead: convenience, expertise, or the need for a stand-in to make decisions in the case of incapacity. Agency relationships occur routinely in society, in both formal and informal matters, and in commercial and personal matters.

2. **Agency** is a fiduciary relationship that arises when one person, the **principal**, manifests assent to another person, the **agent**, that the agent shall act on the principal's behalf subject to the principal's control, and that the agent manifests assent or otherwise consents so to act.

   EXAMPLE: X hires a babysitter to watch his children.

   EXAMPLE: Y retains a headhunter to recruit potential employees.

   EXAMPLE: Z signs a power of attorney granting a relative the ability to sign contracts on her behalf.

   a. The **person** may manifest itself in many forms, including [Restatement (Third) of Agency § 1.04(5)]:
      (1) an individual;
      (2) an organization or association with the capacity to possess rights and incur obligations;
      (3) a government, political subdivision, or entity created by the government; or
      (4) any other entity that has the legal capacity to possess rights and incur obligations.

B. Consequences of Agency Relationship

1. There are four consequences of entering into an agency relationship:
   a. duties arise between the principal and agent;
   b. the agent has the power to bind the principal in contract and act on his behalf, without the principal having to act personally, but under the principal's control;
   c. liability is imposed on the principal for the agent's actions in tort; and
   d. knowledge of the agent is imputed to the principal.

C. Types of Relationship

1. An agency relationship can take many forms, the most common of which are master-servant (employer-employee) and employer-independent contractor.

2. **Master and Servant (Employer and Employee)**
   a. The master-servant relationship is an employment relationship in which the master has the right to control the details of the physical conduct of

the servant in the performance of the service, not only as to the result, but also as to the means to be used to achieve the result.

b. Under the doctrine of *respondeat superior*, a master is generally liable for his servant's torts committed within the scope of his employment.

EXAMPLE: Professor Hurt is an employee of the University of Illinois; a law firm associate is an employee of the law firm.

3. **Employer and Independent Contractor**

a. The employer-independent contractor relationship is an employment relationship.

b. Unlike the master in the master-servant relationship, however, the employer has no right to control the details of the performance of the independent contractor.

c. The distinction between the master-servant relationship and the employer-independent contractor relationship lies in the right to control—the degree to which an employer could intervene in the control of an employee's manner of performance.

EXAMPLE: Professor Hurt is a consultant for a U.S. Attorney; an aging real estate magnate hires an attorney to do her estate planning.

II. CREATION OF THE AGENCY RELATIONSHIP

A. Formation

1. An agency relationship is formed by the principal granting authority to the agent to act for him.

2. There must be a manifestation of the principal's intention to grant authority.

   a. Such manifestation may be express (written or oral), implied, verbal, or by conduct.

B. Required Elements of the Relationship

1. Both parties must assent to the agency [Restatement (Third) of Agency § 1.03]. An agent can neither force an unwilling principal, nor be forced to be an agent against his will.

2. The agent must agree to act on behalf of the principal. The agent may be compensated (this is optional), but he is compensated primarily to advance the interests of the principal.

3. The agent must act under the control of the principal.

C. Capacity

1. **Principal**

   a. Any person who has the capacity to effect his own transactions has the capacity to appoint an agent to act on his behalf [Restatement (Third) of Agency § 3.04].

      (1) An incompetent may not act as a principal. Thus, a minor generally cannot act as a principal except when contracting for necessaries.

      (2) A corporation may act as a principal only as to matters within its corporate powers.

2. **Agent**

   a. Generally, any person with minimum mental capacity may act as an agent.

      (1) Accordingly, both minors and incompetents may act as agents.

   b. The agent will be endowed with the same capacity as the principal.

   c. One may not be an agent for two adverse parties to a transaction unless both parties are fully advised and give their consent. The burden is upon the agent to show full disclosure and consent.

D. Proof of Agency

1. Existence of an agency relationship may be established by circumstantial evidence.

2. Relevant factors include:

   a. the situation of each party; and

   b. their words and actions.

3. The existence of an agency relationship is ordinarily a question of fact for the jury, and the burden of proof rests with the party asserting the relationship.

   a. It is to be determined from all the evidence, direct or circumstantial, and must be proved by a fair preponderance of the evidence.

   b. It will not be implied solely from the showing of a family relationship.

4. While an alleged agent may be called as a witness to testify to facts from which an agency relationship may be found, he may not testify to his conclusions on the matter.

   a. Statements of the alleged agent made out of court are inadmissible to prove agency.

   b. Such statements are not competent as admissions by the principal, binding upon him, in the absence of independent evidence of the authority of the alleged agent to make them.

5. Parties cannot disclaim an agency relationship if, in fact, one exists, even if the disclaimer is contained in a contract between the parties.

6. **Presumption of Agency in Motor Vehicle Operation**

   a. At common law, the owner of a motor vehicle is not presumed liable for the negligent use of the vehicle by another.

   b. A number of states, however, have enacted statutes which create a presumption that the driver of a motor vehicle is operating as the agent of the owner. In such a case, the owner of the automobile is liable for the negligence of any person operating the vehicle with the express or implied permission of the owner.

      (1) If the presumption of agency is rebutted, the owner may be held directly liable for his own negligence in entrusting the car to an unfit person.

E. **Types of Principals**

   1. **Disclosed, Undisclosed, and Partially Disclosed Principals**

      a. A principal is **disclosed** if, at the time of the transaction, the third party has notice that the agent is acting for a principal and has notice of the principal's identity.

         EXAMPLE: A potential customer enters a car dealership that has a sign outside stating that it is "ABC Automotive of Naperville," and he is met by a salesperson that assists him. It is clear that the salesperson is an agent of the disclosed principal, "ABC Automotive."

      b. If the third party has no knowledge of the existence or identity of a principal, the principal is **undisclosed**.

         EXAMPLE: Donald Trump wants to purchase real estate on Michigan Avenue, but is concerned that potential sellers would raise the price if they knew he was the buyer. Because Trump fears that his identity cannot be concealed for very long, he instructs an agent to say nothing about the principal's existence and to negotiate a deal as if the agent were the ultimate purchaser.

c. A **partially disclosed** principal is one whose existence, but not identity, is known to the third party.

EXAMPLE: The result is the same as in the example above, except that because Trump is concerned that possible sellers would raise the price if they knew he was the buyer, he instructs his agent to make it clear that the agent is acting on behalf of a reputable businessman whose existence is disclosed, but whose identity is not.

d. An agent who enters into a contract for an undisclosed or partially disclosed principal is personally liable on the contract.

e. An agent for a fully disclosed principal does not ordinarily incur personal liability.

f. When a third party learns of the identity of a principal, he must elect to go after either the agent or the principal, but not both.

F. Types of Agents

1. General and Special Agents

a. The authority conferred by a principal on his agent may be general in nature (a **general agency**), or limited in scope (a **special agency**).

b. **General Agent**

(1) A **general agent** is employed by a principal to transact all of his business of a particular kind.

EXAMPLE: A principal may employ a salesman to sell his goods of a particular type, or a broker to negotiate all of his contracts of a particular description.

EXAMPLE: A is hired by P to manage his department store; A will have numerous responsibilities in connection with that position and is given the authority to execute all of them.

(2) The authority of a general agent to perform all things usual in the line of business in which he is employed cannot be limited by any private order or direction (secret instructions), not known to the party dealing with him.

c. **Special Agent**

(1) A **special agent** is employed by a principal specifically for one transaction.

(2) A special agent has no authority to bind his principal beyond the terms of the specific authority conferred upon him by the agreement for employment.

EXAMPLE: A home seller engages a real estate agent to sell his home, but to perform no other tasks on his behalf. The agent is a special agent, because his responsibility is to complete only one specific transaction.

      (3) **Types of Special Agents**

          (a) A **real estate agent** is a special agent who may be either an agent or a broker licensed by the state to conduct sales of real property. A listing broker merely has authority to promote property, while a selling agent possesses apparent authority to bind a seller.

              1) When a real estate agent unwillingly becomes agent of both the seller and buyer, liability issues may arise.

          (b) A **salesperson** is an agent who sells chattels and warrant goods under the Uniform Commercial Code, although he usually may not modify terms of a sale.

          (c) An **auctioneer** is a special sales agent with authority to sell goods within the auction's terms, usually to the highest bidder. The auctioneer is the agent of the seller and, as a result, warrants title to the goods.

2. **Subagents**

    a. **Subagents** are persons entitled to do work for the original agent in the relationship. As a consequence, a new agency relationship is created, with the original agent becoming the principal to the subagent.

    b. Where the principal has authorized the agent to appoint subagents, the subagent has the same responsibilities to the principal as the original agent does.

    c. Any breaches of duty by the subagent will be imputed to the agent.

    d. If the subagent has been appointed without the principal's authority, no agency relationship exists between the principal and the subagent.

    EXAMPLE: A property owner hires a contractor to construct a new building, and the contractor, in turn, hires a plumbing company to install the pipes and plumbing fixtures. The plumbing company is the sub-agent and is working for the contractor, and is therefore an agent of the general contractor (the original agent), but not an agent of the principal.

3. **Gratuitous Agents**

    a. A **gratuitous agent** agrees to perform all the duties of an agent without compensation [Restatement (Third) of Agency §1.04(4)].

    b. Although agents generally must be compensated for services provided, consideration is not required in order for there to be an agency relationship; the parties may contractually agree to such an arrangement.

III. DUTIES, RIGHTS, AND REMEDIES

A. Duties of Principal to Agent

1. Absent an agreement to the contrary, the principal is obligated to his agent to:

   a. compensate the agent for services rendered, either for an agreed-upon amount or for the reasonable value of those services;

   b. reimburse the agent for reasonable expenses incurred by him in the scope of his agency;

   c. indemnify and exonerate the agent for any liability that results from his good-faith performance of his duties;

   d. cooperate with the agent in the performance of his duties; and

   e. exercise due care toward the agent.

> **NOTE** Duties begin when the agency relationship is created, and end when the agency relationship is terminated.

2. **Agent's Remedies for Principal's Breach**

   a. The agent may seek the usual remedies available for breach of an agency contract.

   b. The agent retains a lien on any property of the principal of which he has lawful possession, but more than mere custody.

   c. The agent may set off any money owed to him by the principal against monies collected on behalf of the principal.

   d. The principal may use any of the following defenses in the event of his breach:

      (1) Statute of Frauds;

      (2) illegality;

      (3) the agent's disobedience; or

      (4) the agent's contributory negligence (such as in a tort claim).

B. Duties of Agent to Principal

1. **Duty of Care**

   a. Absent an agreement to the contrary, the agent is obligated to show a duty of care to the principal, with a duty to:

      (1) perform the contract and render services with reasonable care;

      (2) obey the principal in all reasonable directions, outside illegal or unethical orders;

      (3) act with the care, competence, and diligence normally exercised by agents in similar circumstances, and if the agent possesses a higher level of skill, to exercise that level of skill; and

      (4) indemnify the principal against loss caused by the agent's wrongful behavior or failure to act with reasonable care.

2. **Duty of Loyalty**

   a. The agent has a duty of loyalty to the principal arising from the fiduciary character of the relationship.

   b. **Self-Dealing**

      (1) An agent who acts for his own benefit, instead of that of the principal, is said to be **self-dealing**.

      (2) An agent must prefer the interests of the principal to his own or those of others in acting for the principal.

      EXAMPLE: Stealing is a form of self-dealing. Taking a box of pens from the law firm's supply closet would thus be self-dealing.

   c. **Usurpation of Business Opportunity**

      (1) An agent may not usurp a business opportunity belonging to the principal.

      (2) A **business opportunity** is one that is so closely related to the principal's business that it could be deemed incidental to that business.

         (a) When a business opportunity is so clearly different that there is no doubt that the principal would not want the opportunity, then the agent is not required to offer the opportunity to the principal.

      (3) An employee may take personal advantage of a business opportunity only if the employer knows and consents.

      EXAMPLE: Dana is an associate at a law firm. Her friend from law school calls and wants her to help him in a custody battle, but he does not want to pay her firm's hourly rates. He offers her $500 to do it in her spare time.

      EXAMPLE: Greg's law firm sends him to look for new office space for the firm. He finds an excellent, undervalued space that would be great for the business his spouse is starting.

   d. **Duty of Confidentiality**

      (1) An agent may not use confidential information obtained from the principal to the detriment of the principal, even if the information has not been obtained through his agency.

         (a) However, an ex-employee may use skills learned on the job in later employment, and he may also solicit former customers so long as he does not reveal confidential information in violation of any contract restrictions.

      (2) **Confidentiality Agreements**

         (a) Because all duties of the agent arising out of the agency relationship end when the agency relationship terminates, employers will often require employees to sign confidentiality agreements that prohibit an employee from sharing the employer's confidential information even after his employment ends.

e. **Duty Not to Compete**

(1) An employee may, while still employed, prepare to enter into competition once his employment ends by setting up his own business, so long as he does not take away from his employer's business by soliciting customers or key employees.

(2) **Noncompete Agreements**

(a) Noncompete agreements are necessary because the duty not to compete ends upon termination of the agency relationship.

(b) Agreements restricting an employee from competition must rest upon a protectable interest, and be sufficiently reasonable in time and geographic scope to be enforceable.

(c) A court may adjust an overreaching agreement to sever the non-enforceable provisions from the enforceable ones, or to reduce the area or time covered by the agreement.

3. **Duty to Account**

a. An agent has a duty to account for money or property received for the principal, and to keep the principal's assets separate from his own assets.

4. **Duty of Candor**

a. An agent must fully disclose to the principal any facts relevant to a transaction that he reasonably believes the principal might want to know.

5. **Dual Agency Rule**

a. When an agent acts for more than one principal in negotiations between those principals, the transaction is voidable by either principal, unless both principals are fully informed of the dual representation and give their consent.

6. **Principal's Remedies for an Agent's Breach of Fiduciary Duties**

a. A compensated agent may be held liable for damages to the principal that result from the agent's breach of his fiduciary duties.

(1) Generally, an uncompensated agent cannot be held liable.

b. An agent may be held liable for damages resulting from a breach of his duty of care, such as negligence, or from a breach of his fiduciary duty of loyalty, such as self-dealing.

c. Any transaction resulting from a breach of the agent's fiduciary duty is voidable by the principal.

d. Where the agent breaches his duty of loyalty to the principal, the appropriate remedy is disgorgement of any profits the agent realized from his disloyalty. If others have also benefited from the breach, the agent is liable for the profits of those third parties, even if the agent did not receive any part of those profits.

(1) The principal need not have suffered a loss in order to recover.

e. Punitive damages may be awarded to the principal if the agent acts with malice or in bad faith.

f. If the agent has intentionally breached his fiduciary duty, the principal may withhold compensation.

C. Agent's Duties and Obligations to Third Parties

1. If a third party knows of the principal's existence and identity at the time of a transaction (i.e., the principal is disclosed), the agent will not incur personal liability unless he takes additional actions to assume personal liability [Restatement (Third) of Agency § 6.01].

   a. To guarantee that he does not assume personal liability, the agent should sign any documents with his name and the principal's name, as well as a notation that he is acting as an agent.

2. If the principal is partially disclosed or left unidentified at the time of the transaction, the agent is presumed to be a party to the contract.

   a. To escape personal liability, the agent must make clear to the third party that he is representing a principal and that he is not a party to the contract.

3. If the existence of a principal directing the agent's actions is unknown, the agent is assumed to be contracting on his own behalf.

4. Disclosure of the principal after the execution of a contract will not relieve the agent of liability. The third party must then elect to sue either the principal or agent.

   EXAMPLE: Trump's agent signs a contract for Chicago real estate without discussing Trump as a principal. After signing, Trump refuses to purchase the real estate. The agent is still on the hook for the contract because, to the sellers, the agent was the principal.

   EXAMPLE: Once the contract is signed and Trump is disclosed as the principal, the sellers could elect to sue either the agent or Trump in the event of breach.

D. Election to Sue Principal or Agent

1. Upon learning of the identity and existence of an undisclosed principal, the third party may be required to elect to sue either the principal or agent. Having made such an election, the third party may not thereafter hold the other liable.

2. To be binding, the election to sue either the principal or the agent must be made with knowledge of the fact of the undisclosed principal.

   a. Suit brought against an agent prior to learning the identity of the principal does not act as a waiver of the third party's rights against the principal (i.e., there is no "election" in such a situation).

IV. POWER OF AGENT TO BIND PRINCIPAL

A. **Authority of the Agent**

1. The general rule is that an agent, acting within the scope of his authority, may bind his principal in contract.

2. Generally, a principal may be bound to contracts executed by an agent if it is within the agent's authority to contract on behalf of that principal.

    a. An agent's authority may be either actual or apparent.

3. **Actual Authority**

    a. **Actual authority** is created by the manifestation of the principal to the agent of the principal's request that the agent act for the benefit of the principal in a particular way, and that the principal agrees to be bound by the actions of the agent.

    b. The consent for actual authority may be in writing, oral, or through any other method of communication.

    c. An agent has actual authority to take actions designated or implied in the principal's manifestations and actions that are necessary or incidental to achieving the principal's objectives, and as the agent reasonably understands them when he determines how to act.

    d. Actual authority may be either express or implied.

    e. **Express Authority**

        (1) **Express authority** arises when the principal directly requests the agent to act on the principal's behalf in a specific matter.

        EXAMPLE: The principal who tells a person to "sell my house for me," or "please bid on the Picasso at the auction," gives a grant of express authority.

        EXAMPLE: If A tells B to purchase Blackacre, B has the express authority to purchase Blackacre, even if A meant to tell B to purchase Whiteacre.

        (2) Inherent in a grant of express authority is the principal's consent to any actions that are incidental to the agent carrying out of his primary grant of authority.

        EXAMPLE: When a principal directs a real estate broker-agent to sell his house, the broker has the inherent authority to place a "For Sale" sign on the front lawn.

        (3) Consent to the authority need not be in writing, and may be demonstrated by merely completing the task.

        (4) The **equal dignity rule** holds that if a contract must be in writing, the grant of authority to an agent to enter into such contract on behalf of the principal must also be in writing. Thus, the writing requirement cannot be escaped merely by granting authority to an agent.

f. **Implied Authority**

(1) **Implied authority** includes the authority to do:

(a) anything necessary to accomplish the principal's express request of his agent; or

(b) those things the agent believes the principal wishes him to do based on his reasonable understanding of the principal's expressed request.

EXAMPLE: When the owner of stock requests his stockbroker-agent to sell the investments at the best price available, the broker has the implied authority to choose which market to use for the sale.

4. **Apparent Authority**

a. **Apparent authority** arises based on the principal's representations made not directly to the agent, but to a third party.

(1) Because of the behavior of the principal, the third party is led to believe the agent is acting with the principal's authority.

b. Under the doctrine of apparent authority, a principal is accountable for the results of third-party beliefs about an actor's authority to act as an agent when the belief is reasonable and is traceable to a manifestation of the principal.

c. A principal may be liable to a third party for knowingly or negligently allowing a purported agent to assume authority or to overextend his legitimate authority.

(1) The overreaching agent will still be held liable to the principal for his unauthorized actions.

d. Only the principal has the ability through his actions to create apparent authority of an agent with respect to third parties; the agent cannot create his own apparent authority with respect to third parties.

e. Apparent authority requires some overt action by the principal.

(1) A principal's holding out may be accomplished by words, conduct, or a failure to act (e.g., failure to notify customers of the termination of an actual agency).

EXAMPLE: If a corporation permits its agent to deal in a manner that leads third parties to reasonably believe the agent is authorized to bind the corporation to contracts, the corporation may be bound even if the agent acts beyond the scope of his actual authority.

EXAMPLE: If a company hires someone as "vice president of marketing," this gives the impression that the person has the authority to purchase advertising.

EXAMPLE: Hiring someone as the manager of a dry cleaning business gives her the apparent authority to promise to have customers' orders done in a certain amount of time.

5. **Estoppel to Deny Existence of Agency Relationship**

   a. A principal may properly deny the existence of an agency relationship, including apparent authority, if there is a lack of a manifestation by the principal that the purported agent holds authority to complete the transaction in question.

   b. A third party may fight an estoppel claim by showing justifiable inducement under the circumstances because:

      (1) the principal intentionally, or carelessly, caused such belief; or

      (2) having notice of such belief, and that it may induce others to change their positions, the principal did not take reasonable steps to notify them of the facts.

      EXAMPLE: A landlord knows that a tenant's 14-year-old son acts as doorman on some afternoons for tips. The landlord thinks it is cute and does not say anything to the boy. One day, the boy is carrying a tenant's packages and drops them on the tenant's foot, requiring medical attention.

B. **Ratification**

   1. **Ratification** allows a principal to grant retroactive authority for his agent's earlier unauthorized actions.

      EXAMPLE: Kara bought Lee's Evidence book for him. After the fact, Lee thanks her, but also tries to subsequently renege when Kara's credit card bill arrives.

      EXAMPLE: Although Trump's agent was given a limit of $20 million for the purchase price of a building, the agent nonetheless signs a contract for $21 million. Trump can agree to honor the contract. Once he does, however, the contract is then binding.

   2. The ratified act must be one that the principal could have authorized at the time of the act, meaning the principal must have been in existence and had the capacity to enter into the agreement.

      a. Accordingly, a principal who was underage at the time of an action cannot ratify it after reaching the age of majority.

      b. Ratification will only grant authority; it does not legitimize an otherwise illegitimate transaction, nor will it grant authority to a nondelegable act.

   3. A person ratifies an act:

      a. by manifesting assent that the act shall affect the person's legal relations; or

      b. through conduct that is justifiable only on the assumption that the person so consents.

   4. Any act done on behalf of the principal, or purported to be done for the principal, may be ratified.

   5. Once an act has been ratified, it has the same effect as if it were originally done by the agent with actual authority.

6. **Limitations on Ratification**

a. Ratification is not effective:

(1) in favor of a person who causes it by misrepresentation or other conduct that would make a contract voidable;

(2) in favor of an agent against a principal when the principal ratifies an act to avoid a loss; or

(3) to diminish the rights or other interests of persons, not parties to the transaction, that were acquired in the subject matter prior to the ratification.

b. A principal may not ratify an act in part; ratification of any part of the act or contract is deemed to constitute ratification of the whole.

c. In order for ratification to be effective, the following conditions are necessary:

(1) the act the principal is seeking to ratify must have been otherwise valid at the time it was performed;

(2) the principal must have been in existence when the act was performed, and he must be legally competent when he attempts to ratify the act;

(3) the act must have been performed on behalf of the principal;

(4) the ratification must have the same formalities as those that would have been required to give authorization initially and, by extension, any formalities that the original act itself would have required; and

(5) at the time of ratification, the principal must know of all material facts concerning the transaction.

EXAMPLE: In the sale of real estate, the same formalities requirement means that the ratification must be in writing, just as the original authorization would have been, in order to satisfy the Statute of Frauds.

d. A ratification will not be effective if, prior to ratification, the ratification would have an adverse effect on third parties in the following circumstances [Restatement (Third) of Agency § 4.05]:

(1) manifestation of intention to withdraw from the transaction by the third party;

(2) a material change in circumstances that would make it inequitable to bind the third party, unless the third party chooses to be bound; and

(3) the specification of a time that determines whether a third party is deprived of a right or subjected to a liability.

EXAMPLE: If A contracts to sell P's house to B without P's authority, and the house is destroyed by fire, P's later ratification of A's act will not bind B. However, if B still wishes to proceed, the changed circumstances will not prevent his doing so.

e. Manifestation of intent can be implied as well as express.

7. **Retroactive Effect of Ratification**

    a.   Generally, a ratified transaction is given retroactive effect, but ratification by a principal who did not have capacity when the transaction took place is effective only from the date of ratification.

        EXAMPLE: One who was a minor at the time of a transaction may ratify it upon reaching the age of majority, but the ratification is effective only from the date of the ratification.

V. VICARIOUS LIABILITY OF PRINCIPAL FOR ACTS OF OTHERS

A. **Relationship between Principals and Agents**
   1. **Employers, Employees, and Independent Contractors**
      a. A **master**, commonly known as an **employer**, is a principal who employs an agent to perform a service in his affairs, and who controls, or has the right to control, the physical conduct of the agent in the performance of the service.
      b. A **servant**, commonly known as an **employee**, is an agent employed by a principal to perform a service in his affairs, and whose physical conduct in the performance of the service is controlled, or is subject to the right of control, by the master.
      c. **Independent Contractors**
         (1) An **independent contractor** is a person who contracts with another to do something for him, but who is not controlled by the other or subject to the other's right to control with respect to his physical conduct in the performance of the undertaking.
            (a) The word servant is frequently used to contrast with independent contractor.
            (b) An independent contractor is someone who contracts to complete tasks for another, but is not a servant in doing his work.
            (c) An agent who is not a servant is, therefore, an independent contractor when he contracts to act on behalf of the principal.
         (2) The following factors are used to determine, for agency purposes only, whether an agent is a servant (employee) or an independent contractor:
            (a) the amount of control the principal exerts over how the agent performs his work;
            (b) whether the agent is engaged in a distinct occupation or business;
            (c) whether the type of work the agent is doing is customarily done under the supervision of the principal;
            (d) the skill required in the agent's occupation;
            (e) who supplies the tools required for the agent's work and the place of performance;
            (f) the length of time the agent is engaged by the principal;
            (g) whether the agent is paid by the job or by the hour;
            (h) whether the principal and agent intend to create an employment relationship; and/or
            (i) whether the principal is in business.

            EXAMPLE: Michael works as a dental hygienist for Dr. Ferry. The doctor sets Michael's hours, provides all the equipment Michael needs to clean a patient's teeth, and supervises his actions. Michael is Dr. Ferry's servant agent, and the doctor is the master.

EXAMPLE: Michael grows bored with his job and tells the doctor he is leaving and wants a severance package. When the doctor refuses, Michael hires an attorney to negotiate on his behalf. Michael tells the attorney how much he believes he is entitled to, but leaves the particulars of the negotiation to the attorney. Hence, the attorney is a non-servant agent and, therefore, an independent contractor.

B. Tort Liability

1. ***Respondeat Superior***

   a. ***Respondeat superior*** is the doctrine that imposes vicarious liability upon a principal for the torts his agent committed in the course of agency.

      (1) The liability of the employer is in addition to, not instead of, the employee's liability. The employer and employee are jointly and severally liable.

      (2) An agent, however, may be held liable for his nonfeasance.

   b. *Respondeat superior* is a strict liability doctrine in that the principal has no defenses.

   c. The employer is liable for harm caused by an employee while he was acting within the scope of his employment.

2. **Scope of Employment**

   a. An employee acts within the scope of his employment when performing tasks assigned by the employer or engaging in a course of conduct subject to the employer's control.

   b. An employee's act is not within the scope of employment when it occurs within an independent course of conduct not intended by the employee to serve any purpose of the employer—i.e., it is done for the employee's purposes only.

   c. Unless the tort occurred, at least in part, to serve the master, the employee will be held liable. An employee may, however, still be acting within the scope of his employment even while disobeying his employer's orders.

   d. **Frolic and Detour**

      (1) Torts committed by the employee on the way to or from work are outside the scope of employment, unless the employer places an employee's travel to and from work within the scope of employment by providing the employee with a vehicle and exerting control over how the employee uses the vehicle so that the employee may more readily respond to the needs of the employer's enterprise.

      (2) An employer will not be liable if the employee has substantially deviated from the authorized route (a **frolic**), but will be liable

if the deviation is slight (a **detour**). However, an employee can return to the scope of employment after a frolic occurs.

(a) The extent of the deviation is a question of fact. In general, courts consider:

1) the advancement of the employer's interests;

2) whether the deviation occurred before or after the employer's objective was served;

3) the scope of the deviation in terms of time and distance; and

4) whether the deviation was in keeping with the type of employment.

(b) An employee need not take the most direct route to his destination in order to be acting within the scope of his employment.

EXAMPLE: A substantial deviation would occur where a garage employee picked up an automobile for repairs and, instead of driving it directly to the garage, the employee became involved in a collision while traveling in the opposite direction towards his home for breakfast. A slight deviation would occur where an employee on his employer's business chose a route longer than the authorized route, but one that was smoother, with less traffic. If the employee drove home for breakfast, but then returned to the authorized route on the way to the garage and an accident subsequently occurred, the employee would have re-entered the scope of employment despite the frolic.

(3) **Employee Driving His Own Automobile**

(a) An employer-employee relationship may be found even though the negligent employee was using his own automobile and choosing his own route and speed at the time of the accident.

EXAMPLE: Professor Hurt's dean asks her to drive to Chicago for an alumni function, and she stops in Kankakee to get lunch. Professor Hurt negligently backs into another vehicle in the Taco Bell parking lot.

EXAMPLE: Where a driver uses his own vehicle for his employer's business with the employer's consent and encouragement, use of the vehicle may be found to be within the scope of the driver's employment.

3. **Intentional Torts**

a. The trend is to extend an employer's liability for an employee's intentional torts to situations where the type of employment provides a peculiar opportunity and incentive for the commission of an intentional tort.

(1) Where argument is likely to be involved in the employee's duties, and such conduct is wholly or partially in furtherance of the employer's business—e.g., the employee is a bouncer, bill collector, or

security guard—liability will be imposed on the employer for those intentional torts that may arise from the argument.

(2) If an employee commits an assault and battery in the course of doing the employer's work, and for the purpose of accomplishing it, then it is no defense to the employer that he had previously instructed the employee not to use force in the performance of his duties, or that the work for which the employee was hired would not incidentally involve the use of force.

(a) Where an employee's purpose in committing an assault and battery is to vent personal anger, however, *respondeat superior* will not apply.

b. **Common Carriers**

(1) An employer is even more likely to be held liable for the intentional torts of his employee in common carrier cases.

EXAMPLE: A cab company has been held liable to a customer for an assault and battery committed by its driver on the customer. Despite the defendant's argument that the servant was not acting within the scope of employment when he committed the tort, the court held that the common carrier was absolutely liable for injuries to a customer caused by the misconduct of a servant while engaged in the performance of his contract of carriage.

C. Other Agents

1. **Independent Contractors**

a. Generally, a principal is not responsible for the tortious conduct of an independent contractor.

EXAMPLE: Paul hires Irreverent Colors to repaint his house. During the job, the painting crew gets into a colorful argument with some neighborhood kids about an upcoming Jets-Bills football game, and the painters end up violently injuring the youths. In a subsequent court action, Paul will not be liable for the torts of the painters because he had no control over them.

b. The following are exceptions to the rule that principals are not liable for the torts of independent contractors:

(1) inherently dangerous activities;

(2) nondelegable duty; and

(3) the negligent selection of a contractor.

c. **Inherently Dangerous Activities**

(1) Work is inherently dangerous where the nature and circumstances of the work to be performed are such that injury to others will probably result unless precautions are taken.

EXAMPLE: Blasting and demolition work are inherently dangerous activities.

d. **Nondelegable Duty**

    (1)   Certain relationships impose a duty of care that cannot be discharged even by the employment of a carefully selected independent contractor.

          <u>**EXAMPLE:**</u> The duty of ordinary care owed by a landlord to a tenant for areas under the landlord's exclusive control may not be satisfied merely by the careful selection of an independent contractor.

    (2)   **Dangerous Disrepair**

        (a)   Where the employer's premises are in a state of dangerous disrepair and an independent contractor is employed to correct the situation, the risk of harm due to the disrepair cannot be delegated to an independent contractor by the owners of the premises.

2. **Police Officers**

    a.   Often, police officers are employed by a private person to perform services such as directing traffic or maintaining order.

    b.   Tort liability depends on the extent to which the private person has the right to control the activities of the officer.

    c.   If the tort arises from an activity for which the officer has been given instructions by the employer, then the employer may be liable.

3. **Borrowed Employees**

    a.   A person who is generally the employee of one employer may become the **borrowed employee** of another.

    b.   Typically, the borrowed employee is one who is doing the work of a third party, but is being paid by the original employer.

    c.   The right to control is the key test.

        (1)   If the employer who loaned the employee does not continue to exercise control over the employee, he will not be liable even though he continues to pay the employee.

    d.   Important factors in determining whether control has been completely transferred to the new employer include:

        (1)   the manner of hiring;

        (2)   the mode of payment;

        (3)   the right to discharge; and

        (4)   the manner of direction of services.

    e.   There is a rebuttable presumption that the original employer maintains the right to control the employee, but if the borrowed employee commits a tort at the bidding of the borrower, vicarious liability attaches to the borrower.

    f.   If the original employer and the borrowing employer jointly control the activities of the employee, they may both be held liable for his tortious acts.

        (1)   Generally, liability will attach to the employer who had the primary right of control over the act at issue.

    4. **Temporary Servants**

       a. A person may be a servant for the commission of one act.

        EXAMPLE: If a service station owner asked someone not usually employed by him to move an automobile, the owner could be held liable for the negligent operation of the vehicle by that person.

D. Delegation

    1. In general, if the authority given involves the agent using his own judgment, he cannot delegate his responsibilities, absent an emergency or the explicit agreement of the principal.

    2. An example of a responsibility that an agent may not delegate is a duty to perform personal services on behalf of the principal to another.

    3. Delegation of such a duty would be a material change in understanding when a principal has hired a particular person to perform a particular purpose.

VI. IMPUTED KNOWLEDGE

A. In General

1. Another consequence of the agency relationship is that the knowledge of an agent is imputed to his principal.

2. For knowledge to be imputed, the agent must have a duty to speak to his principal about the specific item of knowledge.

3. Knowledge is generally not imputed when the agent is acting adversely to the principal and for his own or another's benefit.

   EXAMPLE: Peter wants to sell goods to the government of country X but is concerned that payoffs may be necessary to effect such a sale. Peter employs Allen in country X and advises Allen that he does not wish to know of any commission or other payments Allen may need to pay in order to effect the sale of Peter's goods. Peter may nonetheless be charged with violations of anti-bribery laws since notice may be imputed to Peter of Allen's knowledge of payments made by Allen.

VII. TERMINATION OF THE AGENCY RELATIONSHIP

A. Termination by the Parties

1. Regardless of any remedies available for breach of contract, both the principal and the agent have the power to terminate the agency relationship at any time.

   a. Death or incapacity of the principal or the agent will automatically terminate the agency.

2. Although both the principal and agent have the power to terminate, this does not mean that a party has the right to terminate.

3. The ability to terminate an agency at will does not preclude either party from institution of a breach of contract action.

   EXAMPLE: If P hired A for two years and terminated the relationship after six months, A could sue P for breach of contract.

4. For termination to be effective, the principal must notify the agent of termination unless:

   a. the agency naturally expires upon completion of an action; or

   b. the agency is set to expire at a particular time.

5. Notification need not be express.

6. The agency will end if, by an objective standard of reasonableness, the agent should have understood his authority to be terminated by the principal's actions.

7. To terminate the agent's apparent authority, the principal must notify all third parties with whom the agent has dealt who might expect the agent to still be acting for the principal.

   EXAMPLE: A notice sent by ABC Widget Co. to its suppliers informing them that Alison, the former purchasing agent, is no longer with the company, properly sends notice that she no longer has authority to bind ABC in the purchase of goods.

B. Exceptions

1. An agency is not terminable at the will of either party if:

   a. the agency is coupled with an interest; or

   b. the agent has a power given for security.

2. An **agency coupled with an interest** exists when the agent has an interest in the subject matter of the agency.

   EXAMPLE: Where an insurance policy gives the insurer the right to settle, the agreement binds the insured despite his dissent.

3. A **power given for security** exists when the agency was created for the purpose of payment of a debt owed by the principal to the agent.

   EXAMPLE: An agreement giving a mortgagee the power to collect and apply rents from mortgaged premises.

Conflict of Laws

TABLE OF CONTENTS

VIII. CONSTITUTIONAL LIMITS ON CHOICE OF LAW

IX. RECOGNITION AND ENFORCEMENT OF SISTER STATE AND FOREIGN JUDGMENTS

X. PREEMPTION

I. INTRODUCTION

A. **Conflict of Laws**

1. A problem in Conflict of Laws is usually presented on a bar examination in conjunction with the substantive law of torts, contracts, family law, or wills.

2. If a bar examination question contains any fact or reference associated with two different states, be prepared to discuss the possible applicability of foreign law.

B. **Choice of Law**

1. Traditionally, under the theory of "vested rights," courts applied a rigid rule requiring application of the law of the place where the cause of action arises to all substantive aspects of the case, and the law of the forum (*lex fora*) to all procedural questions [Restatement (First) of Conflict of Laws § 378].

   a. Thus, the characterization of a question as substantive or procedural was often dispositive of the choice of law [Restatement (Second) of Conflict of Laws § 122, cmt. b].

2. These rules have been under attack in recent years, however, and the modern trend is in favor of the significant contacts or governmental interests approaches.

   a. These approaches generally suggest that the law of the state having the most significant relationship with the cause of action should be applied [Restatement (Second) of Conflict of Laws § 2, cmt. c].

II. DOMICILE

A. **In General**

1. **Domicile** is the place where a person has a settled connection for certain legal purposes, either because his home is there or because that place is assigned to him by the law [Restatement (Second) of Conflict of Laws § 11, cmt. a].

2. Each person must have one (and only one) domicile [Restatement (Second) of Conflict of Laws § 11(2)].

    a. The acquisition of a new domicile extinguishes a former domicile [Restatement (Second) of Conflict of Laws § 18, cmt. b].

3. Domicile is an important legal concept in Conflict of Laws because if a person is domiciled in a particular state:

    a. he is liable to personal jurisdiction in its courts, whether or not he can be found and personally served [McDonald v. Mabee, 243 U.S. 90 (1917); Milliken v. Meyer, 311 U.S. 457 (1940)];

    b. matters relating to his personal status, such as the validity of his marriage, adoption, or legitimacy, may be determined by the laws of that state [Williams v. North Carolina, 317 U.S. 287 (1942)];

    c. the transfer of his personal property upon death, and the validity of his will with respect to such property or its distribution in the event of intestacy, is determined by the laws of the domiciliary state [Restatement (Second) of Conflict of Laws § 269];

    d. domicile is considered to be an important "contact" if a court applies a "contacts" approach to choice of law; and

    e. he is likely liable for state inheritance, income, and personal property taxes [Restatement (Second) of Conflict of Laws § 9, cmt. f].

B. **Domicile of Choice**

1. Any person who is legally competent can choose or change his domicile [Restatement (Second) of Conflict of Laws § 15(1)].

2. Two elements must coincide to effect a change of domicile [Restatement (Second) of Conflict of Laws § 15(2)]:

    a. physical presence in the place where domicile is alleged to have been acquired; and

        (1) Actual physical presence in the new domicile is generally required, but need not be for a prolonged period, and need not be a fixed or permanent place of residence in the locality.

            (a) The sufficiency of physical presence is a question of fact [Restatement (Second) of Conflict of Laws § 16, cmt. b].

            EXAMPLE: John moves to Chicago with the intent to remain there. Even though he has been staying in a hotel for three weeks while looking for an apartment, and even though his belongings are still in New York, he has established a new domicile in Chicago.

    b.   an intention to make it his home without any fixed or certain purpose to return to his former place of abode [Restatement (Second) of Conflict of Laws § 18, cmt. b].

        (1)   Thus, an attempt to establish domicile in another state merely to make use of more favorable laws will be unsuccessful if there is no intent to remain indefinitely [Restatement (Second) of Conflict of Laws § 18, cmt. f].

            (a) Similarly, an attempt to retain a former domicile in order to use more favorable tax laws will be ineffective.

        (2)   **Intent** is usually proved by an individual's actions and statements [Restatement (Second) of Conflict of Laws § 20, cmt. b]. Relevant factors are:

            (a) owning real estate;

            (b) voting;

            (c) paying taxes to the state or a town;

            (d) having a bank account; or

            (e) registering an automobile in the state.

3.   There is a presumption that a domicile continues until a new one is affirmatively established; the individual asserting a change in domicile has the burden of proving both physical presence and intent to remain indefinitely [Restatement (Second) of Conflict of Laws § 19, cmt. c].

    a.   A person traveling continually would retain his old domicile [Restatement (Second) of Conflict of Laws § 19, cmts. a, b].

    b.   A new domicile is not established if a serviceman resides in a locality under military compulsion; rather, his domicile at the time of enlistment is presumed to continue, absent an affirmative showing of intent to change [Restatement (Second) of Conflict of Laws § 17, cmt. c].

        (1)   Likewise, a domiciliary of one incarcerated in another state does not lose his original domicile, but may change his domicile to the state of incarceration if he can prove the requisite intent [Restatement (Second) of Conflict of Laws § 17, cmt. b].

4.   A person may simultaneously have two or more residences, but only one domicile at a time [Restatement (Second) of Conflict of Laws § 20, cmt. b].

    a.   Thus, if an individual maintains two "principal" homes—for example, a city home in one state and a country home in another—or if he maintains substantial ties with his old residence, the problem of determining domicile is particularly difficult.

    b.   The home established first is presumed to continue as the domicile unless intent to change the domicile is affirmatively shown [Restatement (Second) of Conflict of Laws § 20, cmt. b(3)].

5.   Domicile is not changed by an extended absence from the state, as long as there is an intent to return to the original domicile [Restatement (Second) of Conflict of Laws § 18, cmt. f].

EXAMPLE: A domiciliary of Florida can live in Pennsylvania for seven years while going to college and law school and retain his Florida domicile if he intends to return to Florida at the end of his schooling.

C. Domicile by Operation of Law

1. **Minors**

   a. At birth, a child is assigned the domicile of his origin, which is the domicile of his parents and generally the place of his birth [Restatement (Second) of Conflict of Laws § 22(1)].

      (1) The domicile of a legitimate child is that of his father; the domicile of an illegitimate child or of one whose father is dead is that of his mother, unless the mother has abandoned the child [Restatement (Second) of Conflict of Laws § 14(2)].

      (2) If the parents are separated or divorced, the child assumes the domicile of the parent with whom he lives [Restatement (Second) of Conflict of Laws § 22, cmt. d].

      (3) If both parents are dead, or if the child is abandoned by both parents or by a surviving parent, the child's domicile will be that of a close relative or other person who stands *in loco parentis* and with whom he lives [Restatement (Second) of Conflict of Laws § 22, cmt. i].

   b. The child's domicile changes whenever the parent's changes, until the child is emancipated, such as upon reaching majority or marrying, when he may establish his own domicile [Restatement (Second) of Conflict of Laws § 22, cmt. f].

2. **Married Persons**

   a. At early common law, the domicile of a married woman was that of her spouse [Restatement (Second) of Conflict of Laws § 21, cmt. a]; later, she was permitted to establish her own domicile if legally separated from her spouse.

      (1) The modern trend allows a person who lives apart from his or her spouse to acquire a separate domicile [Restatement (Second) of Conflict of Laws § 21, cmt. d].

   b. Currently, the law appears to apply a "family domicile" interpretation [Restatement (Second) of Conflict of Laws § 21, cmt. b].

3. **Incompetents**

   a. An infant who is insane has the domicile of his parents [Restatement (Second) of Conflict of Laws § 23, cmt. c].

   b. A person who becomes insane after infancy retains the domicile he had prior to his insanity [Restatement (Second) of Conflict of Laws § 23, cmt. b]. He may, however, change his domicile if, although incompetent for some purposes, he has sufficient mental capacity to choose the place he regards as home [Restatement (Second) of Conflict of Laws § 23(1)].

4. **Corporations**

   a. A corporation is domiciled in the state of its incorporation [Restatement (Second) of Conflict of Laws § 11, cmt. l].

III. WHAT LAW APPLIES

A. In General

1. When a cause of action involves contacts with more than one state, the forum court is confronted with the problem of which state's law to apply [Restatement (Second) of Conflict of Laws § 2, cmt. a]. This problem has three aspects:

    a. which state's law is consulted to characterize the cause of action (e.g., is it a torts or contracts problem);

        (1) The court makes this characterization according to its own law.

    b. which state's law governs which issues; and

        (1) The forum applies its own procedural rules even if it is applying a foreign state's substantive law; the characterization of an issue as procedural or substantive is made according to the forum state's law.

    c. how much of the foreign law is to be applied—only its internal law or its choice-of-law rules as well (the *renvoi* problem).

        (1) The majority view rejects *renvoi*, or reference back to the foreign state's choice-of-law rules, and applies only the foreign state's internal law.

2. If the forum state's statute expressly or impliedly extends to out-of-state transactions, there is no choice-of-law problem, and the forum state applies its own laws.

3. A federal court exercising diversity jurisdiction applies the choice-of-law rules of the state in which it sits [Restatement (Second) of Conflict of Laws § 7, cmt. f].

IV. CHOICE-OF-LAW APPROACHES

A. **The Vested Rights Approach**

    1.   Under this traditional approach, advocated by the First Restatement, the forum state must apply the law of the state in which the rights of the parties "**vest**"—i.e., where the act or relationship giving rise to the cause of action occurred or was created [Restatement (First) of Conflict of Laws § 378].

        a.   Thus, the forum first characterizes the cause of action, for example, as a tort, and then applies the substantive law of the state where the wrong occurred.

B. **The Most Significant Relationship Approach**

    1.   The Second Restatement directs a court to look to all the circumstances surrounding a cause of action and to determine which state has the most significant relationship to each issue raised [Restatement (Second) of Conflict of Laws § 6, cmt. c].

        a.   Thus, the forum state may apply its own law on some issues and the foreign state's law on others [Restatement (Second) of Conflict of Laws § 2].

    2.   *Depeçage*

        a.   Choice of the applicable law depends upon the issue involved, and different issues in the same case may be decided by applying the law of different states [Restatement (Second) of Conflict of Laws § 2, cmt. a].

            (1)   Therefore, the various issues arising from a single tort claim may be resolved by reference to the law of various jurisdictions [Restatement (Second) of Conflict of Laws § 145, cmt. d].

            (2)   This process of applying the law of different states to decide different issues is known as *depeçage*.

        b.   In general, a court will assume that a case is to be governed by the laws of the forum unless a party-litigant timely invokes the law of a foreign state and establishes that such foreign law should apply [Restatement (Second) of Conflict of Laws § 1, cmts. a, b].

    3.   The important principles to be considered are [Restatement (Second) of Conflict of Laws § 6(2)]:

        a.   the needs of the interstate and international systems (choice-of-law rules should further harmony between states and facilitate commerce between them);

        b.   the relevant policies of the forum;

        c.   the relevant policies of other interested states and the relative interests of those states in the determination of the particular issue;

            (1)   The governmental interests approach focuses on the policies underlying the laws of the various states involved and on their respective interests in furthering those policies.

                (a)   Thus, the court must examine the policies behind the substantive laws of the states involved, and then determine which state has a policy interest in having its law applied.

      (b) If only one state has a legitimate interest, its law will be applied because only a "false conflict" is raised.

    (2) If the law prohibits wrongful conduct, the policy of preventing that conduct is at stake when the action occurs within the regulating state.

    (3) If the law allocates loss, the policy is at stake if application of the law protects the state's domiciliary.

  d. protection of justified expectations;

    (1) This would not apply in tort cases.

  e. the basic policies underlying the particular field of law (for example, to validate contracts whenever possible);

  f. certainty, predictability, and uniformity of result; and

  g. ease in the determination and application of the law to be applied.

V. CHOICE-OF-LAW IN SPECIFIC AREAS

A. **Characterization**

1. There are two aspects of characterization: the classification of a given factual situation under the appropriate legal categories and specific rules of law; and the interpretation of the terms employed in the legal categories and rules of law [Restatement (Second) of Conflict of Laws § 7, cmt. b].

   a. In general, the classification and interpretation of conflict of laws concepts and terms are determined in accordance with the law of the forum [Restatement (Second) of Conflict of Laws § 7(2)].

   b. At times, the same legal concept may be classified in different ways in different bodies of law [Restatement (Second) of Conflict of Laws § 7, cmt. d].

   EXAMPLE: In Sampson v. Channell [110 F.2d 754 (1st Cir. 1940)], the court noted that the federal court had characterized the issue of burden of proof as substantive in applying the rule of Swift v. Tyson [41 U.S. 1 (1842)], whereas most courts had characterized the same issue as procedural for choice-of-law purposes. The court then looked to the underlying rule of Erie Railroad Co. v. Tompkins [304 U.S. 64 (1938)] and determined that the purpose of the rule was to ensure substantial uniformity of result between federal and state courts in the same state. Thus, the court held that the burden of proof should be characterized as substantive for Erie purposes in the instant case.

2. By characterizing the suit as falling into one legal category rather than another, the court may decide to apply its own law and may avoid an unjust result.

   EXAMPLE: The plaintiff-passenger was injured in State X while riding in a car rented in State Y, and he sued the lessor in State Y. Under a State Y statute, the lessor was liable for any injuries arising out of the use of its leased vehicles; however, State X had no such statute. If the action was characterized as in tort, the law of the place of injury (State X) would not recognize the action. However, State Y characterized the action as in contract and thus governed by the place the contract was made (State Y), and held the lessor liable.

B. **Torts**

1. Many states continue to follow the traditional rule in tort actions and apply the law of the place where the tort was committed (*lex loci delicti*).

   a. A tort is committed in the state where the injury occurred [Restatement (Second) of Conflict of Laws § 145, cmt. e].

   b. However, when application of the traditional rule would produce an arbitrary or irrational result, even some of these courts may apply the Second Restatement most significant relationship test [Restatement (Second) of Conflict of Laws § 145(1)].

2. Over the past few decades, courts in a number of states have expressly rejected the mechanical application of the *lex loci delicti* doctrine to

multistate tort controversies in general and have substituted in its place the modern rule, under which applicable law is determined by analyzing a number of objective factors via the most significant relationship approach [Restatement (Second) of Conflict of Laws § 145(2)].

3. The domiciles of the parties are considered significant relationships because many tort law policies are formulated with respect to balancing compensation for its plaintiffs against protecting its defendants against excessive liabilities [Restatement (Second) of Conflict of Laws § 145, cmt. e].

   EXAMPLE: A married couple from Pennsylvania gets into an accident in Michigan. On the issue of negligence, Michigan will have the dominant interest. Pennsylvania, however, may have the most significant relationship to the issue of whether the wife may sue the husband.

4. **Wrongful Death**
   a. The Second Restatement holds that, in an action for wrongful death, the local law of the state where the injury occurred determines the rights and liabilities of the parties unless, with respect to the particular issue, some other state has a more significant relationship to the occurrence and the parties, in which event the local law of the other state will be applied [Restatement (Second) of Conflict of Laws § 175].
   b. Accordingly, the law selected by application of this rule determines both the defenses that may be raised on the merits and the measure of damages in a wrongful death action [Restatement (Second) of Conflict of Laws §§ 176, 178].
   c. Usually, the statute of limitations in a wrongful death action is deemed to be so closely identified with the right of action that it thereby qualifies as substantive and is governed by the foreign law [Restatement (Second) of Conflict of Laws § 142, cmt. g].
   d. The general rule provides that the distribution of amounts recovered under a wrongful death statute is ordinarily governed by the law of the state where the tort was committed [Restatement (Second) of Conflict of Laws § 177].

5. **Dram Shop Act**
   a. Some states have statutes (dram shop acts) that impose liability on tavern keepers for injuries caused to an individual by an intoxicated patron; where the injuries occur in a state other than that in which the liquor was served, a choice-of-law problem arises.
   b. If a patron becomes intoxicated in a tavern in a state without a dram shop act and then causes injury in a state that has a dram shop act, a state court may likely not impose liability, under the traditional reasoning that the tavern keeper would have a vested right in his "exemption" from such liability in his own state.

C. **Workers' Compensation**
   1. **Jurisdiction**
      a. Workers' compensation is statutory and usually administered by a state administrative agency empowered to decide cases under its own state statute.

          (1)   However, because the employment relationship may involve more than one state, and since the available benefits vary from state to state, conflicts problems arise as to which state will award benefits.

    b.   Any state that has a legitimate interest in an injury and its consequences may apply its compensation act [Wilson v. Faull, 141 A.2d 768 (N.J. 1958)].

    c.   State statutes usually spell out their applicability in detail, but generally a state would have a legitimate interest if it were where [Restatement (Second) of Conflict of Laws § 181]:

          (1)   the injury occurred;

          (2)   the employment is principally located;

          (3)   the employer supervised the employee's activities from a place of business in the state;

          (4)   the state was that of most significant relationship to the contract of employment;

          (5)   the parties agreed in the contract of employment that their rights should be determined under that state's workers' compensation act; or

          (6)   the state had some other reasonable relationship to the occurrence, the parties, and the employment.

    d.   A stipulation in the employment contract that the law of a particular state shall be applied will be upheld as long as it is reasonable and not violative of the public policy of another state that has a legitimate interest [Restatement (Second) of Conflict of Laws § 181(e)].

2. **Governing Law**

    a.   Compensation claims are filed with a state administrative agency, and the agency applies its own state's law in determining eligibility and compensation.

    b.   Nevertheless, characterization and choice-of-law problems arise, particularly in cases seeking a common law recovery, where independent tort actions are barred or limited by the compensation act of the forum state or the state where the employee was injured or received an award.

3. **Successive Awards**

    a.   Because more than one state may have a legitimate interest in a single injury, an employee may file and receive awards under the Workers' Compensation Acts of different states [Restatement (Second) of Conflict of Laws § 182, cmt. a].

    b.   A subsequent award in another state is barred only if "unmistakable language by a state legislature or judiciary" precludes recovery in another state [Industrial Commission of Wisconsin v. McCartin, 330 U.S. 622 (1947)].

    c.   The amounts paid under a prior award are credited against the subsequent award, so a dual recovery is not had [Restatement (Second) of Conflict of Laws § 182, cmt. b].

EXAMPLE: In Thomas v. Washington Gas Light Co. [448 U.S. 261 (1980)], the petitioner resided in the District of Columbia and was hired there by the respondent, who was principally located in the District. However, while working for the respondent in Virginia, he was injured. He received an award under the Virginia Workers' Compensation Act, and subsequently received a supplemental award under the District's Workers' Compensation Act. On review, the Supreme Court declared, "a state has no legitimate interest within the context of our federal system in preventing another state from granting a supplemental compensation award when that second state would have had the power to apply its workers' compensation law in the first instance. The Full Faith and Credit Clause should not be construed to preclude successive workers' compensation awards." However, only a plurality joined in this opinion, while the concurrence upheld the second award on the grounds that the Virginia Act—which barred additional recovery "at common law or otherwise"—did not contain the "unmistakable language" necessary to bar a recovery outside Virginia.

D. Contracts

1. Contracts fall into three distinct categories for choice-of-law purposes:

   a. contracts that specify the governing law;

      (1) Frequently, contracting parties will expressly stipulate that the laws of a particular state shall govern all rights and obligations arising under a contract [Restatement (Second) of Conflict of Laws § 186].

         (a) Generally, the power of the parties to select jurisdiction is subject to certain definite limitations [Restatement (Second) of Conflict of Laws § 186, cmt. a].

         (b) Such stipulation is thus deemed valid and enforceable unless [Restatement (Second) of Conflict of Laws § 187(2)]:

            1) the chosen state has no substantial relationship to the parties or the transaction and there is no other reasonable basis for the parties' choice; or

            2) it is contrary to a fundamental policy of the forum which has a materially greater interest than the chosen state and which would be the state of the applicable law in the absence of an effective choice of law by the parties.

      (2) Furthermore, the parties' power to choose the governing law is frequently subject to the additional requirement that such state have a significant relationship to the transaction or subject matter of the contract [Restatement (Second) of Conflict of Laws § 187, cmt. f].

      (3) Notwithstanding the generally recognized ability of contracting parties to determine choice of laws, most courts would likely find such a designation invalid in an adhesion contract.

       (a) Furthermore, if the contract stipulates that suit may be brought only in the courts of a specified state, many courts may deem such provision ineffective on the grounds that it is against public policy to exclude a court from jurisdiction [Restatement (Second) of Conflict of Laws § 80, cmt. a].

  b.   contracts that specify no choice of law; and

     (1) Under the traditional rule, the validity and construction of a contract are determined by the law of the place where the contract was made [Gaston, Williams & Wigmore v. Warner, 260 U.S. 201 (1922); Mutual Life Ins. Co. v. Liebing, 259 U.S. 209 (1922)].

       (a) The general rule that the law of the place of the making governs has frequently been modified upon a showing that the contract was executed to have its operating effect or its place of performance in another jurisdiction [Restatement (Second) of Conflict of Laws § 187, cmt. a].

       (b) Where a conflict between the place of making and the place of performance exists, some courts have broadly held that contracts are to be governed by the place of performance [Supervisors v. Galbraith, 99 U.S. 214 (1878)].

       (c) Furthermore, some courts have held more specifically that the law of the place where the contract is to be performed determines the validity and construction [Crossman v. Lurman, 192 U.S. 189 (1904)].

     (2) Problems arising from the mechanical application of the traditional rule have led many states to employ a modern most significant relationship approach to conflicts concerning contracts [Vanston Bondholders Protective Committee v. Green, 329 U.S. 156 (1946)].

       (a) Under this approach, adopted by the Second Restatement in 1971, the determination turns upon the law of the place that has the most significant relation, connection, or contacts with the matter in dispute [Restatement (Second) of Conflict of Laws § 188(1)].

       (b) In the absence of a choice of law by the contracting parties, the concepts to be evaluated and weighed include [Restatement (Second) of Conflict of Laws § 188(2)]:

         1) the place of contracting;

         2) the place of negotiation of the contract;

         3) the place of performance;

         4) the location of the subject matter of the contract; and

         5) the domicile, residence, nationality, place of incorporation, and place of business of the parties.

     (3) Notwithstanding the increasingly frequent use of the modern approach in deciding contract choice-of-law problems, the traditional conflict of laws rule survives in a great many jurisdictions.

    c.   contracts governed by the Uniform Commercial Code.

        (1)   Generally, when a transaction bears a reasonable relation to this state and also to another state or nation, the parties may agree that the law of either state or nation shall govern their rights and duties.

        (2)   Failing such an agreement, the Uniform Commercial Code applies to transactions bearing an "appropriate relation" to the state [UCC § 1-301].

E. Property

1.   In property cases, two characterizations must be made.

    a.   First, the problem must be characterized as to whether or not it involves a property interest (e.g., an agreement to sell land might be characterized as a contract, rather than a property, problem).

    b.   Once it is determined that a property interest is involved, that interest must be characterized as a "movable" or "immovable" interest [Restatement (Second) of Conflict of Laws § 222, cmt. e].

        (1)   If an interest is closely connected with or related to land (e.g., a leasehold or the right to rents), it is **immovable**; if it is not, the interest falls into the **movable** category.

            (a)   Characterization of the interest traditionally has been made by the forum using its own internal law. However, the Second Restatement suggests that characterization should be made according to the law of the *situs* of the property [Restatement (Second) of Conflict of Laws § 189, cmt. c].

        (2)   The law of the *situs* governs all rights in land and other immovables. In applying the law, the forum state refers to the whole law of the *situs,* including its choice-of-law rules [Restatement (Second) of Conflict of Laws §§ 223; 223, cmt. b].

            (a)   Generally, the validity and effect of a conveyance (e.g., the form of the deed or the capacity of the grantor) are governed by the law of the *situs* [Restatement (Second) of Conflict of Laws § 223(1)].

            (b)   Mortgages likewise are deemed so closely related to the land that their creation, validity, and foreclosure are governed by the law of the *situs* [Restatement (Second) of Conflict of Laws § 228].

            (c)   However, the underlying contract or note is usually governed by the law of the place of making [Restatement (Second) of Conflict of Laws § 224, cmt. e].

            (d)   Liens (such as materialmen's or laborers' liens) are also governed by the law of the *situs* [Restatement (Second) of Conflict of Laws § 230].

            (e)   Some courts hold that executory contracts for the sale of land are generally characterized as a contracts problem and governed by the law of the place of making.

        1) However, the Second Restatement provides that in the absence of an effective choice of law by the parties, the validity of a contract for the transfer of an interest in land, and the rights created thereby, are to be determined by the local law of the state where the land is located, unless, with respect to the particular issue, some other state has a more significant relationship to the transaction and the parties, in which event the local law of the other state will be applied [Restatement (Second) of Conflict of Laws § 189].

   (3) Traditionally, questions as to tangible chattels have been resolved under the law of their *situs* at the time of the relevant transaction [Restatement (First) of Conflict of Laws § 255].

     (a) However, most issues dealing with sales of, or security interests in, movables would now be governed by the Uniform Commercial Code.

     (b) Thus, the parties usually may stipulate to the applicable law or, absent such a stipulation, the forum state will apply the law of a state bearing an "appropriate relation" to the transaction [UCC §1-301].

   (4) An intangible—or chose in action—has no *situs*; however, if the intangible is represented by an instrument, the law of the *situs* of the instrument may be applied. If there is no instrument, the law of the place of transfer may be applied, or contracts choice of law may be applied.

F. Trusts

1. In general, the validity of a trust of realty is determined by the law of the *situs* of the land, and the legality of a trust of personalty by the law of the settlor's domicile [Restatement (Second) of Conflict of Laws §§ 278, 269].

   a. Intangible personalty and choses in action included in the trust have a legal *situs* in the settlor's domicile [Restatement (Second) of Conflict of Laws § 271, cmt. b].

2. The Second Restatement establishes a tendency to respect the will of the settlor as to the controlling law of the administration of a trust [Restatement (Second) of Conflict of Laws § 271(a)].

   a. In the absence of such a provision, the administration of a testamentary trust of personalty will be controlled by the state of the testator's domicile [Restatement (Second) of Conflict of Laws 271(b)].

3. Furthermore, the administration of an *inter vivos* trust of personalty will be controlled by the state to which the administration of the trust is most substantially related [Restatement (Second) of Conflict of Laws § 272(b)].

   a. The administration of a trust of an interest in land is determined by the law of the *situs* [Restatement (Second) of Conflict of Laws § 279].

G. **Wills and Administration of Estates**
   1. **Intestate Succession**
      a. The succession to an intestate's personalty—wherever located—is governed by the law of his domicile [Restatement (Second) of Conflict of Laws § 269].
      b. The succession to an intestate's realty is governed by the law of the state where it is located [Restatement (Second) of Conflict of Laws § 278, cmt. b].
   2. **Wills**
      a. Whether one dies testate or intestate is to be determined as to personalty by the law of the decedent's domicile, and as to realty by the law of the *situs* of the realty.
      b. However, any will executed in compliance with the law of the jurisdiction where the testator was domiciled at the time of the execution of the will or at the time of his death is validly executed and will be effectual to pass any property of the testator situated in such state [Restatement (Second) of Conflict of Laws § 278, cmt. e].
      c. Generally, unless the terms of the will indicate a contrary intention, the will's disposition of personalty is interpreted under the law of the testator's domicile [Restatement (Second) of Conflict of Laws § 269(a)].
         (1) Insofar as the will devises an interest in land, it will be construed according to the law of the *situs* [Restatement (Second) of Conflict of Laws § 278].

H. **Corporations**
   1. The law of the state of incorporation determines the existence of a corporation and governs issues relative to its structure, such as the manner of electing directors, their authority and liability, the rights of its shareholders, the attributes of its shares, and the procedure for its dissolution [Restatement (Second) of Conflict of Laws §§ 296-313].

I. **Family Law**
   1. **Validity of Marriage**
      a. The validity of a marriage is generally governed by the law of the state where the ceremony took place, unless another state has the most significant relationship with the marriage (such as the domicile of the parties) and the marriage violates a strong public policy (not merely a law) of the other state [Restatement (Second) of Conflict of Laws § 283].
   2. **Divorce Decree from Sister State**
      a. The domicile of one of the parties to a marriage is a sufficient basis for a state to render a divorce, even if there is no personal service or domicile on the other party [Williams v. North Carolina, 317 U.S. 287 (1942); Restatement (Second) of Conflict of Laws § 285, cmt. a].
         (1) Therefore, where one spouse establishes a valid new domicile in another state and secures a divorce, the state of the

stay-at-home spouse must give full faith and credit to the divorce [Restatement (Second) of Conflict of Laws § 93].

    (2)   However, where only one spouse participates in a divorce proceeding, the stay-at-home spouse has the right to attack the finding of domicile of the procuring spouse, because there has been no contested hearing on the issue of domicile in the rendering state.

        (a) The divorce decree is presumptively valid until attacked [Cook v. Cook, 342 U.S. 126 (1951)].

    b.   Where both spouses participate in the divorce proceedings, jurisdiction must still be based upon the domicile of one of the parties.

        (1)   By participating in the out-of-state divorce, the stay-at-home spouse is barred by the doctrine of collateral estoppel from attacking the validity of the divorce, because the question of domicile has either actually been litigated or could have been litigated in the rendering state [Sherrer v. Sherrer, 334 U.S. 343 (1948)].

3.   **Divorce Decree from Foreign Nation**

    a.   A state need not recognize the validity of a foreign country divorce decree [Restatement (Second) of Conflict of Laws § 98, cmt. b].

    b.   Many states, however, will generally recognize such decrees on the basis of comity if both spouses were represented [Restatement (Second) of Conflict of Laws § 98, cmt. d].

VI. ESCAPE DEVICES

A. **The Substance-Procedure Distinction**
1. **In General**
   a. Because the forum state has a great interest in how cases are presented and tried in its own courts, when presented with a choice-of-law problem, it will usually apply its own procedural rules and practices [Restatement (Second) of Conflict of Laws § 122].
      (1) These "house rules" of litigation, which have little bearing on the outcome, should be governed by forum law both to promote convenience and practicality, and to ensure the proper administration of justice in the forum [Restatement (Second) of Conflict of Laws § 122, cmt. a].
   b. Consequently, the general conflicts principle is that matters of "**procedure**" are determined according to the law of the forum, and matters of "**substance**" are determined according to the forum's "choice-of-law" rules—rules which in some instances will result in the application of the substantive law of a sister state, and in other instances will result in the application of the substantive law of the forum [Restatement (Second) of Conflict of Laws § 122, cmt. b].
   c. Whether a matter is substantive or procedural for choice-of-law purposes is determined according to forum law.
      (1) Frequently, the forum characterizes an issue as procedural because it desires to apply its own law instead of having to use a foreign rule that it regards as less sound [Restatement (Second) of Conflict of Laws § 122, cmt. a].
      (2) The Supreme Court has intimated, however, that there may be some constitutional limits on arbitrary characterizations by state courts. An outrageous characterization by a forum court of a particular issue as procedural may be a violation of the Due Process and Full Faith and Credit Clauses of the United States Constitution [Wells v. Simonds Abrasive Co., 345 U.S. 514 (1953); John Hancock Mut. Life Ins. Co. v. Yates, 299 U.S. 178 (1936); Restatement (Second) of Conflict of Laws § 122, cmt. c].
   d. The forum sometimes will apply its own substantive law as well, either because it will not enforce the penal laws of another state [Huntington v. Attrill, 146 U.S. 657 (1892)], or because application of a particular foreign law would offend some strong public policy of the forum state.
2. **Specific Applications**
   a. **Statute of Limitations**
      (1) The statute of limitations is generally considered to bar the remedy and not the cause of action, and is therefore procedural and governed by the forum law [Restatement (Second) of Conflict of Laws § 142, cmt. e].

        (a)   However, if the foreign statute of limitations is so interwoven with the statute creating the cause of action as to become one of the elements necessary to establish the right, the time fixed is a limitation on the cause of action, and therefore substantive and governed by the foreign law [Restatement (Second) of Conflict of Laws § 142, cmt. g].

    (2)   Generally, if the statute gives a right of action that did not exist at common law, the time fixed is a condition attached to the right and is a limitation of the liability itself.

        (a)   The most common example is the limitations specified in wrongful death statutes, which are usually considered substantive [Id.].

b. **Evidence**

    (1)   Most evidentiary questions are procedural and are controlled by forum law [Restatement (Second) of Conflict of Laws § 138].

    (2)   Forum law determines the competence and credibility of witnesses [Restatement (Second) of Conflict of Laws § 137].

    (3)   However, if an evidentiary ruling would be "outcome determinative," it would be considered substantive (e.g., if violation of a statute is mere evidence of negligence in one state, and is negligence *per se* in the other state) [Restatement (Second) of Conflict of Laws § 138, cmt. c].

c. **Burden of Proof**

    (1)   Burden of proof is generally considered procedural and governed by the law of the forum [Restatement (Second) of Conflict of Laws § 133].

    (2)   However, if the primary purpose of a rule as to burden of persuasion is to affect the outcome (e.g., the plaintiff has the burden of proving lack of contributory negligence), the forum will apply the foreign state's rule [Id.].

d. **Presumptions**

    (1)   Presumptions, because they relate to the manner in which facts are proved, are matters of procedure and governed by the law of the forum [Restatement (Second) of Conflict of Laws § 134].

    (2)   However, a conclusive presumption would be treated as substantive [Restatement (Second) of Conflict of Laws § 134, cmt. a].

e. **Legal Duty Owed**

    (1)   Questions concerning legal duties owed, such as the standard of care the defendant owes the plaintiff, are clearly substantive and are governed by the law of the foreign state.

f. **Sufficiency of Facts and Evidence**

    (1)   The law of the forum determines whether there is sufficient evidence on an issue of fact to warrant its submission to a jury [Restatement (Second) of Conflict of Laws § 135].

g. **Parol Evidence Rule**

(1) The parol evidence rule is not a rule of evidence, but of substantive law [Restatement (Second) of Conflict of Laws § 140, cmt. c].

h. **Measure of Damages**

(1) The law of the state that creates the right of action determines the extent of damages.

i. **Statute of Frauds**

(1) The majority view treats the Statute of Frauds as substantive; thus, the law of the state where the contract was made would generally be applied [Restatement (Second) of Conflict of Laws § 141, cmt. b].

B. *Renvoi*

1. Once the court decides that it must refer to the law of another jurisdiction, the issue becomes how much foreign law applies—only the substantive law or the "whole" law, including its conflicts rule?

2. The doctrine of *renvoi* would apply the whole law, forcing the forum state to use the foreign state's conflict-of-law rules; these rules may refer back to the forum state's rules (remission) or to those of yet a third state (transmission).

3. In either case, the references back, theoretically, could result in an endless ping-pong game in which no state's substantive law was applied.

a. For this reason, the Second Restatement and most states have rejected *renvoi* [Restatement (Second) of Conflict of Laws § 8].

b. However, the Federal Tort Claims Act requires application of "the law of the place where the act or omission occurred," and this has been interpreted to mean the whole law, including its conflicts rules [28 U.S.C. § 1346(b); Richards v. United States, 369 U.S. 1 (1961)].

4. In general, most states follow the Restatement position and look only to the internal substantive law of a foreign jurisdiction.

a. However, the Restatement does require that a state look to the whole law of the foreign state in determining title to land and testate or intestate succession to interests in land or immovables [Restatement (Second) of Conflict of Laws §§ 8, 223, 236, 239, 240].

C. **Limitations on Applying Foreign Law**

1. In certain types of cases, states may decline to exercise jurisdiction for policy reasons.

2. **Penal Laws**

a. Courts will generally not enforce the penal laws of another state. A penal law's purpose is "to punish an offense against the public justice of a state," rather than "to afford a private remedy to a person injured by the wrongful act of another" [Huntington v. Attrill, 146 U.S. 657 (1892)].

3. **Revenue Laws**

a. As a general rule, a state will refuse to enforce the revenue laws of another state [Moore v. Mitchell, 281 U.S. 18 (1930)].

   b.   Such foreign laws or the rights and liabilities based thereon are not given extraterritorial effect by a sister state.

4.   **Public Policy**

   a.   Ordinarily, a state's courts will refuse to enforce a foreign state's rule if it is contrary to a strong public policy of the forum state [Restatement (Second) of Conflict of Laws § 90].

   b.   Conversely, "public policy" has been used to circumvent a limitation in a foreign state's law.

   EXAMPLE: Where State X's recovery in wrongful death actions is limited to $15,000, State Y might ignore the limitation by holding that its public policy of assuring full recovery of damages requires application of State Y's measure of damages.

5.   **Actions Involving Land in Another State**

   a.   Courts of the forum state will not ordinarily entertain cases in which the principal issue is title to land situated in another state because of the local expertise necessary to litigate such actions.

   b.   However, if the court has *in personam* jurisdiction over the parties, it may exercise its equitable power to require one party to convey property to the other.

D.   **Notice and Proof of Foreign Law**

1.   Federal statutes will be judicially noticed, and federal regulations and executive orders published in the Federal Register must be judicially noticed [44 U.S.C. § 1507].

2.   Statutes or session laws either printed by the authority of a sister state or proved to be commonly recognized in its courts are *prima facie* evidence, and the courts shall take judicial notice of them.

3.   Ordinarily, where the applicable law of a foreign state is not shown to be otherwise, it is presumed to be the same as that of the forum.

VII. JURISDICTION OF COURTS: LIMITS ON EXERCISE OF JURISDICTION

A. **Choice of Forum by Agreement**

1. Limitations on the exercise of judicial jurisdiction may be imposed by contract of the parties.

2. Choice of forum by agreement of the parties will be given effect unless it is unfair or unreasonable [Restatement (Second) of Conflict of Laws § 80].

    a. The burden of establishing unfairness or unreasonableness rests on the party who seeks to avoid a choice-of-forum provision [The Bremen v. Zapata Off-Shore Co., 407 U.S. 1 (1972)].

3. The parties cannot by their agreement oust a state of judicial jurisdiction [Restatement (Second) of Conflict of Laws § 80, cmt. a].

B. **Fraud, Force, and Privilege**

1. A state will not exercise judicial jurisdiction over a defendant or his property where such jurisdiction has been obtained by fraud or unlawful force [Jaster v. Currie, 198 U.S. 144 (1905); Restatement (Second) of Conflict of Laws § 82].

2. A state will not exercise judicial jurisdiction when required to refrain by the needs of judicial administration [Restatement (Second) of Conflict of Laws § 83].

    EXAMPLE: A state may grant immunity from service of process to nonresidents whose appearance is necessary for proper judicial proceeding; such immunity is ordinarily granted to witnesses and lawyers in order to encourage their appearance.

3. A state will not exercise judicial jurisdiction when prohibited by international law or by treaty [Id.].

    EXAMPLE: Foreign sovereigns and their ambassadors and ministers are immune from suit.

C. *Forum Non Conveniens*

1. The doctrine of *forum non conveniens* establishes that a state will not exercise jurisdiction where it is a significantly inconvenient forum for the action, provided that a more appropriate forum is available to the plaintiff [Restatement (Second) of Conflict of Laws § 84].

2. It is within the discretion of the trial judge to determine the applicability of the rule as founded upon the following two most important factors [Restatement (Second) of Conflict of Laws § 84, cmts. b, c]:

    a. that the plaintiff's choice of forum should not be disturbed except for weighty reasons; and

    b. that the action will not be dismissed unless a suitable alternative forum is available to the plaintiff.

3. Particularly where the plaintiff is a resident of the chosen forum, his choice will rarely be disturbed [Restatement (Second) of Conflict of Laws § 84, cmt. f].

4.   Other significant considerations are [Gulf Oil Corp. v. Gilbert, 330 U.S. 501 (1947)]:

    a.   the relative ease of access to sources of proof;

    b.   availability of compulsory process for attendance of unwilling witnesses, and the cost of obtaining attendance of willing witnesses;

    c.   possibility of a view of the premises, if appropriate;

    d.   enforceability of a judgment;

    e.   judicial administrative difficulties; and

    f.   all other practical problems.

5.   Usually, if a court finds itself an inappropriate forum, it will stay the action until suit is brought in another forum, or dismiss it conditionally, requiring that the defendant stipulate to accept process and not plead the statute of limitations in another state [Restatement (Second) of Conflict of Laws § 84, cmt. e].

VIII. CONSTITUTIONAL LIMITS ON CHOICE OF LAW

A. In General

1. The Due Process Clause of the Fourteenth Amendment and the Full Faith and Credit Clause of Article IV, which are treated as coextensive for this purpose, impose some minimal limitations on the power of state courts to make choice-of-law decisions [Restatement (Second) of Conflict of Laws § 2, cmt. b].

B. Due Process

1. According to the United States Supreme Court's current doctrine, "[f]or a State's substantive law to be selected in a constitutionally permissible manner, that State must have a significant contact or significant aggregation of contacts, creating state interests, such that choice of its law is neither arbitrary nor fundamentally unfair" [Allstate Ins. Co. v. Hague, 449 U.S. 302 (1981)].

> **NOTE** The term "creating state interests" does not mean "interests" as that term is used in the interest-analysis approach to choice of law followed in some states. "Interest" for constitutional purposes can be based on a state's factual contacts with the underlying transaction, regardless of whether those factual contacts give rise to the state's interest in applying its law in order to implement the policy reflected in that law.

EXAMPLE: Two residents of State A are involved in an accident in State B. The law of State A allows unlimited recovery. The law of State B limits recovery of non-economic damages to $200,000. The State A plaintiff brings suit against the State A defendant in State A. State A is one of the states still applying the traditional approach to choice of law, and holds that tort liability is governed by the law of State B. The fact that the accident occurred in State B is a constitutional contact, and for that reason, State B has a constitutional interest in having its law applied to determine liability for the accident.

EXAMPLE: A resident of State A is driving in State B, where she is severely injured in an accident caused by the negligence of a State B driver. As required by State B law (and the laws of all states), the State B driver's automobile liability insurance policy covers liability under the law of every state into which the vehicle is driven. The State A plaintiff brings suit against the State B driver in State A. The law of State A allows unlimited recovery. The law of State B limits recovery of non-economic damages to $200,000. The plaintiff's residence in State A is a constitutional contact. Because State A has a real interest in applying its law permitting unlimited recovery of non-economic damages for the benefit of the State A resident, and because the State B resident's insurance covers him for unlimited liability for non-economic damages, the application of State A law to allow unlimited recovery can be sustained under the interest and fairness test.

C. Full Faith and Credit

1. The Full Faith and Credit Clause precludes a state from discriminating against claims arising under the law of a sister state [Restatement (Second) of Conflict of Laws § 93].

   a. This means that if a state allows a substantive claim, such as a claim for wrongful death, under its own law, it cannot bar a claim for wrongful death arising under the law of a sister state.

2. A state is not required to accord special treatment to claims arising under the law of a sister state. It can apply neutral rules to these claims, such as its own statute of limitations to determine the timeliness of the claim, and rules relating to the dismissal of a case on grounds of *forum non conveniens*.

   EXAMPLE: The Wisconsin Wrongful Death Act applies only when the death occurs in Wisconsin. Since the effect of the law is to bar a suit under the wrongful death act of a sister state, it is violative of full faith and credit, and the Wisconsin courts must entertain a suit brought under the Illinois Wrongful Death Act [Hughes v. Fetter, 341 U.S. 609 (1951)]. If the suit were barred by the Wisconsin statute of limitations, the Wisconsin court could apply its statute of limitations to bar the suit, even if the suit would not be barred by the Illinois statute of limitations [Wells v. Simonds Abrasives Co., 345 U.S. 514 (1953)].

IX. RECOGNITION AND ENFORCEMENT OF SISTER STATE AND FOREIGN JUDGMENTS

A. Full Faith and Credit

1. The Full Faith and Credit Clause, and its implementing legislation, embody a national policy of maximum recognition of sister-state judgments (including federal court judgments) by sister-state courts [U.S. Const. art. IV, § 1; 28 U.S.C. § 1738].

> **NOTE** The court that issued the judgment is referred to as F-1 (forum 1), and the court where recognition is sought, either by way of an action to enforce the judgment or by way of defense to an action brought there, is referred to as F-2 (forum 2).

2. A state court must recognize a final judgment on the merits issued by a sister-state court, and cannot refuse recognition of the judgment on the grounds that it is contrary to the public policy of F-2, that the judgment is wrong, that the judgment is based on a tax law, or on the grounds that F-2 has an interest in not recognizing the judgment [Restatement (Second) of Conflict of Laws § 93].

   EXAMPLE: A Missouri court entered a judgment in a case where all the facts were connected with Mississippi and where the Missouri court applied Mississippi law to uphold a contract that was invalid under Mississippi law. Suit was brought in Mississippi to enforce the Missouri judgment. As a matter of full faith and credit, the Mississippi court had to enforce the judgment, even though it was based on an incorrect application of Mississippi law [Faunterloy v. Lum, 210 U.S. 230 (1908)].

3. The Full Faith and Credit Clause does not require a court to recognize a judgment of a sister-state court that:

   a. is not a final judgment [Restatement (Second) of Conflict of Laws § 107];

      (1) A judgment is not a final judgment when it is subject to modification in the F-1 court, as in the case of a custody decree (which is always modifiable on the basis of changed circumstances) [Kovacs v. Brewer, 356 U.S. 604 (1958)], or a support judgment that is modifiable retroactively [Barber v. Barber, 323 U.S. 77 (1944)].

> **NOTE** The fact that custody decrees are not entitled to full faith and credit gave rise to conflicting custody orders and constant relitigation of custody issues in different states. These problems were substantially resolved by the enactment of the Uniform Child Custody Jurisdiction and Enforcement Act and the federal Parental Kidnapping Prevention Act.

   b. is not a judgment on the merits [Restatement (Second) of Conflict of Laws § 110]; or

      (1) A judgment not on the merits includes a judgment dismissing the suit as being barred by the statute of limitations or as being against the forum's public policy, and an anti-suit injunction prohibiting a party from filing a suit in another state.

   c. is not valid [Restatement (Second) of Conflict of Laws § 93, cmt. a].

4. There are three circumstances in which the F-2 court can refuse to recognize a final F-1 judgment on the merits:

   a. where the F-1 court lacked jurisdiction in the due process sense [Restatement (Second) of Conflict of Laws § 96], and the F-1 decree was entered *ex parte* so that the party challenging the F-1 judgment in F-2 could not litigate the jurisdictional question in F-1 [Restatement (Second) of Conflict of Laws § 103, cmt. b];

   EXAMPLE: A Nevada court, in a divorce proceeding brought by the husband, issued an *ex parte* divorce decree, dissolving the marriage of a North Carolina couple. In Nevada, jurisdiction is based on the husband's domicile, and the domicile of one of the parties is a constitutional requirement for the exercise of jurisdiction to divorce. The husband returned to North Carolina, and the divorce was put in issue there. North Carolina, consistent with full faith and credit, determined that the husband was not domiciled in Nevada and refused to recognize the Nevada divorce decree [Williams v. North Carolina II, 325 U.S. 226 (1945)].

   b. where the judgment is subject to collateral attack in the F-1 court on grounds such as lack of subject-matter jurisdiction or fraud [Restatement (Second) of Conflict of Laws § 97]; and

      (1) The F-2 court can permit a collateral attack on those grounds, applying F-1 law to determine whether the collateral attack will be sustained.

      EXAMPLE: Under New Jersey law, a magistrate's court did not have subject-matter jurisdiction to condemn a vessel for illegal use unless such use occurred in the county in which the magistrate's court was located. Under New Jersey law, a judgment can be collaterally attacked for lack of subject-matter jurisdiction. A trespass action to recover for seizure of the vessel was brought against a New Jersey sheriff in New York. The New York court could determine independently whether the illegal use occurred in the county where the vessel was seized because, if the illegal use did not occur in that county, the magistrate's court lacked subject-matter jurisdiction to condemn the vessel [Thompson v. Whitman, 85 U.S. 457 (1873)].

   c. where enforcement of the judgment is barred by the nondiscriminatory application of the forum's statute of limitations—that is, the forum must apply the same statute of limitations to the enforcement of viable foreign judgments that it applies to the enforcement of domestic judgments [Restatement (Second) of Conflict of Laws § 118(2)].

      (1) If the judgment has been revised in F-1, the forum must apply its statute of limitations to the revised judgments [Watkins v. Conway, 385 U.S. 188 (1966); Union National Bank v. Lamb, 337 U.S. 38 (1949)].

NOTE There is a special rule for recognition of workers' compensation decrees. A workers' compensation decree in F-1 will not bar an action for additional workers' compensation in F-2 unless the F-1 workers' compensation law includes unmistakable language that is intended to bar subsequent claims for workers' compensation [Thomas v. Washington Gas Light Co., 448 U.S. 261 (1980)].

5. **Race to Judgment**
   a. Where two courts are exercising jurisdiction over the same case and neither chooses to stay its hand, the first final judgment that is rendered is entitled to full faith and credit and must be recognized by the court of the other state, regardless of which suit was filed first [Morris v. Jones, 329 U.S. 545 (1947)].

6. **Last-in-Time Rule**
   a. Where there are conflicting determinations of jurisdiction by different courts, and the parties appeared in both proceedings, the determination of jurisdiction by the second court, even though it may have denied full faith and credit to the judgment of the first court, is binding on the parties and on the first court, as a matter of full faith and credit [Treinies v. Sunshine Mining Co., 308 U.S. 66 (1939)].

7. **Collateral Estoppel Effect to Sister-State Court**
   a. Whether or not to give collateral estoppel effect to a factual finding that was made in an action in a sister-state court is a matter of F-2 law, and F-2 is not precluded by full faith and credit from giving collateral estoppel effect to that finding, even if it would not have collateral estoppel effect under F-1 law [Restatement (Second) of Conflict of Laws § 95, cmt. g].

   EXAMPLE: An airplane that departed from New York crashed in Kentucky. The first case to come to trial was brought in Texas. The court submitted the issue of the carrier's negligence to the jury, which found in favor of the plaintiffs. A wrongful death suit arising out of the accident was brought in New York by New York plaintiffs. Under the New York law of collateral estoppel, collateral estoppel effect would be given to the finding of negligence. Under Texas law, collateral estoppel effect would not be given to the finding of negligence. The New York court gave collateral estoppel effect to the finding of negligence [Hart v. American Airlines, 304 N.Y.S.2d 810 (N.Y. Sup. Ct. 1969)].

X. PREEMPTION

A. In General

1. Federal preemption of state law will be found in four situations:

   a. **Express Preemption**

      (1) Congress may specifically prohibit the states from enacting a particular substantive rule of law, as Congress did when it prohibited the states from imposing vicarious liability on automobile rental companies [49 U.S.C. § 30106]. This statute preempted a New York law, imposing such liability on automobile rental companies.

   b. **Actual Conflict Preemption**

      (1) Whenever a state law is in direct conflict with a federal law, the state law is preempted to the extent of the conflict [Florida Lime & Avocado Growers, Inc. v. Paul, 373 U.S. 132 (1963)].

      EXAMPLE: The federal agency established by Congress to regulate federally chartered savings and loan associations issued a regulation authorizing the savings and loan associations to include due-on-sale clauses in the mortgages they issue. (A due-on-sale clause requires that the buyer pay off the mortgage at the time the buyer sells the home, and so prevents the buyer from transferring the mortgage to the next purchaser.) A state law prohibits due-on-sale clauses in home mortgages. The state law cannot be applied to prevent the enforcement of due-on-sale clauses in mortgages issued by federally chartered savings and loan associations [Fidelity Federal Savings and Loan Ass'n v. de la Cuesta, 458 U.S. 141 (1982)].

   c. **Implied Conflict Preemption**

      (1) When the applicable federal law itself establishes a standard of federal preemption, the law preempts state law that is inconsistent with the federal standard of preemption. For the same reason, a state law regulating a matter in issue that is consistent with the federal statute of preemption is not preempted.

      EXAMPLE: The Federal Arbitration Act [9 U.S.C. §§ 1, et seq.] provides that the arbitrator shall decide all questions under the contract, including questions relating to time limits. It does not prohibit the parties from providing that the law of a particular state will govern their contract. In their contract, the parties provided for arbitration and further provided that the agreement and its enforcement shall be governed by New York law. The New York Court of Appeals concluded that the Federal Arbitration Act did not preempt New York's determination that, in light of the parties' express choice of New York law, the question of the applicability of the New York statute of limitations was for the courts, rather than the arbitrator, to decide [Smith Barney, Harris Upham & Co. v. Luckie, 647 N.E.2d 1308 (N.Y. 1995)].

d. **Field Preemption**

(1)   In limited cases, "the scheme of federal regulation is so pervasive as to make reasonable the inference that Congress left no room for the state to supplement it" [Rice v. Santa Fe Elevator Corp., 331 U.S. 218 (1947)]. This is called **implied field preemption**.

(2)   The Supreme Court, for example, has found implied field preemption with respect to the federal labor relations law [29 U.S.C. §§ 157, 158], which preempts state law with respect to questions of unfair labor practices and employee rights that are within the jurisdiction of the National Labor Relations Board [San Diego Building Trades Council v. Garmon, 359 U.S. 236 (1959)].

(3)   A state law is invalid as a matter of federal supremacy if it conflicts with a federal treaty or interferes with federal power over foreign affairs [U.S. Const. art. VI, cl. 2].

EXAMPLE: An 1881 treaty between the United States and Serbia granted Serbian citizens "most favored nation" rights, including the same right to inherit in the United States that was given to citizens of foreign countries. An Oregon statute denied inheritance rights to nonresident aliens in certain circumstances, including the Serbian heirs of an Oregon decedent. The Court ruled that the Oregon statute was violative of the treaty between the United States and Serbia, and the Serbian heirs were entitled to inherit the property [Kolovart v. Oregon, 366 U.S. 187 (1961)].

Corporations

TABLE OF CONTENTS

I. INTRODUCTION

A. Governing Law

1. This chapter is devised to present the subject of Corporations based on general law. The summary generally follows the Model Business Corporation Act ("MBCA" or "Model Act").

   a. The MBCA has been subject to a number of revisions and alterations, the most recent of which was in 2002. The MBCA, in some form, has been adopted in substance in most states.

B. Characteristics

1. A **corporation** is a legal entity created by complying with the statute governing incorporation; it is strictly a creature of statute, existing only because permitted by statute. There is no common law right to organize a corporation.

2. The law regards a corporation as an entity distinct from its shareholders, whether it is a large public corporation with thousands of shareholders, a small, closely held corporation with two or three shareholders, or a sole proprietorship with one shareholder. A shareholder has rights to corporate property only when a dividend is declared or when the corporation is liquidated; if his stock has voting rights, he participates in managing the corporate assets through his power to elect directors.

3. The major characteristics of a corporation are:

   a. freely transferable shares;

   b. a continuous existence, despite the death of individual shareholders;

   c. limited liability of the shareholders; and

   d. centralized management of assets by directors and officers.

C. Corporate Powers

1. Corporations for profit may be organized under the MBCA for any lawful purpose except for the purpose of banking or insurance.

2. Medical and professional service corporations may be organized under the MBCA.

3. The MBCA sets out a list of powers each corporation inherently has under the MBCA, but generally a corporation may exercise all powers necessary or convenient to effect any or all of the purposes for which the corporation was formed.

II. FORMATION OF CORPORATIONS

A. **Articles of Incorporation**

1. A corporation is ordinarily created by filing the articles of incorporation with the secretary of state.

2. The original incorporator(s) will file the articles; any natural person(s), or any domestic or foreign corporation(s), may act as incorporator.

3. The articles of incorporation can be amended through a lengthy process whereby the board of directors proposes the amendment to the shareholders and the shareholders vote on the amendment. The details of the procedure are discussed in a later section of the outline.

4. **Mandatory Provisions**

   a. Under the Model Act, the articles of incorporation must include:

      (1) the incorporators' names and addresses;

      (2) the name of the corporation;

      (3) the name and address of the initial registered agent; and

      (4) the number of shares the corporation is authorized to issue.

   b. **Purpose**

      (1) A corporation may be formed for the transaction of any or all lawful business for which corporations may be incorporated under the Model Act.

   c. **Name**

      (1) The name must contain the word "corporation," "company," "incorporated," or "limited," or an abbreviation of one of these words.

      (2) The name may not be the same as, or deceptively similar to, the name of any domestic or foreign corporation authorized to transact business in the state, unless the first corporation files written consent with the secretary of state.

      (3) A corporate name may be reserved prior to incorporation by filing it with the secretary of state.

   d. **Stock**

      (1) Relevant information regarding stock includes:

         (a) the total number of shares and the par value, if any, of each class of stock that the corporation is authorized to issue; and

         (b) if more than one class is authorized, the preferences, voting powers, qualifications, and special rights or privileges of each class and series.

      (2) The corporation need not issue as many shares as are authorized; as little as one share may actually be issued.

      (3) The articles of incorporation need not state the number and type of shares actually issued, or the consideration received for the shares.

5. **Optional Provisions**
   a. Under the Model Act, the articles of incorporation may also include:
      (1) the names and addresses of the individuals who will be serving as the initial directors;
      (2) any lawful provision regarding:
         (a) the purpose(s) for which the corporation is being organized;
         (b) managing the business and regulating the affairs of the corporation;
         (c) defining, limiting, and regulating the powers of the corporation, its board of directors, and shareholders;
         (d) a par value for authorized shares or classes of shares; or
         (e) the imposition of personal liability on shareholders for debts of the corporation;
      (3) any provision required or permitted to be set forth in the bylaws;
      (4) a provision eliminating or limiting the personal liability of a director for breach of the duty of good faith; and
      (5) a provision permitting or making obligatory indemnification of a director for certain liability.
   b. If any preemptive rights are to be granted to the shareholders, the provisions applicable to those rights must appear in the articles of incorporation.
   c. If no duration of existence is specified in the articles, the corporation will have perpetual existence.

B. **Organization Meeting and Bylaws**
   1. **Initial Directors Named**
      a. After incorporation, if initial directors are named in the articles of incorporation, they must hold an organizational meeting at a call of the majority of directors to complete the organization of the corporation by:
         (1) appointing officers;
         (2) adopting bylaws; and
         (3) carrying on any other business brought before the meeting.
   2. **Initial Directors Not Named**
      a. If initial directors are not named in the articles of incorporation, the incorporator(s) must hold an organizational meeting at the call of a majority of incorporators to either elect directors and complete organization or elect a board of directors, who will then complete the organization of the corporation.
   3. **Bylaws**
      a. **Bylaws** are internal rules and regulations enacted by the corporation to govern its actions and relations to its shareholders, directors, and officers.
      b. Bylaws may include any provisions for the regulation and management of the affairs of the corporation that are not inconsistent with law or with the articles of incorporation.

    c.   The bylaws often specify:

        (1)   the time and place for the annual shareholders' meeting;

        (2)   the record date for determining the shareholders entitled to vote at meetings or to receive dividends;

        (3)   the number of shareholders necessary to constitute a quorum;

        (4)   the percentage of votes necessary to authorize corporate action; and

        (5)   any restrictions on transferability of shares.

    d.   The power to alter, amend, or repeal the bylaws or to adopt new bylaws, subject to repeal or change by action of the shareholders, will be vested in the board of directors unless exclusively reserved for the shareholders by the articles of incorporation or the shareholders, in amending, repealing, or adopting a bylaw, expressly provide that the board of directors may not amend, repeal, or reinstate that bylaw [MBCA § 10.20].

        (1)   Unless the articles of incorporation provide otherwise, the board of directors may adopt bylaws by their own action in the event of an attack on the United States or any nuclear or atomic disaster, which are subject to amendment or repeal by the shareholders [MBCA § 2.07(a)].

        (2)   The emergency bylaws are not effective after the emergency ends [MBCA § 2.07(b)].

C. Defective Incorporation

1.   A disappointed creditor of a corporation may seek to enforce a corporate liability against persons who knowingly purported to act as shareholders or as agents of the corporation when the corporation did not, in fact, exist.

2.   The success of such an attack depends upon the organizers' compliance with the incorporation statute and the corporation's resulting legal status.

3.   *De Jure* Corporation

    a.   A corporation organized in compliance with the statute is a *de jure* corporation.

    b.   Failure of the organizer(s) to comply with a mandatory statutory provision will preclude *de jure* status.

    c.   Use of the words "must" or "shall" in the statute usually characterizes a mandatory provision.

    d.   In general, corporate existence begins when the articles of incorporation become effective (generally upon being filed with the proper state agency as prescribed by statute); a certified statement of the fact of incorporation by the state is generally considered evidence of *de jure* status.

4.   *De Facto* Corporation

    a.   If statutory compliance is insufficient for *de jure* status, a *de facto* corporation may still have been formed if:

        (1)   a good-faith, colorable attempt was made to comply with the incorporation statute; and

        (2)   the corporate principals, in good faith, acted as if they were a corporation.

b. *De facto* status insulates directors and shareholders from liability except in a direct action by the state.

c. All persons who purports to act as or on behalf of the corporation, knowing there was no incorporation, are jointly and severally liable for all liabilities created while so acting [MBCA § 2.04].

d. The *de facto* doctrine rarely applies today, however, because the state must approve the articles before they are filed, and a statement by the state of the fact of incorporation is conclusive evidence of incorporation.

5. **Corporation by Estoppel**

a. Absent *de jure* or *de facto* status, a corporation may still exist by estoppel.

b. If a creditor always dealt with the principals as if they were a corporation, he will be estopped from later alleging that the corporation is defective if that would unjustly harm the principals.

c. In the same manner, a defendant that has held itself out to be a corporation cannot try to avoid liability by claiming the plaintiff has no cause of action because the defendant is not a legal entity.

d. The estoppel doctrine is not a defense to a tort claim, as the claimant has not previously dealt with the principals as if they were a corporation in a contractual transaction.

e. It may be relevant in contract claims, however, where a prior business relationship exists.

D. *Ultra Vires*

1. The board of directors is not permitted to undertake action that is beyond the corporation's authority, as set forth in the articles of incorporation or bylaws.

2. Under the **ultra vires doctrine**, a corporation cannot be obliged to undertake a contract or activity that is beyond the scope of its powers, as described in the articles of incorporation or bylaws.

3. Under the Model Act, a corporation's power to act may only be challenged [MBCA § 3.04]:

a. in a proceeding by a shareholder to enjoin the act;

b. in a proceeding by the corporation (directly, derivatively, or through a representative) against a current or former director, officer, employee, or agent of the corporation; and

c. in a proceeding by the attorney general based on the grounds that:

(1) the corporation obtained its articles through fraud; or

(2) the corporation has continued to exceed or abuse the authority conferred upon it by law.

4. In addition, the *ultra vires* doctrine has little applicability today, since the articles of incorporation typically authorize the corporation to engage in all legal activities. All that remain are activities that are illegal or that are not directed to any business purpose.

EXAMPLE: Dan, CFO of Acme Corporation, sought a personal loan from Bank to finance the purchase of a new yacht. The board of directors of Acme agreed with Bank that if Dan defaulted on the loan, Acme would guarantee the debt. On that basis, Bank loaned a large sum to Dan. The yacht Dan purchased later sank in the deep ocean, and Dan had allowed insurance on the yacht to lapse. Dan defaulted on his loan to Bank. Bank sued Acme on the guaranty agreement. The guaranty must be paid even though *ultra vires*. The board may be sued for breaching its fiduciary duty in agreeing to the *ultra vires* act.

E. Piercing the Corporate Veil

1. Even if a corporation is properly formed, a court may disregard its separate entity and hold shareholders or affiliated corporations liable on corporate obligations. This is known as **piercing the corporate veil**.

2. As a general rule, a corporation will be looked upon as a separate and legal entity, unless the entity is used to commit fraud or to achieve inequitable results.

   a. One of the strongest reasons for attaining corporate status is the limited liability for the shareholders, meaning that the shareholders are not personally liable for the debts and obligations of the corporation.

      (1) The creditors of the corporation are limited in recovery of any claim to the assets of the corporation.

   b. An individual has the right to use the corporate form to shield him from personal liability, and a corporation has the right to use a subsidiary for the same purpose.

3. **Alter Ego**

   a. To pierce the corporate veil, a plaintiff must demonstrate that:

      (1) there is control so complete that the corporation has no separate will or existence of its own, and in fact the shareholder was the alter ego of the corporation or a mere instrumentality of a parent corporation;

      (2) the corporate form has been used fraudulently or for an improper purpose (e.g., using corporate assets for personal benefit or a commingling of funds); and

      (3) injury or unjust loss resulted to the plaintiff from such control and wrong.

   b. Common ownership of the stock of two or more corporations, together with common management (such as a parent-subsidiary relationship) will not alone render one corporation liable for the acts of the other corporation or its employees.

   c. However, liability may be imposed where [My Bread Baking Co. v. Cumberland Farms, Inc., 233 N.E.2d 753 (Mass. 1968)]:

      (1) the representatives of one corporation actively and directly participate in and apparently exercise pervasive control over the activities of the other corporation, and some fraudulent or injurious consequence of the relationship results; or

(2) there is an intermingling of activity of corporations engaged in a common enterprise, with substantial disregard of the separate nature of the corporate entities, or serious ambiguity about the manner and capacity in which the corporations and their representatives are acting.

d. Where there is common control of a group of separate corporations engaged in a single enterprise, disregard of the separate entities may be warranted to prevent gross inequity if the corporations failed to:

(1) make clear which corporation was taking action in a particular situation, and the nature and extent of that action; or

(2) observe with care the formal barriers between the corporations, with a proper segregation of their separate businesses, records, and finances.

4. **Inadequate Capitalization**

a. Although adequacy of capitalization is a factor considered by the courts, inadequate capitalization alone will not ordinarily lead to disregard of the corporate entity if the corporate formalities are carefully observed.

b. **Adequate capital** is not precisely defined, but generally, capital must be sufficient for the corporation's prospective needs and for meeting corporate debts as they become due.

c. A subsidiary's capital must be sufficient to allow it financial independence from the parent corporation.

(1) A **subsidiary** is a company wholly owned by another company, the **parent.**

5. **Failure to Comply with Corporate Formalities**

a. If, through a defect in incorporation, no corporation was formed, those attempting to act as a corporation may be held personally liable.

b. However, only those active in managing the corporation would be held personally liable, as individual contractors, as agents of a nonexistent principal, or for fraud.

6. **Liability**

a. The corporate veil is more likely to be pierced in a tort action than in a contract action, because in a contract action, a third party is able to investigate whom it is contracting with and can seek guarantees from any parent company of a subsidiary with whom it is contracting.

b. If the corporate veil is pierced, liability is generally imposed only upon shareholders active in management, although it is sometimes imposed on inactive shareholders as well.

c. Liability is for the full amount of the debt, not merely for the amount that would have constituted adequate capital.

d. In a tort suit seeking to impose personal liability on shareholders, the court will look to the amount of liability insurance available in addition to the corporate capital.

e. Corporate officers are not liable for breach of warranty of authority because they are duly authorized agents of a valid corporation.

III. PREINCORPORATION TRANSACTIONS

A. Promoters

1. A **promoter** is one who causes a corporation to be formed, organized, and financed.

   EXAMPLE: Sensei Chu wants to form "Shiro Dojo, Inc.," a corporation created for the purpose of teaching martial arts. Before the corporation is formed, he enters into a commercial lease for property to be used as the future company's dojo. Sensei Chu is a promoter of the corporation.

2. In small corporations, the promoters usually, although not necessarily, become the incorporators, shareholders, officers, and directors of the new corporation.

3. The promoter's function is to set up the corporation and establish it on firm footing.

4. Typically, the promoter will:

   a. manage the initial financing of the corporation;

   b. arrange for a meeting of the investors;

   c. negotiate and prepare the preincorporation agreements;

   d. lease office and factory space; and

   e. contract for the initial needs of the business.

B. Promoters' Relationship to the Corporation

1. Promoters stand in a fiduciary relationship to the corporation, its subscribers for stock, and those who are expected will afterwards buy stock from the corporation.

2. Promoters are under a duty to avoid self-dealing (duty of loyalty) concerning any assets they sell to the corporation.

3. **Duty of Disclosure**

   a. If the cost and manner of acquisition of the assets by the promoter were fully disclosed to an independent board of directors, and the board approved the transaction, the promoter has not breached his fiduciary duty of loyalty and he may keep any profit from the sale.

   b. **Board Approval**

      (1) If the only shareholders of the corporation are the promoters and no further issuance of stock is contemplated, the self-interested transaction is not a violation of the fiduciary duty of loyalty to the corporation.

      (2) Thus, the corporation has no cause of action even if shares are later sold to the public without disclosure, since the corporation is not a party to the resale.

      (3) However, the purchaser may have a cause of action against the promoters for failure to disclose under federal securities law statutes.

          (4)   If the corporation becomes insolvent, a creditor might be able to assert the corporation's rights against the promoters.

    c.   **Additional Shareholders Are Contemplated**

          (1)   If the original promotional scheme contemplates sale of stock to other investors, the corporation has an action for breach of fiduciary duty against a promoter who fails to fully disclose material facts about property transferred in an interested transaction.

          (2)   However, if the new shareholders purchase their shares from the promoters and not the corporation, the corporation has no cause of action.

          (3)   The promoter will not be liable to the corporation if he made full disclosure to:

               (a)   all the original subscribers for shares and obtained their approval; or

               (b)   the shareholders of the established corporation and they ratified the transaction.

    4.   **Promoters' Liability for Breach of Fiduciary Duty**

        a.   In an action for breach of the promoters' fiduciary duty of loyalty, the corporation may either:

          (1)   avoid the transaction; or

          (2)   hold the promoters liable for the secret profits.

C. Promoters' Relationship with Other Promoters

    1.   If there is more than one promoter of a corporation, the promoters are, in effect, joint venturers and owe each other a fiduciary duty.

    2.   As fiduciaries, they cannot make a secret profit on assets that they transfer to the promoters as a group, and must fully disclose to each other information concerning the formation of the corporation.

    3.   There is a mutual agency among the promoters, such that each can bind the others on contracts within the scope of the promotion.

D. Preincorporation Contracts

    1.   Before incorporation, promoters frequently enter into consensual agreements with third parties relative to the proposed corporation.

    2.   As the corporation is not yet in existence, it cannot contract in its own name, nor can the promoters contract on the corporation's behalf as its agents.

    3.   The question then arises as to who is liable on the contracts and who can enforce them.

    4.   Generally, promoters are liable for the contracts entered into on behalf of the corporation not yet formed, but where the contract specifically disclaims personal liability of the promoter, the obligee will not be able to successfully maintain an action against the promoter.

5.   To determine whether the obligee intended to hold the promoter personally liable or to look exclusively to the future corporation, courts examine the circumstances carefully to determine the intent of the parties, including whether the third party had knowledge that the corporation would come into existence and adopt the contract.

EXAMPLE: Carl, owner of an appliance store, urged Patty to purchase an expensive espresso machine for the coffee shop she was planning to open. Patty told Carl that she was forming a corporation to operate the shop, but hadn't completed the paperwork and wanted to wait. Carl told Patty, "That's OK," and that she should simply sign the contract of sale as "president" of the corporation to be formed. Thereafter, Patty was unable to form her corporation or open her coffee shop, and never accepted delivery of the espresso machine. If Carl sued Patty to recover for breach of contract, Patty would probably prevail because, in these circumstances, it appears that Carl intended to look to the future corporation only for payment under the contract. It would have been best for Carl to explicitly memorialize this expectation in the contract.

6.   **Liability of the Promoter**

   a.   **General Rule**

      (1)   As a general rule, the promoter is personally liable on any contract he enters into on behalf of the still nonexistent corporation, absent contrary intent of the parties, unless the corporation expressly or impliedly adopts the contract after formation and discharges the promoter through a valid novation.

   b.   **Promoter Personally Liable**

      (1)   When the corporation forms, it does not automatically become liable on the contract.

      (2)   A promoter's personal liability will continue even after the corporation is formed unless there is:

         (a)   a novation; or

         (b)   an agreement to release liability.

      (3)   **Novation**

         (a)   A **novation** occurs if the corporation adopts the contract and all of the parties agree that the promoter will be discharged from the contract and the corporation substituted in the promoter's place.

         (b)   Even if the promoter is personally liable on the contract, a novation will release him from that liability.

         (c)   The consideration for the promoter's release is the assumption of liability by the corporation [Restatement (Second) of Contracts §§ 424, et seq.].

         (d)   A novation is usually express, by way of a board resolution, but might be implied from the actions of the parties.

(4) **Agency Principles**

  (a) If the promoter signs as an agent, he is generally personally liable because he cannot be an agent for a nonexistent principal.

  (b) A promoter may be personally liable for obligations created by another promoter under normal agency principles, as when the promoters are joint venturers, or when adoption occurs.

  (c) A promoter is not liable, by reason of his promoter status alone and in the absence of an agency relationship between promoters, on preincorporation contracts made by other promoters.

c. **Indemnification**

  (1) Even if the promoter is held liable on the contract, he may be entitled to reimbursement by the corporation if he undertook the contract in good faith, at least to the extent that the corporation benefited from the contract.

7. **Liability of the Corporation**

a. **General Rule**

  (1) As a general rule, a corporation is not liable on any preincorporation agreements its promoters entered into on its behalf, unless it assumes liability by its own act after it comes into existence.

  (2) If the contract was made for the corporation's benefit, concerned a matter on which the corporation could legally contract, and full disclosure was made to an independent board, the new corporation may assume liability.

b. **Novation or Adoption**

  (1) If all the parties agree to substitute the liability of the corporation for that of the promoter, there is a novation and the promoter is discharged.

  (2) Note that, in some states, the corporation cannot become a party to a preincorporation contract by simply adopting it. In those jurisdictions, there must be a novation or a new contract.

  (3) Some courts prefer to view the corporation as having adopted the contract of the promoter. When there is such an adoption, the promoter may remain liable on the contract with the third party, but will be entitled to indemnification from the newly created corporation.

  (4) Adoption can be express or implied.

    (a) **Express adoption** occurs where the contract is explicitly approved or adopted by the board of directors.

    (b) **Implied adoption** occurs where the corporation accepts or acknowledges the benefits of the contract in some manner.

    EXAMPLE: Paul entered into a contract with Furn "on behalf of Acme Corporation, a corporation to be formed," to purchase several thousand dollars' worth of office furniture. Paul subsequently caused Acme to be validly formed. Furn delivered the furniture to Acme headquarters, and corporate employees moved it into the offices and began using that furniture. Acme is liable on the contract to Furn even though the board never formally adopted the Paul-Furn contract.

    c. **Acceptance of Benefits**

        (1)   A corporation may become bound to fulfill a contract made in its name and on its behalf in anticipation of its existence by afterwards accepting the benefits of the contract, at least to the extent of the fair value of the goods or services received.

        (2)   A corporation may be liable under *quasi*-contract or unjust enrichment.

        (3)   If, after incorporation, it accepts an assignment of the rights and obligations of the contract with full knowledge of the terms, the corporation will be liable.

8.   **Liability of a Third Party**

    a.   A third party who enters into a contract with a promoter is liable from the contract's inception.

    b.   The corporation cannot later claim the benefits of the promoter's contract with a third party, unless the third party accepts performance by the corporation.

    c.   The promoter can still usually enforce the contract.

    d.   If the corporation assumes liability for the promoter's contract, it can enforce the contract.

E.   Subscriptions for Shares

1.   A person may become a shareholder of a corporation by agreeing to purchase shares pursuant to a subscription for shares either before or after incorporation.

2.   A **subscription** is, in essence, a contract to buy shares that will be issued.

3.   Under the Model Act, a preincorporation subscription for shares is irrevocable for six months unless the subscription agreement provides otherwise or all subscribers agree to revocation.

4.   Payment terms of preincorporation subscriptions for shares are set out in the subscription agreement, or are determined by the board of directors in the absence of provisions in the agreement.

5.   A call for payment by the board of directors must be uniform as to all shares in a class or series.

6.   If a subscriber defaults in payment under a preincorporation subscription agreement, the corporation may:

    a.   treat the subscriber as a debtor of the corporation and collect from him; or

    b.   rescind the agreement and sell the shares where the debt is not paid within 20 days of written demand for payment upon the subscriber.

IV. FINANCING THE CORPORATION

A. **Sources of Finance**

1. Individuals who invest in a corporation receive securities as tangible evidence of their investment.

2. These are of two types: debt securities and equity securities.

3. **Debt Securities**

   a. **Debt securities** represent money loaned to the corporation, and a person holding debt securities is a creditor of the corporation.

   b. The creditor's rights are fixed by the instrument creating the debt. Usually, he is entitled to repayment of his principal at a specified time, with a return on the principal in the form of interest.

   c. The terms of the instrument may also grant:

      (1) the creditor the right to convert his debt security into an equity security; or

      (2) the corporation the right to prepay the debt before the stated term expires.

   d. Holders of debt securities have priority over equity security holders upon liquidation of the corporation, but they do not ordinarily have the right to vote.

   e. The three major kinds of debt securities are debentures, bonds, and notes.

   f. **Debentures** are unsecured obligations of the corporation. Holders of these debt securities are general creditors.

   g. **Bonds** usually are secured by a mortgage or a security interest in specific assets of the corporation; thus, holders are secured creditors.

      (1) Bonds may be:

         (a) **registered** on the corporate books, in which case the corporation's obligation runs to the registered owner; or

         (b) **bearer bonds**, in which case the corporation pays the interest to the holder of the coupons, and upon maturity, pays the principal to the person holding the bond.

   h. A **note** is a short-term debt security with a duration of less than five years.

      (1) Notes are typically used when dealing with institutional lenders, and are generally not traded or transferred as bonds and debentures may be.

4. **Equity Securities**

   a. **Equity securities** represent the capital of the corporation that is at risk in the business.

   b. Equity security holders have no right to repayment of the amount invested, or to a return on the investment.

   c. Upon liquidation, however, once the creditors are satisfied, all the remaining corporate assets belong to the shareholders (the "right to the residual").

d. Shareholders usually have:

    (1) **dividend rights**—the right to a dividend, if any are declared, at the board's discretion;

    (2) **liquidation rights**—the right to a share of the corporate assets at the end of the corporation's existence; and

    (3) **voting rights**—the right to a voice in the management of the corporation.

e. All shares have equal voting rights unless otherwise provided in the articles of incorporation.

f. The articles may create several classes of shares and delineate the different rights of each.

    EXAMPLE: There can be a Class A preferred and Class B preferred, or a Class A common and Class B common. The relative rights will be set out in the articles of incorporation.

g. **Common Stock**

    (1) Every corporation must authorize and issue at least one class of common stock.

    (2) **Common stock** represents the residual ownership interest in the corporation; upon liquidation, the holders of the common stock divide all the assets remaining after satisfaction of creditors and payment to the preferred shareholders of their liquidation preference.

    (3) Common shareholders have a potentially unlimited return on their investment, but also have the greatest risk of losing their investment.

    (4) Common shareholders have no right to a dividend unless declared by the directors after payment of preferred stock dividends.

    (5) Common shareholders usually have the right to vote, but common stock may be divided into classes, some of which may be nonvoting or, in the election of directors, limited.

h. **Preferred Stock**

    (1) Any corporation may authorize one or more classes of preferred stock, if allowed in the articles of incorporation.

    (2) The articles of incorporation may specify the rights of each series of preferred stock, or may give the board of directors power to create classes of preferred stock with any set of rights ("blank preferred").

    (3) Preferred shareholders are generally entitled to receive fixed dividends before any dividends are paid to common shareholders.

       (a) While the directors ordinarily have discretion as to whether to declare a dividend, if a dividend is declared, the preferred shareholders are entitled to receive their stipulated amount before the common shareholders receive any dividends.

    (4) The articles of incorporation, the bylaws, or a stock contract may make a preferred stock dividend mandatory whenever there are sufficient current earnings to pay it, and such provisions may be enforced.

(5) Likewise, a reasonable provision in the articles or bylaws restricting the accumulation of surplus is enforceable.

(6) **Participating Preferred Stock**

   (a) Usually, preferred shares are **nonparticipating**—i.e., they receive no more than their stipulated dividend.

   (b) However, preferred stock may have the right to participate with the common stock in any further distributions after the stipulated preferred dividend is paid.

   (c) The terms of such participation are fixed by the articles of incorporation.

(7) **Cumulative Dividends**

   (a) The right of preferred shareholders to receive dividends may be cumulative or noncumulative, depending on the provisions in the articles of incorporation.

   (b) **Cumulative**

   1) If the dividend preference is **cumulative**, the shareholders have the right to receive the stated amount each year, whether or not earnings are sufficient to pay it.

   2) If not paid in a particular year, the amount must be added to the stated preference of the succeeding year, and the dividend preferences cumulate until paid.

   3) Usually, the holders of preferred stock cannot force the directors to declare a dividend, but no dividends may be paid on the common stock until all cumulated preferred dividends are paid.

   EXAMPLE: In Year 1, AAA Corporation chose not to declare a dividend. In Year 2, it chose to issue a dividend. In Year 2, owners of cumulative preferred shares have the right to an amount equal to the declared dividend for both Years 1 and 2, and they must receive the cumulative amount before owners of common shares receive anything.

   (c) **Noncumulative**

   1) If the preferred dividend right is **noncumulative**, the shareholders are entitled to a dividend only if and when declared by the board.

   2) Failure to pay a dividend, even if sufficient earnings are available, does not increase the preference amount to be paid in a subsequent year.

   3) Preferred shareholders still have the right to receive their dividend before a dividend is paid on common stock in any year.

(8) **Summary of Preferred Stock Characteristics**

(a) Although preferred stock may have a variety of privileges and limitations, the following characteristics are typical:

1) Preferred stock is usually nonvoting stock, but voting rights may accrue if the dividend is not paid, or if an attempt is made to alter its rights by amending the articles of incorporation.

2) Preferred stock is usually preferred and limited as to liquidation rights.

a) After creditors are paid, assets are distributed to preferred shareholders according to the liquidation preference, or, if none is specified, to the extent of the par or stated value of their stock.

b) Shareholders' preference also extends to any cumulative dividends unpaid as of the liquidation date.

3) Preferred stock is usually redeemable at a stated price at the option of the corporation, or the articles may provide that it is redeemable at the option of the shareholder.

i. **Shares in Series**

(1) The articles of incorporation may provide that any preferred or special class is to be divided into series.

(a) This allows variations in the rights and preferences of the different series within a class.

(2) The series may differ as to:

(a) the rate of dividend and whether it is to be cumulative;

(b) whether the shares are redeemable, and the terms, conditions, and price of a redemption;

(c) special and relative rights on liquidation;

(d) sinking or purchase fund provisions for redemption of shares;

(e) terms and conditions for conversion of shares; and

(f) voting rights.

(3) The articles, if they do not establish series, may vest in the directors the authority to divide classes into series, and to fix the relative rights and preferences of the shares in each series.

(a) Prior to the issuance of series, the board must file a certificate with the secretary of state designating the series and setting out the rights and preferences; the certificate then constitutes an amendment of the articles.

j. **Fractional Shares and Scrip**

(1) A corporation may issue fractional shares. Usually, this is not done in the initial capitalization, but is in connection with stock dividends, reverse stock splits, or corporate reorganizations.

(2) The holder is entitled to voting rights, dividends, and other distributions in proportion to his fractional holdings. As an alternative,

the corporation may pay in cash the value of the fractional shares, or it may issue scrip.

    (3) **Scrip** is a certificate exchangeable for stock or cash, and it is usually transferable. Its holder is not entitled to any rights as a shareholder, and if scrip is not exchanged by a specified date, it usually becomes void.

  k. **Hybrid Securities**

    (1) Occasionally, hybrid securities, combining features of debt and equity securities, are issued.

    (2) Hybrid securities raise difficulties as to how they should be treated for tax purposes.

      (a) If they are debt securities, the corporation can deduct periodic payments to the holders as interest.

      (b) If they are equity securities, then such payments are dividends and not deductible.

    (3) If a security has a fixed maturity at a reasonable future time and a fixed rate of return, it will probably be found a debt security; if it has neither, it is probably an equity security.

    (4) A third test is whether the holder ranks with the general creditors on liquidation, in which case it will be considered a debt security.

  l. **Equity Securities under the Model Act**

    (1) The Model Act does away with the traditional designations of common and preferred stock.

    (2) The rationale of the drafters of the Model Act was that the differences between common and preferred stock are now largely historical, given the recent tendency to grant certain preferential rights to common stock, and to otherwise blur the distinction between the terms.

    (3) Under the Model Act:

      (a) shares may be divided into classes of shares, and classes may be further divided into series; and

      (b) each class and each series is to have distinct designations, preferences, limitations, and rights.

5. **Balancing Debt and Equity**

  a. Extensive debt financing is attractive to corporations for several reasons.

    (1) For tax purposes, the interest paid on debt is deductible by the corporation. Interest payments avoid double taxation of dividends (once as corporate profits, and once as income to the dividend recipient).

    (2) If the corporation becomes insolvent, a holder of debt securities participates with the other creditors in the assets, whereas an equity holder receives a distribution only after all the creditors are satisfied.

  b. Excessive debt financing, however, is risky.

    (1) In the event of insolvency, the shareholder-creditor's claim may be partially or totally subordinated to the claims of other creditors, or it may be reduced to participation with the shareholders in the assets.

(2) If the corporation is undercapitalized and has too high a ratio of shareholder debt to equity, a court may also deny the shareholders limited liability.

B. Securities Issuance

1. The corporation must issue at least one share of stock representing ownership interests in the corporation. This is typically done at the first meeting of the board of directors.

2. The corporation need not issue as many shares as are authorized.

3. **Authority**

   a. A corporation is empowered to issue the number of shares **authorized** by its articles of incorporation.

   b. Any unissued stock authorized under the articles may be issued:

      (1) by vote of the shareholders; or

      (2) by vote of the directors under authority of:

         (a) a provision of the bylaws; or

         (b) a vote of the shareholders.

   c. Such a provision or vote may be adopted before or after the stock is authorized.

      EXAMPLE: Blue Devil Co., Inc. has 1,000 shares authorized in its articles of incorporation. Each of the three shareholders is issued 100 shares, leaving 700 shares authorized but not issued. Only the 300 shares can vote or receive dividends. The other 700 shares are available for future use.

   d. Once issued, shares are outstanding.

      (1) In the hands of shareholders, the shares are authorized, issued, and outstanding.

   e. If the corporation voluntarily repurchases its shares, they are **treasury shares**.

      (1) Treasury shares, although no longer outstanding, are still considered authorized and issued stock, so their repurchase does not empower the directors to issue additional stock.

      (2) Treasury shares may, however, be restored to unissued share status.

      (3) As long as they are treasury shares, the shares have no voting, liquidation, or dividend rights.

   f. If the corporation cancels the shares upon repurchase, they cannot be reissued.

4. **Authorization of Additional Shares**

   a. If the corporation has used all of its authorized shares in its articles of incorporation and needs to sell more, the articles must be amended to authorize more shares.

   b. The authorization of additional shares requires the approval of the board of directors and the shareholders by a majority vote.

5. **Consideration for Shares**

   a. **Amount of Consideration**

      (1) **Par value shares** may not be issued for a consideration worth less than the par value. The amount of par becomes stated capital, an amount that cannot be used for dividends or stock repurchases.

      (2) **No-par shares** may not be issued for a consideration less than their stated value (the value fixed by the board of directors at the time of issue).

      (3) When shares are sold for a price higher than par, the amount above par is known as a **capital surplus**.

      EXAMPLE: If a corporation sells 100 shares, each with a $0.01 par value, for $1.00 per share (instead of $0.01 per share), the money received above par value will be surplus. In this example, that amounts to $100 minus $1.00 (the stated capital) for a result of $99.

      (4) Under the Model Act, there is no longer any provision relating to the concept of par value, and therefore no minimum price at which specific shares must be issued.

         (a) The drafters of the Model Act felt that the problems of unreasonably low prices for stock could not be dealt with by the arbitrary concept of par value.

         (b) The issuance of shares below market value would violate fiduciary duties.

   b. **Valid Consideration**

      (1) Under the Model Act, valid consideration for shares may be:

         (a) money or obligations (promissory notes);

         (b) property, tangible or intangible, actually received by the corporation; or

         (c) services actually performed for the corporation or contracts for future services.

      (2) Unless there is fraud, the judgment of the board of directors or the shareholders, as the case may be, is conclusive as to the value of consideration received for shares.

6. **Shareholders' Preemptive Rights**

   a. **Preemptive rights** are the rights of existing shareholders to acquire unissued or treasury shares in the corporation, or options or rights in proportion to their holdings of the original shares, when the corporation seeks to issue additional stock that would reduce existing shareholders' ownership percentage.

      (1) Under the Model Act, shareholders have no preemptive rights, except to the extent provided in the articles of incorporation [MBCA § 6.30].

      (2) Preemptive rights prevent dilution of a shareholder's voting interest.

   b. When preemptive rights are granted, they are usually granted only to common shareholders and may not apply to stock issued for property or services.

c. A shareholder who does not purchase the stock at the offering price when offered has waived his rights.

d. A shareholder whose rights are violated may:

 (1) enjoin the sale and recover from the purchaser shares bought knowingly in violation of the preemptive right;

 (2) cancel issuance of additional shares to himself; or

 (3) purchase the shares on the open market and recover from the corporation the difference between the offering price and the price he paid.

e. Absent preemptive rights, a shareholder's equity suit may still block issuance of stock that would unfairly dilute or transfer control on a theory of breach of fiduciary duty under some circumstances, such as a sale for less than fair market value.

7. **Share Certificates**

a. The shares of a corporation may be represented by certificates.

b. One's status as a shareholder is not dependent on the issuance of a certificate, which is merely tangible evidence of stock ownership.

c. Shares not represented by a certificate are uncertificated.

d. **Requirements**

 (1) The face of each certificate must state the number of shares and the class and series, if any, that the certificate represents.

 (2) The certificate must be signed by the president or a vice president, and by the treasurer or an assistant treasurer.

  (a) The signatures may be facsimiles if the certificate is signed by a transfer agent, or by a registrar, other than a director, officer, or employee of the corporation.

  (b) If an officer who has signed a certificate ceases to be an officer before issuance, the certificate may still be validly issued by the corporation.

e. **Restrictions**

 (1) In most states, any restriction on the transferability of stock, whether imposed by the articles of incorporation, the bylaws, or any agreement to which the corporation is a party, must be noted conspicuously on the share certificate or it will be ineffective, except against a person with actual knowledge of it at the time he acquired the shares.

 (2) The notation must set forth either the full text of the restriction or a statement of the existence of the restriction, as well as a statement that the corporation will furnish a copy of the restriction to the shareholder upon written request and without charge.

 (3) This requirement is to be construed in light of Uniform Commercial Code ("UCC") Section 8-204, which also specifies that the restriction must be noted conspicuously.

  (a) A term or clause is **conspicuous** when it is so written that a reasonable person against whom it is to operate ought to have noticed it; a printed heading in capitals is conspicuous, as is language in the body of a form in larger or contrasting type or color [UCC § 1-201(10)].

C. Dividends and Distributions

1. A **dividend** is a distribution by a corporation to its shareholders of cash or property of the corporation.

2. A dividend differs from a distribution in redemption of stock in that a dividend is distributed with respect to the shareholder's stock, rather than in exchange for his stock.

3. The articles of incorporation establish the relative rights of different classes of stock (preferred stock, common stock, or different classes of each), including the right to receive a dividend. Within a class of stock, dividends, when paid, are equal per share.

4. **Shareholders' Right to Dividends**

    a. A shareholder has no inherent right to be paid a dividend.

    b. Generally, the board of directors has discretion to decide whether and when to declare a dividend, subject to any restrictions in the articles of incorporation [MBCA § 6.40].

    (1) The directors may legitimately decide to retain corporate earnings to expand the business, to anticipate losses, or to provide for a stable dividend policy in the future, rather than to pay a current dividend.

    c. Under the Model Act, the directors may not declare a dividend if [Id.]:

    (1) the corporation would not be able to pay its debts as they become due in the ordinary course of business; or

    (2) the corporation's total assets would be less than the sum of its total liabilities plus the amount the corporation would need, if it were dissolved at the time of distribution, to satisfy the preferential rights upon dissolution of shareholders whose preferences are superior to those receiving the distribution.

    d. Dividends may be paid only to the extent of surplus.

    (1) **Surplus** is the difference between a corporation's net assets (total assets minus total liabilities) and its stated capital, or the stated value of the corporation's stock multiplied by the number of outstanding shares.

    e. **Contractual Rights to Dividends**

    (1) One means of assuring dividend payments is a provision in the articles of incorporation, the bylaws, or a shareholders' agreement:

    (a) making dividends mandatory when earnings are available for dividends; or

    (b) limiting the amount of earned surplus that may be accumulated.

    (2) Such a provision offers protection to preferred shareholders or to minority shareholders, and will be enforced by the courts.

f. **Bad Faith Refusal to Declare Dividends**

(1) If a shareholder can prove that the directors' refusal to declare a dividend amounted to fraud, bad faith, or an abuse of discretion, a court of equity can intervene to compel declaration.

(2) The court would look at all the circumstances surrounding the corporate policy decision in light of the corporation's financial condition and requirements.

(3) Factors relevant to the issue of bad faith are:

(a) intense hostility of the controlling faction against the minority;

(b) exclusion of the minority from employment by the corporation;

(c) high salaries, bonuses, or corporate loans made to the officers in control;

(d) the fact that the majority group may be subject to high personal income taxes if substantial dividends are paid; and

(e) the existence of a desire by the controlling directors to acquire the minority stock interests as cheaply as possible.

(4) The plaintiff must show that such factors were the motivating causes in order to prove bad faith.

g. **Remedies**

(1) Once the plaintiff-shareholder has proven his contractual right to dividends, or abuse of discretion of the directors, the court may issue a decree for specific performance of the contract or a mandatory injunction ordering a dividend.

5. **Declaration and Payment of Dividends**

a. **Procedure**

(1) Once the directors have voted to declare a dividend, they may fix a **record date** for determination of the shareholders entitled to receive dividends [MBCA § 6.40].

(a) The date is fixed in accordance with the articles of incorporation, the bylaws, or by resolution. The record date may be no more than 70 days prior to the action to be taken.

(2) If no record date is fixed, the record date will be at the close of business on the day the directors vote to declare the dividend.

b. **Shareholders' Rights after Declaration**

(1) **Debtor-Creditor**

(a) As soon as a dividend has been declared, a debtor-creditor relationship arises between the corporation and the shareholders, and the funds to pay the dividend are considered segregated from other corporate funds.

(b) A shareholder may enforce his dividend right as a creditor of the corporation.

(2) **Revocation**

(a) A valid declaration of a lawful dividend generally cannot be revoked without the shareholders' consent.

   (b) If funds are not legally available to pay the dividend, however, the declaration may be revoked.

   (c) If the declaration was conditional (e.g., in the discretion of the directors or officers), it may be revoked; similarly, a declaration not yet disclosed to shareholders may also be revoked.

  (3) **Transfers of Shares**

   (a) Dividends declared before a sale of stock belong to the seller, even if not paid until after transfer of the stock.

   (b) Dividends on shares held in trust are disposed according to the trust's terms, or, if the trust is silent, the ordinary cash dividends are paid to the life tenant.

 c. **Unclaimed Dividends**

  (1) Any dividend owed by a corporation to a shareholder is presumed abandoned if, within some statutorily prescribed time after declaration, it has not been claimed or the owner has not corresponded in writing with the corporation concerning the dividend.

  (2) If stock is abandoned—i.e., the holder has not claimed dividends, corresponded in writing, or otherwise indicated an interest, and the corporation does not know the location of the owner—the dividends and stock are presumed abandoned.

  (3) Most jurisdictions have a statute which provides that unclaimed dividends escheat to the state.

6. **Liability for Improper Dividends**

 a. **Directors**

  (1) Directors who vote to authorize a dividend that is in violation of the state corporation statute will be held personally liable for the amount of the dividend payment in excess of the amount that could legally have been paid, but only to the extent that it has not been repaid to the corporation.

  (2) If the corporation is insolvent, or is rendered insolvent by payment of the dividend, the directors who voted for the dividend are liable to the extent that the corporation is not repaid.

  (3) Directors are not liable if the dividend could properly have been paid at the time of authorization, even though circumstances later made it improper.

  (4) A good faith exception exists, in that the director will not be liable if he relied upon corporate financial records and acted reasonably and in good faith [MBCA § 6.40].

  (5) Any director against whom a claim is successfully asserted is entitled to contribution from the other directors who voted for the dividend and who are not entitled to the good faith defense [MBCA § 8.33].

b. **Shareholders**

    (1) A shareholder who receives a dividend when the corporation is insolvent, or is rendered insolvent by its payment, is liable to the corporation for:

        (a) the amount of the dividend; or

        (b) the amount of the dividend in excess of what could lawfully have been paid.

    (2) The shareholder is liable only for the amount paid to him.

    (3) A shareholder who pays more than his proportionate share is entitled to contribution from the other shareholders; unless the articles of incorporation provide otherwise, the other shareholders' liability for contribution is in proportion to the amounts paid to them.

D. Redemption and Repurchase of Shares

1. A **repurchase** is a voluntary agreement by the corporation to buy its own shares of either common or preferred stock.

    a. Authorization in the articles of incorporation is not required; repurchase is governed by the agreement.

    b. Repurchased shares are either retired or held as treasury stock.

    c. A corporation cannot repurchase shares if it is insolvent or if repurchase of common stock would impair the rights of preferred shareholders.

    d. A corporation may repurchase shares to prevent takeover by looters, but a repurchase solely to keep management in power could be enjoined, and the directors voting for it held personally liable for resulting corporate losses.

2. **Redemption** occurs when a corporation has the right to compel a shareholder to sell his shares back to it.

    a. This right must be stated in the articles of incorporation.

    b. It usually applies only to preferred stock, and generally must be made ratably among all the shares in the class.

    c. A redemption call forms a contract, which a shareholder can enforce by suing for the redemption price.

V. MANAGEMENT AND CONTROL

A. **In General**

1. A hierarchy of authority allocates power between:

   a. the **shareholders**, who own the corporation; and

   b. the **directors**, who manage the corporation.

2. The highest authority is the state incorporation statute, which, in the event of a conflict with mandatory provisions, prevails over the articles of incorporation, which in turn prevails over conflicting bylaws, which prevail over shareholders' agreements.

3. The statutory scheme is designed to effectuate the concept of centralized management by granting a majority of the board of directors the power to manage the corporation's assets and affairs.

4. Unless the articles of incorporation or bylaws provide otherwise, the directors elect officers of the corporation, who make the day-to-day management decisions. The directors are not mere agents of the shareholders, and need not follow the shareholders' wishes; rather, the directors owe a duty to the corporation to manage its affairs prudently.

5. The shareholders do, however, have indirect power to manage the corporation through their right to elect the board of directors.

6. In addition, shareholders must approve fundamental changes such as merger, amendment of the articles of incorporation, sale of all or most assets, and dissolution.

B. **Shareholders**

1. Shareholders have the right to:

   a. elect and remove directors;

   b. approve any amendments to the articles of incorporation;

   c. amend the bylaws; and

   d. approve fundamental changes in the corporation, such as a merger, sale of substantially all assets, or dissolution.

2. Management may seek shareholder ratification of actions if the directors have a conflict of interest.

3. **Shareholder Meetings**

   a. Shareholder action is usually taken at a meeting [MBCA §§ 7.01-7.20].

   b. **Annual Meeting**

      (1) A meeting of shareholders is to be held annually for the election of directors and the transaction of any other business.

      (2) Shareholders' meetings need not be held within the state, but unless a bylaw specifies otherwise, they are held at the corporation's registered office.

(3) If the annual meeting is not held either six months after the end of the fiscal year or 15 months after the last meeting, a court may order an annual meeting to be held on application of any shareholder.

(4) The bylaws normally specify the date of the annual meeting. The hour, place, and manner of conducting the meeting are also fixed or determined by the bylaws.

c. **Special Meetings**

(1) Special meetings of the shareholders may be called by the president, the directors, or upon the written application of the holders of 10% of the shares entitled to vote.

(2) Special meetings may also be called by anyone authorized to do so by the articles of incorporation or the bylaws.

d. **Notice of Shareholders' Meetings**

(1) Written notice stating the place, date, hour, and purpose(s) of the meeting must be given by the clerk to each shareholder entitled to vote not less than 10, and not more than 60, days prior to the meeting.

(2) Notice may be waived in writing either before or after the meeting.

e. **Record Date and Shareholder List**

(1) A record date for determining the shareholders entitled to receive notice or to vote may be fixed by the articles of incorporation, the bylaws, or the board.

(2) Under earlier versions of the Model Act, the record date was to be no more than 50 days prior to the meeting; the current Model Act now provides a 70-day time limit.

f. **Quorum**

(1) Unless the articles of incorporation or the bylaws provide otherwise, a majority of the shares entitled to vote at a meeting constitutes a **quorum** [MBCA § 7.25].

(a) If a transaction must be voted on by a class, a majority of the shares in that class constitutes a quorum.

4. **Voting**

a. **Consent in Lieu of Meeting**

(1) Any shareholder action that may be taken at a meeting can be taken without a meeting if all of the required number of shareholders entitled to vote on the matter act by written consent, or as otherwise provided by the articles of incorporation.

(2) If provided by the articles, each eligible shareholder must be given 10 days' written notice.

b. **Qualification of Voters**

(1) Unless a statute or the articles of incorporation provide otherwise, each share is entitled to one vote, and each fractional share is entitled to a proportionate vote [MBCA § 7.21].

      (2)   The articles may deny or limit the voting rights of a class.

      (3)   Only the shareholders of record on the record date are eligible to vote [Id.].

      (4)   A transferee of shares after the record date may demand a proxy from the record holder, or designate how he should vote.

      (5)   Some ownership-related issues to consider include the following:

          (a)   Jointly owned stock may be voted by either co-owner, but if co-owners disagree and each tries to vote, the vote is split 50-50.

          (b)   Stock owned by a partnership may be voted by any partner, but in the event of disagreement, it is voted under the terms of the partnership, or by the majority of partners.

          (c)   Stock owned by a corporation may be voted by the officer or agent prescribed by the bylaws, or as the board of directors determines.

      (6)   Stock may not be voted if any installment on the subscription has been duly demanded and is overdue and unpaid.

      (7)   No corporation may directly or indirectly vote any of its own stock [Id.].

  c. **Nonvoting Shares**

      (1)   The articles of incorporation may deny or limit the voting rights of any designated class.

      (2)   Even if stock is designated as nonvoting, its holders are entitled to vote, as a class, on proposed amendments to the articles that would adversely affect their rights.

5. **Proxy Voting**

  a. By statute, in most states, every shareholder entitled to vote may do so by proxy.

  b. The term **proxy** means the grant of authority by a shareholder to another person to vote the shareholder's stock; it may also mean the instrument granting the authority, or the agent to whom authority is granted (also called the **proxy holder**).

  c. Most states require that the proxy be in writing, and that it be executed within a specified period of time before the meeting or vote at issue.

  d. Appointment of a proxy must be in writing executed by the shareholder or the shareholder's authorized agent.

  e. A proxy is generally valid for 11 months, unless it states some other duration.

      (1)   Under the Model Act, a proxy is valid for 11 months from the date of its execution [MBCA § 7.22].

  f. Unless coupled with an interest, a proxy is freely revocable by the shareholder unless the instrument specifically states otherwise [Id.].

      (1)   Under the Model Act, a proxy is deemed to be coupled with an interest if the proxy holder is [Id.]:

          (a)   a pledgee;

          (b)   a person who has purchased or agreed to purchase the shares;

      (c)   a creditor or employee of the corporation whose contract provides for the granting of a proxy; or

      (d)   a party to a voting agreement.

g.   A shareholder may revoke a proxy by:

    (1)   notifying the person given the proxy;

    (2)   giving it to another person; or

    (3)   his personal attendance and vote at the shareholders' meeting.

h.   If stock is held in the name of two or more persons, a proxy executed by any one of them is valid unless, before or at the exercise of the proxy, the corporation receives specific written notice to the contrary from any of the co-owners.

    (1)   One spouse or one co-trustee can execute a proxy without having to submit proof of his authority to do so.

i.   A proxy purporting to be executed by or on behalf of a shareholder is deemed valid unless challenged before or at its exercise; the burden of proving invalidity is on the challenger.

6.   **Shareholder Voting Agreements and Voting Trusts**

a.   To consolidate voting power in order to gain or strengthen control of corporate affairs, shareholders may arrange to vote their stock collectively. This can be done through either a voting agreement or a voting trust.

b.   **Shareholder Voting Agreements (Pooling Agreements)**

    (1)   Shareholder voting agreements are, in essence, contracts designed to ensure the shareholders will vote in concert with regard to issues designated by the agreement [MBCA § 7.31].

       (a)   Such agreements are ordinarily used by minority shareholders to marshal the aggregate number of votes necessary to be elected to the board, or to veto corporate action of which they disapprove.

    (2)   Absent fraud or other illegal objective, shareholder voting agreements are generally considered valid and enforceable in court.

    (3)   A shareholder voting agreement does not involve a transfer of legal title to the shares; it merely binds the shareholders to vote according to its terms.

    (4)   The agreement may provide that the shares are to be voted in a particular way, or that the shares will be voted as the parties agree in the future, or that the shares will be voted according to an agreed procedure (e.g., by arbitration).

       EXAMPLE: Linkletter Co. has 100 shares of outstanding common stock. John owns 46 shares, while Alice, Mike, and George own only 18 shares each. Alice, Mike, and George sign a pooling agreement that requires each of them to vote all of their shares as any two of them decide, giving them the potential to outvote John.

(5) Such agreements are often used to ensure election of certain directors, but may cover other matters as well.

(6) The Model Act authorizes voting agreements either between two or more shareholders, or between one or more shareholders and one or more other persons, and simply provides that the agreement will be enforceable in accordance with its terms.

(7) To assure that the agreement will be enforceable against a transferee of the shares, the agreement should be accompanied by stock transfer restrictions conspicuously noted on the share certificates.

(8) A voting agreement may always be revoked by unanimous vote of the shareholder participants.

c. **Voting Trusts**

(1) Voting trusts are generally subject to stricter statutory regulation than are voting agreements.

(2) A voting trust involves a transfer of legal title to the shares to a trustee who votes them for a specified period according to the trust terms.

(3) Equitable ownership remains with the shareholders, and they are entitled to any dividends or distributions, and to all other rights except voting [MBCA § 7.30].

(4) To create the trust, shareholders execute a written agreement specifying the terms and conditions of the trust, and transfer their shares to the trustee.

EXAMPLE: Using the example above, Alice and Mike enter into a voting trust with George, instead of a pooling agreement among the three. The voting trust legally transfers all voting rights to George for a set period of time, which means that George has the exclusive right to vote all of his shares plus the shares of Alice and Mike in whatever way he feels is best, without consulting Alice or Mike, or obtaining their approval.

(5) The trustee must keep a written record of the names and addresses of all those participating in the trust, and must issue certificates of beneficial interest.

(6) A copy of the instrument creating the voting trust must be kept at the corporation's offices, and is subject to the right of examination by shareholders.

(7) A voting trust can be used to ensure that the shareholders will not become deadlocked or that control will be exercised fairly, by appointing an equal number of trustees to represent each faction of the shareholders, and neutral trustees to resolve deadlocks.

(8) The duration of a voting trust is limited to 10 years; however, any of the parties may extend the trust (as to their shares) for one or more additional periods, each not to exceed 10 years [MBCA § 7.30].

(9) A voting trust can be revoked by unanimous vote of the shareholder participants.

(10) A voting trust expires at the time set by the trust instrument, or when the purpose for which the trust was created has been fully accomplished.

(11) A trust may be terminated if its purpose becomes impossible to accomplish.

EXAMPLE: The termination of a trust established to provide a neutral trustee to break deadlocks may be ordered after a finding that the trustee was neither impartial nor independent.

7. **Election of Directors**

   a. **Election of Directors to Ensure Representation**

   (1) In **straight voting**, each share has one vote for each director; thus, a majority shareholder can elect the entire board of directors.

   (2) To ensure representation of certain shareholders on the board, stock can be classified for the purpose of electing directors under the Model Act and by many states.

   EXAMPLE: If X owns 25% and Y owns 75% of the common stock, X's stock can be designated Class A Common with the right to elect one-quarter of the directors, and Y's can be designated Class B Common with the right to elect three-quarters of the directors. Thus X, although a minority shareholder, is still assured representation.

   b. **Cumulative Voting**

   (1) Representation of minority shareholders can be made more likely by cumulative voting, which grants each share as many votes as there are directors to be elected, and allows the shareholder to allocate his votes as he chooses.

   (a) Cumulative voting must be provided for in the articles of incorporation [MBCA § 7.28].

   (b) The formula for calculating cumulation is:

   $$\frac{\text{Shares Voting}}{(\text{Directors to Be Elected} + 1)} + 1$$

   EXAMPLE: ABC Corporation has three shareholders with 100 shares each. Two directors are to be elected in an election with cumulative voting. For any shareholders to determine one of the directors would require the following amount of shares:

   $(300/(2+1)) + 1 = 101$

   Therefore, no single shareholder of ABC Corporation could guarantee the election of a particular director.

   However, if three directors are to be elected, then a shareholder with 76 shares could determine the election of one director:

   $(300/(3+1)) + 1 = 76$

Therefore, in an election of three directors, each shareholder of ABC Corporation could guarantee that the board member of his choice is elected.

(2) Cumulative voting is usually permissive.

(3) The impact of cumulative voting can be reduced by staggering director's terms, reducing the number of directors, or classifying shares.

c. **By Term of Office**

(1) The articles of incorporation may provide for staggered terms if there are nine or more directors [MBCA § 8.06].

(2) Under this provision, only one-third to one-half of the directors is up for election at any meeting [Id.].

(3) This plan prevents the replacement of a majority of the board at any given annual meeting.

EXAMPLE: If X Corporation has nine directors, they might be divided into three classes of three directors each, and one class of three would be elected each year.

(4) Although the benefit of this type of classification is the assurance of continuity, that continuity may also be a drawback, since the board is insulated from shareholder pressure for change.

8. **Shareholders' Right to Information**

a. **Statutory Right**

(1) Shareholders of record are entitled to examine the original, or attested copies, of:

(a) the articles of incorporation;

(b) the bylaws;

(c) the records of all meetings of incorporators and of shareholders; and

(d) the stock and transfer records, which must contain the names and addresses of all shareholders and the amount of stock held by each.

(2) The corporation is required to furnish to its shareholders annual financial statements, including:

(a) a balance sheet as of the end of each fiscal year; and

(b) a statement of income for that fiscal year, which is to be prepared on the basis of generally accepted accounting principles.

(3) A shareholder may inspect and copy records only if:

(a) the demand is made in good faith and for a proper purpose;

(b) he describes with particularity his purpose and the records he desires to inspect; and

(c) the records are directly connected with his purpose.

(4) Enforcement of a shareholder's statutory inspection right is through an equitable proceeding.

b. **Common Law Right**

    (1)   A shareholder also has a common law right to inspect corporate records, and this may be used to examine books of account and other records unavailable under the statute.

    (2)   However, the common law inspection right is an equitable remedy and thus is discretionary with the court.

    (3)   Some courts have held that the shareholder has the burden of proving that he sought examination in good faith and for a proper purpose. Other courts will weigh the reasonableness of the shareholder's request against the interests of the corporation.

c. **Federal Securities Laws on Disclosure**

    (1)   The shareholders' right to information is also protected by federal securities regulations.

    (2)   Unless an exemption to registration is available, the Securities Act of 1933 ("'33 Act") requires that all issuers proposing to offer securities through any means of interstate commerce file a registration statement with the Securities and Exchange Commission ("SEC").

    (3)   Public companies are required to make continued disclosures to shareholders by filing reports and other disclosures with the SEC.

C. Directors

1. Number

a. The minimum number of directors is set by statute, and states vary with regard to the requisite number.

b. Under the Model Act, only one director is required, although more may be provided for [MBCA § 8.03].

c. The articles of incorporation or bylaws may provide for a variable range in the size of the board of directors.

2. Qualifications

a. A director need not be a resident of the state of incorporation, or a shareholder of the corporation, unless required by the bylaws. The articles or bylaws may, however, prescribe further qualifications [MBCA § 8.02].

3. Election

a. The initial directors are chosen by the incorporators, and hold office until their successors are elected by shareholders at their first annual meeting.

b. Directors are usually elected at the annual meeting for a one-year term [MBCA §§ 8.03, 8.05].

    (1)   If the next annual meeting is not held, or if there is a deadlock so that successor directors are not elected, the directors remain in office until their successors are elected and qualify as directors.

4. Vacancy

a. Unless the articles provide otherwise, any vacancy on the board of directors, however occurring, is filled in the manner prescribed in the bylaws, or, in the absence of such a bylaw, by the shareholders [MBCA § 8.10].

5. **Removal**

   a. Unless otherwise stated in the articles of incorporation, the entire board of directors, or any individual directors, can be removed, with or without cause, by a majority of the shares entitled to vote in the election of such directors. The removal of one or more directors can be accomplished only at a meeting called for that purpose, with notice given of the purpose of that meeting [MBCA § 8.08].

   b. However, a director elected by a particular class may be removed only by a majority of the shares entitled to vote in the class that elected him.

   c. If the corporation has cumulative voting and less than the entire board is to be removed, no director can be removed if the votes against his removal would be sufficient to elect him if they cumulatively voted at an election of the entire board.

6. **Meetings of the Board**

   a. **Time and Place**

      (1) Meetings of the board may be held anywhere, either within or outside the state.

      (2) The bylaws may specify the time and place for meetings, but absent such a bylaw, the directors may select the time and place [MBCA § 8.21].

   b. **Notice**

      (1) Unless otherwise provided by the bylaws, regular meetings of the board may be held without notice if the time and place of the meetings are fixed by the bylaws or by the board [MBCA § 8.22].

      (2) Special meetings may be held only upon at least two days' notice to the directors.

         (a) The bylaws should prescribe what constitutes proper notice and may set a longer or shorter period required for notice.

      (3) A notice, or waiver of notice, of a special directors' meeting need not specify the purpose of that meeting, unless required by the bylaws.

      (4) Notice of a meeting need not be given to any director who signs a waiver of notice either before or after the meeting; the waiver must be filed with the minutes of the meeting [MBCA § 8.23]

      (5) A director's attendance at a meeting constitutes a waiver of required notice unless the director protests the lack of notice either before or at the beginning of the meeting [Id.].

   c. **Quorum of Directors**

      (1) A quorum is the number of directors that must be present for the board to be legally competent to transact business [MBCA § 8.24].

      (2) Unless otherwise provided in the articles of incorporation or the bylaws, a majority of the directors then in office constitutes a quorum.

   d. **Vote of Directors**

      (1) Once a quorum is present, a vote of the majority of directors present at the meeting constitutes an act of the board, unless the

articles of incorporation or bylaws require a greater margin, or even a unanimous vote [Id.].

(2) Thus, a minority of the board can act for the corporation if not all directors are present at the meeting.

EXAMPLE: If there are five directors on the board, and only three attend a validly called meeting, the votes of two directors—a majority of those present—will constitute a valid act of the board.

e. **Director Participation**

(1) A directors' meeting should be a collective, deliberative proceeding at which directors listen to the ideas and arguments of other directors, and then vote in the best interests of the corporation.

(2) Therefore, a director cannot vote by proxy, even if the proxy holder is another director.

(3) In order to vote, a director must be present at the meeting.

(4) If not prohibited by the articles of incorporation or bylaws, a director may participate in a meeting by conference telephone or similar device, provided that all those participating in the meeting can hear each other at the same time.

(5) A director must be free to vote according to his best judgment. Therefore, any agreement by a director to vote in a certain way—even if that agreement has all the formalities of a binding contract—is void as against public policy.

7. **Action of Directors without a Meeting**

a. Action that may be taken at a meeting can be taken without convening if all the directors sign written consents setting forth the action to be taken [MBCA § 8.21].

b. The consents must be filed with the records of directors' meetings, and will have the effect of a unanimous vote [Id.].

8. **Defects in a Meeting**

a. Defects in quorum, notice, or voting may be cured by post-meeting ratification, where a majority of the directors:

(1) signs a writing that approves the resolution; or

(2) fails to object after knowledge of the resolution is acquired.

9. **Action by Committee**

a. The board does not ordinarily run the corporation on a day-to-day basis; it may delegate its powers to officers and executive committees.

b. If the articles of incorporation or bylaws so provide, the board may elect an executive committee or other committee of directors.

c. Under the Model Act, the board may delegate to one or more committees all the authority of the board, except the power to [MBCA § 8.25]:

(1) authorize the payment of any dividend or distribution to shareholders;

(2) approve or recommend to shareholders actions or proposals required to be approved by shareholders;

(3)   fill vacancies on the board of directors or any of its committees; or

(4)   adopt, amend, or repeal the bylaws.

d.   Except as otherwise provided in the articles or bylaws, the directors shall determine the time and place of conducting committee business. In addition, except as otherwise provided in the articles or bylaws, a majority of the committee members shall constitute a quorum and the committee may act by unanimous written consent in lieu of a meeting.

e.   Delegation of authority to a committee does not relieve directors of any responsibility imposed on them by law.

10. **Directors' Objections to Actions**

a.   A director who objects to a course of action to be taken by the board of directors, or a committee of the board of directors, must dissent by an affirmative act at the time of the meeting at which the vote on the action is taken.

b.   A director who votes in favor of a corporate action may not later dissent.

c.   The Model Act provides three methods by which a director present at a meeting may dissent from action:

(1)   objection at the beginning of the meeting to holding the meeting or transacting business at the meeting;

(2)   dissent or abstention from the action entered in the minutes of the meeting; or

(3)   delivery of written notice of dissent or abstention to the presiding officer of the meeting before adjournment, or to the corporation immediately after adjournment.

d.   A director who is present at a meeting and makes no objection is deemed to have assented to all corporate action taken at the meeting.

11. **Right to Inspection of Books and Records**

a.   Generally, directors may inspect the corporation's books and records.

b.   A court may enjoin such inspections if the director is, or would be, misusing the information—for instance, by delivering customer lists to a competitor.

12. **Compensation**

a.   Unless the articles of incorporation or bylaws state otherwise, the board of directors may fix the compensation of directors [MBCA § 8.11].

D. **Officers**

1.   Directors delegate the day-to-day management of the corporation to officers.

2.   A previous version of the Model Act required that a corporation have at least four officers:

a.   a president;

b.   one or more vice presidents;

c.   a secretary; and

d.   a treasurer.

3.   However, the latest versions of the Model Act does away with these requirements and provide that a corporation shall have the officers described in its

bylaws or appointed by the board of directors in accordance with the bylaws [MBCA § 8.40].

4. One person may simultaneously hold more than one office in a corporation.

5. Officers are elected or appointed by the board of directors in accordance with the bylaws.

6. **Authority of Corporate Officers**

   a. The powers of a corporate officer are, like the powers of an agent, either actual or apparent.

   b. The major corporate officers are charged with performing duties as follows:

      (1) the president is charged with managing the corporation's day-to-day affairs;

      (2) the vice president is charged with performing the functions of the president when the president is unavailable;

      (3) the secretary is charged with taking minutes at directors' and shareholders' meetings, as well as the safekeeping of the corporation's books and records; and

      (4) the treasurer is charged with receiving, depositing, and retaining receipts for corporate income and expenditures.

   c. A corporation may repudiate an agreement or transaction entered into by an officer or agent who lacked proper authority. However, adequate authority will be found when officers have actual or apparent authority.

   d. **Actual Authority**

      (1) **Express Authority**

         (a) Express actual authority of an officer may originate in board approval of actions by resolution at a board meeting.

         (b) Express actual authority may also originate in the state corporation statute, the articles of incorporation, or the bylaws.

      (2) **Implied Authority**

         (a) A corporate officer or agent may enter into any transaction for which he has been expressly or implicitly authorized under the certificate of incorporation, the bylaws, an employment contract, or a corporate resolution.

         (b) Corporate officers have the implied authority to enter into transactions that are reasonably related to performing the duties for which they are responsible.

            1) This may be based upon past practices, or by looking at what kinds of authority people in that position usually have in similar businesses.

            2) The president generally has the power to purchase assets, such as equipment or inventory; sell goods, used equipment, and possibly land in the ordinary course of business; hire employees; and establish salary levels.

            3) A vice president in charge of sales probably has the power to hire employees for that function.

(c) Where a particular corporate officer has previously entered into a type of transaction without objection by the board, he is deemed to have been implicitly authorized to bind the corporation with regard to subsequent, similar undertakings.

e. **Apparent Authority**

(1) Where a corporation should have recognized that a third party would be likely to view the officer or agent in question as possessing the authority to bind the corporation to the agreement in question, it cannot avoid the transaction based on the concept of apparent authority.

(a) Under agency principles, the corporation manifests authority to the third party in such a way that the third party has a reasonable belief that the officer or agent had actual authority.

f. **Ratification**

(1) Acts of a corporate officer or agent that have not been properly authorized may be ratified by the board.

(2) Ratification may be explicit (i.e., by passing a resolution that confirms the transaction) or implied (i.e., by acceptance of the benefits of an agreement).

g. **Officer Liability**

(1) The personal liability of a corporate officer on corporate contracts or debts is the same as that of any agent.

(a) If it is disclosed or known that the officer is acting only as an agent of the corporation, the corporation alone is liable.

(b) If an obligation runs solely against the corporation, the only action available against the officer is an action for fraud, or for breach of an express or implied warranty that the officer was acting within his authority.

(c) If the officer expressly agrees to be personally bound on or to guarantee the contract, that agreement is enforceable against the officer, even if no consideration was furnished personally to the officer.

1) Usually the officer must sign twice—both as an agent and individually.

(2) If the corporation does not, in fact, exist or is defectively incorporated, the purported officer may be held personally liable.

7. **Vacancies and Removal**

a. Any vacancy in an office may be filled in the manner prescribed in the bylaws, or, absent such a bylaw, by the directors.

b. Any officer or agent may be removed by the board of directors whenever, in its judgment, the best interests of the corporation will be served by such removal.

c. The Model Act specifically states that such a removal may be made with or without cause by the board, which reflects the current majority rule [MBCA § 8.43].

d. Under the Model Act, removal from office does not impair the ex-officer's right to sue the corporation for breach of contract; however, election or appointment to an office does not in itself create contract rights [Id.].

VI. FIDUCIARY AND OTHER DUTIES OF MANAGEMENT AND CONTROLLING SHAREHOLDERS

A. **Duty of Care**

1. In general, directors, officers, and incorporators of a corporation must perform their duties:

    a. in good faith;

    b. in a manner reasonably believed to be in the best interests of the corporation; and

    c. with such care as a person in a like position would use under similar circumstances.

2. Although some states have, by statute, codified standards for director behavior, specific application of the standard is still governed largely by case law.

3. **Standard of Care**

    a. A director has a duty to act in good faith, in the honest belief that he is acting in the best interests of the corporation on an informed basis.

    b. The duty of care usually applies to officers as well as directors.

    EXAMPLE: Multiple employees of a midsize grocery chain alert the vice president of operations about a rodent problem in an Evanston store. The vice president tells the store manager to get an exterminator, but then he never actually follows up on the issue. The manager quits without ever handling the problem. Two months later, the media gets wind of it and splashes the story all over the news. The company's stock falls 10%. The vice president may be liable for the loss, because he knew about the problem and failed to take appropriate steps to correct it.

4. **Business Judgment Rule**

    a. The business judgment rule shields directors from liability and insulates board decisions from review.

    b. The business judgment rule creates a rebuttable presumption that directors are honest, well-meaning, and acting through decisions that are informed and rationally undertaken in good faith.

    c. Usually, a director or officer who makes a good faith error of business judgment will not have breached his duty of care.

    d. Under the Model Act, a director is entitled to rely on information, opinions, reports, records (including financial statements), and other financial data presented or prepared under authority delegated by the board of directors, by [MBCA § 8.30]:

        (1) one or more officers or employees of the corporation whom the director or officer reasonably believes to be reliable and competent in the matter;

        (2) legal counsel, public accountants, or other persons as to matters that the director or officer reasonably believes to be within that

person's professional or expert competence, or as to which the person merits confidence; or

    (3)   a duly constituted committee of the board upon which he does not serve.

e.   The director or officer is not considered to be acting in good faith if he has knowledge concerning the matter in question that would cause his reliance to be unwarranted.

f.   The business judgment rule does not apply where there is an inexcusable lack of attention, diligence, or good faith.

g.   Directors are protected by the business judgment rule in voting on a takeover or liquidation threat, despite a director's self-interest in maintaining control of the corporation, unless self-interest is the sole and primary purpose for the director's resistance.

h.   A director or officer is not required to make decisions solely in the interests of the corporation, but when considering the best long-term and short-term interests of the corporation, he may consider the effects of any action (including changes in control) on employees, suppliers, and customers of the corporation or its subsidiaries; communities in which officers or other establishments of the corporation or its subsidiaries are located; and other pertinent factors.

5.   **Statutory Liabilities**

    a.   In the absence of good faith action or reliance on the enumerated items, directors are subject to the following liabilities under the Model Act:

        (1)   **Improper Declaration of Dividend**

            (a)   A director who votes for or assents to the declaration of any dividend or other distribution of the assets of a corporation to its shareholders contrary to statutory provisions or any restrictions contained in the articles of incorporation is liable, together with all other assenting directors, to the corporation for the amount of the distribution.

        (2)   **Distributions during Liquidation**

            (a)   A director who votes for or assents to any distribution to the shareholders during the liquidation of the corporation without payment of or adequate provision for all known debts, obligations, or liabilities of the corporation will be liable, with the other assenting directors, for the value of the assets so distributed.

        (3)   **Improper Redemption and Repurchase of Shares or Purchasing Corporation's Shares**

            (a)   A director who votes for, or assents to, the purchase of the corporation's own shares, contrary to the statutory provisions, is liable, together with the other assenting directors, to the corporation for the amount of consideration paid for those shares.

      (4)   **Failure to Give Notice to Barred Creditors**

          (a) If a dissolved corporation proceeds to bar any known claims against it, directors who fail to take reasonable steps to cause the required notice to be given to any known creditor of the corporation will be jointly and severally liable to the creditor for all loss and damage caused.

  b. **Contribution**

      (1)   Any director against whom such a claim is successfully asserted is entitled to contribution from the other directors who voted for, and the other officers who participated in, the wrongful action, and who did not meet the good faith standard.

      (2)   A director or officer may also be entitled to indemnification.

      (3)   A director may also receive contribution from the shareholders who accepted any improper dividend or distribution knowing that the dividend or distribution was wrongful.

6. **Responsibility for Acts of Others**

  a. A director or officer can be liable for negligently selecting or supervising subordinates.

  b. He would not be liable, however, for the negligence of a person at the same level of responsibility, unless he participated in the negligence, or was negligent in not discovering and correcting the problem.

7. **Burden of Proof**

  a. In a suit for breach of duty of care, the plaintiff has the burden of rebutting the business judgment rule.

B. Duty of Loyalty

1. The fiduciary duty of officers, directors, and employees requires that they be loyal to the corporation and not promote their own interests in a manner injurious to the corporation.

2. A conflict of interest constituting a breach of the duty of loyalty may arise where the individual:

  a. has business dealings with the corporation;

  b. takes advantage of a corporate opportunity; or

  c. enters into competition with the corporation.

3. **Business Dealings with the Corporation**

  a. A conflict of interest is inherent whenever a director or officer contracts with the corporation to buy or sell goods or services, or has a personal or financial interest in the transaction.

      (1)   A **personal interest** could mean, for example, profit where a director has a direct financial interest or profit for a close family member.

  b. A conflict would arise if a director were on the board of two corporations transacting business with each other. This is known as **interlocking directors**.

c. Such transactions are not void, but are, at most, voidable by or on behalf of the corporation unless the interested person can prove that:

(1) the material facts of the conflict were disclosed and fully described to the board, and the transaction was validly approved by a majority of disinterested directors;

(2) the material facts of the conflict were disclosed and fully described to the shareholders, and the transaction was validly approved by a majority of disinterested shareholders; or

(3) a court determines the transaction was fair and reasonable to the corporation.

d. If a transaction is fair to the corporation at the time it is authorized, the fact that a director is directly or indirectly a party to the transaction is not grounds for invalidating the transaction or the director's vote. The person asserting the validity of the transaction generally has the burden of proving fairness unless the material facts of the transaction and the director's interest or relationship were known to:

(1) the board or a committee of the board, and the board or committee authorized the transaction by affirmative vote of a majority of disinterested directors; or

(2) the shareholders entitled to vote, and those shareholders authorized the transaction without counting the votes of any shareholders who were interested directors.

e. A contract will stand if an independent corporate fiduciary in an arm's-length bargain would have bound the corporation to the transaction [Murphy v. Washington American League Baseball Club, Inc., 324 F.2d 394 (D.C. Cir. 1963)].

f. **Remedy**

(1) A corporation may rescind a transaction that is not fair.

(2) If rescission is not feasible, the corporation may recover damages for losses as a result of entering into the transaction with an interested director.

4. **Corporate Opportunity**

a. The fiduciary duty of loyalty prohibits directors and officers (and sometimes employees) from taking for their own benefit any business opportunity that properly belongs to the corporation, unless:

(1) the opportunity is fully disclosed to the corporation, the corporation is first given a chance to pursue the opportunity, and the corporation decides not to pursue the opportunity; or

(2) the corporation could not have taken the opportunity.

b. It is often difficult to determine what is, in fact, a corporate opportunity.

c. The focus is on the fairness in the particular circumstances of taking advantage of an opportunity for personal profit when the interests of the corporation justly call for protection.

    d.   Factors considered are:

        (1)   whether the business constituting the opportunity is closely related to that of the corporation;

        (2)   whether the board had expressed an interest in acquiring that type of business;

        (3)   whether the individual became aware of the opportunity while acting in his capacity as a director or officer; and

        (4)   whether he used any corporate funds or facilities in discovering or developing the opportunity.

    e.   If the opportunity is rejected by the corporation, by a vote of the board or otherwise, it usually ceases to be considered a corporate opportunity and may be acted upon by the officer or director.

    EXAMPLE: Where managerial employees first learn in confidence of a chance to acquire certain assets in the corporation's line of business while they are employed by the corporation, they violate their duty of loyalty and usurp a corporate opportunity by subsequently forming their own corporation and buying those assets.

    f.   **Remedy**

        (1)   If a director has usurped a corporate opportunity, the court may:

            (a)   hold the individual to be a constructive trustee for the corporation, and order him to convey to the corporation any property, income, or profits derived through his misappropriation; or

            (b)   assess any damages suffered by the corporation.

5.   **Competition with Corporation**

    a.   Competition by a director or officer will not necessarily be a breach of fiduciary duty if he acts in good faith.

    b.   As a general rule, directors and officers may engage in independent business, but if the independent business competes with the corporation, equitable limitations will apply.

        (1)   In the absence of any contrary agreement or understanding, corporate officers are not precluded, upon the termination of their employment, from entering into competition with their corporate employer, or from using the intangible knowledge and skill they acquired while employed.

        (2)   Covenants not to compete, however, will be enforced if they are reasonable as to time and area of application.

    EXAMPLE: Use of corporate personnel, facilities, information, or funds to develop or acquire a competing business would constitute a breach.

    EXAMPLE: A corporate executive would be breaching his fiduciary duty to the corporation by engaging in disloyal activities as part of an effort to establish a business that competes with his employer. Because he is bound to act solely for his employer's benefit in all matters within the scope of his employment, an executive employee is barred from actively competing with his employer during the tenure of his employment, even in the absence of an express covenant so providing.

  c. **Remedy**
   (1) The remedy for such a breach would be:
    (a) the profits earned in competition;
    (b) a constructive trust on the competitor's property; or
    (c) damages for injury to the corporation.
   (2) The corporation may also be entitled to recover the salary paid to the director or officer during the period of wrongful competition.

 6. **Burden of Proof**
  a. In a suit for breach of duty of loyalty, the defendant has the burden of disproving a breach of loyalty.

C. Indemnification
 1. **Permissible**
  a. A corporation may indemnify an individual who is a party to a proceeding because he is a director against liability incurred in the proceeding if [MBCA § 8.51]:
   (1) he conducted himself in good faith and reasonably believed:
    (a) in the case of conduct in his official capacity, that his conduct was in the best interests of the corporation; and
    (b) in all other cases, his conduct was not opposed to the best interests of the corporation; or
   (2) he engaged in conduct for which broader indemnification is otherwise permitted or required according to the articles of incorporation.
  b. Termination of a proceeding by a judgment, order, settlement, or conviction, or a plea of *nolo contendere*, is not, by itself, determinative as to whether the director met his standard of conduct.
  c. However, a corporation may not indemnify a director in connection with:
   (1) a proceeding by, or in the right of, the corporation (except reasonable expenses incurred if the director has met his relevant standard of conduct); or
   (2) any proceeding with respect to conduct for which the director was found liable on the basis that he received a financial benefit to which he was not entitled (i.e., a breach of duty of loyalty).

 2. **Mandatory**
  a. A corporation must indemnify a director who was successful, either on the merits or otherwise, in the defense of any proceeding to which he was a party because he was a director of the corporation against reasonable expenses incurred by him in connection with the proceeding [MBCA § 8.52].

3. **Court-Ordered**

   a. A director who is a party to a proceeding because he is a director may apply to the court for indemnification, or an advance on expenses [MBCA § 8.54].

   b. The court will order indemnification, or an advance, if it determines that the director is entitled to mandatory indemnification or indemnification as set forth in the articles of incorporation, if indemnification or an advance is fair and reasonable in view of the relevant circumstances.

4. **Insurance**

   a. Corporations may purchase directors and officers insurance [MBCA § 8.57].

5. **Limiting Liability**

   a. The articles of incorporation may contain provisions eliminating or limiting the liability of a director to the corporation or its shareholders for money damages for any action or failure to act as a director, other than liability for [MBCA § 2.02]:

   (1) the amount of a financial benefit received by the director to which he is not entitled;

   (2) an intentional infliction of harm on the corporation or shareholders;

   (3) authorizing an unlawful distribution; or

   (4) intentional violation of criminal law.

D. **Duties of Controlling Shareholders**

1. Majority or controlling shareholders of a corporation have a fiduciary duty to refrain from exercising their control to obtain a benefit from the corporation not shared proportionally with the minority shareholders.

2. Examples of improper conduct include:

   a. causing the board of directors to guarantee, or enter into, a loan made by or with a majority shareholder;

   b. causing the board of directors to issue additional stock to a controlling shareholder at less than fair market value for the purpose of diluting the minority's interest;

   c. causing the board of directors to enter into a contract with a majority shareholder, or an entity affiliated with a majority shareholder, on unfair terms; and

   d. causing the board of directors to dissolve the corporation, merge it with a company owned by the controlling shareholders, or sell its assets, for the purpose of excluding the minority shareholders from participation in a profitable business.

3. A majority shareholder's fiduciary duty is usually enforceable by the corporation, by means of a shareholder's derivative action, or by an individual shareholder's action for a direct breach of fiduciary duty to him.

   a. The controlling shareholder has the burden of proving the entire fairness of the transaction.

4. **Sale of Control**

   a. The general rule is that, even though sellers of a controlling block of shares receive a control premium above the fair market value, the sellers do not share that premium with all shareholders (the "no sharing" rule).

b.   In selling their control, courts may impose fiduciary duties on controlling shareholders because control is a corporate asset in which all shareholders have an interest.

EXAMPLE: A shareholder would be liable for a sale to a buyer if the shareholder knew the buyer was a corporate looter or competitor that intended to merge the acquired entity into his own.

EXAMPLE: A controlling shareholder sells his stock in a steel company to a syndicate of steel users who thereby gained a steady supply of steel at fixed prices during wartime instead of continuing to pay a premium to the company for a supply commitment. The court holds that the shareholder's receipt of a price substantially in excess of market price and book value was a premium received for sale of a corporate asset—the supply commitment premium—for which he was held accountable to the minority shareholders [Perlman v. Feldman, 219 F.2d 173 (2d Cir. 1955)].

c.   Courts will scrutinize a sale of control in three instances:

(1)   if the seller is, in effect, selling an office of the corporation;

(2)   if the buyer offered to purchase the entire corporation, but the seller reframed the transaction as just a purchase of seller's shares; or

(3)   if the seller sells to someone who he knows will loot the corporation.

d.   If the corporation is publicly held, any tender offer for control is subject to the federal Williams Act, creating a statutory "equal opportunity" rule.

5.   **Remedies**

a.   For negligence in selling control, the shareholder will be liable for the damages suffered by the corporation.

b.   For breach of fiduciary duty, he may be liable for damages, or his profit or premium.

c.   Shareholders may also seek an injunction.

E.   **Rule 10b-5 and Insider Trading in Securities**

1.   Corporate executives, shareholders, and employees have a fiduciary duty to disclose material facts they learn that affect the value of the corporation's stock, and to refrain from trading in stock using inside information.

a.   The duty to disclose extends to existing shareholders in connection with a sale or purchase of the corporation's stock. The insider must abstain from trading or disclose.

2.   **At Common Law**

a.   At common law, the majority rule was that a director, officer, or other corporate insider owed no fiduciary duty to shareholders, and therefore was under no duty to disclose inside information when trading in corporate stock.

(1)   Various exceptions to this rule arose, and some states enacted statutes to prevent fraud in insider trading.

b. Several courts, however, have held that insider trading constitutes a breach of the fiduciary duties owed to the corporation, on the theory that inside information is a corporate asset and cannot be exploited for personal gain.

    (1) Under this theory, a constructive trust can be imposed on any profits received by officers and directors in such trading [Diamond v. Oreamuno, 248 N.E.2d 910 (N.Y. 1969); Brophy v. Cities Services Co., 70 A.2d 5 (Del. Ch. 1949)].

c. While insider trading is now primarily regulated by federal law, this common law theory has the advantage of not requiring that the suit be brought by a purchaser or seller (as it is under Rule 10b-5); in addition, it applies to all corporations, not just those registered under the Securities Exchange Act of 1934 (as in Section 16(b)).

3. **Under Federal Law**

    a. **Rule 10b-5**

        (1) State law governing insider trading in corporate securities has largely been eclipsed by federal law—the Securities Exchange Act of 1934 ("1934 Act").

        (2) Causes of action can be brought under Rule 10b-5 against:

            (a) those who have made misrepresentations or omissions in connection with the purchase or sale of securities (action for false or misleading statements); and

            (b) those who traded in the stock while under a duty either to disclose or to abstain from trading until the inside information they possess is disclosed (insider trading action).

        (3) **General Rule—False and Misleading Statements**

            (a) SEC Rule 10b-5 (promulgated under Section 10(b) of the 1934 Act), the federal anti-fraud rule, prohibits, in connection with the purchase and sale of any security (whether or not such security is listed on a national exchange):

                1) the use of any device, scheme, or artifice to defraud;

                2) omissions and misstatements of a material fact; or

                    a) A **material fact** is a fact that would have been necessary in order to make the statements actually made not misleading in light of the circumstances in which they were made.

                3) any act, practice, or course of business that operates or would operate as a fraud or deceit.

            (b) **Elements**

                1) Elements of a Rule 10b-5 action are:

                    a) a misrepresentation or omission of a material fact;

                    b) knowledge by the defendant of the misrepresentation or omission, or reckless disregard of the truth (negligent misrepresentation is not sufficient) [Ernst & Ernst v. Hochfelder, 425 U.S. 185 (1976)];

      c)   scienter (intent to deceive, manipulate, or defraud);

      d)   reliance of the plaintiff, which is generally assumed if the fact was material; and

      e)   damages.

            i)   Damages are the difference between the price at which the plaintiff either bought or sold the stock, and the price of the stock within a reasonable time after the insider information was made public.

2) In Connection with Purchase or Sale

    a)   Privity is not required, and the defendant need not be a buyer or seller as long as his fraud was in connection with the transaction in which the plaintiff was a buyer or seller.

3) Public and Private Corporations

    a)   Rule 10b-5 applies to all securities of any corporation, whether registered securities or not, as long as some means of interstate commerce was used in connection with the purchase or sale of securities.

(4) Enforcement

(a)   Enforcement may be by an SEC suit for injunction.

(b)   The SEC may impose civil fines and seek criminal penalties.

(c)   Courts have also implied a private cause of action for money damages where the plaintiff either purchased or sold stock in connection with the alleged fraud.

    1)   The plaintiff must have purchased, sold, issued, or received securities. When one refrains from taking action on the basis of information improperly obtained or disclosed, no sale or purchase is made.

    EXAMPLE: Joan wants to sell her stock in Hot Air Balloon Rides Corp., but decides against it when the president tells her that the company is about to sign a big contract with Birthday Balloons Unlimited. Even if the president's statement was in violation of Rule 10b-5, Joan still would have no right to sue him because she did not purchase or sell the stock.

    2)   A plaintiff has standing to sue for equitable relief even if he is merely a target of the fraud.

(5) Insider Trading Action

(a)   Rule 10b-5 has been applied to insider trading actions as well as actions for false or misleading statements.

(b)   In a 10b-5 insider trading action, manipulation or deception is established by having confidential information and trading on the basis of that information.

1) Thus, an insider is liable for inside trading only where he fails to disclose material nonpublic information before trading on it and thus makes secret profits.

2) An established trading program, in writing, that grants someone the authority to sell or purchase stock on given dates or at given prices will negate the "on the basis of" element of insider trading.

EXAMPLE: Martha Stewart's defense in her obstruction of justice trial was that she knew she was not violating insider-trading laws by selling ImClone stock because she had a "stop-loss" order in place with her broker to sell if the stock went below $60.

(c) **Insiders**

1) An **insider** is anyone who:

a) learns of material, non-public information about the corporation as a consequence of his corporate position; or

b) has a fiduciary relationship to the corporation or the plaintiff.

2) Insiders typically include officers, directors, controlling shareholders, or employees of the corporation.

a) A confidential relationship also exists with **constructive insiders**—outside counsel, accountants, or bankers.

(d) **Tipper and Tippee**

1) **Tippers**, or insiders who make selective disclosures of material inside information, can be liable for the profits of their **tippees** if they (the insiders) made the disclosure for the purpose of obtaining direct or indirect pecuniary gain (money, gift, benefit, etc.).

2) Tippees may be liable if a tipper breached his duty and a tippee traded on the material inside information, knowing that the tipper acted improperly.

a) In other words, the duty of a tippee who has no independent duty to the corporation is derivative; a breach by the insider tipper must be shown.

b) Information accidentally transmitted, such as a conversation overheard in a public place, does not give rise to a breach of duty to the accidental tippee (unless the tippee overhears what he knows or should know is a tip in breach of a duty).

EXAMPLE: A securities analyst for Entra International Corp. learns from Entra's president that the company is in confidential negotiations to purchase Extra Domestic Corp. He passes the information on to investors, who know about its secret nature.

c) Outsiders who develop information on their own have no duty.

EXAMPLE: In the movie Wall Street, Budd Foxx follows a well-known investor around town one day, noting to whom the investor spoke, what buildings he entered, etc. He came to a conclusion about the investor's intentions and traded on that assumption. This is not insider trading.

(e) **Misappropriation**

1) Under the **misappropriation** theory, a person may be prosecuted by the government under Rule 10b-5 even when he has no duty to the issuer, or shareholders of the issuer, when he has traded on market information in breach of the duty of trust and confidence owed to the source of the information.

2) Both the classic theory and the misappropriation theory leave open a loophole that a "brazen thief" would not be liable for insider trading because he owes no duties to anyone from whom he acquired information. Recently, the Second Circuit held that a computer hacker who traded on information that he acquired by "deceptive" hacking would be liable [SEC v. Dorozhko, 574 F.3d 42 (2d Cir. 2009)].

EXAMPLE: Members of an investment banking firm and an employee of a financial printer were liable for trading on nonpublic information gained in the course of their employment. The employees were found to have a duty to their employers and their employers' corporate clients not to misappropriate confidential information entrusted to the defendants' employers by the clients [SEC v. Materia, 745 F.2d 197 (2d Cir. 1984)].

EXAMPLE: Financial reporter R. Foster Winans was held liable for revealing financial information he intended to publish in his Wall Street Journal column, "Heard on the Street," to others who traded on the basis of this advance information. Although the confidential information did not come directly from the corporations whose stock was traded and no duty to those corporations was breached, the court found a sufficient breach in the use of material nonpublic information belonging to Winans' employer, The Wall Street Journal [United States v. Carpenter, 791 F.2d 1024 (2d Cir. 1986)].

(6) **Damages**

    (a) Damages are usually measured by the price at which the stock was actually traded and its true value at that time.

        1) This means the stock's price at a reasonable time after the omitted information was made public or the misinformation was publicly corrected.

    (b) Rescission, or other equitable relief, such as disgorgement of profits, may also be granted in appropriate cases.

(7) **Causation**

    (a) There is no requirement of privity between the plaintiffs and defendants in Rule 10b-5 actions because identification of buyers and sellers is difficult on the open market.

    (b) However, some courts apply a **contemporaneous trading rule**—i.e., the defendants are liable to all those who traded in the opposite direction at approximately the same time [Wilson v. Comtech Telecomm. Corp., 648 F.2d 88 (2d Cir. 1981)].

b. **Recovery of Short-Swing Profits under Section 16(b)**

(1) A *per se* rule of invalidity is applied to short-swing profits made by insiders on in-and-out transactions within a short period of time.

(2) Section 16(b) of the Securities Exchange Act of 1934, which seeks to prevent unfair use of information and internal manipulation of price, applies to directors, officers, and large shareholders of corporations that have at least one class of equity stock registered under Section 12 of that same act.

(3) Under Section 16(b), any profit is recoverable if:

    (a) made by an officer, director, or beneficial owner of more than 10% of a class of equity security;

    (b) derived from any sale of a security; and

    (c) occurring no more than six months from a purchase of the same security.

(4) This federal cause of action requires two transactions in the stock, whereas recovery under common law or Rule 10b-5 is for a single transaction.

(5) To be liable, an officer or director need only have been in office at the time of purchase or sale. Conversely, once a director or officer ceases to be a director or officer, he may be liable for sales made within six months of purchase, even though he is no longer a director or officer.

(6) A 10% beneficial owner must have been a 10% beneficial owner at both times (i.e., he must have owned more than 10% prior to the purchase and prior to the sale).

(7) A violation of Section 16(b) is a strict liability offense.

    (a) Intent is irrelevant, and there need be no showing that the defendant knew of and acted on material inside information.

EXCEPTION: Certain involuntary sales are exempt from the rule, including structural reorganization, reincorporation, and reclassification, as well as other transactions that have the same effect on holders of the reclassified class or series.

EXCEPTION: The rule protects pre-IPO investors and shareholders whose shares may be reclassified before the IPO from violating the rule upon selling their shares in the IPO or within six months after reclassification.

EXCEPTION: This protects purchases and sales made pursuant to an integrated plan to acquire shares, such as a stock option plan that has already been approved, or a compensation plan that entitles an individual to purchase additional shares.

(8) As under common law, the damages are payable to the corporation. A shareholder may sue, however, if the corporation does not.

(9) The profit recoverable is maximized by matching the lowest-priced purchases with the highest-priced sales within the preceding or succeeding six-month period.

DIFFERENCES BETWEEN 10B-5 ACTION AND 16(B) ACTION	
10b-5	**16(b)**
Applies to all corporations.	Applies only to publicly traded companies.
Applies to all purchases and sellers.	Applies only to directors, officers, and 10% beneficial owners.
Requires a purchase or sale.	Requires a purchase and sale.
Requires intent to deceive.	No intent required; strict liability.
Direct and derivatives actions; SEC action.	Derivative action.

VII. CLOSE CORPORATIONS AND SPECIAL CONTROL DEVICES

A. Characteristics

1. A **close corporation**, or **closely held corporation**, is defined as one having:

   a. a small number of shareholders;

   b. no ready market for the corporate stock; and

   c. substantial majority shareholder participation in the management, direction, and operations of the corporation.

2. Close corporations are often small businesses whose owners want to keep ownership and control in a few hands; the owners may, in effect, have a partnership relationship, but desire incorporation to achieve limited liability and potential tax benefits.

3. The only ready market for close corporation stock is for the controlling stock, and there may be limitations on the transferability of stock, such as a shareholders' repurchase agreement.

4. Majority rule is the traditional principle in corporate decision-making; those shareholders disagreeing can sell their stock.

5. In a close corporation, a dissident shareholder is often impeded by transfer restrictions, lack of a ready market, and difficulties in determining a fair stock price.

6. A dissident shareholder may be an employee as well as a shareholder; if he sells his stock, he may lose his job, besides being compelled to sell to the majority shareholders at an unrealistically low price.

B. Statutory Provisions—Control of Management

1. Although most jurisdictions have no special close corporation statute, close corporations may wish to avail themselves of certain general provisions of the corporations statute to alleviate the problems peculiar to them.

2. In addition to protective mechanisms intended to protect minority shareholders, such as preemptive rights, voting agreements, voting trusts, and cumulative voting, the bylaws may provide that a quorum requires a larger percentage than a majority, and may even require unanimous attendance.

3. The articles of incorporation or bylaws may set a voting requirement of a percentage greater than a majority (a **supermajority**), or a unanimous vote.

   a. Such higher requirements protect the minority, but can create a danger of deadlock by minority veto.

4. To equitably balance ownership and voting in a close corporation, shareholders may want to avail themselves of statutory provisions permitting classification of stock, preemptive rights, and preferred stock.

C. Special Agreements Allocating Authority

1. Generally, it is improper for shareholders to enter into agreements determining matters usually held to be within the directors' discretion (e.g., selection and salary of officers, or payment of dividends). This rule may

not, however, apply to close corporations where shareholders (who are often also directors and/or officers) may enter into enforceable agreements controlling such matters, at least so long as:

  a. all of the shareholders are parties to the agreement;

  b. the agreement is reasonable in length and scope; and

  c. there is no harm to outsiders (e.g., creditors).

2. The Model Act requires that such agreements be included in the articles of incorporation [MBCA § 8.01(b)].

3. The Model Act and the laws of some states even allow a close corporation to do away with a board of directors entirely and have the shareholders run the corporation as though they were directors.

D. Resolution of Disputes and Deadlock

1. Because close corporations are likely to suffer from deadlock of shareholders or directors, the articles of incorporation may provide for a remedy, such as arbitration or a buyout agreement in the event of irreconcilable conflict.

2. The articles may also provide for dissolution at the option of a specified percentage of the shares, or upon some other contingency.

3. Any such option must be conspicuously noted on the shares.

4. When shareholders manage a close corporation and it is suffering or threatened with irreparable injury from deadlock, a court may appoint custodians.

5. A receiver may be appointed in the event of bankruptcy.

6. A court may also appoint a disinterested provisional director to aid a hopelessly deadlocked board.

E. Stock Transfer Restrictions

1. Restrictions on stock transfers are often used in close corporations to control who can become a business associate, which may be necessary to comply with exemptions from securities laws and to preserve small business ("S") tax status.

2. Any restriction on transfer must be set forth in the articles of incorporation, the bylaws, or a separate agreement, and must be noted conspicuously on the share certificates.

3. The validity of stock transfer restrictions is generally upheld if adopted for a lawful purpose, but such restrictions may also infringe on the public policy of promoting the alienability of property and contract interests.

4. In general, preventing outsiders from obtaining ownership and maintaining the proportionate interests of shareholders are considered valid purposes for such restrictions.

5. **Options and Buy-Sell Agreements**

   a. **Right of First Refusal**

      (1) The **right of first refusal** obliges a shareholder to offer shares first to the corporation or other shareholders before they may be sold to outsiders.

(2) The option may be triggered by a proposed sale or transfer, death, bankruptcy, or termination of employment.

(3) Options may be successive (first to the corporation, then to shareholders), and may allow some shareholders to buy more than their proportionate share if others do not exercise their options.

(4) The agreement should specify whether the selling shareholder can vote his stock on the question of corporate repurchase of his shares.

(5) It is important that the price at which the option is to be exercised is capable of ascertainment; otherwise, the agreement may be held unenforceable because of lack of definiteness.

b. **Buy-Sell Agreements**

(1) A **buy-sell agreement** is similar to a first option, but is mandatory, requiring the offeree shareholders or corporation to buy the stock upon the triggering event (e.g., death, disability, termination of employment, or proposed sale).

(a) Such agreements, usually funded by a life insurance policy on each shareholder, have the advantage of assuring a purchaser, which is especially important for an illiquid estate.

(2) An agreement may provide for the corporation to buy the shares, or may allow the other shareholders to buy proportionally.

(3) Provision should be made for fixing the value of the stock. This may be a set price or book value at the time of the buyout, or it may be determined by a procedure such as capitalization of earnings, or appraisal by an outside party.

F. **Fiduciary Duty of Shareholders in a Close Corporation**

1. When it comes to shareholders' fiduciary duties, close corporations differ from both general partnerships and larger corporations.

2. In a general partnership, all investors have fiduciary duties and are able to force dissolution if unhappy.

3. In a corporation, however, shareholders do not have fiduciary duties to one another, their capital is locked in, and their shares may be illiquid.

4. In a close corporation, courts are willing to say that managing shareholders owe a fiduciary duty to the corporation and possibly directly to other shareholders.

5. The fiduciary duty may be applied to all shareholders alike, and thus prohibits a minority shareholder from acting to harm the corporation.

6. Some courts will grant a shareholder relief if he is a victim of shareholder "oppression," which may include terminating the employment of a minority shareholder, voting off the board of directors, instituting a "no dividend" policy but increasing the salary of remaining shareholder-employees, and not holding meetings.

VIII. FUNDAMENTAL CHANGES IN CORPORATE STRUCTURE

A. Overview

1. Shareholder approval is required to make fundamental changes in the corporate structure, although the board of directors may pass a resolution recommending accepting or rejecting the proposed changes.

2. The following are fundamental changes to the corporate structure:

   a. amendment of the articles of incorporation;

   b. mergers and consolidations;

   c. sale of all assets; and

   d. dissolution.

B. Amendment of Articles of Incorporation

1. A corporation may amend its articles of incorporation in any respect if the amendment would be a legal provision in original articles filed on the date of amendment [MBCA § 10.01].

2. The Model Act requires only a majority vote to effect a change.

3. **Procedure**

   a. **Board Resolution**

      (1) The board of directors must adopt a resolution setting forth the proposed amendment and direct that it be submitted to a vote at a meeting of the shareholders [MBCA § 10.03].

         (a) If shares have not yet been issued, the amendment is deemed adopted upon the resolution by the board [MBCA § 10.02].

   b. **Written Notice**

      (1) Each shareholder of record is to be given either the proposed amendment or a summary thereof.

      (2) Notice must be given in the same manner as the giving of notice for a shareholders' meeting.

   c. **Vote**

      (1) The vote is held at the meeting. There is no limitation on the number of amendments that may be submitted and voted upon at any one meeting.

4. **Amendments Authorized by Majority Vote of Board of Directors**

   a. Without the approval of shareholders, a corporation may authorize amendments of its articles of incorporation [MBCA § 10.05]:

      (1) to extend the duration of the corporation;

      (2) to delete the names and addresses of the initial directors, initial registered agent, or registered office;

      (3) if the corporation has only one class of shares outstanding, to:

         (a) change each issued and unissued authorized share of the class into a greater number of whole shares of the class; or

          (b)   increase the number of authorized shares of the class to the extent necessary to permit the issuance of shares as a share dividend;

     (4)   to effect a change to the business designation or geographic designation of its corporate name;

     (5)   to reflect a reduction of the authorized shares of any class;

     (6)   to delete a class of shares from the articles when there are no remaining shares of the class (because the corporation has acquired all the shares of the class and the articles prohibit the corporation to reissue the shares); or

     (7)   as otherwise provided in the articles of incorporation.

5. Restatement of Articles

a. A corporation may restate its articles as enacted or amended by a resolution adopted by the board of directors; the same verification and filing procedures apply [MBCA § 10.07].

6. Filing and Effect

a. Articles of amendment, setting forth the amendment and its due adoption, must be signed by the president or any vice president, and by the secretary or an assistant secretary, and submitted to the secretary of state [MBCA § 10.06].

b. The amendment becomes effective when the secretary of state issues a certificate of amendment.

c. Restated articles must likewise be signed and submitted, and must set forth all matter that would be required or permitted to be set forth in original articles.

d. From the effective date, the restated articles supersede the original articles.

7. Dissenters' Appraisal Rights

a. A shareholder who is adversely affected by an amendment of the articles and who objects to the action is entitled to an appraisal and payment for his stock.

b. Unless the articles provide otherwise, a shareholder's rights are deemed adversely affected only when the amendment:

     (1)   alters or abolishes any preferential right of his stock;

     (2)   creates, alters, or abolishes any right in respect of redemption of his stock;

     (3)   alters or abolishes any preemptive right in respect of his stock; or

     (4)   excludes or limits his right as a shareholder to vote on a matter, except as such a right may be limited by voting rights given to new shares then being authorized of an existing or new class.

c. The procedure for exercising appraisal rights is discussed below.

C. Mergers, Consolidations, and Share Exchanges

1. In a **merger,** one corporation is absorbed into another corporation, which survives.

   EXAMPLE: A Corporation and B Corporation merge; A Corporation survives.

2. In a **consolidation**, two corporations combine to form a new corporation, and both of the former corporations cease to exist.

    EXAMPLE: A Corporation and B Corporation consolidate into C Corporation.

3. In a **share exchange**, one corporation acquires all of the outstanding shares of one or more classes or series of another corporation, pursuant to a plan of exchange adopted by the board of directors of each corporation.

4. **Board Resolution for Merger**
    a. Two or more domestic corporations may merge into one of the corporations under a plan of merger that must be approved in accordance with statutory procedures.
    b. The board of directors of each corporation must adopt a **plan of merger** that sets forth:
        (1) the names of the corporations preparing to merge, and the name of the surviving corporation;
        (2) the terms and conditions of the proposed merger;
        (3) the manner and basis for converting shares, obligations, and securities into cash or other property; and
        (4) a statement of changes in the articles of incorporation of the surviving corporation.

5. **Board Resolution for Share Exchange**
    a. When a corporation desires to acquire the shares of another corporation in a **share exchange**, the board of directors of each corporation must adopt resolutions setting forth:
        (1) the names of the corporations whose shares will be acquired, and of the corporation that will acquire those shares;
        (2) the terms and conditions; and
        (3) the manner and basis of exchanging shares.
    b. In the resulting organizational scheme, the acquirer will be the parent of a wholly owned subsidiary.

6. **Shareholder Approval**
    a. For mergers, consolidations, and share exchanges, the plan must be submitted to a shareholder vote for approval unless such approval is not required. The Model Act requires a vote of the majority of the shareholders.
    b. The meeting notice must specify that the purpose, or one of the purposes, of the meeting is to consider a proposed plan of merger or consolidation, and a copy or summary of the plan must be included in the notice.
    c. Class voting is required if set forth in the articles of incorporation.
    d. Generally, the shareholders of the acquiring corporation do not have to approve the merger unless the articles of incorporation specify that such approval is necessary.
    e. If the consideration for the merger is stock of the acquirer, and will result in the issuance of more than 20% of the common stock outstanding, then the shareholders of the acquirer are required to vote.

7. **Filing of New Articles**

    a. If the plan is approved, the articles of merger or consolidation must be executed in duplicate by each corporation by its president or vice president and its secretary or assistant secretary. Duplicate originals are to be delivered to the secretary of state, and, if in accordance with law, a certificate of merger or consolidation will be issued.

8. **Short-Form Merger**

    a. A simpler procedure exists for merger of a subsidiary corporation into its parent.

    b. A parent owning at least 90% of the outstanding shares of each class of its subsidiary may merge the subsidiary into itself without the approval of shareholders of either the parent or the subsidiary.

    c. The board of the parent must approve a plan of merger, stating the terms and conditions of the merger and the manner of determining its effective date, and a copy of the plan must be mailed to each shareholder of record of the subsidiary corporation.

    d. Articles of merger, signed by the president or vice president and the secretary or assistant secretary must be filed with the secretary of state, and become effective upon the issuance of a certificate of merger.

9. **Effect of Merger or Consolidation**

    a. Upon the effective date, the participating corporations become a single corporation, and the surviving or new corporation succeeds to all the rights, privileges, immunities, and powers of the former corporations.

    b. The surviving or new corporation also succeeds to the liabilities and duties of the former corporations, and is responsible for any debts, liens, or suits against its predecessor, including tort liabilities.

    c. By operation of law, title to any property is transferred to the surviving or new corporation.

    d. The surviving or new corporation is entitled to issue stock or bonds to complete the merger or consolidation.

10. **Dissenters' Rights**

    a. Shareholders dissenting from the merger, consolidation, or share exchange have appraisal rights, which are discussed in detail below.

D. **Sale of Substantially All Assets**

1. Instead of merging with another corporation, a corporation may choose to acquire the other corporation by buying all its assets.

2. Historically, corporations attempted to avoid shareholder votes for mergers by merely selling assets. Consequently, merger statutes now typically cover sales of "all or substantially all" assets not in the ordinary course of business, thereby requiring shareholder approval.

3. **Authorization**

    a. Shareholder approval is required for sale of all, or substantially all, assets not in the ordinary course of business.

    b.   A corporation may authorize at a meeting duly called for that purpose, the sale, lease, or exchange of all, or substantially all, of its property and assets (including goodwill), upon such terms and conditions as it deems expedient.

    c.   Shareholder authorization is required if the disposition of assets would leave the corporation without significant continuing business activity—i.e., retention of less than 25% of total assets and 25% of either income (before taxes) or revenue from continuing operations.

    d.   Notice of the time, place, and purpose of the meeting must be given to all shareholders, whether or not they are entitled to vote.

4.   **Dissenting Shareholders' Appraisal Rights**

    a.   Shareholders dissenting from a sale, lease, or exchange of all, or substantially all, property and assets are entitled to the same appraisal rights as dissenters from a merger or consolidation, and must follow the same procedures.

5.   **Liabilities**

    a.   When a corporation sells or transfers all of its assets to another corporation, the purchaser is generally not liable for the contractual or tort liabilities of the seller unless the purchaser expressly or impliedly agrees to assume them.

    b.   Some courts will impose "successor liability" if the purchaser is merely a continuation of the seller and the seller's management, or if the transaction is a fraudulent attempt to escape liability.

E. Recapitalizations

1.   An existing corporation may choose to change its capital structure by adjusting the amount or priority of the debt and equity securities of the corporation.

2.   Recapitalization may be accomplished, for example, by adjusting the amount of each type of security, or changing the priority of different classes of stock.

F. Dissenting Shareholders' Appraisal Rights

1.   Shareholders may dissent from:

    a.   an amendment of the articles of incorporation that materially and adversely affects their rights;

    b.   a sale of all assets other than in the ordinary course of business; or

    c.   a merger or consolidation if the shareholder has the right to vote or is a shareholder in a subsidiary being merged with its parent.

2.   Dissenting shareholders have the right to require the corporation to appraise their shares and buy them at fair market value.

    a.   This effects a workable compromise between the desire of the majority to make a fundamental change in the corporation, and the desire of the dissenter not to be forced into a corporate situation radically different from that which he anticipated when he bought his stock.

b. Some courts further protect minority shareholders by holding that controlling shareholders should not be able to freeze out minority interests in the absence of a valid business purpose.

3. Shareholders must follow a specific procedure to exercise their appraisal rights.

4. **Notice and Objection Required**

a. Notice of the shareholders' meeting must contain a statement of the rights of existing shareholders, and the prerequisites for appraisal rights are:

(1) a dissenting shareholder must file with the corporation, before the shareholders' vote, written objection to the proposed action, stating that he intends to demand payment for his shares if the action is taken; and

(2) the dissenting shareholder must not vote his shares in favor of the proposed action.

b. Failure of the dissenting shareholder to comply with these requirements results in loss of any appraisal rights.

5. **Procedure**

a. If the action is approved, the corporation must notify each shareholder who filed an objection and did not vote in favor of the action that the action has taken effect.

b. The notice must state where and when demand for payment must be made and supply the shareholder with a form for demanding payment.

c. The time for demand must not be less than 30 days from the mailing of the notice.

d. If the shareholder believes the amount remitted by the corporation for his shares is less than the fair value, he may send the corporation his own estimate of value and make a demand for the deficiency.

6. **Appraisal Proceedings**

a. If the corporation and the dissenter still fail to agree as to the value of his stock, the corporation may petition a court for a determination of value.

b. To do so, the corporation must file within 60 days of receiving a demand for payment from the shareholder.

c. All dissenting shareholders who have not agreed on a price must be made parties to the action, and the corporation must give them all notice.

d. **Value**

(1) The court may appoint a special master to receive evidence and recommend a fair value.

(2) The value of the shares is determined as of the day preceding the vote approving the action, and excludes any value arising from an expectation of the action.

(3) The judgment should include interest from the date of the vote on the proposed action.

e. **Costs**

(1) The costs of the proceeding (except counsel and expert fees) are assessed against the parties as the court deems equitable, but the costs of giving notice are charged to the corporation.

G. Dissolution

1. Dissolution is the extinguishing of corporate existence; it requires affirmative action by the corporation itself or by the courts, and does not occur because of bankruptcy or inactivity.

2. Although dissolved, a corporation may continue to exist for a limited time for limited purposes (i.e., prosecuting or defending lawsuits).

3. **Voluntary Dissolution by Written Consent of Shareholders**

   a. A corporation may be voluntarily dissolved by the written consent of all of its shareholders by executing and filing a statement to that effect with the secretary of state.

   b. Upon this filing, the corporation must cease doing business except insofar as is necessary to wind up its affairs.

   c. Its corporate existence continues, however, until the secretary of state issues a certificate of dissolution, or a decree dissolving the corporation has been entered by a court of competent jurisdiction.

4. **Voluntary Dissolution by Vote of Shareholders**

   a. Dissolution may take place by the corporation's filing of articles of dissolution with the secretary of state pursuant to a vote of two-thirds of each class of stock outstanding and entitled to vote thereon, and with the approval of the board of directors, or pursuant to provisions in the articles of incorporation.

   b. Notice of voluntary dissolution must be given to the secretary of state.

   c. The articles of dissolution must set forth the pertinent information concerning authorization and other provisions for dissolution, and the effective date.

   d. The articles take effect when filed, or on a specified date within 30 days thereafter.

   e. At any time before filing, however, the corporation may authorize abandonment of the dissolution proceedings.

5. **Involuntary Dissolution**

   a. **Judicial Dissolution**

   (1) A court may dissolve a corporation:

   (a) in a proceeding by the attorney general, if it is established that:

   1) the corporation obtained its articles of incorporation through fraud; or

   2) the corporation has continued to exceed or abuse the authority conferred upon it by law;

          (b)   in a proceeding by a shareholder, if it is established that:

               1)   the directors are deadlocked and irreparable injury to the corporation is threatened or being suffered, or the business and affairs of the corporation can no longer be conducted to the advantage of the shareholders;

               2)   the directors, or those in control, have acted in a manner that is illegal, oppressive, or fraudulent;

               3)   the shareholders are deadlocked in voting power and have failed for at least two consecutive annual meetings to elect successors to directors whose term has expired; or

               4)   the corporate assets are being misapplied or wasted;

          (c)   in a proceeding by a creditor, if it is established that:

               1)   the creditor's claim has been reduced to judgment, the execution on the judgment has returned unsatisfied, and the corporation is insolvent; or

               2)   the corporation has admitted in writing that the creditor's claim is due and the corporation is insolvent; or

          (d)   in a proceeding by the corporation to have its voluntary dissolution continued under court supervision.

      b.   **Administrative Dissolution**

          (1)   The secretary of state can commence a proceeding to administratively dissolve a corporation if:

               (a)   the corporation does not pay franchise taxes or penalties within 60 days after they are due;

               (b)   the corporation fails to deliver its annual report within 60 days after it is due;

               (c)   the corporation is without a registered agent or office for 60 days or more;

               (d)   the corporation does not notify the secretary of state within 60 days that its registered agent or office has been changed, the agent resigned, or the office discontinued; or

               (e)   the corporation's period of duration in the articles has expired.

          (2)   The corporation must receive notice of the administrative dissolution and it has a right to correct the ground for such dissolution.

6.   **After Dissolution**

      a.   After dissolution, or expiration of the duration stated in the articles of incorporation, the corporation's existence continues to allow it to:

          (1)   prosecute and defend lawsuits;

          (2)   gradually settle and close its affairs;

          (3)   dispose of and convey its property; and

          (4)   make distributions to its shareholders of any assets remaining after the payment of its debts and obligations.

b.   The corporation may not, however, continue the business for which it was established.

c.   The secretary of state normally has the power to revive a corporation after dissolution for any purpose, irrespective of the period of time having elapsed since dissolution and of the method of dissolution.

IX. TAKEOVERS AND CORPORATE CONTROL TRANSACTIONS

A. **Tender Offers**

1. An individual, group, or corporation seeking to acquire another corporation normally attempts to do so by negotiating with the board of directors.

2. If this fails, the would-be acquirer will often go directly to the shareholders and make a tender offer.

3. A **tender offer** is a public (usually published) solicitation by a bidder (the individual, group, or corporation) of the publicly held shares of the corporation to be acquired (the target).

4. The offer is usually made at a premium over the current market price of the target's shares, and is held open for a limited period of time.

   EXAMPLE: Marketco's stock currently trades at $1 per share. Tuner Inc. offers to purchase Marketco's shares at $1.15 per share, provided that a majority of shareholders agree.

5. If the shareholders do not tender the minimum number of shares specified in the offer by the end of the offer period, the bidder will withdraw the tender offer.

6. The bidder also need not accept the tender of more shares than any maximum number of shares specified in the tender offer.

7. Target companies have developed a number of defensive tactics against takeover attempts:

   a. One technique involves finding a more acceptable bidder (a **white knight**).

   b. Another is creating classes of stock that increase in rights if any person acquires more than a specified percentage of shares, making the acquisition more expensive to the bidder (**poison pills**).

8. Defensive tactics must be reasonable in relation to the threat posed to the corporation.

B. **State Regulation**

1. State laws have attempted to protect the interests of the minority and target management.

2. These anti-takeover statutes prevent the acquirer from exercising control of the shares unless the prior shareholders approve, despite the acquirer's possession of a controlling block of shares. If the acquirer fails to win voting rights from the prior shareholders, the target corporation may redeem the control shares.

C. **Federal Regulation of Tender Offers**

1. The Williams Act, passed in 1968, amending the Securities Exchange Act of 1934, was implemented to protect investors, and to give the market early warning of an impending tender offer. The Williams Act has the following elements, all relating to the provision of information:

a. **No Secret Purchases**

  (1) A party that directly or indirectly acquires more than 5% ownership of a corporation must disclose, within 10 days of passing the 5% threshold, certain information, such as:

    (a) the party's identity and number of shares held;

    (b) the source and amount of funds for making share purchases;

    (c) any arrangements the party has with others concerning shares of the target; and

    (d) the party's purposes in acquiring the shares, and intentions regarding the target.

b. **Tender Offer Disclosure**

  (1) A bidder must disclose, on the day it commences its tender offer, the information required by 5% owners and:

    (a) the purpose of the tender offer;

    (b) the bidder's plans for the target;

    (c) past negotiations between the bidder and the target;

    (d) the bidder's financial statements (if material);

    (e) regulatory approvals that may be necessary; and

    (f) any other material information.

c. **Timing**

  (1) The SEC requires tender offers to be kept open for at least 20 business days. If the offeror increases the price, then the offer must be kept open for at least 10 days after the announcement of the increase.

  (2) Anyone who has tendered his shares before the end of the offer period may withdraw his tendered shares within the first 15 days of the tender offer or 10 days following the commencement of a competing bid.

d. **Equal Treatment**

  (1) During the offer period, shares can only be bought through the offer. The buyer must:

    (a) make the same price offer to everyone; and

    (b) take the shares *pro rata* if there are too many sellers.

e. **False or Misleading Statements**

  (1) Section 14(e) of the Securities Exchange Act of 1934 prohibits any false or misleading statements or omissions, as well as any fraudulent, deceptive, or manipulative acts, in connection with any tender offers.

2. **Requirements for Section 16(b) Actions**

a. In a Section 16(b) action, both the target corporation and the tendering and non-tendering shareholders may sue for damages.

b. The plaintiff must prove injury caused directly by the defendant, or through reliance on the defendant's misrepresentations or omissions.

c. To obtain injunctive relief under Section 16(b), the plaintiff must show a substantial probability that a violation has occurred, or that an irreparable injury will occur.

X. SHAREHOLDER LITIGATION

A. **Direct and Derivative Suits**

1. There are two basic types of shareholder actions [MBCA §§ 7.40-7.47].

2. One is a **direct suit**, in which a shareholder sues on his own behalf to redress an injury to his interest as a shareholder.

   a. If the harm affects multiple shareholders, the plaintiff may maintain his direct suit as a class action, in which he sues as the representative for the injured shareholders; a class action is governed by the provisions of Rule 23 of the Federal Rules of Civil Procedure.

   b. Many states have similar rules governing class actions.

3. The second type of action is a **derivative suit**, in which a shareholder sues on behalf of the corporation to redress a wrong to the corporation when it fails to enforce its right. A derivative suit is an equitable action, and often involves breach of fiduciary duty.

4. Because there are conditions precedent to derivative suits, it is important to determine if a cause of action is direct or derivative.

5. Causes of action held to be direct include suits to:

   a. compel payment of dividends;

   b. enforce the right to inspect corporate records;

   c. protect preemptive rights;

   d. enforce the right to vote; and

   e. recover for breach of a shareholders' agreement, a preincorporation agreement, or a contract with a shareholder.

6. In a direct suit, the damages go to the shareholder bringing the suit; in a derivative suit, the damages go to the corporation.

B. **Derivative Suits**

1. Shareholders' derivative suits are governed by Federal Rule 23.1, and many states have adopted rules similar to the federal rule for use in state court practice.

2. A derivative action may not be maintained if it appears that the plaintiff does not fairly and adequately represent the interests of the shareholders similarly situated in enforcing the right of the corporation [MBCA § 7.41; Fed. R. Civ. P. 23.1].

3. **Conditions Precedent**

   a. **Contemporaneous Ownership**

      (1) In a derivative suit, the plaintiff must allege in his complaint that he was a shareholder at the time of the transaction complained of, or that his shares thereafter devolved upon him by operation of law (e.g., inheritance) from a person who was a shareholder at that time [Fed. R. Civ. P. 23.1].

      (2) The plaintiff must also allege that the action is not a collusive one to confer jurisdiction on a court of the United States that it would not otherwise have.

(3) The purpose of the contemporaneous ownership requirement is to prevent a **strike suit**, in which a person buys a few shares simply so that he may threaten to bring a shareholders' derivative suit, seeking a private settlement with corporate management.

b. **Demand upon Directors**

(1) Since a derivative suit is based on a corporate cause of action, a shareholder must first attempt to persuade the board of directors to enforce the corporation's right, by making a written demand upon the board.

(2) A derivative proceeding may not be commenced until 90 days after the demand was made, unless [MBCA § 7.42]:

    (a) the shareholder has been notified that the demand has been rejected by the corporation; or

    (b) irreparable injury to the corporation would result by waiting for the expiration of the 90-day period.

(3) A shareholder's complaint must allege with particularity his efforts to secure from the board of directors such action as he desires.

    (a) The complaint in a derivative suit must be verified under oath [Fed. R. Civ. P. 23.1].

(4) If demand upon the directors would be futile (e.g., if a majority of the directors are the alleged wrongdoers), it will be excused, but the reasons must be alleged with particularity in the complaint.

    (a) Demand is considered **futile** when:

        1) a majority of the board is interested in the transaction;

        2) the directors fail to inform themselves of the transaction; or

        3) the directors fail to exercise their business judgment in approving the transaction.

c. **Dismissal**

(1) Upon a motion by the corporation, a court will dismiss a derivative proceeding if a majority of independent directors, or a majority of a committee consisting of two or more independent directors (a special litigation committee appointed by the board of directors), has determined in good faith, after conducting a reasonable inquiry upon which its conclusions are based, that a derivative proceeding is not in the best interests of the corporation [MBCA § 7.44].

    (a) The independent directors on the special litigation committee must have been appointed by a majority vote of independent directors present at a meeting of the board of directors.

(2) If a derivative proceeding is commenced after a determination has been made to reject the shareholder's demand, the complaint must allege with particularity facts establishing either that:

    (a) a majority of the board of directors did not consist of independent directors at the time the determination was made; or

            (b)   the determination was not made in good faith after conducting a reasonable inquiry that the derivative proceeding was in the best interests of the corporation.

    d. **Demand upon Shareholders**

        (1)   If the board is not disinterested, or if, after demand, the board refuses to act, some jurisdictions require the shareholder to make a demand upon the corporate shareholders, unless that effort would be futile because a majority of the shareholders are also involved in the wrongdoing. In other jurisdictions, no demand on shareholders is required; demand on the directors is sufficient.

4. **Defenses**

    a.   Since shareholders in a derivative suit stand in the shoes of the corporation, they are subject to the same defenses that could have been raised against the corporation.

    b.   Some courts have held that if a shareholder consented to, acquiesced in, or ratified the wrongful act with knowledge of all the material facts, he cannot later attack that act [Swafford v. Berry, 382 P.2d 999 (Colo. 1963)].

        (1)   Other courts, however, have reasoned that shareholder misconduct should not preclude the corporation's recovery [Atkinson v. McCabe Hanger Mfg. Co., 55 N.Y.S.2d 274 (N.Y. Sup. Ct. 1945)].

    c.   Since a derivative suit is an equitable action, the equitable defenses, such as laches and unclean hands, may be interposed.

    d.   Judgment on the merits is *res judicata* as to any subsequent action for the same claim.

5. **Intervention**

    a.   Other shareholders may wish to intervene in either direct or derivative suits involving their corporation.

    b.   The trend is to require that intervenors in a derivative suit be contemporaneous shareholders.

    c.   A person is entitled to intervene when he [Fed. R. Civ. P. 24(a)(2)]:

        (1)   claims an interest relating to the property or transaction that is the subject of the action; and

        (2)   is so situated that the disposition of the action may as a practical matter impair or impede his ability to protect that interest, unless the applicant's interest is adequately represented by existing parties.

6. **Expenses**

    a.   In its discretion, the court may order the corporation to pay expenses, including counsel fees, to a successful derivative action plaintiff [MBCA § 7.46].

    b.   In some jurisdictions, fees and disbursements are allowable only out of the fund that resulted from the successful litigation.

    c.   Other courts have awarded expenses even if no fund has been created—e.g., where the shareholder established violation of federal securities law [Mills v. Electric Auto-Lite Co., 396 U.S. 375 (1970)].

7. **Compromise and Dismissal**
   a. Court approval is generally required for the compromise or dismissal of any class action or derivative suit [MBCA § 7.45].
   b. Notice of the proposed compromise or dismissal must be given to all members of the class in such manner as the court directs [Fed. R. Civ. P. 23(c), 23.1].
   c. The purpose of this rule is to ensure that the defendants do not buy off the representatives, thereby enriching them rather than the class or corporation.

XI. LIMITED LIABILITY COMPANIES

A. **Purpose and Characteristics**

1. A **limited liability company** ("LLC") is an unincorporated association, without perpetual duration, having one or more members, and is organized and operated pursuant to a state's LLC statute.

2. Limited liability companies can be formed to conduct any type of business.

3. A limited liability company is treated like a corporation for limited liability purposes in protecting its members, managers, and agents from liability for the obligations of the company, but if properly organized, it has the attributes of a partnership for federal income tax purposes.

4. A professional limited liability company is organized for the sole purpose of rendering those professional services enumerated, and has, as its members, individuals who are licensed or otherwise duly authorized to render the professional services for which the limited liability company is organized.

5. Notwithstanding the limitations on liability of members in general, members are held personally liable for their own negligence and other actionable conduct in rendering and supervising others in the conduct of professional services.

6. A member will not be liable for any debts or claims against the professional limited liability company, or the acts or omissions of the professional limited liability company or any other member or employee not under the member's supervision.

B. **Organization and Permitted Ownership**

1. A limited liability company must file articles of organization with the secretary of state in which it is organized.

2. The articles of organization must contain the information specified in the state's LLC statute, which generally includes:

   a. a statement that the entity is an LLC;

   b. the name of the LLC; and

   c. the address of the LLC's registered office and that of its registered agent.

3. LLC names, which must be distinguishable from the name of any other LLC organized or doing business, must contain the word "limited company" or "limited liability company," or the abbreviations "L.C." or "L.L.C.

   a. In addition, the name must not include any word or phrase (a long list is set forth in the act) that implies or infers association with a government entity.

4. LLCs are governed by the **operating agreement**, a document similar to a corporation's bylaws that governs the LLC's internal affairs.

5. **Permitted Ownership**

   a. One or more individuals or entities are required to form a limited liability company.

   b. The limited liability company may admit initial and subsequent members (other than assignees) only with the consent of all of the members, unless an operating agreement provides otherwise.

    c.   Except as otherwise provided in the articles of organization or an operating agreement, assignees of membership interests may become members by the consent of a majority in interest of the remaining members.

C. Control and Management

1. Absent an operating agreement or a controlling provision in the articles of organization to the contrary, control of a limited liability company lies with the members in proportion to their equity in the LLC at the time a vote is taken.

2. Typically, however, members enter into an operating agreement that sets forth how a limited liability company will be operated, and how its profits and losses will be shared.

3. The members of a limited liability company may agree to appoint one or more managers to operate the business, in which case the limited liability company is **manager-managed**.

    a.   If the members decide not to appoint managers, the limited liability company is **member-managed**.

4. The managers may or may not be members of the limited liability company, and have as much power and authority as given to them by the members.

5. Managers of an LLC owe the duties of care and loyalty similar to those owed by directors to a corporation.

    a.   However, most states and the Uniform Limited Liability Company Act (ULLCA) permit the operating agreement of an LLC to alter the fiduciary duties of managers or members [ULLCA (2006) § 105(d)(3)].

    b.   Under the ULLCA, if not manifestly unreasonable, an operating agreement may [Id.]:

        (1)   identify specific conduct that does not violate the duty of loyalty; and

        (2)   alter or eliminate aspects of the duty of loyalty, including the duty to refrain from competing with the company.

6. Managers of an LLC owe a duty not to engage in grossly negligent or reckless conduct, intentional misconduct, or a knowing violation of the law. However, some states reject the gross negligence requirement, instead using the business judgment rule used by corporations.

D. Owner Liability and Ownership Rights

1. No member, manager, or agent of a limited liability company will have any personal obligation for the debts, obligations and liabilities of the company.

    a.   Note that a member or manager could still be held directly liable for their own conduct, just not for the debts, obligations and liabilities of the LLC.

2. Courts may pierce the veil of a limited liability company, however, under circumstances similar to those of a corporation: alter ego liability (when the LLC is a mere instrumentality) and inadequate capitalization.

    a.   Note that liability based on failure to comply with corporate formalities is not likely because LLCs must follow fewer formalities, and because many state statutes explicitly prohibit this as a ground for liability. The Uniform Limited Liability Company Act is one such statute, stating that, "the failure of a limited liability company to observe any particular formalities relating to the exercise of its powers or management of its activities is not a ground for imposing liability on the members or managers for the debts, obligations, or other liabilities of the company."

3. Members may bring direct actions against the LLC, when injured personally by the LLC, or derivative actions on behalf of the LLC, in the same way that a shareholder may bring a derivative action on behalf of the corporation.

4. **Classes of Ownership Interest**

   a. A limited liability company has complete flexibility in structuring classes of membership interests, each with different management and control rights, capital and other obligations, preferences with respect to distributions and other economic benefits, voting privileges, and other privileges the members wish to address.

5. **Transferability of Interests**

   a. Absent a contrary provision in an operating agreement, a member may assign all or a part of his economic interest in the limited liability company.

   b. Such assignment, however, will not permit the assignee to become a member or to have a voice in management of the limited liability company unless the assignee is admitted as a member to the limited liability company in accordance with an operating agreement or by the consent of a majority in interest of the remaining members.

E. **Dissolution**

   1. Under the ULLCA, a LLC is dissolved, and its activities and affairs must be wound up, upon [ULLCA (2006) § 701]:

      a. the occurrence of an event that the operating agreement states will cause dissolution;

      b. the consent of all the members;

      c. the passage of 90 consecutive days where the LLC has no members unless, before the end of the 90 days, transferees owning the rights to receive a majority of distributions as transferees consent to admit a specified person as a member and that person becomes a member;

      d. upon application of a member and the entry of a court order dissolving the company on the grounds that:

         (1) the conduct of the company's activities and affairs is unlawful;

         (2) it is not reasonably practicable to carry on the company's activities in conformity with the certificate of organization and the operating agreement; or

         (3) the managers or members in control of the LLC have acted (or

will act) in a manner that is illegal or fraudulent or have acted in a manner that is oppressive and is directly harmful to the applicant; or

    e.   the signed filing of a statement of administrative dissolution by the Secretary of State.

F. Income Tax Treatment

1. If properly structured in accordance with the terms of the Uniform Limited Liability Company Act, a limited liability company should be classified as a partnership for federal income tax purposes.

2. State taxing authorities follow federal classification of limited liability companies and should tax a limited liability company as a partnership if federal classification would permit the same.

G. Advantages and Disadvantages of a Limited Liability Company

1. The limited liability company combines the limited liability protection of a corporation with the pass-through tax treatment of a partnership. There is no limit on the number of members of a limited liability company, as there is with an S corporation.

2. In addition, unlike an S corporation, there is no restriction on the type or character of those who may be members of a limited liability company, and a limited liability company can create and own wholly owned subsidiaries, which may include S corporations.

3. Members of a limited liability company may partially or fully participate in the management and control of the business without losing the protection of limited liability.

4. Considerable flexibility exists in control, management, voting, and sharing of economic benefits.

5. Allocation of items of income, gain, loss, deduction, and credit for income tax purposes follows the Subchapter K partnership rules, and members' tax bases for reporting losses allocated from the limited liability company are increased by recourse and nonrecourse third-party loans to the limited liability company. In addition, no formalities must be observed to preserve the limited liability of the members.

XII. BENEFIT CORPORATIONS

A. **Introduction**

1. Since 2010, there is a growing trend among state legislatures to amend their corporate statutes so as to allow for a new type of corporation known as a "benefit corporation" (or B-corporation).

2. Approximately half of all states have enacted such legislation.

3. Benefit corporations are for-profit corporations whose corporate purpose includes the benefiting of the public.

B. **Purpose and Organization**

1. Dual-purpose corporate entity:

    a. A benefit corporation must be organized not only for the purpose of lawfully pursuing the economic interests of its shareholders but also for the purpose of creating a general public benefit.

2. "General public benefit" defined:

    a. A "general public benefit" is defined as a "material, positive impact on society and the environment taken as a whole."

3. Specific public benefit purposes

    a. In addition to the general public benefit purpose that it must have, a benefit corporation has the right to name specific public benefit purposes that its directors would also be obligated to pursue.

    b. Specific public benefit purposes include such things as the following: environmental conservation efforts; promotion of the arts, sciences, or education; providing goods or services to individuals or communities in need; and funding of other corporations and businesses that work toward benefiting society and the environment.

C. **Duties and Liability**

1. In their governance and management of the benefit corporation, directors and officers must take into account the effects of their decisions on not only the economic interests of the corporation and its shareholders but also:

    a. the corporation's employees;

    b. the public at-large;

    c. the environment; and

    d. the ability of the corporation to pursue and create a general public benefit (as well as any specific public benefit named in the articles of incorporation).

2. In a benefit corporation, because the pursuit of a general public benefit is not secondary to the pursuit of profits, directors have protection against claims of corporate waste when pursuing non-profitmaking activities that would not otherwise exist in a traditional corporation.

3. The failure to pursue a general public benefit or any specific public benefit named in the articles of incorporation does not expose the corporation (or

its directors and officers) to monetary liability; however, it does provide the grounds for bringing a benefit enforcement proceeding and for the court to issue a mandatory injunction that such public benefits be pursued.

D. Benefit Report

1. Generally, benefit corporations are required to provide their stockholders with annual benefit reports that shall also be made available to the public.
2. The annual benefit reports should include:
   a. how the corporation attempted to benefit the public and the extent its efforts made an effect;
   b. any specific public benefits that were pursued, if any were other than what is stated in its charter; and
   c. any problems or events that kept the corporation from pursuing its purposes.
3. Statutory provisions usually provide that the benefit report should be prepared using a comprehensive, credible, independent, and transparent third-party standard.

Family Law

TABLE OF CONTENTS

I. GETTING MARRIED

A. **Nature of Marriage**

1. A **marriage** is the civil status or relationship created by the legal union of two persons. The relationship imposes on the spouses certain duties and responsibilities that are in effect during the marriage, with certain rights accruing at legal termination of the marital relationship and upon the death of one of the spouses.

2. The law of domestic relations today is actually a complex mixture of rights and duties arising from:

   a. the "status" of the spouses as married persons, with many rights and obligations dictated by statute and case law;

   b. the spouses' voluntary contractual agreements with each other as independent parties; and

   c. the sharing of life and life's work that occurs in marriage, which has given rise to an understanding of marriage as a merger or intimate partnership relationship.

3. The right to marriage has been deemed a fundamental human right under the U.S. Constitution, and a state may not unreasonably interfere with, or restrict, a person's right to marry. Equal protection and due process principles protect the freedom to marry.

   a. In Obergefell v. Hodges, 576 U.S. ___ (2015), the United States Supreme Court held that, under both the Due Process Clause and the Equal Protection Clause of the Fourteenth Amendment, the fundamental right to marry is guaranteed to same-sex couples.

   b. Under Obergefell, states are required to license a marriage between two people of the same sex and to recognize a marriage between two people of the same sex when their marriage was lawfully licensed and performed out of state.

   c. State laws that directly and substantially interfere with the right to marry must be narrowly tailored to promote a compelling state interest [Zablocki v. Redhail, 434 U.S. 374 (1978); Turner v. Safley, 482 U.S. 78 (1987); Loving v. Virginia, 388 U.S. 1 (1967)].

   d. The right to obtain a divorce is also protected by principles of due process [Boddie v. Connecticut, 401 U.S. 371 (1971)].

4. The state's interest in regulating marriage is greatest at its beginning and end. The spouses' right to privacy generally prevails during the marriage, particularly as to matters regarding their intimate relationship and choices about procreation [Griswold v. Connecticut, 381 U.S. 479 (1965)].

B. **Breach of Promise to Marry**

1. Generally, there is no cause of action in tort for breach of a promise to marry (or for "seduction"), and likewise, tort claims for deceit, misrepresentation, or to recover for emotional distress in connection with

a breach of a promise to marry, are not actionable.

2.   At common law, a promise to marry was legally enforceable, with damages for breach. However, this cause of action has been abolished in most jurisdictions by statutes known as **anti-heart balm acts**.

C.   **Gifts in Contemplation of Marriage**

1.   A gift is complete and irrevocable, such that the gift recipient becomes the new owner of the asset, if:

   a.   the donor intends, unconditionally, to make a gift to the donee at that time;

   b.   the property is delivered to the donee; and

   c.   the donee accepts the property.

   EXAMPLE: Angela is so overwhelmed with love for her new boyfriend, Brad, that she buys him an expensive watch. When he protests that they may be "rushing things," she insists, "I just want you to have it." To Angela's joy, he decides to accept it and wears it constantly. Upon their breakup a year later, she insists on return of the watch because she regrets giving it to him. Brad has no legal obligation to return the watch as the unconditional gift was complete upon his receipt and acceptance of it.

2.   It is possible to attach an enforceable condition on a gift that obligates the recipient to return the gift after it is given. A gift may be given presently, but its retention conditioned on whether a future event occurs. The donor's intent is critical. Most states treat engagement rings as gifts conditioned on a future marriage, and the ring must be returned if the wedding does not take place.

3.   A gift is made in consideration (or contemplation) of marriage under circumstances indicating that the donor intended the gift:

   a.   to be subject to a condition subsequent—namely, that the donor and donee later marry; and

   b.   would not have been made without expectation of marriage.

   EXAMPLE: An engagement ring is ordinarily considered a gift in consideration of marriage, unless the facts indicate to the contrary, such as if the donor should insist, "no matter what happens, I want you to have this."

4.   If the marriage does not take place, the donor will generally be able to compel the return of the ring or other gift made in contemplation of marriage.

   a.   The modern trend generally favors a no-fault. This means that a court will not assess who cancelled the marriage, or who is "at fault" for canceling the marriage.

      (1)   Thus, it is immaterial why the marriage did not occur; the fact that the condition subsequent did not occur should be sufficient to revoke the gift.

   b.   The current law departs from the older view, where the question of whether the ring or other gift must be returned turned on an assessment of fault.

EXAMPLE: Bob gave Gail an engagement ring when she agreed to marry him. Later, Bob had an affair with another woman. After she found out, Gail buried the ring in Bob's backyard, and told him to find it himself if he wanted it back. Bob could not locate the ring and brought an action to recover its value. Regardless of who is at fault for the breakup, Gail is liable to Bob for the value of the ring.

D. **Premarital Agreements**
   1. **Nature and Validity**
      a. **Premarital** (also called prenuptial or antenuptial) **agreements** are contracts made by the parties prior to marriage and in contemplation of marriage, generally attempting to alter or extinguish the spouses' property and/or support rights otherwise recognized by law.
      b. Under the Uniform Premarital Agreement Act ("UPAA"), a valid premarital agreement becomes effective upon a formal marriage between the parties [UPAA § 4].
         (1) If the marriage is later declared void, the agreement remains effective to the extent necessary to avoid an inequitable result [UPAA § 7].
      c. The current view is that premarital agreements are generally valid devices to resolve disputes between spouses in the event of divorce, as well as a means for estate planning in the event of death.
      d. However, states have adopted different standards for enforcing prenuptial contracts.
         (1) A slight majority of states have adopted, in part, the UPAA regarding formation and enforceability of premarital agreements that deal with divorce. Its principles have been influential.
         (2) However, states have adopted different rules on a number of issues.
            (a) States disagree about whether the proponent or challenger of the agreement has the burden of proof and what standard of proof is required for enforcement.
            (b) States also disagree on the required elements for enforcement.
         (3) Collecting the approaches across the various jurisdictions, the issues considered for enforcement are:
            (a) Have basic contract formation rules been satisfied?
               1) All states require this.
            (b) Was there procedural fairness when the contract was formed?
               1) To satisfy procedural fairness, all states require disclosure of certain financial information.
               2) Procedural fairness for an enforceable prenuptial contract includes special disclosure requirements in addition to the standard contract formation elements such as voluntariness.

    (c)   Are the terms in the agreement substantively fair?

        1)   Some states will evaluate a prenuptial agreement for substantive fairness, as well as for procedural fairness. In contrast, other states consider only procedural fairness.

        2)   Under the UPAA, the challenger must not only show that the agreement was "unconscionable," but also that he should have received disclosure of the assets and liabilities of the other party, and that he did not voluntarily waive such disclosure.

e.   In general, although it is certainly possible, it is difficult to successfully challenge enforcement, as modern law emphasizes the importance of freedom to contract.

2. Contract Elements and Defenses

a.   Antenuptial agreements are contracts, and thus must meet all of the usual requirements for valid contracts, including capacity to contract, voluntariness, offer, acceptance, and consideration. The mutual promises to marry and adjustment of the parties' rights is sufficient consideration.

b.   The parties must have capacity to contract—such that neither party is a minor or mentally infirm—and must enter the contract voluntarily.

c.   In most states, an antenuptial agreement must be in writing and signed by the parties, consistent with the UPAA and the Statute of Frauds (where applicable).

d.   An amendment to or revocation of the agreement after the marriage must also be in writing, but is enforceable without additional consideration [UPAA § 5].

3. Procedural Fairness

a.   All states examine whether there are any procedural defects surrounding the agreement such that it should not be enforced. In addition, several states also look at the reasonableness or fairness of the substantive provisions of the agreement.

b.   Factors considered relevant to procedural fairness may include [In re Marriage of Matson, 705 P.2d 817 (Wash. Ct. App. 1985)]:

    (1)   the fullness of disclosure of net worth;

    (2)   the availability of independent counsel or knowing and voluntary waiver of such representation;

    (3)   the timing of the presentation of the agreement, giving sufficient time to review before the wedding; and

    (4)   the relative bargaining power of the parties, and their relative levels of financial or legal knowledge.

c. Voluntariness

    (1)   All states and the UPAA allow a challenge to enforcement of the contract if a party can prove that he did not execute the agreement voluntarily.

    (2)   Voluntariness is evaluated under the usual common law standard in contract situations. The agreement will be enforced

unless the challenger can show that the agreement was the product of fraud or duress.

(3) Courts generally have not found that presenting the agreement to the spouse on the eve of the wedding, and threatening to call it off if the agreement is not signed, constitutes sufficient duress to invalidate the agreement for lack of voluntariness [see In re Yannalfo, 794 A.2d 795 (N.H. 2002); In re Marriage of Spiegel, 553 N.W.2d 309 (Iowa 1996)].

(a) However, pressured timing is relevant and may contribute to a duress claim if combined with other facts.

(4) Most states do not require independent counsel as a precondition to enforcing an agreement against an objecting party, but the assistance, or at least availability, of counsel may be a factor in the assessment of voluntariness.

(a) The UPAA does not require the assistance of independent counsel for each party. Limited language skills and lack of practical alternatives for one party may be factors showing unconscionability, however, in the absence of independent counsel [In re Marriage of Shirilla, 89 P.3d 1 (Mont. 2004)].

EXAMPLE: Barry, a professional sports figure, presented a premarital agreement to his Swedish bride-to-be the day before their Las Vegas wedding and told her that their marriage was conditioned on her signing the agreement. He was represented by counsel, but she was not, and her English was limited. The wife challenged the agreement upon their subsequent divorce, but the California court found she had not carried her burden of proof on involuntariness under the UPAA [In re Marriage of Bonds, 5 P.3d 815 (Cal. 2000)].

(5) The presence of only one spouse's attorney at the signing of an agreement drafted by that attorney may further be considered a coercive circumstance for the unrepresented party [Peters-Riemers v. Riemers, 644 N.W.2d 197 (N.D. 2002)].

EXAMPLE: When the owner of a major sports franchise married a Bolivian woman, he required her to sign a prenuptial agreement by which she waived all rights in his estate if they were not living together at the time of his death. He presented the agreement to her on the eve of their wedding. Looming criminal charges threatened her with deportation, so without consulting an attorney, she signed the agreement in the hope that their marriage would ease her immigration problems. Several years later, the couple separated. At her husband's death, the wife attempted to elect against his will, which left her nothing. She argued that the prenuptial agreement was signed under duress and that public policy should allow her to elect against the will. The wife has a strong argument for duress given her imminent deportation, pressured timing, and lack of an attorney.

d. **Lack of Adequate Disclosure**

   (1) Prenuptial agreements can also be challenged for lack of adequate financial disclosure. The disclosure standard, as set forth in the UPAA and typically followed under state laws, is that before execution of the agreement, the challenger:

      (a) was not provided a fair and reasonable disclosure of the property or financial obligations of the other party;

      (b) did not voluntarily and expressly waive, in writing, any right to disclosure of the property or financial obligations of the other party beyond the disclosure provided; and

      (c) did not have, or reasonably could not have had, an adequate knowledge of the property and financial obligations of the other party.

   (2) While full financial disclosure is not required in every case, such as where the parties have a fairly accurate knowledge of each other's financial condition, a party may demand it.

   (3) Many jurisdictions have indicated that a "fair and reasonable disclosure" requires the parties to provide each other with a general approximation of their income, assets, and liabilities, preferably in a written schedule [see, e.g., Blige v. Blige, 656 S.E.2d 822 (Ga. 2008)].

      EXAMPLE: Husband had told Wife her engagement ring was worth more than $20,000, and she had signed a premarital agreement with the understanding that this was to be one of her assets upon divorce. She could not invalidate the agreement when she discovered upon their divorce that the ring was actually cubic zirconium, since this was an asset under her control that she could have had appraised.

4. **UPAA Approach**

   a. To find an agreement unenforceable (other than for lack of voluntariness), the UPAA requires two elements:

      (1) the agreement was unconscionable (at the time of the signing); and

      (2) there was a lack of adequate disclosure (i.e., procedural unfairness).

   b. The unconscionable standard is basically the same as under contract law.

      (1) As in commercial contract situations, the term contemplates a large disparity in sophistication and resources that results in a one-sided agreement due to inequity in bargaining power.

      (2) Thus, unconscionability recognizes both a concern for substantive unfairness because the content or terms of the deal is unfair, and a concern for procedural unfairness because of flaws in the bargaining process.

c. The UPAA view examines only the circumstances surrounding the execution of the agreement, not its fairness at the time of enforcement. In contrast, some states will evaluate fairness at the time of contract enforcement as well as at formation.

d. Some interpretations of the unconscionability provision in the UPAA or similar state laws reflect the view that there is a confidential relationship between persons who are engaged to be married, which imposes a higher duty toward each other than between contracting parties in the usual arms-length commercial bargaining situation [see, e.g., Mallen v. Mallen, 622 S.E.2d 812 (Ga. 2005)].

5. **Majority Approach**

a. In most states, courts will evaluate a premarital agreement for the substantive fairness of its provisions. Accordingly, in most states, an antenuptial agreement can be invalidated based on a finding of either procedural or substantive unfairness.

b. In contrast, the language of the UPAA itself requires both procedural and substantive unfairness (as described above) in order to invalidate a premarital agreement. States generally have not followed this aspect of the UPAA. This important difference is one example of how, even among the jurisdictions that have adopted the UPAA, there are differing versions of some provisions, and differing interpretations on many of the issues related to substantive and procedural fairness.

c. Although it is unlikely as the standards are similar and overlapping, the UPAA unconscionability standard tracks contract law and may be more difficult to prove than the arguably lesser demands of a substantive unreasonableness standard. In other words, it is possible that a fact situation could be substantively unfair but not necessarily rise to the level of unconscionability.

d. In contrast to the UPAA, some states will evaluate the agreement at the time of enforcement, allowing the court to take into account changed circumstances such as changes in employment prospects, health, or the birth of children since the time of signing [see, e.g., In re Yannalfo, 794 A.2d 795 (N.H. 2002)].

e. The American Law Institute's Principles of the Law of Family Dissolution ("ALI Principles") have not been officially adopted, but reflect aspects of the law of many states. The ALI Principles attempt to clarify some of the issues that have remained most unsettled under the UPAA.

(1) The ALI Principles, which apply to both prenuptial and post-nuptial agreements, articulate a balance between the parties' autonomy and concerns for fairness at the time of execution as well as at the time of enforcement.

(2) In a departure from the norm, the ALI Principles place the burden of proof on the party seeking enforcement, not on the challenger.

(3) The ALI Principles are consistent with the majority of states in

that they require substantive fairness and procedural fairness. However, the ALI Principles also propose some reforms that have not yet been adopted, such as greater disclosure in the absence of independent counsel and a 30-day waiting period between presentation of the agreement and the wedding [ALI Principles § 7.04].

(4) In addition to these suggested enhancements of procedural safeguards, the ALI Principles approach substantive fairness by asking whether the agreement would "work substantial injustice," thus encouraging substantive judicial review of the agreement [ALI Principles § 7.05].

6. **Subject Matter**

   a. The subject of the agreement may include any provisions that do not violate public policy [UPAA § 3], but states differ on what the public policy exception means.

   b. Agreements concerning property division are permissible.

   c. **Waiver of Alimony**

      (1) The majority view and modern trend permits waiver of alimony by agreement. However, some states permit only property division provisions, and will not enforce a waiver of spousal support. Even when permissible, states tend to more closely scrutinize agreements waiving spousal support upon divorce [see, e.g., Lane v. Lane, 202 S.W.3d 577 (Ky. 2006)].

      (2) The UPAA limits the parties' freedom to contract regarding support only in the extreme case [UPAA § 6].

         (a) Under the UPAA, if the premarital agreement modifies or eliminates spousal support so as to cause one party to the agreement to require public assistance, the court may require the other party to pay sufficient support to avoid that result.

   d. Under the UPAA, the rights of children to support may not be adversely affected by a premarital agreement [UPAA § 3(b)]. In virtually all states, an agreement that abrogates, or even limits, the obligation of a parent to support his minor children during or after the marriage is against public policy and is invalid.

   EXAMPLE: Jack and Jill were engaged. Jack had been married previously and had three teenage children whom he hoped to send to college. Jack does not want more children, but Jill is younger than Jack and is still of childbearing age. Jack talks her into signing a prenuptial agreement by which she promises not to bear his children during their marriage. If Jill becomes pregnant, the agreement provides that she will forfeit all right to spousal or child support. These provisions are not enforceable.

   e. Nonmonetary provisions dealing with such matters as division of household duties, the frequency of sexual relations, childbearing, or childrearing have seldom been enforced, although permitted by the

UPAA. An agreement altering the grounds for divorce, as recognized under state law, will not be enforced.

f. A premarital agreement may alter the spouses' ownership and powers of management of property during marriage and the expectations of creditors with respect to debts of the spouses and access to what would otherwise be marital or community property [Schlaefer v. Financial Mgmt. Serv., 996 P.2d 745 (Ariz. Ct. App. 2000)].

7. **Choice of Law**

a. Parties may designate, in the premarital agreement, which state's law will govern in the event of a dispute regarding enforceability, and that choice will generally control if consistent with jurisdictional rules.

b. If the agreement does not address the issue, some states will apply the law of the state in which the agreement was signed.

c. Others, generally following different choice-of-law rules for agreements, apply the law of the state with which the parties have the most significant relationship.

EXAM TIP Due to the inconsistency of court decisions in this area, often even within the same state, a thorough discussion of facts in the question bearing on both procedural and substantive fairness will probably earn the most points, unless the question provides or excludes a specific standard to follow. The majority rule, however, favors upholding these agreements despite challenges on either substantive or procedural fairness grounds.

E. **Legal Requirements for Marriage**

1. **Formal Marriage**

a. The majority of states require a formal marriage, meaning that there must be a state-issued marriage license and solemnization (a ceremony) by a state-authorized official. There is a presumption of validity of marriages and a policy of recognizing them.

b. **Marriage License Requirements**

(1) **Application for License**

(a) Both parties must generally appear before the clerk of the local probate or family court to obtain a marriage license.

(b) Most states no longer require a premarital blood test to show the absence of sexually transmitted diseases, but they may require that the applicants receive information about sexually transmitted and/or genetically transmitted diseases.

(2) **Waiting Period**

(a) Many states impose a short waiting period between the filing of the application for a marriage license and the issuance of the license.

(b) Statutes generally permit a judge to waive the waiting period upon request for good cause shown.

(3) **Duration of Marriage License**

(a) The license is typically valid for a limited period of time, specified by statute.

(b) If the marriage is not solemnized within that period, the parties must reapply.

c. **Solemnization**

(1) **Performance by Authorized Official**

(a) Once a marriage license is issued, the ceremony may be performed by an authorized official prior to the expiration of the license. State law determines who may solemnize a marriage.

(b) Typically, judges, retired judges, county clerks, public officials authorized to solemnize marriages (e.g., justices of the peace), and clergy (according to the prescriptions of any religious denomination or Indian nation or tribe) are authorized to perform a marriage ceremony.

d. **Failure to Comply with Formalities**

(1) Lack of authority on behalf of the official performing the ceremony generally does not render the marriage invalid. Most states will forgive the mistake under a **substantial compliance doctrine**.

(2) In many states, even the failure to obtain a marriage license will not invalidate the marriage, as long as the parties are eligible to marry and married in good faith that the marriage was valid.

(3) Other states will insist on strict formalities. Even so, the would-be spouses may yet get relief as **putative spouses** (discussed below).

e. **Proxy Marriages**

(1) A **proxy marriage** is one solemnized through agents standing in for and acting on behalf of one or both parties.

(2) Proxy marriages have most often been performed and recognized during wartime.

2. **Informal or Common Law Marriage**

a. In a minority of states, a marriage may be entered into without satisfying the licensing requirements and without a ceremony through the doctrine of common law marriage, recognized either by statute or case law [see, e.g., Utah Code Ann. § 30-1-4.5; Piel v. Brown, 361 So. 2d 90 (Ala. 1978)].

(1) Most states today do not recognize common law marriages. However, the doctrine is relevant nationwide because most states, even those that do not themselves recognize common law marriages created within the state, will nonetheless recognize a common law marriage validly created in another state, unless the circumstances violate an important state public policy.

b. The requirements for such marriages are generally as follows:

(1) **expression of intent**;

(a) The common law requires a present intention to be married.

(b) The parties must mutually consent and contract to become a married couple in the present, not upon the happening of some future, intervening event. There must be a present assumption of the marital status rather than an agreement for a future union.

(c) Intent to be married can be demonstrated expressly, such as in an exchange of words or vows. Alternatively, intent can be implied based on upon the parties' behavior—i.e., acting like a married couple.

(2) **cohabitation**;

(a) The cohabitation requirement means that the parties must live together on an ongoing basis and consummate the relationship.

(b) **Cohabitation** has been defined in various domestic relations contexts as consisting of more than a common residence and a sexual relationship. It requires carrying out certain mutual responsibilities in the everyday maintenance of the home and a financial relationship, as well as the intimate relationship between the parties [Konzelman v. Konzelman, 729 A.2d 7 (N.J. 1999); Pellegrin v. Pellegrin, 525 S.E.2d 611 (Va. Ct. App. 2000)].

(3) **holding out**;

(a) The parties must represent themselves to others as a married couple and not merely as partners.

(b) Evidence that the parties have a reputation in the community as being married will be persuasive, as well as any legal or financial documents prepared by the couple representing themselves as spouses.

(4) **legal capacity**; and

(a) The parties to a common law marriage must have the requisite age and capacity, and none of the restrictions to the validity of a marriage may exist (e.g., consanguinity or prior existing marriage).

(b) Legal capacity may arise subsequently, however, when an existing impediment is removed, such as by the death or divorce of the spouse of the prior marriage. Once legal capacity exists, a common law marriage may then arise if all of the other elements exist (i.e., intent, cohabitation, holding out).

(5) **burden of proof**.

(a) The burden of proving a common law marriage is on the party asserting it, and typically, the elements must be proven by clear and convincing evidence (as opposed to the usual preponderance of the evidence standard).

(b) The burden may be especially heavy when a party claims that he was the common law spouse of a deceased person, so as to be able to share in the estate of the deceased.

3. **Covenant Marriage**

   a. A few states, in recent years, have attempted to stem the tide of divorce by enacting statutes providing a category of marriage called **covenant marriage**, in which the parties pledge a life-long commitment and mutually agree to limit the grounds on which they may divorce [see La. Rev. Stat. Ann. § 9:272; Ariz. Rev. Stat. Ann. § 25-901].

   b. The parties to a covenant marriage typically must sign a "declaration of intent" that commits them to premarital counseling and to additional counseling or mediation before seeking separation or divorce.

F. **Legal Impediments to Marriage**

1. **Nonage**

   a. In most states today, a marriage license will not be issued without the consent of a parent or guardian if either party is under 18. Some states require court approval if the minor is under age 16, but prohibit marriage entirely for those under 14, although there may be exceptions if the minor is pregnant.

2. **Consanguinity and Affinity**

   a. A marriage license generally will not be issued for marriages between relatives who are ancestor and descendant, brother and sister, uncle and niece, or aunt and nephew, whether of the whole blood or half blood.

   b. Few states still extend the prohibition to the same relationships by marriage (**affinity**). Where the parties are related only by marriage and not by blood, restrictions on their marriage have no genetic basis and are now disfavored.

   c. There is a split among the jurisdictions regarding marriage between first cousins.

3. **Mental Incapacity, Lack of Consent, and Fraud**

   a. The inability of a party to consent to a marriage due to mental incapacity or infirmity will render the marriage invalid. If a person cannot understand the nature of the marriage contract, he cannot enter into a marriage.

   b. A person under conservatorship may have the mental capacity to marry, even though the person does not have the power to manage his own property. In some states, the conservator's permission to marry must be obtained prior to issuance of the marriage license.

   c. Incapacity may also result if either party is heavily under the influence of alcohol or drugs. State law may require, however, that there is no cohabitation once the party or parties recover from the intoxication and discover that a wedding occurred.

   d. Fraud must be proven in the same manner as fraud in other contexts under state law. Thus, the misrepresentation or failure to disclose must be intended to induce the other party to enter the marriage, and must be material, i.e., must cause reliance, or in some states, go to the essence of the marriage contract, in order to invalidate a marriage.

   (1)   In the latter states, to void the marriage, the fraudulent misrepresentation must:

        (a) be related to the essential purposes of marriage, including procreation; and

        (b) either prevent a party from entering into a true marital relationship, or having entered it, preclude the performance of customary and legal marital duties.

           EXAMPLE: Harold knew he was impotent when he asked Wanda to marry him, but he did not disclose this fact to her. She had told him she wanted to have children, and he was afraid she would not marry him if he told her the truth. Wanda would have grounds for annulment.

   (2)   Courts typically have not found certain types of misrepresentation to meet this test, such as:

        (a) chastity; or

        (b) misrepresentation as to a party's wealth.

  e.   To invalidate a marriage, duress must be sufficient to override a party's free will. Threats of physical force may be required, and courts are reluctant to invalidate a marriage on this ground if the party had opportunity to escape the situation [Phipps v. Phipps, 57 S.E.2d 417 (S.C. 1950)].

4. Physical Incapacity

  a.   The ability to consummate the marriage is a common law requirement for marriage.

5. Prior Marriage Still in Force

  a.   A person who has already been married is incapable of entering into another valid marriage unless the former spouse has died or the prior marriage has been judicially terminated.

  b.   The fact that the second marriage was made in good faith and under a reasonable belief that the former spouse was dead will not render the marriage valid.

  c.   Where a party has entered more than one marriage, there is a strong presumption in most states that the party's latest marriage is valid, and any earlier marriage was dissolved.

  d.   By statute or case law in many states, and in accord with the Uniform Marriage and Divorce Act ("UMDA") view, a subsequent marriage that is initially invalid because one of the parties had a prior marriage in force will become valid upon the removal of the impediment of the prior marriage by death or dissolution. The following requirements typically must be met for this to occur:

   (1)   at the time of the subsequent marriage, one of the parties to it believed, in good faith, that:

        (a) the other spouse to the former marriage was dead;

(b) there had been a divorce; or

(c) there had been no former marriage;

(2) after the subsequent marriage, the parties lived together as a married couple; and

(3) they continued to live together as a married couple after the impediment had been removed.

e. Bigamy is a crime in many states. A ban on polygamy has been upheld as constitutional even where it is a widely held religious belief [Reynolds v. United States, 98 U.S. 145 (1878); State v. Holm, 137 P.3d 726 (Utah 2006)].

(1) Some states thus hold that a bigamous marriage is absolutely void for policy reasons and cannot be "revived" by such corrective measures as obtaining a divorce from the first spouse [Toler v. Oakwood Smokeless Coal Corp., 4 S.E.2d 364 (Va. 1939)].

6. **Putative Spouses**

a. Many states recognize a **putative spouse doctrine**, under which a putative spouse is granted divorce-like remedies at the dissolution of the relationship, even if the marriage is void because of a flaw in the marriage formation process. The doctrine provides an alternative when no marriage has been validly created.

b. To qualify as a **putative spouse**, there must be a ceremonial marriage, and at least one spouse must have a good faith belief in the validity of the marriage.

(1) The putative spouse doctrine has been applied to voidable marriages that were properly performed but where at least one party is unaware of an impediment to the marriage (such as a prior marriage still in force) [Dawson v. Hatfield Wire & Cable Co., 280 A.2d 173 (N.J. 1971)].

NOTE A putative marriage may later become a legally valid marriage if an impediment, existing at the time of the marriage, is subsequently removed and the parties continued to live together in a good faith belief in the validity of the marriage [see, e.g., Mont. Code Ann. § 40-1-404].

c. In some states, a putative spouse acquires the rights conferred upon a legal spouse, including inheritance rights, rights in property acquired during the putative marriage, and the right to maintenance following termination, even if the marriage was legally prohibited or held invalid. In others, the courts may be willing to apply equitable remedies, such as equitable reimbursement or recovery for unjust enrichment.

d. The putative spouse doctrine operates only until knowledge of the fact that the putative spouse is not legally married terminates his status and prevents acquisition of further rights [see, e.g., Colo. Rev. Stat. § 14-2-111]. An annulment proceeding may be invoked to sort out the rights of the parties, but the acquisition of those rights may cease upon the new awareness of the putative spouse before the proceeding is instituted.

EXAMPLE: A Roman Catholic couple was ceremonially married and later divorced. Some years later, they resumed their relationship and went to their priest to arrange a second wedding ceremony. The priest told them they were "still married in the eyes of God" and no new ceremony was necessary. Upon the death of the husband in a work-related accident, the wife was initially denied workmen's compensation benefits because she was not legally married to the deceased, but the state supreme court allowed her claim on the basis of her good faith belief in the continued validity of her marriage until her husband's death, particularly in light of her sixth-grade education [Parkinson v. J. & S. Tool Co., 313 A.2d 609 (N.J. 1974)].

G. Annulment

1. Challenges

a. If the validity of a marriage is questioned, a party, and in some instances a third party, may seek a judgment declaring the invalidity of (**annulling**) the marriage. A marriage may generally be annulled regardless of whether the marriage is void or voidable.

b. The primary difference between a void marriage and a voidable one is that only the aggrieved party may bring the action to annul a voidable marriage during the life of both parties, as discussed below.

2. Grounds

a. Most states distinguish between invalid marriages that are void and those that are voidable, but they may differ on which grounds fall into each category, particularly in instances of nonage.

b. In either case, the grounds for annulment must have existed at the time of the marriage ceremony, not arising later.

c. **Void Marriages**

(1) A void marriage is of no legal effect. Although there is technically no need for a court decree of annulment in the case of a void marriage, a party may request a judicial determination of invalidity by means of an annulment action in order to clarify the rights of the parties.

(2) A void marriage may be collaterally attacked by a party to the marriage, the state, or an interested third party in any proceeding, even after the death of either party to the purported marriage.

(3) Void marriages are those in which the state has such a strong interest in enforcing the prohibition that the parties' desires are considered irrelevant. In most states, those impediments are:

(a) bigamy; or

(b) consanguinity (incest).

> **EXAMPLE:** Harriet married Walter, who was raised in foster care. They did not know they were first cousins when they married in a state that prohibits such marriages. Walter died intestate. At that point, Walter's half-brother came forward to claim his intestate share as Walter's closest living relative.

He has been searching for Walter for years and done genealogical research revealing Harriet's relationship to them. The probate court can rule on Walter's brother's claim that Harriet is not Walter's surviving spouse in the intestacy proceeding.

d. **Voidable Marriages**

(1) A voidable marriage is valid until and unless the aggrieved party obtains an annulment. If a voidable marriage is confirmed or ratified by the aggrieved party, or if one of the parties to the marriage dies, the validity of the marriage may not be questioned or attacked by any person [In re Estate of Davis, 640 P.2d 692 (Or. Ct. App. 1982)].

(2) Voidable marriages generally result from the following impediments, intended for the protection of the disadvantaged party but waivable by that party:

(a) nonage;

(b) impotence of the other spouse;

(c) temporary lack of capacity to consent due to alcohol or drugs, duress, or fraud; or

(d) mental incompetence.

EXAMPLE: Herbert Haft, a wealthy Washington, D.C. developer who had previously gone through a highly publicized and contentious divorce and estrangement from his children, lay dying at age 83 in a hospital intensive care unit. To the horror of his family, he married his girlfriend from his hospital bed two weeks before his death. The children wanted to challenge the validity of his marriage after their father's death. Although the marriage was voidable, they did not have standing to bring an action to void the marriage after their father's death.

3. **Effects of Annulment**

a. **Alimony and Property Division**

(1) Some states' annulment statutes give the courts power to divide property or order support as in divorce cases [see, e.g., Utah Code Ann. § 30-1-17.2].

(2) In some states, even without statutory authority, the court may, under equitable principles, order conveyance of property or restitution as justice may require. This may involve returning the parties to the condition they were in at the time the "marriage" commenced.

b. **Legitimacy of Children**

(1) By statute in most states, children born of a prohibited marriage are considered legitimate as to both parents. Upon annulment, the court thus has the same power to make orders relating to the care, custody, and maintenance of minor children of the parties as in the case of a divorce.

H. Validity of Out-of-State Marriages

1. **Principles of Comity**

   a. Most states have adopted the view of Section 283(2) of the Restatement (Second) of Conflict of Laws that a marriage which satisfies the requirements of the state where contracted "will everywhere be recognized as valid, unless it violates the strong public policy of another state which had the most significant relationship to the spouses and the marriage at the time of the marriage." Thus, out-of-state marriage will usually be recognized as valid, but there are exceptions.

   b. States differ as to what constitutes a "strong" enough public policy that the state will not only prohibit such marriages from being contracted in the state but will also not recognize those validly contracted elsewhere.

      (1) States generally recognize marriages of first cousins married in a state where such marriages are legal.

      (2) Common law marriages contracted outside the state have typically been recognized in states that prohibit them for residents, unless evasion of state law is suspected.

2. **Evasion of State Law**

   a. Most states do not recognize marriages entered into by their residents who leave the state to contract a marriage that would not be valid if contracted within the state, with the intention of continuing to reside in the state while attempting to evade its public policy against such marriages.

   b. By the same token, states generally will not recognize marriages contracted within the state by parties residing, and intending to continue to reside, in another jurisdiction if the marriage would be void if contracted in the other jurisdiction.

      EXAMPLE: Alfred and Bertha are first cousins who both reside in State A, which does not allow first cousins to marry. To avoid this prohibition, they traveled to another state that does not prohibit the marriage of first cousins, and in that other state, they obtained a marriage license and got married. They then immediately returned to State A, where they have been telling people they are married and otherwise holding themselves out as married. Because they purposefully traveled out of state to avoid the policy of their home state, they do not have a valid marriage in State A.

I. Rights of Unmarried Partners

1. Unmarried cohabitants generally have no legally recognized "status" unless they meet the requirements for common law marriage or putative spouses.

   a. The spousal support, community property, or equitable distribution statutes available to married couples will generally not be applied to an unmarried couple.

2. **Express and Implied Contracts**

   a. Most states have followed the principle of Marvin v. Marvin [557 P.2d 106 (Cal. 1976)] in recognizing express and implied contracts between cohabitating persons by which they agree to support each other (pay "palimony") or share property, so long as there is consideration to support the contract other than the furnishing of sexual services because that would constitute an illegal contract. Marvin held that:

(1) courts should enforce express oral or written contracts between nonmarital partners;

(2) in the absence of an express contract, a court should inquire into the conduct of the parties to determine whether that conduct demonstrates an implied contract, partnership agreement or joint venture, or some other tacit understanding between the parties; and

(3) courts may also employ the doctrine of *quantum meruit*, or equitable remedies such as constructive or resulting trusts, when warranted by the facts of the case.

(a) A constructive trust may be imposed where, for example, one partner provided the down payment on a home that was purchased in the name of both parties or of the other partner alone. Virtually all states recognize this remedy.

(b) *Quantum meruit* is the most limited option, as recovery would be limited to the value of domestic services rendered, and only if rendered with expectation of remuneration. In the absence of express agreement, a court may assume that household services are rendered to a partner without expectation of compensation. Thus, the value of business services rendered may more likely be returned under this doctrine than the value of domestic services [see, e.g., Tapley v. Tapley, 449 A.2d 1218 (N.H. 1982)].

b. Under any of these theories, a partner's rights generally fall short of the full panoply of rights for a divorcing or surviving spouse that would be accorded those deemed to have entered a valid marriage.

c. The ALI Principles have recommended a more "conscriptive" approach that would impose marital obligations and rights on cohabiting couples unless they contract out of them, rather than requiring such couples to affirmatively contract for these rights, but very few states follow this approach to date.

3. States that are willing to enforce cohabiting partners' agreements or expectations generally do not distinguish between heterosexual and homosexual couples in this regard, so long as they are able to sever the "illegal," or sexual, components of the agreement from those that could be enforced between any two unrelated parties [Posik v. Layton, 695 So. 2d 759 (Fla. Dist. Ct. App. 1997)].

4. A minority of states recognize only written agreements to share property between unmarried partners [Kohler v. Flynn, 493 N.W.2d 647 (N.D. 1992)].

5. A minority of states have refused to enforce any agreements between nonmarital partners on the basis that such relief would undermine the state policy of fostering marriage and would encourage "meretricious" relationships [see Hewitt v. Hewitt, 394 N.E.2d 1204 (Ill. 1979)].

6. **Tort Recovery**

        a.   A majority of jurisdictions would be unlikely to extend tort recovery for emotional distress to a cohabitant, even a cohabiting fiancée, who witnesses a serious accident injuring or killing the other cohabitant. Compensation for loss of consortium is likewise available only to the legally recognized spouse of the injured party, and not to a fiancée or cohabitant.

           (1)   This reluctance is likely based on the difficulties of determining which cohabitants should be allowed to recover and problems of proving the importance of the relationship [Elden v. Sheldon, 758 P.2d 582 (Cal. 1988); Dunphy v. Gregor, 642 A.2d 372 (N.J. 1994)].

           (2)   Courts may also take the position that allowing cohabitants rights to recover in such situations would undermine the strong public policy in support of marriage.

EXAM TIP To distinguish a common law marriage from a putative marriage or from an unmarried cohabiting relationship, consider the parties' state of mind. A common law marriage cannot be entered without present ability and intent. (The requirements closely mirror those for a formal marriage, but the official ceremony and license is missing. If valid when and where entered, a common law marriage creates full marital rights.) A putative spouse legitimately thinks he is legally married because there was a ceremony, and he is unaware of an impediment or procedural flaw. (The putative spouse may have equitable spousal inheritance rights at the death of the other party, but rights of property division and support are generally determined by annulment remedies.) Unmarried partners know they are not married because there has been no legal ceremony and either they cannot marry or at least one of them doesn't intend to. (They may have statutory, contractual, or equitable rights that vary greatly in different states.)

II. LEGAL EFFECTS OF THE ONGOING MARITAL RELATIONSHIP

A. **Family Privacy**
1. **Common Law Doctrine**
   a. Under the common law, a family's home is subject to privacy, and its internal affairs generally cannot be regulated or interfered with by the government or the courts [McGuire v. McGuire, 59 N.W.2d 336 (Neb. 1953)].
2. The spousal right to privacy and law regarding reproductive choices are covered in detail in the Constitutional Law outline.
3. Law regarding the interspousal evidentiary privilege is covered in the Evidence outline.

B. **Spousal Property Rights during Marriage**
1. **During Life**
   a. **Title Rules**
      (1) Most states are so-called "separate property" states where the spouse with title to property is the legal owner. Neither spouse has a vested interest in property over which they do not have formal title. During ongoing marriage there is no "marital property" that would prevent a title-holding spouse from conveying marital property to a third party during the marriage.
      (2) In contrast, spouses in one of the few community property states have a present interest in community property before termination of the marriage.
         (a) Community property states have a number of presumptions with respect to the ownership of property and its character-ization as community or separate.
         (b) Community property states also have special rules on the spousal power to manage community property during the marriage that affect the power of conveyance, but where the property is held in one spouse's name alone, there may be a presumption that that spouse has the power to convey the property without joinder by the other spouse.
   b. **Married Women's Property Rights**
      (1) Today, a married woman retains her rights to her separate prop-erty held before or acquired after her marriage. She has the power to contract with her spouse or with third parties, to grant or receive conveyances of real or personal property, and to sue and be sued in her own right.
   c. **Co-Ownership**
      (1) Often spouses choose to own property jointly, in a form that may avoid potential difficulties upon the death of one of the parties. Concurrent estates recognized at common law include joint tenancies, tenancies in common, and tenancies by the entirety.

(a) The tenancy in common does not carry inherent survivorship rights.

(b) A tenancy by the entirety, recognized in a significant minority of states, is the only form of joint ownership that requires an existing marital relationship between the co-owners. Unlike joint tenants, a tenant by the entirety cannot unilaterally destroy the other tenant's right of survivorship nor alienate his interest in the property without the other spouse's consent.

(c) Generally, rights of survivorship are implied if the grant specifies a "joint tenancy."

(2) Some states have enacted statutes that convert a conveyance to spouses in the form of a tenancy by the entirety into a joint tenancy with rights of survivorship or a tenancy in common.

(3) A tenancy by the entirety is converted into a tenancy in common by a judgment terminating a marriage, unless the court orders otherwise through an order of equitable distribution.

(4) In many common law states today, the default for transfers of real property to a married couple is a tenancy in common, unless a joint tenancy is expressly declared.

d. **Transfers between Spouses**

(1) Transfers of real and personal property between spouses are generally valid to the same extent as if they were unmarried.

(a) When one spouse transfers money or other property to the other without consideration, there is a rebuttable presumption that it is a gift. Likewise, if one spouse pays the consideration for property to a third person who conveys it to the other spouse, it is presumed to be a gift. A resulting trust does not arise in such a transfer unless there is clear proof that a gift was not intended at the time of the conveyance.

(b) For the protection of third parties, however, statutes may provide that when spouses live together, no transfer or conveyance of goods and chattels between the spouses will be valid against any third person unless the transfer is in writing and filed in the same manner as security interests where possession of the property is to remain with the person giving security.

e. **Transfers to Third Parties**

(1) A married person may transfer real or personal property that he owns separately.

(2) Joint property may pose difficult issues, depending on the form of title.

(a) Property owned as tenants by the entirety cannot be transferred without the consent of the other spouse, but other jointly owned property generally can be.

1) The spouse can transfer only his own interest in such property, however, severing the joint ownership.

   (b) In community property states, property that is subject to joint management requires both spouses to join in the conveyance, so creditors generally require this for their protection, although some community property may be eligible for conveyance by one spouse alone.

  (3) Once a divorce proceeding is commenced, courts typically have the power to issue interim orders to prevent transfers or dissipation of assets by a spouse before entry of the final decree.

   (a) If the transfer could not be prevented or the property recovered, a divorce court may adjust property rights in other assets to compensate, but this may be not feasible.

   (b) Thus, some states treat the spouses as potential creditors of each other with respect to marital assets, bringing the transfer of marital property to a third party in anticipation of divorce under the state fraudulent conveyance law if intended to defraud the spouse.

2. Upon Death

 a. Virtually all non-community property states today have effectively abolished dower and curtesy, which provided certain property rights to a surviving spouse. Instead, there are now family protection devices such as homestead and an elective share for a spouse who is not provided for, or feels inadequately provided for, in the deceased spouse's will.

 b. Dower and curtesy were not needed in the community property states due to the protections afforded a surviving spouse under the community property system, which generally affords the surviving spouse half of all community property.

 c. Elective share, intestate inheritance, and family allowance issues are addressed in the Wills outline.

NOTE Spousal rights upon death may differ significantly from rights upon divorce, because relatively fixed rules in the probate code govern the spousal share in cases of intestacy or election against the decedent's will regardless of the survivor's circumstances or needs, whereas a spouse's share of property upon divorce is generally unpredictable due to the degree of discretion given to courts in divorce cases. Rights upon death, like rights at divorce, can be altered by agreement between the parties, however.

C. Support Obligations

1. Duty of Both Spouses

 a. Spouses have a legal duty to support each other. Courts first ascertain which of the spouses or parents is able to provide support, and then place the obligation on that person without regard to gender-based distinctions. This approach has been adopted by statute or case law in many states, and may be mandated by equal protection principles [Orr v. Orr, 440 U.S. 268 (1979)].

b. The duty of support is generally not enforceable by a spouse directly during the marriage, however. Most states provide civil remedies and criminal penalties for nonsupport and desertion, allowing the state to enforce family support obligations so that needy individuals do not become public charges.

2. **Liability for Debts and Necessaries Contracted for by Needy Spouse**

a. A corollary to the duty of support is the **necessaries doctrine**, which is a tool for creditors. There is a reciprocal obligation on the part of each spouse to provide for necessaries furnished to the other spouse based on the respective spouses' needs and financial ability [see, e.g., Landmark Med. Ctr. v. Gauthier, 635 A.2d 1145 (R.I. 1994)].

b. The majority of states recognize a doctrine of necessaries whereby a spouse's liability for obligations incurred by the other spouse arises in three primary situations:

   (1) where the debtor-spouse has express or apparent authority to pledge the other's credit for household expenses;

   (2) where the non-needy spouse neglects, fails, or refuses to furnish the needy spouse with necessaries which are then supplied to that spouse by a third person with expectation of payment; and

   (3) where one spouse has incurred medical expenses beyond his sole ability to pay.

   EXAMPLE: A husband becomes ill and is admitted to the hospital and receives medical treatment. Husband later receives a hospital bill of $10,000 for which he has no insurance. Husband is unable to pay the bill. Assuming she has the money, the wife can be held liable to the hospital because the medical bills were a necessity for the husband, and the husband is unable to pay.

c. Some states have "family expense" statutes that impose joint liability on both spouses [see, e.g., Wash. Rev. Code § 26.16.205].

d. Others impose primary liability on the spouse who directly incurred the debt or liability and secondary liability on the other spouse [Landmark Med. Ctr. v. Gauthier, 635 A.2d 1145 (R.I. 1994); Marshfield Clinic v. Discher, 314 N.W.2d 326 (Wisc. 1982)].

e. A few states have abrogated the doctrine of necessaries entirely, holding neither spouse liable for debts incurred by the other spouse, absent an express agreement with the creditor [Govan v. Med. Credit Servs., Inc., 621 So. 2d 928 (Miss. 1993); Emanuel v. McGriff, 596 So. 2d 578 (Ala. 1992)].

f. Once there is a separate support decree, in most states a spouse's legal obligation is set by the decree, and the spouse would no longer be liable to third persons for necessaries furnished to the other spouse.

3. **Contract Liability**

a. Contract liability is generally based on which spouse contracted the debt, unless it is a contract for necessaries.

b.   Contracts may be made, and liabilities incurred, by either spouse, and may be enforced against that person to the same extent as if the spouse were unmarried. Generally, the liabilities of each spouse are determined by the express terms of their agreements with creditors and other third parties.

c.   In general, a mutual agency relationship is not implied in law merely from a marital relationship. Courts typically employ agency theory on a case-by-case basis to determine whether one spouse has the power to bind the other in particular transactions. The tension in the law is between protecting creditors from collusive behavior of the spouses intended to shield assets from the creditor, and protecting an innocent spouse from spendthrift or other irresponsible behavior by the other spouse that may erode the value of the marital estate.

D.   Tort Liability

1.   Interspousal Immunity

a.   The modern view favors complete abolition of interspousal immunity, such that certain suits between spouses are generally permitted. Virtually all states have at least partially abolished the doctrine [Bozman v. Bozman, 830 A.2d 450 (Md. 2003)].

(1)   States have taken different positions on whether such suits should be allowed for intentional torts committed by one spouse upon another, or for negligence actions, particularly involving insured motor vehicles [see Restatement (Second) of Torts § 895F].

(2)   Such situations have typically been assessed with regard to whether abolition of immunity would tend to disrupt the peace and harmony of the marital home or possibly encourage collusive fraud upon insurance companies.

2.   Torts against the Marital Relationship

a.   Most states have abolished:

(1)   the common law tort of alienation of affections against a third party who causes separation from the plaintiff's spouse, resulting in loss of consortium; and

(2)   the common law tort of criminal conversation against a third party who has sexual intercourse with the plaintiff's spouse.

b.   **Elements of Tort Recovery**

(1)   A spouse may recover consequential damages that derive from an underlying tort against the other spouse.

EXAMPLE: A spouse may recover medical and other expenses which he is required to pay as a result of a tort committed against the other spouse, and may also recover damages for loss of earning capacity, and loss of consortium.

(2)   Thus, if the spouse fails to prove negligence or other tortious conduct by the third party, there can be no recovery for these elements of damages.

      c.   **Loss of Consortium**

         (1)   Loss of consortium refers to the loss of benefits that one spouse is entitled to receive from the other, including companionship, cooperation, aid, affection, and sexual relations.

         (2)   Today, most states permit this form of recovery for either spouse as an element of damages in a negligence action for injuries to the other spouse.

   3.   **Vicarious Tort Liability**

      a.   A spouse is not vicariously liable for torts committed by the other spouse. This is a departure from prior law, under which a husband was liable for his wife's torts.

E. Criminal Liability and Domestic Violence

   1.   Spouses can be held accountable for criminal conduct, including rape.

   2.   All 50 states and the District of Columbia make protective orders available as a civil remedy to victims of domestic violence.

   3.   Typically, the following acts may give rise to a protective order:

      a.   attempting to cause, or intentionally, knowingly, or recklessly causing bodily injury or a sexual offense;

      b.   placing another in reasonable fear of imminent serious bodily injury;

      c.   false imprisonment; or

      d.   physical or sexual abuse of minor children.

F. Postnuptial Property Agreements

   1.   The rules applying to postnuptial agreements are generally the same as those applicable to prenuptial agreements.

   2.   The law encourages spouses who have decided to change or end their marital relationships to use separation agreements to settle their affairs. An agreement is generally negotiated after the cause for separation has occurred and while the parties are separated.

   3.   The UPAA, governing premarital agreements, does not by its terms apply to postnuptial agreements, but some states have extended the same principles to postnuptial agreements.

   4.   States differ as to whether they find a confidential relationship between the parties before marriage as they do after marriage.

      a.   Separation agreements must be fairly and voluntarily made, and will be upheld in the absence of fraud, duress, concealment, or overreaching.

      b.   In addition, there may be a requirement of full and fair financial disclosure between the parties.

   5.   The agreement may be used to settle all property rights and claims of the spouses, including child support and custody. However, the court retains the authority to make appropriate orders contrary to the agreement where necessary to protect the best interests of the children affected.

6. The ALI Principles differ from the UPAA by placing the burden of proof on the party seeking to enforce the agreement, rather than on the party challenging its validity. The ALI Principles also make lack of disclosure sufficient to invalidate an agreement and requires a 30-day waiting period before signing. The ALI Principles look at fairness at the time of enforcement, not at the time of signing, and spell out factors to be weighed in a fairness analysis.

7. **Contract Principles Govern**

   a. The agreement is a contract between the parties and is governed by ordinary contract principles. If intended as a complete and final settlement (i.e., fully integrated) it will bar all further claims by either party. It must be supported by consideration, and each party's waiver of rights in the property or estate of the other spouse is sufficient consideration.

8. **Modification or Termination of Agreement**

   a. The agreement may only be modified by mutual consent of the parties.

   b. The parties may expressly or impliedly agree to terminate or revoke the agreement. If both parties act in a manner inconsistent with the terms of the agreement, a court may find mutual consent to terminate the agreement.

   c. Subsequent cohabitation by the parties after reconciliation will void the agreement, only if such intent is manifested by the parties.

III. PARENTS AND CHILDREN

A. **Establishing Parenthood**

1. **Presumption of Marital Legitimacy and Paternity**

   a. Paternity may be established because of marriage.

      (1) Common law rules, supplemented by statutes in many states, reflect a strong presumption that children born to or conceived by a woman while she is married are the children of the woman and her husband.

      (2) This presumption may only be rebutted on facts proving, by clear and convincing evidence, that the mother's husband was not the father. There are varying state laws on whether and when evidence of biological paternity will be allowed to rebut the presumption. Many states will allow DNA evidence to challenge the husband's paternity within a few years of the child's birth.

      (3) The doctrine of estoppel may operate to confirm the marital presumption of paternity.

         (a) When the mother's husband learns he is not the biological father, but nevertheless continues to support and hold out the child as his own, he is estopped from denying paternity [Watts v. Watts, 337 A.2d 350 (N.H. 1975)].

         (b) Similarly, the mother may be estopped from seeking child support from a different man after she has deliberately allowed another man to believe he was the father of her child and has accepted child support from him.

      (4) Most states have enacted statutes providing that children born to parents whose marriage was invalid are, nevertheless, legitimate. Under the Uniform Parentage Act ("UPA"), as adopted in some states, every child is deemed to be the legitimate child of both natural parents regardless of the parents' marital status.

   b. **Actions Brought by a Putative Father**

      (1) In the interest of preserving intact families, states may take a different view of assertions of parenthood by an alleged ("putative") father when the child has a presumed father.

      (2) In Michael H. v. Gerald D. [491 U.S. 110 (1989)], the U.S. Supreme Court upheld a California statute that precluded a biological father from bringing a paternity action when the mother of his child was married at the time of the child's birth and she did not join in the paternity petition. There was no substantive due process violation even though the father, wishing to establish his paternity, had had a significant residential relationship with his child.

      (3) In the wake of the Michael H. opinion, many states have enacted statutes that give an unmarried father no more than two years to establish his paternity when his alleged child has a presumed father, deeming a two-year period sufficient to resolve the issue

without subjecting the child to a long period of possibly unsettled circumstances [see UPA §§ 607(a); 607, cmt.].

   c.   The UPA provides presumptions of paternity, which may only be rebutted by results of genetic testing introduced in a paternity proceeding, if the man and the child's natural mother [UPA §§ 201(b), 204]:

       (1)   are or have been married to each other, regardless of whether the marriage is or could be declared invalid, and the child was conceived or born during such marriage or within 300 days after its termination;

       (2)   married each other after the child's birth and the man voluntarily asserted his paternity, such as by agreeing to be named as the child's father on the birth certificate; or

       (3)   for the first two years of the child's life, resided in the same household with the child and the man openly held out the child as his own.

2. Establishing Maternity

   a.   Traditionally, maternity was considered simple and obvious, resulting only from natural birth or adoption.

   b.   Due to issues arising from assisted reproduction methods and surrogacy arrangements, as discussed below, the UPA now recognizes that maternity may also be established by adjudication [UPA § 201(a)].

3. Establishing Paternity of Unwed Father

   a. Actions to Establish Paternity

       (1)   The issue of paternity may become the subject of litigation in a variety of circumstances, including actions involving visitation rights, adoption, distribution of decedents' estates, and, most commonly, the duty of child support.

       (2)   Proceedings to establish paternity of a child born out of wedlock generally may be brought by the mother or a state social service agency, acting on behalf of the mother.

   b. Statute of Limitations

       (1) Actions Brought by or for Child

          (a)   Most states allow paternity actions to be brought at any time prior to the child reaching the age of 18. However, many states require that a paternity action be instituted prior to the death of the putative father.

          (b)   The constitutionality of statutes of limitations on actions to determine the parentage of a child has been addressed by the United States Supreme Court, which struck down a one-year period of limitation on the ability of an infant to determine paternity, and thereby obtain parental support [Mills v. Habluetzel, 456 U.S. 91 (1982)], and a two-year period of limitation after the child's birth [Pickett v. Brown, 462 U.S. 1 (1983)]. The Court noted that any limitation on a nonmarital child's right to obtain support must be substantially related to the state's interest in avoiding the litigation of stale or fraudulent claims.

    c. **Evidence of Paternity**

      (1) **Types**

         (a) Evidence to establish paternity may include the following:

           1) evidence that there was sexual intercourse between the mother and the defendant at or near the time of conception and that the child was likely born as a result;

           2) medical evidence regarding the defendant's paternity based upon genetic tests performed by experts; and

           3) any other relevant evidence.

         (b) In recent years, many states have replaced their earlier blood grouping tests with the more accurate results of HLA (human leukocyte antigen, or tissue typing) tests, and increasingly, DNA testing.

      (2) **Level of Accuracy of Test Results**

         (a) Where relevant, the court may require the child, the mother, and the defendant to submit to tests performed by qualified experts to determine whether the defendant may be excluded as being a parent.

         (b) The test results are admissible only where they definitely exclude the defendant as the father. Under UPA Section 505, genetic testing results create a rebuttable presumption of paternity if the results show that the man has at least a 99% probability of being the father.

    d. **Burden of Proof**

      (1) Many states permit a finding of paternity to be made by a preponderance of the evidence, although some require a higher standard of clear and convincing evidence. The U.S. Supreme Court has held that the Due Process Clause of the Fourteenth Amendment does not require a state to adopt a standard of proof more rigorous than a preponderance of the evidence [Rivera v. Minnich, 483 U.S. 574 (1987)].

      (2) Where a married woman is seeking to prove that someone other than her husband is the father of her child, a higher standard of proof must be met because of the presumption of legitimacy discussed above. This presumption can only be overcome by clear and convincing evidence that someone other than her husband is the child's father.

4. **Acknowledgment or Legitimation**

    a. Federal law provides that a valid, unrescinded, unchallenged acknowledgment of paternity is to be treated as equivalent to a judicial determination of paternity [42 U.S.C. § 666(a)(5)(C)].

    b. The father may voluntarily legitimize the child in various ways under state laws. Most states permit the establishment of paternity by the filing of an acknowledgment of paternity executed by both parents and filed with a court or other office.

5. **Rights of Children Born Out-of-Wedlock**
   a. **Support**
      (1) Nonmarital children are constitutionally guaranteed equal rights to support as marital children.
   b. **Inheritance**
      (1) In addition, by statute in most states today, a nonmarital child is given the same rights to inherit from the intestate estate of the mother as a marital child, and also from the child's natural father if the decedent's paternity of the child is properly shown.
      (2) The state may require, however, that paternity have been proved during the life of the alleged father in order to inherit from him [Lalli v. Lalli, 439 U.S. 259 (1978)].
   c. **Wrongful Death**
      (1) Nonmarital children also have equal rights to sue for a parent's wrongful death and recover applicable wrongful death benefits.

B. **Nature of Parental Rights**
1. **Custody and Control of Children**
   a. If both parents are living, competent, and have not been found to be unfit, they are entitled to custody of the minor and to direct his education and medical care. If one parent dies and the remaining parent is competent and not unfit, the remaining parent has these rights, superior to all others.
   b. For a non-parent to seek custody or visitation rights over a child with living parent(s), significant deference must be given to a legal parent's objection to visitation [Troxel v. Granville, 530 U.S. 57 (2000)]. However, in Troxel, the Supreme Court did not specify what weight must be given to a parent's decision, as the statute under scrutiny gave no weight to the mother's decision regarding grandparent visitation, and thus was unconstitutional. The court suggested that a requirement of a finding of parental unfitness or harm to the child to override a parent's decision likely would satisfy the constitution's demands.
      (1) Some states have statutes permitting third parties to seek visitation rights while the child is in the custody of a parent, but these statutes are subject to the parental rights recognized in Troxel.
      (2) Third parties seeking custodial or visitation rights who show a substantial, *in loco parentis* relationship with the child—i.e., in the nature of a surrogate parent who has exercised custody over the child in place of the legal parent—are treated more favorably and may have standing to sue for custody, but still have to overcome the parental preference [Simpson v. Simpson, 586 S.W.2d 33 (Ky.1979); Rhinehart v. Nowlin, 805 P.2d 88 (N.M. Ct. App. 1990)].
   c. Statutes in a majority of states preserve the right of parents to administer "reasonable" corporal punishment to their children.

2. **Education of Children**

   a. The U.S. Constitution implies a right of privacy within the family that protects parental decisions regarding childrearing as well as the decision whether or not to have children. These rights may conflict with the government interest in matters affecting the family, such as compulsory education of children.

   b. The Supreme Court has found that:

      (1) states may require up to an eighth-grade education, but not more, where the parents' religious beliefs require the children to be kept home [Wisconsin v. Yoder, 406 U.S. 205 (1972)];

      (2) states may not forbid the teaching of languages other than English to children in the eighth grade or below [Meyer v. Nebraska, 262 U.S. 390 (1923)]; and

      (3) parents have a right to choose between public and private school for their children to satisfy compulsory education requirements [Pierce v. Society of Sisters, 268 U.S. 510 (1925)].

3. **Medical Decisions**

   a. Statutes in all states require the consent of parents to medical care for their children except in emergency situations. Parents who refuse to allow "necessary" medical procedures to save the life of their child may be found guilty of neglect, and a guardian may be appointed to make medical decisions.

   b. A Georgia statute permitting a parent to have his child institutionalized for mental health care has been upheld [Parham v. J.R., 442 U.S. 584 (1979)].

   c. State statutes may grant "mature" minors capacity to make certain medical decisions without their parents' consent, including treatment for substance abuse and abortions.

C. **Support Rights and Obligations**

1. **Parental Obligation to Support Child**

   a. As a general rule, a parent's obligation to support a child is terminated when the child reaches the age of majority (18 in most states).

      (1) In many states, a court may, upon divorce, order child support to extend beyond the age of majority where a child is still dependent due to physical or mental incapacity or is attending high school or even college [see, e.g., Gnirk v. Gnirk, 589 A.2d 1008 (N.H. 1991)].

      (2) Some states require parents to continue to support a child beyond the age of majority where the child is incapable of self-support by reason of mental or physical disability.

      (3) States differ in their approach to postsecondary education support. States will generally recognize the parents' voluntary agreement to provide for support beyond the age of majority (for example, by antenuptial agreement or separation agreement). Even in the absence of an agreement, some states will impose such an obligation. Other states, however, have not allowed courts to include such provisions in their divorce decrees.

  b. **Emancipation**

   (1) A minor child who is legally emancipated need not be supported by the parent. See below for further discussion of emancipation in connection with termination of parental rights.

 2. **Obligation to Support Parent**

  a. Some states impose a statutory duty on adults to support their parents or other close relatives who are in danger of becoming public charges.

  b. Support obligations of this nature are typically not enforceable directly by the individual relative but are for the benefit of government agencies that have expended funds for the individual's support.

D. Tort and Contract Liability

 1. **Torts Committed by Child**

  a. **Liability of Child**

   (1) Except where the age of a child prevents the child from forming the state of mind necessary for the commission of the tort, a child is generally liable for his own torts.

   (2) A child is liable for negligence where the child has failed to exercise the degree of care expected of the ordinary child of comparable age, knowledge, and experience.

  b. **Liability of Parent**

   (1) All states have enacted parental responsibility laws that make parents either civilly or criminally liable for the acts of their children. While all states have some form of statutory civil remedy against parents, states vary greatly in their restrictions on liability.

   (2) Most states limit responsibility to situations of malicious or intentional acts by the child, and more than 25% of states restrict liability only to property damage. Some states impose strict liability on the parents for willful damage to property of another by an unemancipated minor, up to a specified dollar amount.

 2. **Torts Committed against a Child**

  a. **Parent-Child Immunity**

   (1) Most states have abolished the common law parent-child immunity doctrine such that it is not an absolute bar to suits against the parent by the child. However, states vary in the types of suits that are permitted.

    (a) Some states have abolished parent-child immunity only for intentional personal injuries to the child, some for any negligently caused injuries, and some have done so only with regard to motor vehicle negligence actions or other actions covered by insurance.

   (2) The Restatement (Second) of Torts provides that a parent or child is not immune from tort liability to the other solely by reason of their relationship, but there may be a privilege that protects certain aspects of the parent-child relationship, such as parental control over and discipline of the child [Restatement (Second)

of Torts § 895G]. Courts will respect the reasonable exercise of discretion by a parent, so long as the parent's behavior toward the child does not constitute abuse or neglect.

b. **Recovery for Injury to the Child**

(1) An action by a minor who is injured by the negligence of another may typically be commenced by a parent, next friend, or guardian who brings suit on behalf of the minor.

(2) A second cause of action may arise in favor of the parent to recover for consequential damages as a result of the injury to the child. The parent may sue for loss of the services of the child, loss of consortium, medical expenses paid by the parent, and related matters.

3. **Minor's Contract Liability**

a. The age of majority in most states today, for most purposes, is 18 years. Persons over 18 thus have full legal rights—e.g., they can marry without parental consent, make a will, form a contract, and select their own domicile apart from their parents.

(1) There are some exceptions where a higher age may be set by statute, however, such as the purchase of alcoholic beverages.

b. Conversely, minors under age 18 do not have full capacity to contract. There is no "mature minor" exception to distinguish adolescents from younger children in this regard.

(1) Under the common law, a contract entered into by a minor is generally voidable at the option of the minor. This rule of law was designed to protect minors from improvident bargains and injustice, but the contract may be disaffirmed even if the minor is sophisticated and the contract is highly beneficial to the minor.

(2) Where the minor has in his possession the value transferred under the contract, the minor may be required to return it as a condition of the minor's ability to disaffirm.

c. Contracts for necessaries may not be avoided by the minor, but the minor is liable for the reasonable value of the necessaries, rather than the contract price.

d. A minor has until a reasonable time after reaching the age of majority to disaffirm the contract. Failure to disaffirm the contract during this time period may constitute a ratification of the contract.

E. **Termination of Parental Rights**

1. Parental rights and obligations involving a child may be terminated by actions of the child (emancipation), the parent (relinquishment), and/or the state (involuntary termination).

2. **Emancipation**

a. The earnings of the child belong to the parent. Children with successful careers, such as in the entertainment industry, may wish to become emancipated in order to enter contracts and manage their finances like adults and remove their parents' control over these matters. Disputes may also arise over the parents' childrearing practices, remarriage, and so on, causing the child to leave home and become self-supporting or supported by others.

b. The financial independence and maturity of the child are generally important considerations in a finding of emancipation. However, a child who voluntarily leaves the custodial parent's home, or who willfully fails to abide by the reasonable rules of the custodial parent, may be found to have forfeited the right to support [Angel v. McLellan, 16 Mass. 28 (1819)].

(1) More recent cases tend to focus more on the dependency of the child for support than on whether the parents disapprove of their child's behavior, such as bearing a child out of wedlock.

EXAMPLE: A daughter left home to marry at age 15 with her parents' consent, but requested support from the county child services agency when her husband filed for divorce. The agency sued her parents for the cost of her care, and the courts found the parents were again obligated to support her. Her marriage was only one factor to be considered, with the primary one being her need for support [Berks County Children & Youth Servs. v. Rowan, 631 A.2d 615 (Pa. Super. Ct. 1993)].

c. A minor who marries before the age of majority is generally emancipated under state law unless, in some states, neither the minor nor the minor's spouse can provide sufficient support [see, e.g., Utah Code Ann. § 15-2-1; Neb. Rev. Stat. § 43-2101].

3. **Voluntary Relinquishment of Parental Rights**

a. Parental rights may be lost by the parent's voluntary relinquishment of parental rights.

b. States typically have statutory formalities such as that an affidavit for voluntary relinquishment of parental rights must be:

(1) signed by the parent after the birth of the child, but usually not earlier than a specified period after the birth (such as 48 hours), to give the parent some time for reflection after the birth;

(2) objectively confirmed such as an oath in front of witnesses [see, e.g., Tex. Fam. Code § 161.103(a)]; and

(3) the affidavit may be required to state whether the relinquishment is revocable, irrevocable, or irrevocable for a stated period of time, or the state may permit only irrevocable relinquishment.

F. **Involuntary Termination**

1. **Due Process Concerns**

a. **Notice of Termination of Parental Rights**

(1) Parental rights cannot be terminated without notice and hearing. Such due process protections are extended only to legal and biological parents, not foster parents, even if they have formed deep emotional ties with the child [Smith v. Organization of Foster Families for Equality & Reform, 431 U.S. 816 (1977)].

(2) An unwed father has a right to notice and hearing before termination of his parental rights [Stanley v. Illinois, 405 U.S. 645 (1972)], but these rights depend on his having made some efforts to establish a relationship with or take responsibility for the child [Quilloin v. Walcott, 434 U.S. 246 (1978); Michael H. v. Gerald D., 491 U.S. 110 (1989)].

b. **Standard of Proof**

(1) The involuntary termination of parental rights generally puts the parental right to custody and care of the child before the issue of the child's "best interest."

(2) Termination must be based upon a finding of parental unfitness proved by clear and convincing evidence [Santosky v. Kramer, 455 U.S. 745 (1982)].

c. **No Right to Appointed Counsel**

(1) The Supreme Court has declined to find a constitutional right to counsel for indigent parents contesting termination of parental rights [Lassiter v. Dep't of Soc. Serv. of Durham, 452 U.S. 18 (1981)].

2. **Considerations**

a. A finding of parental unfitness may result from proof of at least one of the following conditions:

(1) **abandonment**, where the parent has failed to maintain a reasonable degree of interest, concern, or responsibility for the child's welfare for a specified period of time;

(a) Traditionally, abandonment requires proof that the parent subjectively intended to abandon the child; proof of behavior suggesting a loss of interest in the child is not sufficient in states with this standard [In re Adoption of Walton, 259 P.2d 881 (Utah 1953)].

(b) Some states use an objective test for abandonment. The inquiry under this test is whether the parent has demonstrated either a commitment to maintaining the parent-child relationship or a lack of such commitment, based on factors such as whether the parent has paid support or visited the child [see, e.g., Father in Pima County Juvenile Action No. S-114478 v. Adam, 876 P.2d 1121 (Ariz. 1994)].

(2) **neglect**, where the child has, for example, been denied the care, guidance, or control necessary for his physical, educational, moral, or emotional wellbeing; or

(3) **abuse**, where inadequately explained serious physical injury to a child may constitute evidence sufficient for the termination of parental rights, and expert testimony may be required regarding the causes of the child's injuries or behavior and effects of emotional or physical abuse.

b. In determining whether to terminate parental rights, a court may also consider, in addition to the negative factors justifying a finding of unfitness:

(1) the child's positive emotional ties to his parents and to anyone else who has had custody of the child;

(2) the parent's efforts to adjust his circumstances or conduct to make it in the child's best interests to remain in, or return to, the parent's home, including regular contact with the child and with the child's custodian; and

(3) the extent to which a parent has been prevented from maintaining a meaningful relationship with the child by the unreasonable actions of the other parent or any other person or by the economic circumstances of the parent.

G. Adoption

1. Parties

a. Who May Be Adopted

(1) Usually, the object of adoption is a minor. A minor child is considered free for adoption if the child has no living parents, or the rights of the parents have been terminated.

   (a) Many states require the consent of the minor where the minor is above a particular age, such as 12, although a court may override a minor's refusal to consent upon a finding of good cause.

(2) In many states, an adult may adopt another adult, but there may be restrictions on adopting close blood relatives. The Uniform Adoption Act recognizes adoptions of adults, but does not permit an adult to adopt his spouse.

b. Who May Adopt

(1) Persons who have the right to adopt have a legally protectable interest in the adoption, and therefore also have the right to object to another person's petition to adopt.

(2) In order to adopt another, the adopting person generally must be of the age of majority.

(3) In most states, a married person may not adopt a child unless both spouses join in the adoption petition, unless the court excuses this requirement (or unless the other spouse is already the parent of the child).

(4) Statutes in many states today allow a single person to adopt. Foster parents and grandparents may have standing to petition for adoption where the parents' rights have been terminated.

2. Consent

a. Parental Consent

(1) Consent of the natural parents is generally required for adoption unless they have waived their rights or been deemed "unfit" by clear and convincing evidence.

   (a) In the case of a child born to unmarried parents, the consent of the biological father may be required (in addition to the consent of the mother), as a matter of equal protection, where the father has established an ongoing parent-child relationship with the child [Caban v. Mohammed, 441 U.S. 380 (1979)].

    (b)   The biological father has a due process right to be heard at a meaningful time and in a meaningful manner with regard to his interest in the child [Lehr v. Robertson, 463 U.S. 248 (1983)].

  (2)   Many states have statutory requirements for the timing and form of consent. Some statutes require that the parents identify the specific adoptive parents, whereas other states recognize "blanket" consents to adoption.

b.   **Revocation of Consent**

  (1)   The consent of a parent may be revoked upon proof of fraud or duress prior to the adoption decree. Some states impose time limits on revocation for other reasons.

  (2)   The Uniform Adoption Act would allow revocation of consent within 192 hours (eight days) after the child's birth.

  (3)   After the decree has been entered, revocation is generally limited to instances where there has been some substantial defect in the adoption process (such as a lack of the required notices or consents).

3. **Procedure**

a.   Where a child has living parents, the rights of the natural parents must first be terminated, either voluntarily or involuntarily, prior to adoption. In some states, termination of the rights of the natural parents and the approval of the adoption may be accomplished in one judicial proceeding.

b.   Replacement of the bond of natural parenthood with that of adoptive parents is subject to considerable scrutiny by the state, whether the adoption is handled by a state-run agency, a private agency, or private individuals.

  (1)   Some states do not permit private (non-agency) placements for adoption other than with relatives. Other states require that non-agency adoptions be subject to investigation and oversight by a social services or child welfare agency.

  (2)   Typically, persons rejected for adoptive parent status have no right to sue, unless perhaps the would-be adoptive parents have stood in loco parentis to the child, having had care and custody of the child, perhaps through foster care.

4. **Standard for Adoption**

a.   A court will decide whether to grant a petition for adoption based on a determination of the child's best interests.

b.   Neither the state nor any other entity in the state that receives funds from the federal government and is involved in adoption or foster care placements may [42 U.S.C. § 1996b]:

  (1)   deny to any person the opportunity to become an adoptive or foster parent on the basis of the race, color, or national origin of the person or of the child involved; or

(2) delay or deny the placement of a child for adoption or into foster care on the basis of the race, color, or national origin of the adoptive or foster parent or the child involved.

    c. Religion may be a consideration, but is typically not an exclusive one.

5. **Effect of Decree**

    a. A decree of adoption generally has the following effects:

        (1) it creates the relationship of parent and child between the adopting parent or parents and the adopted person, as if the adopted person were the natural child of such adopting parent or parents for all purposes, including inheritance;

        (2) it ends all legal relationships between the adopted person and the natural parents for all purposes, including inheritance, except for prohibitions against marriage, incest, and cohabitation;

        (3) the adopting parents or their relatives inherit the estate of an adopted child if he dies intestate; and

            (a) The natural parents inherit nothing.

        (4) the adopted child's name will be changed and a new birth certificate will issue, including the names of the adopting parents and deleting the names of the natural parents.

    b. Some jurisdictions have refused to permit an adult adoptee to inherit through his adopted parent where it would frustrate the probable intent and expectations of a testator or settlor [see, e.g., First Nat'l Bank of Mackey, 338 N.W.2d 361 (Iowa 1983)].

    c. The decree is not revocable or modifiable unless parental rights are terminated. Thus, a stepparent who adopts the spouse's child does not lose rights or responsibilities upon divorce from the spouse.

6. **Confidentiality of Records**

    a. Adoption records are generally confidential and may not be opened unless leave of court, for cause shown, is obtained.

    b. However, many states today allow an adopted person and the adopting parents access to certain types of information concerning the natural parents (such as medical information) without revealing the identity of the parties, or may even have procedures for accessing information as to identity after the child reaches adulthood.

7. **Equitable Adoption or Parenthood by Estoppel**

    a. Adoption was not recognized at common law and is said to be a statutory creation, but in many jurisdictions today, a court in equity may specifically enforce an unperformed contract for adoption. Some courts require proof of a contract between the natural parents and the putative parent when the child is a minor who cannot contract [In re Estates of Williams, 348 P.2d 683 (Utah 1960)].

    b. Other courts look at whether the putative parent led the child to believe he was legally a member of the family and apply an estoppel theory where the child has performed services for the putative parent.

      c.   The issue generally arises when at least one of the would-be adoptive parents dies, and the child, perhaps now grown, seeks to share in the estate (in abrogation of the statutory requirements for both adoption and inheritance). The effects of equitable adoption are generally limited to recognition of the child's inheritance rights. Courts have been reluctant to find equitable adoption in non-inheritance instances, including those:

          (1)   involving claims of child support upon a stepparent who did not legally adopt the spouse's child [Pierce v. Pierce, 645 P.2d 1353 (Mont. 1982); Estate of Ford, 82 P.3d 747 (Cal. 2004)]; and

          (2)   claims by a *de facto* parent to custody or visitation [A.H. v. M.P., 857 N.E.2d 1061 (Mass. 2006)].

      d.   The ALI Principles, however, would recognize as a **parent by estoppel** a nonparent who has lived with the child since the child's birth, holding out and accepting full and permanent responsibilities as parent, as part of a prior co-parenting agreement with the child's legal parent to raise a child together, "each with full parental rights and responsibilities, when the court finds that recognition of the individual as a parent is in the child's best interests" [ALI Principles § 2.03(1)(b); see, e.g., W. v. W., 779 A.2d 716 (Conn. 2001)].

H.   Alternatives to Adoption

   1.   **Artificial Insemination**

      a.   **Definition**

          (1)   Artificial insemination is a technique by which semen is artificially transferred to the body of a woman in order to make her pregnant.

      b.   **Husband as Donor**

          (1)   Where artificial insemination occurs by means of the husband's semen, few legal issues should develop, as the husband would be the biological father of any child conceived and, thus, subject to all rights and obligations of a father.

          (2)   The UPA appears to equate providing sperm for artificial insemination with the husband's consent [UPA § 703].

      c.   **Third-Party Donor**

          (1)   Where the woman is married but a third-party donor is used, the UPA provides that the child is the legal child of the mother's husband if he consented in writing.

          (2)   The latest version of the UPA also covers the situation where the mother is not married by providing that the donor is not a parent of a child conceived by means of assisted reproduction [Id.].

             (a)   The commentary further explains that the donor cannot sue to establish his parental rights, nor can he be required to provide child support. However, in a state that has not adopted the UPA, there could be a different result.

(3) By analogy, a woman who donates her eggs with the intent to relinquish any parental rights and who does not carry or give birth to the child, would not be the legal parent of any resulting child.

(4) Same-sex couples necessarily have children with the assistance of third-party donors.

(a) Legal recognition of the non-biological parent's rights in this situation may be accomplished by adoption.

2. **Surrogacy**

a. **Nature of Motherhood**

(1) Traditionally, while there might be difficulties determining who was the father of a given child, motherhood was a given if it was known who gave birth to the child. The birth mother was also necessarily the genetic mother of the child.

(2) As various means of assisted reproductive technology have developed, establishing the rights of motherhood, like fatherhood, has become more problematic where one woman gives birth and another intends to raise the child. It is generally agreed that a child can have only one "legal" mother (except perhaps in cases of lesbian couple adoptions), just as there can be only one legal father.

b. **Role of Surrogate Mother**

(1) The term **surrogate mother** generally refers to a woman who is artificially inseminated with the semen of a person to whom she has agreed to relinquish the child after birth. Thus, the surrogate mother is the biological or "natural" parent of the child because her egg is used. The surrogate mother may receive, in return, a sum of money, as well as payment of medical expenses associated with pregnancy and childbirth. The terms of the contract often specify that the surrogate mother will not assert any parental rights to the child, and that parental rights will inure to the person who has supplied the semen.

(2) Surrogate mother may also be used to describe the situation where an egg is taken from party A, fertilized outside of the body, and then implanted into party B, as discussed below under the topic of *in vitro* fertilization. In this case, the birth mother has no genetic relationship to the child.

(a) The Uniform Parentage Act of 2002 prefers the term **gestational mother** for this arrangement.

(b) The ABA's Model Act Governing Assisted Reproductive Technology uses the term **gestational carrier**.

c. **Legal Effects of Surrogacy Contract**

(1) Whether a surrogacy contract is legally enforceable is unclear in many states. The contract may simply be viewed as an illegal contract to sell a child for adoption, violating public policy. More likely, courts will consider the genetic relationships and/or the parties' intent in sorting out their rights.

    (2) **Surrogate as Mother**

        (a) In one well-known case, a state supreme court refused to enforce the surrogacy contract on the grounds of public policy, but upheld the trial court order giving custody of the child to the sperm donor and allowed the surrogate mother, who was also the natural mother, to seek visitation rights (based on the best interests of the child) [In re Baby M, 537 A.2d 1227 (N.J. 1988)].

        (b) The Baby M case was superseded by statute [In re Adoption of Children by G.P.B., 736 A.2d 1277 (N.J. 1999)], but a presumption that the birth mother is the legal mother still exists in most states.

    (3) **Intended Parents are Legal Parents**

        (a) The California Supreme Court, on the other hand, upheld the validity of a surrogacy contract, rejecting the surrogate mother's claims that the agreement requiring her to give up the child at birth constituted an invalid waiver of her parental rights under the adoption laws [Johnson v. Calvert, 851 P.2d 776 (Cal. 1993)]. Johnson treats the parties who had intent to create the child as the "natural" parents, even if the "intended mother" has no genetic relationship to the child.

    (4) **Genetic Parents are Legal Parents**

        (a) A third view looks solely to genetics, treating the genetic parents as the legal parents of the child.

    (5) The UPA takes the unequivocal position that "gestational agreements" should be recognized, under judicial supervision, with consents handled in a manner similar to adoption.

        (a) Another statutory view would treat such contracts as self-executing if at least one of the intended parents contributed a gamete to the embryo.

        (b) Statutes in a number of states allow enforcement of surrogacy contracts only if the surrogate/gestational mother performs her services free of charge. The ABA Model Act permits compensation for the gestational carrier's time, labor and health risks, as well as medical and other expenses, but forbids compensation related to desired characteristics of the child that is produced.

3. ***In Vitro* Fertilization and Embryo Implantation**

   a. ***In Vitro* Fertilization**

     (1) *In vitro* fertilization refers to the medical procedure by which a woman's egg is removed from her body, fertilized outside of her body in a test tube by means of a man's semen, and then implanted into a woman. It should be noted that the recipient of the fertilized

egg may be the same woman whose egg was originally removed for fertilization purposes or the recipient may be a different woman (the latter situation sometimes is referred to as "gestational surrogacy").

(2) The law in this area is developing and the legal issues are murky. The following possibilities arise:

(a) where the process occurs with the egg and semen of a wife and husband, and the fertilized egg is implanted into the wife, the child ought to be viewed as the legitimate child of the wife and husband;

(b) where the semen is that of a third party donor and the egg is implanted into the woman from whom it was taken, the process ought to be treated in the same way as artificial insemination by donor; and

(c) where an egg of one woman is fertilized and then implanted into a different woman with the agreement that the woman will serve as a "gestational surrogate," the law of surrogacy applies.

b. **Frozen Embryos**

(1) Alternatively, the fertilized egg may even be frozen for future use. Where *in vitro* fertilization has occurred using the eggs of a wife and the semen of her husband, and the fertilized eggs ("preembryos") were frozen for future use, a subsequent divorce between the parties may result in a dispute over rights to the frozen preembryos. Presumably, the disposition of the preembryos should be governed by any prior agreement of both parties [Kass v. Kass, 696 N.E.2d 174 (N.Y. 1998)].

(2) Where the parties have made no agreement concerning the disposition of their unused preembryos, either potential parent's interest in avoiding procreation (an interest of constitutional dimension) may prevent their transplantation into a third person or require their destruction [see Davis v. Davis, 842 S.W.2d 588 (Tenn. 1992); J.B. v. M.B., 783 A.2d 707 (N.J. 2001)].

IV. DIVORCE PROCEEDINGS

A. **Jurisdiction and Venue**
1. **Subject-Matter Jurisdiction**
   a. **Domicile and Residency Requirements**
      (1) **Domicile**
         (a) Subject-matter jurisdiction is established over the marital status by virtue of the domicile of one of the parties within the state at the time of filing the action, whether or not the parties lived there as a couple.
         (b) If a state has a domicile requirement and it was met, then the Full Faith & Credit Clause would require other states to recognize that divorce decree [Williams v. North Carolina, 217 U.S. 287 (1942)].
         (c) **Domicile** generally requires both physical presence in the state and the intent to make the state a permanent home.
         (d) The parties cannot confer jurisdiction by consent on a state in which neither party is domiciled [see Jennings v. Jennings, 36 So.2d 236 (Ala. 1948)].
      (2) **Residency**
         (a) In addition, some states impose a jurisdictional requirement that one of the parties must have resided in the state for a specified period of time prior to the filing of the divorce action.
         (b) A one-year durational requirement has been upheld as constitutional [Sosna v. Iowa, 419 U.S. 393 (1975)].
         (c) Residency is different from domicile. **Residency** refers to living in a particular place for a period of time, whereas domicile is established where a person lives in a state with the intent to make it his permanent home, with no present intent to live permanently elsewhere.

         EXAMPLE: Margaret has lived in State X all her life and intends to remain there permanently. She accepts temporary employment in State Y and lives there for a year, planning to return to State X afterwards. Although Margaret satisfies the residency requirement, Margaret cannot file for divorce in State Y because it is not her domicile.
      (3) **Special Provisions for Military Personnel**
         (a) Some jurisdictions have adopted statutes that either specifically allow persons who have resided on military bases within a state for a specified period of time to maintain a divorce action in that state or provide that, for divorce purposes, such persons are deemed to be residents of the state in which the base is located [Lauterbach v. Lauterbach, 392 P.2d 24 (Alaska 1964)].

(b) Most of the courts that have considered this issue have decided that the state can base jurisdiction for divorce on something other than traditional domicile, but some courts have construed such statutes as requiring domicile in addition to residence on the base.

2. **Personal Jurisdiction**

a. Although domicile establishes subject-matter jurisdiction for purposes of granting the divorce, personal jurisdiction over the defendant is necessary for the court to enter or enforce any decrees *in personam*, including the entry of orders imposing support obligations, orders relating to out-of-state property, or the institution of contempt proceedings to enforce such orders.

b. Personal service on the defendant within the state hearing the case is one way of establishing *in personam* jurisdiction.

c. Personal jurisdiction can also be obtained by use of a long-arm statute against a nonresident defendant-spouse. In addition to proper service of process, in order for the court to enter an *in personam* order, the defendant-spouse must have sufficient minimum contacts with the state such that entry of such an order is consistent with due process principles (i.e., sufficient minimum contacts such that the suit does not offend traditional notions of fair play and substantial justice) [Kulko v. Superior Court of California, 436 U.S. 84 (1978)].

d. Substituted service (such as service by publication in cases where the whereabouts of the defendant is unknown), where necessary, may be sufficient under state long-arm statutes.

3. **Venue**

a. Proper venue is set by statute, usually in the county where either party resides.

b. Venue is not jurisdictional, and objection is generally waived if not made within the time for the defendant's response.

B. Procedure

1. While annulment essentially declares that the marriage never really took place, both legal separation and dissolution of marriage (divorce) acknowledge the existence of a marriage and seek to dissolve it.

2. **Comparison of Legal Separation and Divorce**

a. If either spouse wishes to obtain some form of legally enforceable property division or support without the religious or social stigma of divorce, the options are either to make a consensual agreement or to pursue an action for legal separation.

b. Legal separation, sometimes also called a "divorce from bed and board," a "divorce *a mensa et thoro*," or a limited divorce, was permitted in many states before full divorces were recognized. Fault grounds needed to be proven, but the grounds might be somewhat broader than for a full or absolute divorce.

    c.   Separation statutes typically give courts the authority to divide property, order payment of spousal and child support, and award custody. The only true difference between legal separation and divorce, then, is that only an absolute divorce bestows on the former spouses the right to remarry.

3. **Commencement of Action**

    a.   Actions for dissolution of marriage or legal separation are generally commenced and conducted as in other civil cases.

    b.   However, states may have particular pleading requirements, particularly for the complaint, in domestic relations actions.

4. **Financial Disclosure**

    a.   Where a spouse seeks alimony, child support, property division, counsel fees, or expenses, a statement of income, expenses, assets, and liabilities generally must be filed by both parties with the court.

    b.   States may differ on the specifics of when and how such information must be produced.

5. **Default or Summary Judgment**

    a.   Generally, no judgment may be entered by default or on the pleadings in a marital action. The moving party must generally testify as to the grounds for dissolution of the marriage.

    b.   However, as a matter of due process, a default may be entered if the defendant fails to appear after adequate notice and the moving party has established the required jurisdictional and substantive basis for a divorce [Boddie v. Connecticut, 401 U.S. 371 (1971)].

6. **Mediation**

    a.   State statutes may recommend or require that the parties use a form of alternative dispute resolution before entry of a final divorce decree. Even if the parties decide to continue to pursue the divorce, a mediator can help them reach a settlement agreement with a minimum of rancor, which is particularly important when children are involved.

    b.   The ABA publishes Model Standards of Practice for Family and Divorce Mediation ("Model Standards"). A mediator's substantial misconduct is a basis for setting aside a settlement agreement.

        (1)   A mediator must be impartial and disclose potential conflicts of interest [Model Standards, Standard IV].

        (2)   A mediator must explain the mediation process and make sure that the parties have enough information to ensure informed decision-making [Model Standards, Standard III].

        (3)   A mediator may not coerce or improperly influence any party to make a decision [Model Standards, Standard I].

        (4)   A mediator should recognize and control any situation, such as domestic violence, that would result in unfairness or prejudice to one of the parties [Model Standards, Standard X].

7. **Consultation with and Counsel for the Child**

   a. The judge may interview the child in chambers to determine the child's wishes regarding custody [UMDA § 404]. States may vary in the age at which the child's wishes are taken into account, but often the age is 12.

      (1) However, the child's wishes are only one of many factors that must be considered by the judge in determining the best interests of the child.

   b. Some states allow the trial judge to appoint legal counsel to represent the child in contested custody cases in order to advocate for the child. This trend reflects concerns that children should not be fought over as if they were property, but should be granted an opportunity to be heard concerning decisions affecting their custody.

8. **Interim Rights during Pendency of Proceedings**

   a. While a marital action is pending, the court can make temporary orders for custody or support and has general equity powers to issue temporary restraining orders or preliminary injunctions or other orders necessary to protect the parties' interests.

      (1) For example, the court may order temporary alimony (alimony *pendente lite*), counsel fees and expenses pending final decision, or order the seizure or attachment of property.

      (2) The court may also order one party to vacate the marital residence, and may enter a temporary child custody order.

   b. Additionally, during the pendency of an appeal, the court may grant and enforce the payment of maintenance as it deems reasonable and proper.

   c. The court may be asked to provide protection from threats or harassment by one of the parties. Many states provide statutory remedies for a family or household member who has been threatened by, or been the victim of, physical abuse by another family or household member.

      (1) The relief available may include damages, a court order enjoining that person from restraining or assaulting the applicant or from entering the applicant's dwelling (including the family home), or whatever relief the court may find appropriate.

C. Grounds

1. **Fault**

   a. Today, many states permit divorce on no-fault grounds, but have retained fault grounds as well.

   b. Fault grounds still recognized in many states include desertion, adultery, impotence, cruelty, imprisonment, habitual intoxication, or drug addiction. The general understanding of each of these grounds is as follows:

      (1) **Desertion**

         (a) A spouse may obtain a divorce when the other spouse, without reasonable cause, abandons marital cohabitation with the intent to desert and willfully persists for a continuous and set period of time, including any period during which an action was pending between the spouses for dissolution or legal separation.

    1) Voluntary or consensual separation negates the requisite intent.

  (b) Actual abandonment of the marital abode is generally not necessary to prove desertion.

  (c) Constructive desertion may be established where one spouse forcibly and without consent puts the other out of the house, or the latter leaves because of justifiable fear of immediate bodily harm, and the separation continues for the requisite period of time.

(2) Adultery

  (a) Adultery is a ground for dissolution of marriage in all states that recognize fault-based grounds.

  (b) Because there is a natural secrecy to the act of adultery, circumstantial rather than direct evidence is usually permissible. Evidence of an adulterous disposition plus an opportunity to commit adultery may be sufficient. However, the uncorroborated testimony of either party is generally not sufficient to prove adultery without further evidence.

(3) Impotence

  (a) **Impotence** is the inability of one party to perform the act of sexual intercourse.

    1) It may also be grounds for annulment if the fact was concealed before the marriage.

  (b) Sterility, the inability to conceive or to father children, is not a fault ground for divorce in most states.

(4) Cruelty

  (a) Most commonly, **cruelty** as a ground for divorce consists of a pattern of physical abuse committed by one spouse upon the other which causes physical injury. However, a single egregious act of physical violence may be sufficient.

  (b) An activity carried on by one spouse, such as harsh words, which is designed to hurt the other spouse's health and does, in fact, impair health may warrant a finding of mental cruelty, even though no physical abuse is involved.

  (c) Some states make mental cruelty a separate fault ground from physical cruelty, under a term such as "indignities." This usually requires a course of conduct that makes life unbearable or intolerable. This can overlap with, but is distinct from, no-fault grounds of irretrievable breakdown.

(5) Felony Conviction

  (a) Conviction of certain heinous crimes or even any felony may be grounds for dissolution.

(b) In some states, a period of incarceration of one year or more is required.

(6) **Intoxication or Excessive Use of Addictive Drugs**

(a) Some states recognize a ground for divorce where one party is an alcoholic or drug addict.

2. **No-Fault Divorce**

a. All states today provide no-fault grounds for divorce in some form, but they differ on the extent to which these have replaced the fault grounds. Many states retain both fault and no-fault schemes.

b. Some states allow a divorce upon one party's insistence that the marriage is irretrievably broken due to incompatibility or irreconcilable differences, and neither the other party nor the court can deny the requested divorce once these are shown.

c. Other states impose a somewhat slower and more considered procedure under which the parties must live separate and apart for a specified period of time, and the court must find that the marriage in fact is irretrievably broken.

(1) Generally, **irretrievable breakdown** is defined as estrangement due to marital differences with no reasonable prospect of reconciliation. The standard for determining the existence of an irretrievable breakdown is broad, and the court, where permitted, should examine all evidence that bears on the viability of the marriage.

(2) The mandated period of separation is generally one year or less. In some states, a lengthy period of voluntary separation, one year or more, may be sufficient in itself for a court to grant a no-fault divorce. Other states require a separation of only a few months, or impose the separation requirement only where there are children of the marriage.

(3) In some states, proof of serious mental disorder resulting in the defendant's confinement in a mental institution, may also be sufficient grounds for a no-fault divorce.

d. Some states do not require or shorten the mandatory separation period if both parties consent to the divorce.

D. Defenses

1. Some affirmative defenses may be used to defeat a plaintiff's petition for dissolution. These defenses must be affirmatively pleaded by the defendant in order to be used at trial; otherwise, the conduct of the petitioner is not a bar to the action or a proper basis for the refusal of a judgment.

2. **In Fault-Based Divorce Actions**

a. **Collusion**

(1) **Collusion** is an agreement between the spouses, express or implied, whereby one of them wrongfully asserts that the other has committed a breach of marital duty in order to obtain a divorce.

(2) It implies an agreement whereby evidence is fabricated or suppressed in an attempt to deceive the court and obtain dissolution of the marriage in the absence of any legitimate legal grounds.

b. **Connivance**

    (1) **Connivance** is conduct by the plaintiff facilitating the commission of a marital wrong, usually adultery, by the defendant.

    (2) Unlike collusion, in the case of connivance, the marital wrong is actually committed.

c. **Condonation**

    (1) Where one spouse knowingly forgives the other's marital wrong (usually adultery), by words or conduct, so that the marital relationship—i.e., cohabitation—is continued, such forgiveness may bar an action founded upon that marital wrong. Condonation is a question of fact which must be determined by an examination of all the evidence.

    (2) Condonation can be either conditional or unconditional. It is conditional if made contingent on the erring spouse not resuming the misconduct. A conditional condonation does not preclude the injured spouse from raising the initial misconduct as a ground for divorce where the conditions imposed on forgiveness have been violated.

d. **Recrimination**

    (1) Under the fault approach to divorce, there must be only one guilty party and one innocent spouse entitled to relief.

        (a) Thus, where both spouses were guilty of fault grounds, the court would deny a divorce to either on the ground of recrimination.

    (2) States began to treat recrimination as an affirmative defense rather than a complete bar, or limited it to mutual charges of adultery.

    (3) In many states today, if both spouses allege and prove fault grounds, the court may grant a divorce to each.

3. **In No-Fault Divorce Actions**

a. In states that require a minimum period of separation as the basis for a no-fault divorce, the separation need not be consensual.

b. It is also not a defense to a no-fault divorce in most states today that one spouse does not believe that the breakdown is irretrievable or the differences irreconcilable. No-fault divorce recognizes that the desire of one party to quit the marriage is sufficient, so a no-fault divorce may be granted without any attempt at reconciliation.

    (1) Even if the difficulties might be curable and one spouse believes that the marriage can be saved, most states will not deny the other spouse a divorce [Hagerty v. Hagerty, 281 N.W.2d 386 (Minn. 1979); Eversman v. Eversman, 496 A.2d 210 (Conn. App. Ct. 1985)].

c. Where the states' no-fault regimes may differ most is in the treatment of marital fault or misconduct in making property division or alimony determinations.

V. THE DIVORCE DECREE

A. Contents of Decree

1. In General

a. A decree granting a divorce (or other type of dissolution as well, in most states) may include orders determining and disposing of existing property rights between the parties, custody and visitation rights, child support, spousal maintenance, reasonable attorney's fees, costs and expenses, and any other related matters.

b. The decree may include and deal with the enforcement of agreements voluntarily entered into between the parties.

c. State statutes may allow the court to award costs to the party in whose favor the order or decree is entered or to divide them equitably, depending on resources and needs. Otherwise, each party generally pays his own costs.

2. Statement of Reasons

a. State statutes may specify where the order may set forth only general findings and where the order must state specific reasons for the court's decision. A court generally has a duty to make sufficient findings to inform the parties of the reasoning underlying the court's conclusions, and to allow for effective appellate review. However, a trial court has discretion in how much detail to provide.

b. Some states require that, before entering an order of dissolution in a no-fault divorce, a court must make a specific finding that all reasonable efforts to effect a reconciliation have been made.

B. Settlement Agreements

1. Validity

a. Even if they have not previously entered a premarital agreement or post-nuptial property agreement, spouses contemplating divorce frequently reach agreement on such matters as the division of property, future alimony and child support payments, and custody and visitation rights.

b. Like premarital and marital agreements, spousal agreements made during the divorce process are generally valid if voluntarily made and will be upheld in the absence of fraud, duress, concealment, or overreaching.

2. Merged into the Decree

a. When the divorce is actually granted, the terms of such settlement agreements are typically incorporated into and made part of the decree unless the agreement provides to the contrary, or unless the court finds the agreement should be set aside on grounds of fraud or duress.

(1) The court, before entry of judgment, has considerable latitude to reject or modify an agreement it finds unconscionable.

(2) The lack of independent counsel for each party at this stage may be a significant factor supporting a finding that a proposed

agreement is substantively and procedurally unfair in some states. A spouse who has representation may be found to have a fiduciary duty toward a spouse who does not [Terwilliger v. Terwilliger, 64 S.W.3d 816 (Ky. 2002)].

b. Unless the parties agree otherwise, by default the agreement is deemed merged into the decree.

(1) The agreement is thereafter not enforceable as a contract obligation, but can be enforced only by remedies available for enforcement of judgments, including contempt proceedings.

(2) The terms of the agreement as merged into the judgment generally cannot be modified. However, provisions fixing child support and custody are always modifiable to protect children's welfare.

(a) The court also has an inherent power of modification regarding an alimony award in cases of changed circumstances, unless the parties' agreement provides that no alimony is payable or that alimony payments are nonmodifiable and such provisions are made part of the decree.

3. **Where the Contract Survives the Decree**

a. The parties to a divorce action can and regularly do provide that the separation agreement will be incorporated into the decree but not merged into the decree. In such a case, contract obligations and remedies survive, and the terms may be enforced either by an action on the contract or through available statutory remedies such as wage attachment or contempt proceedings.

b. On the other hand, the parties can provide that the separation agreement survives wholly independent of the decree, in which case only contract remedies are available for breach.

C. **Property Division**

1. **In General**

a. The majority of states today follow an **equitable distribution scheme** to divide spousal property upon divorce.

b. In divorces today, the financial interests of the parties are settled more substantially through property division at the time of divorce than by means of spousal support (alimony) payments.

2. **Convergence of Community Property and Separate Property Systems at Divorce**

a. At divorce, the property regimes in the community property states and the separate property states are now substantially the same.

(1) At divorce, separate property states have largely adopted the community property regime.

(2) At the same time, most community property states have adopted a rule of equitable (rather than equal) distribution of property at divorce, like separate property states.

b. Although there are jurisdictional variations, most separate property states have adopted the community property system's dual-classification approach of differentiating jointly owned property (called community property in community property states and marital property in separate property states) from property owned by a spouse individually (called separate property).

c. Note, however, that there are still important differences in the property regimes in effect at death and during an intact marriage, as discussed earlier. Most notably, the doctrine of equitable distribution is not applicable at death or during marriage in separate property states.

d. The community property system views the marriage as a community in which each spouse is an equal partner. Generally, the spouses own undivided one-half interests in all community property during marriage and at death. At divorce, however, community property division is based on what is "equitable," with only a few of the community property states mandating an equal division of property.

e. Specific rules govern the characterization of spousal property as separate or community, the transmutation of property from one classification to the other, and division of such property at divorce (or death of a spouse). Discussed in more detail below, key rules from the community property regime are:

(1) Property owned before marriage, acquired after dissolution of the marriage, or acquired by gift or inheritance to one spouse during the marriage is that spouse's separate property. In contrast, property acquired during the marriage is presumed to be community (or marital) property to which both spouses have a claim.

(2) Generally, earnings from the labor of either spouse or from the appreciation of community property are community property, whereas passive gains from separate property remain separate.

(3) Commingling separate and community property may require the application of certain presumptions to determine ownership rights.

3. **Equitable Distribution**

a. **Policy Considerations**

(1) **Economic Justice between the Parties**

(a) Equitable distribution is flexible in that it allows the court to take into account numerous factors related to the financial situation of each spouse, rather than presuming a 50-50 split.

(b) Under modern law, fault has been eliminated from consideration in property distribution in many states, at least with respect to matters that are not related to the parties' finances (such as dissipation of assets, as discussed below). Neither the ALI Principles nor the UMDA allow marital fault to be considered [see, e.g., ALI Principles § 4.09, cmt. (e)].

(2) **Predictability of Results**

(a) Whereas there are fairly clear rules governing the characterization of property, there is wide discretion allowed in its final division, leading to varying results not only among different states but even within the same state.

    (b) The ALI Principles would remove some of this discretion from the determination, opting instead for a more "equal" division of marital property.

    (c) Some states do have a presumption or "starting point" of an equal division. Other states explicitly reject this approach.

  b. **Steps in Process**

    (1) Regardless of which system is used, there are three basic steps to property division:

        (a) identify the divisible property;

        (b) value it; and

        (c) divide it.

    (2) **Identification and Classification of Assets and Debts**

        (a) The first step in property division is to identify what property (and debt) is divisible upon divorce.

        (b) A minority of states have an all property approach, also called the hotchpot or "kitchen sink" approach. In these states, all property owned by either spouse, however and whenever acquired, is divisible between the parties. The court has authority to divide all of the property regardless of title and previous ownership.

        (c) **Dual Classification**

           1) However, a majority of states have adopted the dual-classification system from the community property regime that differentiates between marital and nonmarital property. Separate property, once identified, is generally not divisible and must be assigned to the owner spouse. Marital property is divisible between the spouses.

           2) The classification rules, described below, are in place in the majority of states, but do not apply in the "all property" states.

        (d) Certain presumptions apply in general, and there are particular rules for items that may be highly contested because they are mixed marital property or difficult to value.

    (3) **Valuation of Assets**

        (a) The value of the property must then be determined by either stipulation or appraisal.

        (b) The time at which valuation is determined is generally as of the date of the parties' separation, but in some states is the date of the trial or hearing.

    (4) **Division of Assets**

        (a) In the last step, the court determines what would be an equitable distribution of all divisible property between the parties, considering a number of factors. In contrast, a few states mandate equal division.

c. **Defining Marital Property**

(1) In both community property and common law (marital property) states, formal title does not determine ownership at divorce. Instead, states have widely adopted a presumption that property acquired during the marriage is marital property subject to division, with certain separate property exceptions, regardless of title.

(2) The burden of proof to rebut the presumption is generally on the spouse claiming separate property.

(3) The earnings of each spouse, and property acquired with those earnings or through the labor of a spouse, are presumptively marital or community property in the absence of an enforceable agreement to the contrary.

(4) **Increased Value of Separate Property**

(a) The fact that a separate asset appreciates in value during the marriage does not, in itself, transform that asset into marital property.

(b) In most states, the increase during marriage of a separate asset will be separate if the increase was due to market forces, not the labor of either spouse.

EXAMPLE: Before marriage, Husband purchased antique furniture worth $20,000. During the marriage, its value increased by $5,000. Upon divorce, both the original $20,000 in value and the $5,000 increase are the Husband's separate property. Separate wealth that increases by luck is the good fortune of the original owner, not his spouse.

(c) If the value of a separate asset is increased through marital funds or significant labor of one or both spouses, then the portion attributable to such labor is marital property. Courts may separate the increase into components, or alternatively characterize the increase as all marital if the increase was primarily attributable to spousal labor (or all separate if primarily from passive forces).

(d) A few states treat any increases in value during marriage as marital property, regardless of the ownership of the asset itself.

d. **Nonmarital Property**

(1) Marital property generally does not include property:

(a) acquired by gift (except between spouses, in some states) or inheritance; or

(b) excluded by valid agreement of the parties.

(2) There is also a temporal aspect to the acquisition of nonmarital property, which includes property:

(a) acquired prior to marriage or in exchange for property acquired prior to the marriage; or

(b) acquired after the marriage effectively ends, which may be the date:

1) of the final separation of the parties, in a minority of states;

2) the divorce action was commenced; or

3) in the majority of states, when a final divorce decree is entered.

e. **Mixed Character, Commingled, or Transmuted Property**

(1) The court may consider whether the parties mixed, changed, or "transmuted" the character of the property from separate to marital or vice versa by agreement or behavior during the marriage.

(2) Title does not generally determine ownership at divorce. However, in identifying marital versus separate property, it can be relevant (although not determinative). If spouses mix together separate and marital property, the question of what the character of the asset is arises.

(a) Taking separate property and combining it with marital property, or taking marital property and combining it with separate property, may imply a gift to the other estate. However, a spouse can trace the contribution to its source and prove its character as either separate or marital, notwithstanding the commingling.

EXAMPLE: Husband owns a separate property stock account worth $10,000. During marriage, he sells the stocks and deposits the $10,000 proceeds from the sale into a joint bank account titled in both spouses' names, so that the bank account now has a total of $15,000. Shortly afterward, Husband files for divorce. The transfer to a joint bank account may imply a gift to the marriage, but Husband can refute that and trace to the source, preserving the separate character of the $10,000 deposit.

(3) However, if commingling is so pervasive that it is no longer possible to separately identify the character of the contribution, resulting in a loss of identity of the contributed property, the contributed property takes on the classification of the estate that received the contribution. If marital and nonmarital property is commingled into newly acquired property, the commingled property will be presumed marital property.

EXAMPLE: Referring to the fact situation described above, imagine instead that Husband and Wife stayed together for five years after stock proceeds were put into the joint account. The parties continued to use the joint account, making new deposits and new withdrawals monthly to pay basic expenses. At divorce, there is $10,000 in the account. The marital presumption shifts the burden of proof to Husband to prove the $10,000 is his separate property. He cannot meet this test, because it is not possible to demonstrate that the $10,000 from the stock deposit remains in the account. Instead, the $10,000 currently in the account likely came from multiple new deposits, and the stock money has been spent. The commingling resulted in a loss of the identity of the separate property.

f. **Dividing Property**

(1) In determining how the property should be divided, the court may equitably distribute it, meaning that there is no requirement that the distribution be equal, although in some states there is a presumption that an equal distribution is an equitable distribution. In others, the court should consider certain factors in determining how the assets should be allocated to each spouse.

(2) Most community property states, with the exception of California, Louisiana, and New Mexico, apply equitable distribution principles such that equal division of community property is not required.

(3) Factors that may generally be considered in determining what division would be equitable, in addition to the length of the marriage and the standard of living enjoyed by the spouses during the marriage, relate primarily to the contributions, both monetary and nonmonetary, of each party during the marriage, and the current financial circumstances of each party.

(4) Contributions of each spouse may include those made:

(a) by one spouse to the education, training, or increased earning power of the other spouse;

(b) to the acquisition, preservation, or appreciation of marital property, or conversely, to the depreciation or dissipation of assets and acquisition of debt; or

1) **Dissipation** is the use of marital property for the sole benefit of one spouse for something unrelated to the marriage.

(c) to the family's quality of life, such as services as a home-maker or child-care giver.

1) The value that courts assign to homemaking services varies from state to state. Some states recognize a rebuttable presumption that the value of such services is equal to that of the breadwinner's.

(5) Financial circumstances or need of each spouse at the time the division of property is to become effective, and in the future, may include:

(a) age, health, vocational skills and employability, assets, liabilities, and needs;

(b) sources of income, including medical, retirement, insurance, and other benefits;

(c) the value of property set aside for each spouse, and the tax ramifications and expenses of the transfer or sale of particular assets, where relevant; and

(d) opportunities for future acquisition of assets and income.

g. **Classification and Division of Particular Types of Assets**

(1) **Marital Residence**

(a) The marital residence is usually the largest asset in the marital estate. Sometimes it must be sold in order to make an equitable distribution where there are insufficient assets of other types to offset a spouse's share in the residence.

(b) Difficulties of allocation may arise if the house was purchased prior to marriage but marital earnings were used to pay off the mortgage and build equity in the house.

1) If a spouse's separate funds are used to make improvements to the property, a gift to the community may be presumed, but this may be rebutted, and in some circumstances reimbursement may be required upon divorce.

2) Appreciation of the property is apportioned in the same manner as the ownership of the house if solely due to market forces, but if appreciation is due to spousal labor, the increase is marital property to that extent.

(2) **Pensions and Other Retirement Accounts**

(a) Pension and retirement benefits accumulated by either spouse during the marriage are subject to equitable distribution, whether the accounts are vested (the employee has a definitive and presently existing legal right to the asset) or nonvested (some contingency must occur such as working for the employer a certain number of years before legal entitlement attaches). These include deferred compensation agreements, profit-sharing benefits, and military retirement benefits, to the extent allowed by federal law.

1) A **defined contribution plan** is one in which the employee and/or the employer make periodic financial contributions into a retirement account owned by the employee.

EXAMPLE: Wife contributes 3% of her income to a 401(k) plan offered by her employer, to which the employer also contributes 2% of her income. All such contributions, and any increases in value during the marriage, are marital property.

2) A **defined benefit plan** is a retirement account for which the promised retirement benefit is calculated by a formula defined in the pension plan provisions.

EXAMPLE: Husband works for State, which offers a retirement pension that vests after 10 years of employment, with the amount of the benefit increasing at specified increments.

(b) Premarital contributions or post-separation increases or contributions to the plan are generally not deemed marital property. Upon divorce, the total retirement benefit owed to the employee-spouse is allocated into marital and nonmarital shares; only the marital share is subject to equitable distribution.

EXAMPLE: Wife worked for Employer for five years prior to her marriage. She has been married for five years when her separation and divorce require distribution of the marital share in her 401(k) plan. The marital share in the present value of the account is 50%, and 50% belongs to Wife alone. Assuming an equal division of the marital share, Wife's total share of the value of the account at divorce is 75%. Any post-separation contributions Wife makes in the future are hers alone.

(c) Difficulties in calculation of the benefit to be divided may arise from a number of circumstances affecting defined benefit plans in particular, including the fact that the final benefit cannot be determined with certainty until the date of retirement because of variables including the total years in service, the final salary of the employee-spouse, and any changes in the pension benefit formula.

    1) The value of the marital portion of the future benefit may be estimated as of the time of divorce for purposes of offsetting that value against other assets available for distribution to the other spouse.

    EXAMPLE: Wife might relinquish her marital share in Husband's pension benefits in exchange for full ownership of the marital residence.

    2) Under a deferred distribution method, the marital share will be divided between the spouses at the time the employee-spouse actually retires.

    3) A **qualified domestic relations order** ("**QDRO**") recognizes the rights of an alternate payee to receive all or a portion of the benefits that would otherwise be payable to the spouse who participated in the employer's pension or retirement plan.

    4) The employer's plan administrator qualifies the order, calculating the amounts payable and ascertaining that the order does not alter the terms of the plan.

    5) A transfer to a spouse subject to a QDRO is not a taxable event.

(3) Stock Options

(a) Stock options granted to either spouse during the marriage, whether vested or nonvested and whether or not their value is ascertainable, are presumed to be marital property. If earned as employment compensation, their status as marital or nonmarital property depends on when acquired and whether the work for which the options are compensation was performed during the marriage.

(b) A vested employee stock option is acquired when granted, but an unvested employee stock option may require more complex analysis. Most states apply a "time rule" formula to determine when unvested employee stock options are acquired.

  1) Unvested employee stock options granted for future employment services are generally acquired over time as the stock options vest, and the question is whether the spouses were living together as a marital unit at the time of acquisition [In re Marriage of Short, 890 P.2d 12 (Wash. 1995)].

(c) In making the allocation between the parties, the court may recognize that the value of the options may not be determinable at the time of the judgment of dissolution or declaration of invalidity. The court may consider, in addition to the usual factors in equitable distribution, all the circumstances underlying the grant of the stock options, including whether the grant was for past, present or future efforts, and the length of time from the grant of the option to the time the options are exercisable. The actual division of the options may not occur until a future date, and valuation may be difficult, given their market volatility.

EXAMPLE: Bob was hired by Microchip Corporation and was offered, as part of his compensation package, an option to purchase 20,000 shares of Microchip. At the time Bob was hired, 5,000 shares were fully vested and could be exercised at any time. The rest of the shares would vest only after Bob had worked at Microchip for 18 months, and only if Bob was still employed at the company at that time. After Bob had worked at Microchip for one year, he and his wife separated. The 5,000 shares that vested during the marriage are marital property; the rest of the shares are separate property solely owned by Bob.

(4) **Professional Degrees and Licenses**

(a) Most states have held that a professional degree or license is not a property interest subject to equitable distribution [In re Marriage of Graham, 574 P.2d 75 (Colo. 1978)].

(b) A few have used a partnership theory to find that a spouse's contribution toward the other spouse's acquisition of the degree or license entitles the contributing spouse to a share of the lifetime earnings the professional accomplishment represents. As a marital asset, however, a professional license is difficult to value.

(c) Even if a degree is not considered divisible marital property, it may be considered in the division of other marital property, as well as in an alimony or reimbursement award for a spouse who contributed to the support of the family while the degree-earning spouse was in school or training.

(5) **Professional Practice and Goodwill**

    (a) A professional practice or corporation, unlike a spouse's degree or license, is subject to disposition as a marital asset. The practice must be valued for its tangible assets and its goodwill, which represents the reputational value of the business.

    (b) The majority of states distinguish between personal and enterprise goodwill. **Enterprise goodwill** is transferable with the business, and thus is not personal to a particular member. Enterprise goodwill should generally be included in the value of the practice, and may be divisible property because it is an asset of the business.

    (c) On the other hand, **personal goodwill** is that generated solely by the reputation and professional expertise of the owner-spouse. To the extent that clients would follow the owner-spouse if he dissociated from the business or practice, that is personal goodwill, and is not marital property [Washburn v. Washburn, 677 P.2d 152 (Wash. 1984)].

(6) **Personal Injury Claims**

    (a) The "analytic" approach—used by the majority of states—assesses what losses the damages compensate for and classifies the proceeds accordingly as either separate or marital property.

        1) To the extent the damages replace lost wages that would have been earned during marriage or medical expenses that were incurred during marriage, those damages are marital property.

        2) To the extent the damages replace future wages or pain and suffering or future medical expenses, those damages are the separate property of the injured spouse.

    (b) In some states, a damages claim for personal injury to a married person is not considered marital property on the basis that the interest is personal to the injured spouse. This approach is sometimes called the "unitary" view.

    (c) The "mechanistic" approach applied in some states looks to the timing of the injury, and classifies the damages according to whether the cause of action arose during the marriage or not.

(7) **Lottery Winnings**

    (a) Lottery winnings of a spouse may be marital or separate property depending on the usual principles such as the date of acquisition and whether community/marital earnings were used to purchase the ticket. Presumably, lottery winnings during the marriage are marital property.

(b) Whether payments distributed during marriage on a lottery win that occurred before marriage, or payments distributed after the marriage on a win that occurred during the marriage, are marital property may depend on the various ownership presumptions applied in the state.

(8) **Expectancies**

(a) Contingent expectancies are subject to equitable distribution if they were acquired through spousal effort during the marriage.

(9) **Fraudulently Transferred Property**

(a) Property owned by a party during the marriage but fraudulently transferred in contemplation of the divorce can also be included as a marital asset. A court will consider whether the transfer constitutes economic misconduct, and if so, it may award the harmed spouse a greater share of the remaining property.

h. **Division of Debts**

(1) In many states, the court is also authorized to assign marital debts and liabilities to one or other of the spouses as equity demands.

(2) Debts are generally characterized using the same principles that govern the characterization of assets, such that debts incurred during marriage are marital debts, while those incurred before or after are separate debts of the spouse who incurred them [ALI Principles § 4.09, cmt. (g)].

(3) Debts will generally be divided according to the same equitable principles considered in property division.

(4) The ALI Principles, however, begin with a presumption of equal division, unless the debts exceed the assets, in which case the presumption of equal division will not apply if the court finds that it is just and equitable to assign the excess debt unequally (e.g., because of disparities in financial capacity, participation in the decision to incur the debt, or consumption of goods or services that the debt was incurred to acquire) [ALI Principles § 4.09, cmt. (h)].

(5) The dischargeability of debts in bankruptcy is frequently an issue, as many divorces are accompanied by bankruptcy filings.

i. **Final Order**

(1) In fashioning an order that will effectuate the purposes of equitable distribution, courts are given broad equitable powers and may make an in-kind distribution, order the sale of property, or impose liens on property as security.

(2) Property transfers from one spouse to the other pursuant to an equitable distribution order are not deductible to the transferor for tax purposes nor included as income to the transferee, unlike alimony payments.

(3) An order for property division, unlike an alimony award, is not modifiable.

D. Alimony / Spousal Maintenance

1. Alimony, referred to more commonly today as maintenance or spousal support, may be awarded to one of the spouses as part of a divorce decree. Alimony may be awarded to either spouse, after consideration of all relevant factors set forth below [Orr v. Orr, 440 U.S. 268 (1979)].

2. **Types of Alimony**

   a. **Periodic Alimony**

      (1) A periodic alimony order requires a certain amount of money to be paid at set intervals, usually monthly.

      (2) The obligation will continue until the recipient dies, remarries, or the court modifies the order.

   b. **Lump Sum Alimony**

      (1) Under appropriate circumstances, the court may make an award of lump sum alimony. Lump sum alimony is distinguished from the normal alimony award in that it is for a fixed amount, rather than a periodic obligation with no aggregate limitations.

      (2) Unlike a periodic alimony order, an award of lump sum alimony is a final order which may not be modified even if the lump sum is payable in installments.

   c. **Rehabilitative Alimony**

      (1) Rehabilitative alimony may be awarded to a spouse for a limited period of time.

      (2) The purpose is to support as necessary until the recipient spouse can become self-supporting by entering the work force.

3. **Grounds**

   a. **Purpose and Prerequisites**

      (1) The modern trend is to limit alimony awards in favor of encouraging the recipient spouse to become self-supporting within a reasonable time. Alimony is generally based on economic need, and in some circumstances may be used to achieve fairness even if the claimant is not clearly in need.

      (2) Under the ALI Principles, which do not reflect the mainstream view, spousal maintenance is viewed as compensation for loss rather than relief of need [see ALI Principles §§ 5.04, et seq.].

      (3) Some jurisdictions also employ a *quasi*-contract or unjust enrichment approach.

      (4) Under the UMDA, an alimony order may be made only if the court finds that the spouse who is seeking alimony [UMDA § 308]:

         (a) lacks sufficient property to provide for his reasonable needs; and

         (b) is unable to support himself through appropriate employment, or is the custodian of a child whose condition or circumstances make it appropriate that the custodian not be required to seek employment outside the home.

b. **Factors**

(1) Rules governing the factors to be considered in making an award of spousal maintenance vary from state to state, but they generally require the trial court to consider:

    (a) the parties' respective financial resources and needs;

    (b) the contributions each has made to the marital relationship, whether financially or by providing care within the home; and

    (c) the duration of the marriage.

(2) Some state statutes require or allow consideration of spousal misconduct, whereas others exclude it.

(3) Some specifically require the court to consider one spouse's support for the other's education or training and may mandate reimbursement for such contributions.

c. **Modification or Termination**

(1) **Modification**

    (a) Under the UMDA, modification of spousal support is allowed only upon a showing of a substantial and continuing change in circumstances making the prior order unconscionable [UMDA § 316(a)].

    (b) Most jurisdictions are not as stringent as the UMDA, but may place a heavy burden on the party requesting the modification, such as requiring a "substantial change in circumstances that rendered the original award unreasonable and unfair" [Hecker v. Hecker, 568 N.W.2d 705 (Minn. 1997)].

    (c) Courts may consider whether the change in circumstances was anticipated at the time the original award was made and the good faith of the party asking for the modification [see, e.g., Pope v. Pope, 559 N.W.2d 192 (Neb. 1997)].

    (d) States may refuse modification involving a "voluntary reduction of income" by the party requesting a reduction in the obligation.

(2) **Termination**

    (a) Spousal maintenance generally terminates:

        1) after a specified term;

        2) on death of either spouse; or

        3) automatically on remarriage or cohabitation [see Stroud v. Stroud, 641 S.E.2d 142 (Va. Ct. App. 2007)].

            a) However, in cases of cohabitation instead of remarriage, alimony may be suspended rather than terminated, and reinstated when the cohabitation ends.

    (b) The court is unlikely to reinstate a spousal maintenance award based on the annulment of the recipient spouse's remarriage. Although an annulment legally "erases" a marriage, the weight of modern authority does not permit reinstatement of alimony based on annulment of the marriage that terminated the alimony obligation.

  d. **Enforcement**

   (1) State statutes generally provide that a court may enforce spousal support by wage garnishment and a variety of other means. Some states require income attachment orders in virtually every case.

   (2) In many states, failure to pay support may result in suspension or revocation of any state licenses issued to the obligor.

E. Equitable Reimbursement

1. Some states recognize a right of a spouse to be reimbursed under specified circumstances for contributions made during the marriage to the education, training, or increased earning capacity of the other spouse.

2. This remedy, which is called "reimbursement alimony" in some states and **equitable reimbursement** in others, may be ordered in addition to any right to alimony or equitable distribution.

F. Child Support and Custody

1. **Child Support**

  a. In connection with the entry of a custody order, the court may require either parent to pay periodic sums for the support of his minor children during the period of their minority. A child support order is generally entered only against the noncustodial parent.

  b. Child support orders are issued after consideration of the state's child support guidelines, if any. These guidelines are generally a mathematical formula based on the income of the parents.

   (1) There is a rebuttable presumption that the amount of child support, if computed consistent with the guidelines, is the proper amount of support to be ordered.

   (2) Statutes typically specify factors and conditions that may warrant variation from the guidelines, but the court must typically justify the deviation in the order.

  c. States have disagreed on whether a college education is a necessity [see Middlebury College v. Chandler, 16 Vt. 683 (1844); Esteb v. Esteb, 244 P. 264 (Wash. 1926)]. Several states now have statutes granting courts authority to include post-high school education expenses in a child support order. These statutes have been challenged on equal protection grounds in states that do not require intact families to provide a college education for their child [Curtis v. Kline, 666 A.2d 265 (Pa. 1995)]. Most states have upheld them, however.

2. **Child Custody**

  a. While both parents of a minor are living and are competent and fit, they are jointly entitled to the custody of the person of the minor. The parents have equal powers, rights, and duties concerning the minor. If one parent is dead and the surviving parent is competent and fit, the surviving parent is entitled to custody. If the parents live apart, the court may award the custody of the minor to either parent.

b. **Presumption in Favor of Parents**

    (1)   In any dispute as to the custody of minor children involving a parent and a non-parent, there is a presumption that it is in the best interests of the child to be in the custody of one of the parents.

    (2)   Thus, a third person such as a grandparent or stepparent will generally be able to obtain custody if they are able to overcome the parent custody presumption, such as by showing that the parents are not fit for custody.

c. **Equality between Parents**

    (1)   As between the parents, custody is now awarded on a sex-neutral basis.

    (2)   In custody determinations between the father and mother of a minor child, the court must exercise its sound discretion to decide as to which parent, if either, the custody of such child should be committed. Regard is had to the best interests and welfare of the child and the fitness of the parent.

    (3)   In order to provide continuity and stability to the child, courts will evaluate the established bond and caregiving history between parent and child, such that one parent's history of serving as the "primary caretaker" of the child is an important factor and may result in assigning primary custody to that parent.

d. **Best Interest of Child**

    (1)   Under the UMDA, the best interest of the child is determined by examination of all relevant factors, including the following [UMDA § 402]:

        (a) the wishes of the child's parent or parents as to his custody;

        (b) the wishes of the child as to his custodian;

        (c) the interaction and interrelationship of the child with his parent or parents, his siblings, and any other person who may significantly affect the child's best interest;

        (d) the child's adjustment to his home, school, and community; and

        (e) the mental and physical health of all individuals involved.

e. **Joint Custody**

    (1)   **Joint custody** generally refers to shared physical custody (both parents have parenting time) and/or shared decision-making power (also called **legal custody**). Sharing either or both aspects qualifies as "joint" custody.

        (a) A typical joint custody structure is where one parent has primary physical custody, the other has significant periods of physical custody, and both parents share decision-making power.

(2) Upon divorce, some states apply a presumption in favor of joint custody, whereas others do not award it unless the parents expressly agree.

    (a) There are two aspects to custody:

        1) the right to physical custody; and

        2) the right to make important decisions relating to the child, such as those concerning health, religion, and education.

    (b) It is generally agreed that requiring hostile parents (those who cannot communicate and make arrangements for the child amicably) to share custody can be harmful to their children [Taylor v. Taylor, 508 A.2d 964 (Md. 1986); Braiman v. Braiman, 378 N.E.2d 1019 (N.Y. 1978); Word v. Remick, 58 S.W.3d 422 (Ark. Ct. App. 2001)].

(3) Joint custody does not necessarily mean equal parenting time. Shared physical custody means that the child will reside for set periods of time with each of the parents with each parent having full custodial rights.

f. Marital Fault

(1) The fact that a parent was guilty of misconduct in connection with the divorce action will be relevant only insofar as the parent's moral fitness affects the child's welfare.

(2) Likewise, a parent's nonmarital relationships should not be relevant to a determination of child custody, unless they are shown to negatively affect the child.

g. Additional Factors

(1) The desires of a child of sufficient age and understanding are considered, but are not controlling. Many states require the judge to take the child's preference into account if he has reached a certain age (which varies by state) [ALI Principles § 2.08, cmt. (f)].

(2) A policy against separating siblings may also be a factor in determining the best interests of the child.

(3) Domestic violence by one parent against the other is a factor to be considered, and is generally influential when shown to negatively affect the child. It may specifically be a factor in awarding legal custody, as the violent history may make it harmful to mandate shared parental decision-making. Violence against the child clearly is harmful and an abusive parent may well have his custody rights limited.

(4) **The Friendly Parent**

    (a) Some courts will consider whether a parent is willing to cooperate and facilitate the child's relationship with the other parent.

h. Conditions to Award

(1) A court may attach reasonable conditions on the custodial rights of the parties to ensure that the child's best interests and welfare are protected.

(2) For example, the court may order parents to attend counseling sessions or to submit periodic reports or plans regarding custody to the court. Similarly, a court may order a custodial parent not to remove a child from the state without prior court approval.

3. **Visitation**
   a. **By Noncustodial Parent**
      (1) The noncustodial parent will generally be granted reasonable visitation rights unless the court finds that visitation is detrimental to the best interests of the child.
      (2) The UMDA provides for reasonable visitation by the noncustodial parent unless it "would endanger seriously the child's physical, mental, moral, or emotional health" [UMDA § 407].
   b. **By Third Persons**
      (1) By the 1990s, in many states a court could grant visitation rights upon divorce or annulment to grandparents, stepparents, or other adults who had established a substantial relationship with the child, if such an arrangement was deemed in the best interests of the child.
      (2) The statutory law on visitation rights by third persons has been reconsidered in light of Troxel v. Granville [530 U.S. 57 (2000)], in which the Supreme Court struck down a Washington state statute that permitted a court to award visitation to a grandparent over the child's mother's objection after the death of the child's father. The court held that significant deference must be given to a legal parent's objection to visitation, but did not specify a standard. Several jurisdictions' grandparent-visitation statutes have been found unconstitutional in the wake of Troxel, but the current standard for grandparent-visitation rights varies from state to state.

4. **Modification of Orders**
   a. **Standard for Modification**
      (1) **Child Support**
         (a) In most jurisdictions, modifications of child support orders may be made only upon a showing of a substantial and continuing change in circumstances making the prior order unreasonable.
         (b) Under the UMDA, modification of a child support order is allowed "only upon a showing of changed circumstances so substantial and continuing as to make the terms unconscionable" [UMDA § 316(a)].
            1) Under any standard, however, the changes must be more or less permanent, rather than temporary [Id.].
         (c) Under the UMDA, a modification of support can be made retroactive only from the date of service of the motion to modify on the other party. Federal law requires the same result with respect to retroactive modification of child support orders [42 U.S.C. § 666(a)(9)].
      (2) **Child Custody**
         (a) **Change of Circumstances Requirement**
            1) The prevailing view is that a court may modify a custody order upon proof of a material and substantial change

in circumstances such that a change in custody will be conducive to the best interests of the child. Even if there is a substantial change in circumstances, a court may not modify a custody order unless the change will serve the child's best interests [UMDA § 409(b)].

a) The burden of proving a change in circumstances, as well as the child's best interest, is upon the party seeking modification of the custody order.

b) Most states require that the change in circumstances be unforeseen. The UMDA, for example, specifies that there must be facts that have arisen since the prior decree or that were unknown to the court at the time of entry of the prior decree [Id.].

2) In a few states, a court need not identify a material or substantial change in circumstances to modify a custody order. Rather, the court must merely find that a change in the custody order is consistent with the best interests of the child.

3) However, stability of the child's existing placement is a consideration that favors the existing custodial structure. Most states disfavor modification when sought shortly after a custody decree has been entered; the principle of *res judicata* and the belief that children's interests are served by stable custody arrangements both mitigate against frequent change.

a) Thus, if a modification petition is filed within two years of the original decree, the UMDA authorizes a modification hearing only if the evidence suggests "there is reason to believe that the child's present environment may endanger seriously his physical, mental, moral or emotional heath" [UMDA § 409(a)]. Some states follow this rule.

b) Some states impose a waiting period of six months or a year before a parent may bring a request for modification after the last custody award.

c) In states that do not have statutory standards restricting early modification, case law typically disfavors it unless the evidence shows that the child is at risk.

(b) **Parent's Cohabitation or Remarriage**

1) In some states, appellate courts have held that a custodial parent's post-decree nonmarital cohabitation represents a change of circumstances sufficient to warrant a modification hearing [see Todd v. Casciano, 569 S.E.2d 566 (Ga. Ct. App. 2002); Word v. Remick, 58 S.W.3d 422 (Ark. Ct. App. 2001)].

a) In these states, an appellate court would likely find that the trial court did not err in hearing evidence on modification. However, even in states that authorize a hearing in these circumstances, modification is typically disallowed unless the petitioner shows that the nonmarital cohabitation has an adverse impact on the children [see UMDA § 402; Todd v. Casciano, 569 S.E.2d 566 (Ga. Ct. App. 2002)].

2) A child's custody preference is relevant to a custody determination, and alteration of a child's custody preference thus can constitute a substantial change of circumstance [see Butland v. Butland, 1996 Ohio App. LEXIS 2773 (Ohio Ct. App. 1996); Mulkey-Yelverton v. Blevins, 884 P.2d 41 (Wyo. 1994)].

(c) **Relocation**

1) The most difficult modification questions may involve a custodial parent's wish to relocate to another state or anywhere that will make it difficult for the other spouse to maintain frequent in-person contact with the child.

2) Many courts have balanced the impact on visitation by the noncustodial parent against the benefits of the move to both the children and the custodial parent, with an overall trend toward leniency for the wishes and needs of the parent with whom the child has been primarily living [ALI Principles § 2.17, cmt. (d)].

   a) Some states are favorably disposed to allowing the custodial parent to relocate with the child. Some permit the custodial parent and child to move, unless the parent's motives for moving are vindictive [Aaby v. Strange, 924 S.W.2d 623 (Tenn. 1996)].

   b) Others will permit the custodial parent to relocate unless the evidence shows that the move will be detrimental to the child [In re Marriage of Pape, 989 P.2d 1120 (Wash. 1999)].

   c) Some courts have emphasized the availability of an alternative reasonable visitation schedule. If such an alternative exists, the court will almost always grant the relocation request [see Schwartz v. Schwartz, 812 P.2d 1268 (Nev. 1991)].

   d) Other states display an anti-relocation viewpoint and require the parent who wishes to relocate to show that the proposed move serves the child's best interests [Pollock v. Pollock, 889 P.2d 633 (Ariz. Ct. App. 1995)].

5. **Uniform Child Custody Jurisdiction and Enforcement Act**

   a. **Enactment and Purposes**

      (1) As a constitutional matter, a court taking jurisdiction of a custody matter need not, except as a matter of comity, give full faith and credit to the decree of a sister state because such a decree is

almost always modifiable, and therefore not a final judgment [May v. Anderson, 345 U.S. 528 (1953)].

(2) However, nearly all the states have adopted the Uniform Child Custody Jurisdiction and Enforcement Act ("UCCJEA"). The UCCJEA attempts to avoid relitigation of custody decisions of other states, to facilitate the enforcement of foreign custody decisions, and to deter abductions of children undertaken to obtain custody awards.

b. **Initial Jurisdiction**

(1) Physical presence or personal jurisdiction over a party or a child is neither necessary nor sufficient for a state to make a child custody determination.

(2) A court has jurisdiction under the UCCJEA to make an initial child-custody determination only when [UCCJEA § 201(a)]:

(a) it is the home state of the child or had been within six months of the commencement of the proceeding, and, if the child is absent from the forum state, a parent continues to live in the forum state;

(b) another state does not have such home-state jurisdiction, or else the home-state court has declined to exercise jurisdiction, the child and his parent(s) have a significant connection with the state other than mere physical presence, and substantial evidence is available in the state regarding the child's welfare;

(c) all other states having jurisdiction under either of the above provisions have declined to exercise jurisdiction on the ground that the state is the more appropriate forum to determine custody of the child; or

(d) no court of any other state would have jurisdiction under any of the above provisions.

c. **Exclusive, Continuing Jurisdiction**

(1) Once a state has made a valid child-custody determination under UCCJEA Section 201 or Section 203, relating to jurisdiction to modify a determination, that state has exclusive jurisdiction over the determination.

(2) Such jurisdiction continues until [UCCJEA § 202]:

(a) a court of the state determines that neither the child nor the child and one parent or person acting as parent have a significant connection with the state, and substantial evidence is no longer available in the state regarding the child's welfare; or

(b) a court of the state or of another state determines that the child, the child's parents, and any person acting as a parent do not presently reside in the state.

d. **Jurisdiction to Modify Determination**

(1) A court that has made an initial child-custody determination but does not have exclusive, continuing jurisdiction, may modify the determination only if it has jurisdiction to make an initial determination under Section 201.

(2) A court may not modify a child-custody determination made by a court of another state unless the forum court has jurisdiction to make an initial determination and [UCCJEA § 203]:

    (a) a court of the other state determines it no longer has exclusive, continuing jurisdiction or that a court of the state would be a more convenient forum; or

    (b) the forum court or a court of the other state determines that the child and the child's parents or any person acting as parent do not presently reside in the other state.

e. **Temporary Emergency Jurisdiction**

    (1) A state has temporary emergency jurisdiction if the child is present in the state and [UCCJEA § 204]:

        (a) the child has been abandoned; or

        (b) it is necessary in an emergency to protect the child because the child (or a sibling or parent of the child) is being subjected to or threatened with mistreatment or abuse.

    (2) The UCCJEA does not govern proceedings pertaining to the authorization of emergency medical care for a child [UCCJEA § 103].

f. **Inconvenient Forum**

    (1) A state that has jurisdiction to make a child-custody determination may decline to exercise its jurisdiction at any time if it determines that it is an inconvenient forum under the circumstances, and that a court of another state is a more appropriate forum [UCCJEA § 207(a)].

    (2) The following factors should be considered [UCCJEA § 207(b)]:

        (a) whether domestic violence has occurred and is likely to continue, and which state could best protect the parties and the child;

        (b) the length of time the child has resided outside the state;

        (c) the distance between the courts of the two states;

        (d) financial circumstances of the parties;

        (e) any agreement of the parties as to which state should assume jurisdiction;

        (f) the nature and location of the evidence required to resolve the pending litigation;

        (g) the ability of the court of each state to decide the issue expeditiously and the procedures necessary to present the evidence; and

        (h) the familiarity of the courts in each state with the facts and issues in the pending litigation.

g. **Jurisdiction Declined by Reason of Conduct**

    (1) If a court has jurisdiction because a person seeking to invoke its jurisdiction has engaged in unjustifiable conduct, the court should decline to exercise its jurisdiction unless [UCCJEA § 208(a)]:

(a) the parents and any persons acting as parents have acquiesced in the exercise of jurisdiction;

(b) court of another state otherwise having jurisdiction determines that the state is a more appropriate forum; or

(c) no court of any other state would have jurisdiction.

(2) If a court declines to exercise jurisdiction on this grounds, it may fashion a remedy to ensure the safety of the child and to prevent a repetition of the unjustifiable conduct, and it may assess fees and costs against the party who unjustifiably sought to invoke its jurisdiction [see, e.g., 23 Pa. Cons. Stat. §§ 5428(b)-(c)].

6. **Termination of Custody Order**

   a. A custody order in a divorce proceeding is terminated by the death of the custodial parent, and the surviving parent is usually entitled to custody unless the latter is determined to be unfit.

   b. A custody order also will terminate when a child attains the age of majority or otherwise becomes emancipated.

7. **Enforcement of Custody or Visitation Orders**

   a. A court may use its contempt power to enforce a custody or visitation award.

   b. Many states provide for specific civil sanctions for violation of a parenting plan or custody order; violation may also be a crime [see ALI Principles § 2.19, Reporter's Notes to Comment (a)].

8. **Enforcement of Child Support Orders**

   a. All states have adopted the Uniform Interstate Family Support Act ("UIFSA"). This was to facilitate enforcement of support orders across state lines, making it easier to obtain jurisdiction over an obligor who moves.

   b. UIFSA establishes broad long-arm jurisdiction over nonresidents in order to facilitate one-state proceedings whenever possible. When jurisdiction over a nonresident is obtained, the tribunal may obtain evidence, provide for discovery, and elicit testimony through use of the "information route" provided in the Act.

   c. The principle of **continuing, exclusive jurisdiction** means that if only one tribunal has issued a child-support order, the order of that tribunal controls and must be recognized.

   d. Contrary to prior law, UIFSA takes the position that a responding state should enforce a child support obligation irrespective of another state's law. Tolerance for the laws of other States and nations, in order to facilitate child support enforcement, is a prime goal of the Act, which also contains provisions to help ease the transition to the new system.

   e. The state that enters the original order will retain jurisdiction for modification, provided the child or one of the parties continues to live in the state or the parties agree in writing that the matter be heard in another state.

   f. An order issued in one state may be registered for enforcement in another. It may also be registered for modification if:

      (1) the issuing state no longer has jurisdiction;

(2)   the petitioner is a nonresident of the forum state; and

(3)   the forum state has personal jurisdiction over the respondent.

g.   After a support order issued in another state has been registered in a second state, the responding court in the second state may modify the order only if a petitioner, who is a nonresident, seeks modification, and all the parties have filed written consents in the issuing tribunal for a court in the second state to modify the support order and assume continuing, exclusive jurisdiction over the order [UIFSA § 611].

9.   **Parental Kidnapping Prevention Act (PKPA)**

a.   Under the PKPA, states must enforce any custody or visitation order made by a court of another state that is consistent with the PKPA [28 U.S. Code § 1738A(a)].

(1)   A custody or visitation order is consistent with the PKPA if [28 U.S. Code § 1738A(c)]:

(a)   the issuing court has jurisdiction under the law of that state; and

(b)   one of the following conditions is met:

1)   the state in which the issuing court is located is the home state of the child on the date of the commencement of the proceeding;

2)   the state in which the issuing court is located had been the child's home state within six months before the date of the commencement of the proceeding and the child is absent from that state because of his removal or retention by a contestant or for other reasons, and a contestant continues to live in the issuing state; or

3)   the child is physically present in the issuing state and has been abandoned, or it is necessary in an emergency to protect the child because the child, a sibling, or parent of the child has been subjected to or threatened with mistreatment or abuse.

b.   If a custody or visitation order is made consistent with the PKPA, the order from the issuing court continues as long as the court retains jurisdiction under the laws of that state, and the issuing state remains the residence of the child or of any contestant [28 U.S. Code § 1738A(d)].

c.   A court of a non-issuing state may modify a custody determination of the child made by a court of another state if [28 U.S. Code § 1738A(f)]:

(1)   it has jurisdiction to make such a child-custody determination; and

(2)   the court of the issuing state no longer has jurisdiction, or it has declined to exercise such jurisdiction to modify the custody determination.

G. Effects of Final Divorce Decree

1. Once a divorce has been decreed, either party may generally marry again as if the party had never been married.

2. Each divorced party loses the right to intestate inheritance and to take an elective share from the estate of the other party. Unless a will expressly provides otherwise, a divorce or annulment revokes any disposition or appointment of property made by the will to a former spouse and any provision naming the former spouse as executor or trustee. Property that is prevented from passing to the former spouse will pass as if the former spouse predeceased the testator.

H. Recognition of Foreign Divorce Decree

1. Only One Spouse Participated

a. Where only one spouse participates in a divorce proceeding, the stay-at-home spouse has the right to attack the finding of the domicile of the procuring spouse because there has been no contested hearing on the issue of domicile in the rendering state [Williams v. North Carolina, 325 U.S. 226 (1945)].

b. When the procuring spouse returns to his original domicile soon after the divorce, or more conclusively, buys a round-trip ticket originally, the stay-at-home spouse will probably be able to attack the out-of-state decree successfully in the state of original domicile under the principle established by the Williams case.

(1) However, the decree is presumptively valid until attacked.

2. Both Spouses Participated

a. By participating in an out-of-state divorce, the spouse is barred by the doctrine of collateral estoppel from attacking the validity of the divorce, because the question of domicile has either actually been litigated or could have been litigated in the rendering state [Sherrer v. Sherrer, 334 U.S. 343 (1948)].

b. The Court extended this doctrine in Coe v. Coe [334 U.S. 378 (1948)], barring a later attack where the defendant merely entered an appearance in the rendering state and admitted jurisdiction. Consent jurisdiction not only binds the parties, but also protects the decree from collateral attack to the extent that it is protected in the rendering state [Johnson v. Muelberger, 340 U.S. 581 (1951)].

3. Divisible Divorce

a. The Supreme Court has upheld the right of a state to continue a support order after an out-of-state divorce decree had purportedly terminated it by granting no alimony [Estin v. Estin, 334 U.S. 541 (1948)].

(1) An out-of-state court in an *ex parte* action has no *in personam* jurisdiction over the other spouse, and thus cannot order or alter economic incidents to a divorce.

b. However, an *ex parte* out-of-state decree that serves to terminate the marital status has been found sufficient to divest a person of the rights of a surviving spouse under an the ex-spouse's pension plan [Stilwell v. Continental Illinois Nat'l Bank & Trust Co., 202 N.E.2d 477 (Ill. 1964)].

4. **Divorce Decree from Foreign Nation**

   a. A state need not recognize the validity of foreign-country divorce decrees.

   b. However, states will generally recognize such decrees on the basis of comity if both spouses were represented and there was a hearing in the court of the foreign country.

Partnership

TABLE OF CONTENTS

VII. LIMITED PARTNERSHIPS

I. CREATION OF GENERAL PARTNERSHIPS

A. Introduction

1. These notes on general partnerships are based on the Revised Uniform Partnership Act ("RUPA") and on general principles of partnership law followed by a majority of jurisdictions. The RUPA has been enacted in some form by almost all the states.

2. Partnerships have the following characteristics:

   a. unlimited liability for partners;

   b. partners have the right to co-manage the partnership;

   c. fiduciary duties exist between and among the partners and the partnership; and

   d. partners share in profits.

3. A partnership is an entity distinct from its partners [RUPA § 201(a)].

4. A **general partnership** is an association of two or more persons to carry on as co-owners of a business for profit [RUPA § 101(6)].

   a. **Person** is defined as [RUPA § 101(10)]:

      (1) an individual;

      (2) a corporation;

      (3) a business trust;

      (4) an estate;

      (5) a trust;

      (6) a partnership;

      (7) an association;

      (8) a joint venture;

      (9) a government;

      (10) a governmental subdivision;

      (11) an agency;

      (12) an instrumentality; or

      (13) any other legal or commercial entity.

   b. **Business** includes every trade, occupation, and profession [RUPA § 101(1)].

B. Formation

1. All that is required to create a partnership under the Revised Uniform Partnership Act ("RUPA") is "two or more persons who associate to carry on a business for profit." RUPA specifically states that intentionally does not matter.

   a. Partnership may be inferred from the conduct of the parties.

   b. No "agreement" or "consent" is required to form a partnership.

      (1) If individuals just act like partners, the law will treat them like partners, even if they had no idea that they were acting like partners and no intent to do so.

(2) Where there is an official agreement or contract (which is not required), it may be oral.

    c. In the absence of any agreed terms, RUPA will fill in those partnership terms.

2. A partnership may be formed:

    a. for a specific undertaking;

    b. for a term; or

    c. at will.

3. **Partnership versus Joint Venture**

    a. Joint ventures are similar to partnerships.

    b. As a general rule, a **joint venture** is described as an association contemplating a single transaction or a related series of transactions, as compared to a partnership, which is generally said to be carrying on a business.

    c. The fact that the individuals involved refer to themselves as either "partners" or "joint venturers" is not determinative of their relationship, but is a factor to be considered.

    d. Although the RUPA does not specifically apply to joint ventures, courts have applied the same rules of law.

4. **Capacity**

    a. Any person who has the capacity to enter into a contract can enter into a partnership agreement.

    b. Partnerships, societies, and other associations can also enter into partnerships with other persons or entities.

    c. A corporation can be a partner in any business enterprise that it would have the power to conduct by itself, so long as the enterprise is appropriate under the corporation's articles and bylaws.

    d. A minor can enter into a partnership, but he may void the partnership agreement on the basis of his infancy. His investment in the business, however, is subject to the claims of creditors, and in some jurisdictions, his investment is subject also to the claims of partners who have not dealt with him fraudulently.

C. Tests of Partnership

1. The key test of whether a partnership has been formed is the intent of the parties to enter into a partnership relationship, no matter what it is called.

2. An express agreement is the best indication of intent.

3. If the partnership agreement was merely implied, other factors must be considered. The court may consider such evidence as the sharing of profits, the management practices of the entity, the amount and type of services rendered by the parties, and the record title to any real or personal property used by the entity.

EXAMPLE: Law students Bella and Edward brainstorm one night about a social networking website. They tell their nerdy computer-geek friend Jacob about it, and they agree that Jacob will create the site, which will be designed by Bella and Edward.

4. **Sharing of Profits**

    a.   Under the RUPA, a person's receipt of a share of the profits of a business is *prima facie* evidence that he is a partner in the business [RUPA § 202(c)(3)].

    b.   No such inference may be drawn, however, if the profits were received in payment:

        (1)   of a debt, by installments or otherwise;

        (2)   for services as an independent contractor, of wages, or of other compensation to an employee;

        (3)   of rent;

        (4)   of an annuity or other retirement or health benefit to a beneficiary, representative, or designee of a deceased or retired partner;

        (5)   of interest or other charge on a loan, even if the amount of payment varies with the profits of the business; or

        (6)   for the sale of the goodwill of a business or other property by installments or otherwise.

    c.   It is not statutorily required that there is a sharing of losses to create a partnership.

    d.   In the absence of a contrary agreement, the partners share losses in proportion to their share of the profits.

5. **Sharing of Gross Returns**

    a.   The sharing of gross returns does not in itself establish a partnership, whether or not the persons sharing the returns have a joint or common right or interest in any property from which the returns are derived [RUPA § 202(c)].

    EXAMPLE: Bella and Edward agree to give Jacob one-fifth of the profits.

    EXAMPLE: Bella and Edward agree to pay Jacob $15 an hour.

    EXAMPLE: Bella's dad gives Bella and Edward $10,000 to start the site, to be repaid out of ad revenue until paid in full.

6. **Common Property**

    a.   Joint tenancy, tenancy in common, tenancy by the entirety, joint property, common property, or part ownership does not in itself establish a partnership, regardless of whether the owners share any profits made through use of the property [RUPA § 202(c)].

    EXAMPLE: If two persons, in undertaking a real estate development, took title to the property as tenants in common, they would not thereby form a partnership.

7. **Control**

    a.   Partners, as co-owners of the business, must have the power of ultimate control.

    b.   If a person shares in the profits, but lacks any power to control, he is probably an agent, and is receiving his profit share merely as an incentive or a bonus, unless the agreement shows a contrary intent.

D. Partnership by Estoppel

1. Even if a voluntary partnership does not exist, liability may be imposed on a person who has let it appear that he is in a partnership if a creditor is thereby misled [RUPA § 308].

2. When a person, by words or conduct, represents himself to be a partner in an existing partnership, or with one or more persons who are not actual partners, he is liable to anyone who has extended credit in reliance on the representation of partnership [RUPA § 308(a)].

    a. A person is likewise liable if he has consented to such a representation by another [Id.].

3. If the representation is made privately, it may be relied upon only by those to whom it was made.

4. If the representation is made publicly (e.g., by newspaper), the "purported partner" is liable to anyone who has knowledge of it and has relied upon it [RUPA § 308].

    a. The particular way in which the representation came to the third party's attention need not have been with the purported partner's consent, as long as he made or consented to some sort of public representation.

5. If partnership liability results, the purported partner is liable as though he were a partner; if no partnership liability results, he is liable jointly with the others consenting to the representation [RUPA § 308(a)].

6. **Agency Created by Holding Out**

    a. When a person has been represented to be a partner in an existing partnership, or with others who are not actual partners, he is an agent of those consenting to the representation, and he can bind them as if he were, in fact, a partner [RUPA § 308(b)].

    b. If all the members of an existing partnership consent to such a representation, any liability is a partnership obligation; otherwise, the person acting and the partners consenting to the representation are jointly and severally liable [Id.].

II. RELATIONSHIP BETWEEN PARTNERS AND THIRD PARTIES

A. Powers

1. Every partner is an agent of the partnership for the purpose of its business [RUPA § 301(1)].

2. The act of a partner for apparently carrying on in the ordinary course of business of the partnership binds the partnership, unless [Id.]:

   a. the partner has no authority to act in the matter; and

   b. the person with whom he is dealing has knowledge that he has no such authority.

3. **Authority**

   a. A partner may have **express authority** to act by the terms of the partnership agreement, or by consent of the other partners.

   b. A partner may have **apparent authority** based on the nature and course of business of the partnership, or on the custom in similar partnerships in the same area.

   c. However, an act of a partner that is not apparently for carrying on in the ordinary course of business of the partnership does not bind the partnership unless authorized by the other partners [RUPA § 301(2)].

4. **Knowledge That Authority Is Lacking**

   a. Partnership agreements may include specific restrictions on authority. If a partner acts in contravention of such a restriction, and the third party has knowledge of the restriction, the partnership will not be bound.

   b. Restrictions on authority are ineffective against a third party without knowledge of the restrictions. Although a partner may be in breach toward his other partners, he would still have to honor any agreement made with a third party.

   c. A person has **knowledge** of a fact not only when he has actual knowledge thereof, but also when he has knowledge of such other facts in the circumstances showing bad faith.

5. **Statement of Partnership Authority**

   a. A partnership may file a statement of partnership authority, which [RUPA § 303]:

      (1) must include:

         (a) the name of the partnership;

         (b) the street address of its chief executive office and of an office in the state, if such an office exists;

         (c) the names and mailing addresses of all the partners, or of an agent appointed and maintained by the partnership; and

         (d) the names of the partners authorized to execute an instrument transferring real property held in the name of the partnership; and

      (2) may state the authority, or limitations on the authority, of some or all of the partners to enter into transactions, or any other matter, on behalf of the partnership.

b. The effect of filing a statement of authority is as follows:

(1) Except for transfers of real property, a grant of authority contained in a filed statement of partnership authority is conclusive in favor of a person who gives value without knowledge to the contrary, so long as and to the extent that a limitation on that authority is not contained in another filed statement. A filed cancellation of a limitation on authority revives the previous grant of authority.

(2) A grant of authority to transfer real property held in the name of the partnership is also conclusive in favor of a person who gives value without knowledge to the contrary, so long as and to the extent that the authority is contained in a certified copy of a filed statement recorded in the office for recording transfers of that real property, and no certified statement containing a limitation on that authority is of record in such office.

(a) A person who is not a partner is deemed to know of a limitation on the authority of a partner to transfer real property held in the name of the partnership if a certified copy of the filed statement containing the limitation on authority is of record in the office for recording transfers of that real property. The recording of a certified copy of a filed cancellation of a limitation on authority revives the previous grant of authority.

(3) A person who is not a partner is not deemed to know of a limitation on the authority of a partner merely because the limitation is contained in a filed statement.

c. Unless previously canceled, a filed statement of partnership authority is canceled by operation of law five years after the date on which the statement, or the most recent amendment, was filed with the secretary of state.

B. Notice to Partner

1. Generally, notice to any partner of any matter relating to partnership affairs constitutes notice to the partnership [RUPA § 102].

2. A person has **notice** of a fact when the notification:

   a. comes to the person's attention; or

   b. is duly delivered at the person's place of business, or at any other place held out by the person as a place for receiving communications.

3. If a partner acting in a particular matter has acquired knowledge while a partner—or if his knowledge was otherwise acquired but is present in his mind when acting for the partnership—that knowledge is imputed to the partnership.

4. If a partner not acting for the partnership in a particular matter has knowledge that he could and should have communicated to the acting partner, that knowledge also will be imputed to the partnership.

5. An exception to this rule of imputation of notice or knowledge is made if a fraud on the partnership is committed by, or with the consent of, that partner.

C. Liability

1. Nature of Liability

a. All partners are liable jointly and severally for all obligations of the partnership, whether arising under tort, contract, or otherwise [RUPA §§ 305, 306].

b. An action may be brought against any one or more of the partners, but a partner will not be bound by a judgment unless he has been served with notice.

c. Therefore, unless one of the partners is no longer subject to jurisdiction, all of the partners must be joined in the action.

   (1) However, a judgment may be satisfied against any one of the partners.

d. The RUPA also permits any partner to enter into a separate obligation to perform a partnership contract, in which case the partner's liability is several.

EXAMPLE: A partner might endorse a partnership note.

e. Many jurisdictions have common name statutes, which provide that a partnership, or any other unincorporated association, may sue and be sued in the name that it has assumed or by which it is commonly known.

f. At common law, all partners were required to be named in a lawsuit and served with process; however, in states that have enacted common law statutes, service on one partner is generally held sufficient.

2. Extent of Liability

a. Even though a partnership obligation is joint, each partner is individually liable for the entire amount of the partnership's obligation.

b. A partner is entitled to indemnification by the partnership for any payments he makes on its behalf.

c. If a partner is forced to pay the entire debt, or more than his *pro rata* share, and the partnership is unable to indemnify him, he is entitled to **contribution** from his co-partners and may seek it through an accounting action.

d. A **dormant partner**—i.e., one who is not active in managing partnership business and who is not known to the world as a partner—is nonetheless liable on partnership obligations.

   (1) This is based on the rule that an undisclosed principal is still liable for the acts of his agent.

e. An **incoming partner**—i.e., one admitted as a partner into an existing partnership—is not personally liable for any partnership obligation incurred before the person's admission as a partner [RUPA § 306].

3. Partnership Liability for Acts of Partners

a. A partnership is liable for loss or injury caused to a person, or for a penalty incurred, as a result of a wrongful act, omission, or other actionable conduct of a partner acting in the ordinary course of business of the partnership or with authority of the partnership [RUPA § 305(a)].

b. If, in the course of the partnership's business or while acting with authority of the partnership, a partner receives or causes the partnership to receive money or property of a person who is not a partner and the money is misapplied by a partner, the partnership is liable for the loss [RUPA 305(b)].

4. **Retiring Partner**

a. Usually, a retiring partner remains liable on all obligations incurred before his retirement.

b. A retiring partner can be discharged from liability by an agreement with the continuing partners and the partnership creditor.

c. An agreement to discharge a retiring partner from liability may be inferred from the course of dealing between a creditor having knowledge of the dissolution and the partners continuing the business.

d. The remaining partners may agree to assume the obligations of the retiring partner, who will then become a surety.

e. If a partnership creditor, knowing of the agreement, consents to any material alteration in the nature or time of payment of the obligations, the retiring partner is released from any liability.

III. RELATIONSHIP BETWEEN PARTNERS

A. Partnership Agreement

1. Relations among the partners and between the partners and the partnership are governed by the partnership agreement. To the extent the partnership agreement does not otherwise provide, the RUPA governs relations among the partners and between the partners and the partnership.

2. The partnership agreement may not [RUPA § 103(b)]:

   a. vary the rights and duties of filing the statement of partnership, except to eliminate the duty to provide copies of statements to all of the partners;

   b. unreasonably restrict the right of access to books and records;

   c. eliminate or reduce a partner's fiduciary duties, but it may:

      (1) identify specific types or categories of activities that do not violate these duties, if not manifestly unreasonable; and

      (2) specify the number or percentage of partners that may authorize or ratify, after full disclosure of all material facts, a specific act or transaction that otherwise would violate these duties;

   d. eliminate or reduce the obligation of good faith and fair dealing, but it may prescribe the standards by which the performance of an obligation is to be measured, if the standards are not manifestly unreasonable;

   e. vary the power to dissociate as a partner, except to require the notice of a partner's will to dissociate to be in writing;

   f. vary the right of a court to expel a partner;

   g. vary the requirement to wind up the partnership business because of an event that makes it unlawful for the partnership to continue, or on the basis of a judicial determination to wind up the business;

   h. vary the law applicable to a limited liability partnership; or

   i. restrict the rights of a person, other than a partner and transferee of a partner's transferable interest.

B. Contributions, Profits, and Losses

1. **Partners' Contributions and Shares**

   a. Partners make contributions to the partnership in cash or otherwise (e.g., a contribution of labor).

   b. Each partner is entitled to be repaid his contributions, whether made by way of capital or through advances to the partnership property, and to share equally in the profits and surplus remaining after all liabilities (including those to partners) are satisfied [RUPA § 403(b)].

      (1) A partner has no right to receive a distribution in kind [RUPA § 402].

   c. Concomitantly, each partner must contribute toward the losses—whether of capital or otherwise—sustained by the partnership, according to his share in the profits [RUPA § 401(b)].

   d. Partners may agree to share the profits other than equally, and would then share the losses in the same ratio, unless specifically agreed otherwise.

EXAMPLE: Bella, Edward, and Jacob are involved in a partnership and have no agreement as to profits and losses. Bella, Edward, and Jacob will each take one-third of the profits and one-third of the losses.

EXAMPLE: Bella, Edward, and Jacob have a partnership agreement that states that Bella and Edward will each take 25% of the profits and Jacob will take 50% of the profits. The agreement is silent as to losses. Therefore, Bella and Edward will each take 25% of the losses, and Jacob will take 50% of the losses.

2. **Rights**

a. **Right to Indemnity**

(1) The partnership must indemnify every partner with regard to payments made and liabilities incurred by that partner in the ordinary course of the partnership's business or for the preservation of its business or property [RUPA § 401(c)].

b. **Right to Interest**

(1) A payment made by a partner, incurred in the ordinary course of the partnership business or as an advance beyond the amount of capital he agreed to contribute, constitutes a loan that accrues interest from the date of the payment or advance [RUPA § 401(e)].

c. **Right to Compensation**

(1) In general, a partner is not entitled to compensation for services performed for the partnership, except reasonable compensation for services rendered in winding up the partnership business [RUPA § 401(h)].

(2) However, a partner's agreement may provide for salaries to be paid.

(a) Such an agreement should spell out the source of payments (i.e., from the partner's share of profits or from partnership income) and the work and time required in exchange.

(3) In the absence of an express agreement, the right to compensation may still be implied from other agreements regarding the conduct of the business, or from the course of dealing among the parties.

d. **Right to Accounting**

(1) The accounting action is equitable in nature, and determines each partner's investment, the partnership's profits or losses, and the share of profits to which each partner is entitled.

(2) The RUPA expands on the Uniform Partnership Act by permitting that, during any term of the partnership, a partner may maintain a legal or equitable action, including an action for an accounting [RUPA § 405].

(3) An accounting is not a prerequisite to the availability of other remedies.

e. **Management and Control**

(1) All partners have equal rights in the management and conduct of

the partnership business [RUPA § 401(f)].

    (a) This may be changed by agreement.

        EXAMPLE: Votes might be assigned varying weights to correspond to capital contributions or shares in the profits.

  (2) Any differences arising as to matters connected to the ordinary course of partnership business may be decided by a majority of the partners, but no act in contravention of any agreement between the partners may be accomplished properly without the consent of all the partners [RUPA 401(j)].

f. **Property Rights of a Partner**

  (1) The property rights of a partner consist of:

    (a) his interest in the partnership (i.e., economic rights); and

    (b) his right to participate in management.

  (2) A partner is not a co-owner of partnership property and has no interest in partnership property that can be transferred, either voluntarily or involuntarily [RUPA § 501].

  (3) **Transfer**

    (a) A partner's only transferable interest is his share of profits and losses of the partnership and his right to receive distributions. Such interest is deemed personal property [RUPA § 502].

    (b) A partner's economic or financial interest in the partnership is transferable (unlike his interest in specific partnership property) [RUPA § 503(a)].

    (c) Such a transfer does not by itself dissolve the partnership, but it also does not entitle the transferee, in the absence of a contrary agreement, to [Id.]:

       1) participate in the management or conduct of the partnership business; or

       2) require access to any information concerning the partnership, or to inspect the partnership books or records.

    (d) The transferee is merely entitled to receive the distributions to which his transferor would have been entitled [RUPA § 503].

    (e) In the event of a dissolution of the partnership, the transferee is entitled to receive his transferor's interest in distributions, and may require an accounting only from the date of the last accounting [RUPA §§ 503(b), (c)].

  (4) **Encumbrances**

    (a) A judgment creditor can subject the partner's transferable interest to a charging order [RUPA § 504].

    (b) Upon application, a court can charge the debtor-partner's transferable interest to satisfy the judgment, and may then, or later, appoint a receiver of his share of the distributions due him from the partnership [Id.].

(c) Before foreclosure or sale of the debtor's interest, the other partners may redeem his interest with their separate property or, with the consent of all other partners, with partnership property [Id.].

(d) A judgment creditor of an individual partner may not attach and execute upon partnership real estate to satisfy his claim against the partner.

(e) Ordinarily, a claimant may not take action against a partner's personal assets unless the partnership assets fail to satisfy the claimant's judgment.

C. Fiduciary Duties

1. Concerning partnership matters, partners have a fiduciary relationship to one another and owe the partnership and the other partners a duty of loyalty and a duty of care [RUPA § 409(a)]. A partnership may maintain an action against a partner for a breach of the partnership agreement or for the violation of a duty to the partnership, causing harm to the partnership [RUPA § 410a].

2. **Duty of Care**

   a. Each partner owes to the partnership a duty of care in the conduct and winding up of the partnership business [RUPA § 409(c)].

   b. Such duty is limited to refraining from engaging in grossly negligent or reckless conduct, intentional misconduct, or a knowing violation of the law [Id.].

3. **Duty of Loyalty**

   a. **Good Faith**

      (1) A partner must discharge his duties to the partnership and the other partners exercising his rights consistent with the obligation of good faith and fair dealing [RUPA § 409(d)].

   b. **Duty Not to Compete**

      (1) A partner must not compete with the partnership in the conduct of its business [RUPA § 409(b)(3)].

         (a) If he does so, he must account to the partnership for his profits.

      (2) A partner must refrain from dealing with the partnership in the conduct or winding up of the partnership business as, or on behalf of, a party having an interest adverse to the partnership [RUPA § 409(b)(2)].

      (3) A partner may not exploit a **business opportunity** of the partnership unless he has made full disclosure and received the approval of his other partners.

         (a) If no conflict of interest or business opportunity is involved, a partner may engage in other enterprises, unless the partnership agreement specifies otherwise.

         EXAMPLE: If a partner in a law firm receives a referral fee, the fee belongs to the partnership.

         EXAMPLE: A friend wants a former law school classmate of hers to do some legal work for her in his spare time, even though he is an associate at a general service law firm.

EXAMPLE: A law professor owns a restaurant or writes a novel.

   c. **Duty to Disclose**

     (1)   Each partner and the partnership shall furnish to a partner, and to the legal representative of a deceased partner or partner under legal disability [RUPA § 408(c)]:

        (a) without demand, any information concerning the partnership's business and affairs reasonably required for the proper exercise of the partner's rights and duties under the partnership agreement; and

        (b) on demand, any other information concerning the partnership's business and affairs, except to the extent the demand or the information demanded is unreasonable or otherwise improper under the circumstances.

   d. **Duty to Account**

     (1)   Under the RUPA, every partner must account to the partnership for any benefit, and holds as trustee for the partnership any profit, derived by him without the consent of the other partners from any transaction connected with the conduct and winding up of the partnership business or from any use by him of its property [RUPA § 409(b)(1)].

     (2)   This is also true of a deceased partner's representative engaged in the winding up of partnership affairs.

  4. **Duty to Keep Books and Right of Inspection**

   a.   The partnership books and records must be kept, subject to any agreement between the partners, at the partnership's principal office, and every partner shall, on reasonable notice, have access to and may inspect and copy any of the books and records [RUPA § 408].

   b.   As a fiduciary, the partner who keeps the books is bound to keep them complete and accurate.

D. New Members

  1.   No person can become a member of a partnership without the consent of all partners [RUPA § 401(i)].

  2.   When a new member is admitted to the partnership by consent, the new partner's liability for obligations and torts arising before his joining is only his contribution to the partnership; the new partner is not personally liable for any such charges that arose prior to him joining the partnership.

E. Suits between Partners

  1.   A partner may maintain an action against another partner or the partnership, with or without an accounting as to the partnership business, to enforce the partner's rights under the partnership agreement, under the RUPA, and any other rights otherwise protectable, whether or not arising under the partnership relationship [RUPA § 4010(b)].

IV. PARTNERSHIP PROPERTY

A. Partnership Property

1. **Property Originally Brought In**

    a. All property originally brought into the partnership stock on account of the partnership is partnership property.

    b. Any property—cash, contributions in kind, goods, labor, or skill—brought into the business at its formation is the **capital** of the partnership.

2. **Property Subsequently Acquired**

    a. Unless a **contrary intention** appears, all property subsequently acquired by purchase or otherwise on account of the partnership is property of the partnership and not that of the partners individually [RUPA § 203].

3. **Property Purchased with Partnership Funds**

    a. Unless a contrary intention appears, property purchased with partnership assets belongs to the partnership, even if not acquired in the name of the partnership, or of one or more partners with an indication (in the instrument transferring title to the property) of the person's capacity as a partner or of the existence of a partnership [RUPA § 204(c)].

    b. Any receivables, judgments obtained, contracts, or profits are partnership property.

    c. Factors considered in establishing a contrary intention are:

        (1) the terms of the partnership agreement or any other relevant express or implied agreement;

        (2) the partnership's records;

        (3) the payment of taxes, repair bills, or insurance premiums;

        (4) the conduct of the partners;

        (5) whether the property was used or improved by the business; and

        (6) how title to the property was held.

    d. As a corollary to this, it is presumed that property acquired in the name of one or more of the partners, without an indication of the person's status as a partner and without use of partnership funds, is separate property, even if used for partnership purposes [RUPA § 204(d)].

4. **Real Property**

    a. Any estate in real property may be acquired in the partnership name.

    b. This is a departure from common law, which did not allow real estate to be held in a partnership name.

    c. However, the RUPA does not require that title be taken in the partnership name.

        (1) Again, if property is acquired with partnership funds, it is presumed to be partnership property even if held in one partner's name.

B. Conveyance of Real Property

1. Title in Name of Partnership

a. If title to real property is in the partnership name, any partner may convey title by a conveyance executed in the partnership name [RUPA § 302].

2. Title in Name of One or More Partners

a. If title to real property is in the name of one or more of the partners, with an indication of their capacity as partners or of the existence of the partnership, but the record does not disclose the name of the partnership, the partners in whose name the title stands may convey title to the property.

3. Title in Name of Third Persons

a. If title is in the name of one or more third persons (e.g., in trust for the partnership), without an indication (in the instrument transferring the property to the third person) of their capacity or of the existence of a partnership, the property may be transferred by an instrument of transfer executed by the persons in whose name the property is held.

4. Partners' Interests Held by Third Person

a. If a person holds all of the partners' interests in the partnership, all of the partnership property vests in that person. The person may execute a document in the name of the partnership to evidence vesting of the property in him, and he may file or record the document.

5. Recovery of Partnership Property Improperly Conveyed

a. A partnership may recover partnership property from a transferee only if it proves that execution of the instrument of initial transfer did not bind the partnership, and:

(1) as to a subsequent transferee who gave value for property transferred under RUPA Section 302(a)(1) or 302(a)(2), the partnership proves that the subsequent transferee knew or had received notification that the person who executed the instrument of initial transfer lacked authority to bind the partnership; or

(2) as to a transferee who gave value for property transferred under RUPA Section 302(a)(3), the partnership proves that the transferee knew or had received notification that the property was partnership property, and that the person who executed the instrument of initial transfer lacked authority to bind the partnership.

b. A partnership may not recover partnership property from a subsequent transferee if the partnership would not have been entitled to recover the property, under these provisions, from any earlier transferee of the property.

V. DISSOCIATION, DISSOLUTION, AND WINDING UP

A. Dissociation

1. Dissociation is the withdrawal of a partner from the partnership.

   a. Older versions of the RUPA did not contain the concept of dissociation and merely used the term dissolution to denote a change in the relationship caused by a partner's ceasing to be associated in carrying on of the business.

2. **Events of Dissociation**

   a. A partner is dissociated from a partnership upon the occurrence of any of the following [RUPA § 601]:

      (1) the partnership having notice of the partner's express intention to withdraw as a partner;

      (2) an event delineated in the partnership agreement as causing the partner's dissociation;

      (3) the partner's expulsion pursuant to the partnership agreement;

         (a) The partnership agreement may provide for expulsion of a partner either automatically or by a designated vote; no power of expulsion exists if not expressly given in the agreement.

         (b) The power must be exercised in accordance with the agreement's terms and in good faith.

      (4) the partner's expulsion by a unanimous vote of the other partners, if, among other things:

         (a) it is unlawful to carry on the partnership business with such partner;

         (b) a partner transfers all, or substantially all, of his transferable interest other than a transfer of security—*e.g.*, for collateral purposes—or a court order charging the partner's interest that has not been foreclosed;

         (c) within 90 days after the partnership notifies a corporate partner that it will be expelled because it has filed a certificate of dissolution or equivalent, the corporate partner's charter has been revoked, or its right to conduct business has been suspended by the jurisdiction of its incorporation, there is no revocation of the certificate of dissolution or no reinstatement of its charter or right to conduct business; or

         (d) a partnership that is a partner has been dissolved and its business wound up;

      (5) a judicial determination, after application to the court by the partnership or another partner because:

         (a) the partner engaged in wrongful conduct that adversely and materially affected the partnership business;

         (b) the partner willfully or persistently committed a material breach of the partnership agreement or of a duty owed to the partnership or other partners; or

(c) the partner engaged in conduct relating to partnership business that makes it impracticable to reasonably carry on the business in partnership with the partner;

(6) the partner's bankruptcy or other financial insolvency;

(7) the partner's incapacity or death;

(8) in the case of a partner that is a trust or trustee, the distribution of the trust's entire transferable interest in the partnership;

(9) in the case of a partner that is an estate or representative of an estate, distribution of the entire transferable interest in the partnership; or

(10) the termination of a partner who is not an individual, partnership, corporation, trust, or estate.

3. **Power to Dissociate**

a. A partner has the power to dissociate at any time, rightfully or wrongfully, by expressly stating the intention to do so [RUPA § 602].

4. **Wrongful Dissociation**

a. In the event of a willful dissociation, a partner's action is wrongful only if [Id.]:

(1) it is in breach of an express provision of the partnership agreement; or

(2) in the case of a partnership for a definite term or particular undertaking, it occurs before the expiration of the term or the completion of the undertaking by virtue of:

(a) a partner's express will to withdraw, unless the withdrawal follows within 90 days after another partner's dissociation by death, bankruptcy, or insolvency, incapacity, distribution by a trust or estate that is a partner of such trust or estate's entire transferable interest in the partnership, or termination of a partner who is not an individual, partnership, corporation, trust, or estate;

(b) the partner's expulsion following judicial determination;

(c) the partner's dissociation by becoming a debtor in bankruptcy; or

(d) in the case of a partner who is not an individual, trust, or estate, the partner is expelled or otherwise dissociated because the partnership willfully dissolved or terminated.

b. A partner who wrongfully dissociates is liable to the partnership and the other partners for damages caused by the dissociation. This liability is in addition to any other obligation the partner has to the partnership or to the other partners.

5. **Effect of Dissociation on Rights and Duties of Dissociating Partner**

a. Upon a partner's dissociation, that partner's [RUPA § 603]:

(1) right to participate in the management and conduct of the partnership business terminates;

(2) duty of loyalty for future events terminates; and

(3) duty of loyalty and duty of care continue only with regard to matters that arose before the partner's dissociation.

b. Under older versions of the RUPA, the withdrawal of a partner resulted in dissolution of the partnership.

6. **Buyout of Dissociating Partner's Share of Partnership**

   a. If a partner is dissociated from a partnership without a dissolution and winding up of the partnership business, the partnership shall cause the dissociated partner's interest in the partnership to be purchased for a buyout price [RUPA § 701].

      (1) The buyout price for a dissociated partner's share of the partnership must be equal to the greater of either of the following amounts, plus interest from the date of dissociation to the date of payment:

         (a) the liquidation value of the partnership's assets; or

         (b) the value of the partnership's assets based on a sale of the entire business as a going concern without the dissociating partner's participation as if the partnership were wound up as of such date.

      (2) Damages for wrongful dissociation and all other amounts owed by the dissociating partner, whether or not currently due to the partnership, must be offset against the buyout price. Interest must be paid from the date the amount owed becomes due to the date of payment [RUPA § 701(c)].

      (3) A partner whose interest is being purchased must be indemnified by the partnership against all partnership liabilities, except liabilities incurred by an act of the dissociated partner following dissociation [RUPA § 701(d)].

      (4) A partner who wrongfully dissociates before the expiration of a definite term or the completion of a particular undertaking is not entitled to payment of any portion of the buyout price until the expiration of the original term or the completion of the undertaking originally agreed upon, unless the dissociating partner establishes to the satisfaction of the court that an earlier payment will not cause undue hardship to the business of the partnership. Any deferred payment must be secured and will bear interest [RUPA § 701(h)].

      (5) If no agreement for the purchase of a dissociated partner's interest is reached within 120 days after a written demand for payment, the partnership must pay, or cause to be paid, in cash to the dissociated partner the amount the partnership estimates to be the buyout price plus accrued interest, reduced by any offsets and accrued interest [RUPA § 701(e)].

      (6) If a deferred payment is authorized, the partnership may tender a written offer to pay the amount it estimates to be the buyout price plus accrued interest, reduced by any offsets as above, stating the time of payment, the amount, the type of security for payment, and the other terms and conditions of the obligation [RUPA § 701(f)].

7. **Dissociated Partner's Power to Bind Partnership**

   a. For two years after a partner dissociates without resulting in a dissolution and winding up of the partnership business, the partnership is bound by an act of the dissociated partner that would have bound the partnership before dissociation only if, at the time of entering into the transaction, the other party [RUPA § 702]:

    (1)   reasonably believed that the dissociated partner was then a partner; and

    (2)   is deemed not to have knowledge or notice of the dissociation.

  b.   If the partnership becomes liable for any obligation that the dissociated partner incurs after dissociation, then the dissociated partner will be liable to the partnership for such damages [RUPA § 702(b)].

    EXAMPLE: A partnership has an open account with a vendor. An ex-partner orders inventory, and the vendor has no reason to believe that the ex-partner has exited the partnership.

8.   **Continuing Obligations of Dissociating Partner**

  a.   A partner's dissociation does not by itself discharge the partner's liability for partnership obligations incurred before dissociation. A dissociated partner is not liable, however, for a partnership obligation incurred after dissociation [RUPA § 703(a)].

  b.   A partner who dissociates without resulting in a dissolution and winding up of the partnership business is liable to the other party in a transaction entered into by the partnership or surviving partnership within two years after the partner's dissociation, but only if the partner would have otherwise been liable for the obligation had he remained a partner and, at the time of the transaction, the other party [RUPA § 703(b)]:

    (1)   reasonably believed that the dissociated partner was then a partner;

    (2)   did not have notice of the partner's dissociation; and

    (3)   is not deemed to have had knowledge of the dissociation by virtue of a statement of authority or statement of dissociation.

    EXAMPLE: Trump has exited the TUV Partnership. A vendor continues filling TUV's orders under the impression that Trump remains liable if TUV does not pay.

  c.   The partners continuing the business may agree with the partnership's creditors to release the dissociated partner from liability [RUPA § 703(c)].

  d.   If a creditor has notice of a partner's dissociation and, without the dissociating partner's consent, agrees to a material alteration of the nature or time of payment of a partnership obligation, the dissociated partner will be released from liability for that obligation [RUPA § 703(d)].

9.   **Termination of Dissociating Partner's Ability to Bind Partnership**

  a.   A dissociated partner, or the partnership, may file a statement of dissociation with the Department of State stating [RUPA § 704]:

    (1)   the name of the partnership; and

    (2)   that the partner is dissociated from the partnership.

  b.   A person who is not a partner is deemed to have notice of the dissociation 90 days after a statement of dissociation has been filed [RUPA § 704].

c. The continued use of a dissociated partner's name in the ongoing partnership business does not by itself make the dissociated partner liable for future obligations of the partnership occurring after the date of dissociation [RUPA § 705].

B. Dissolution, Winding Up, and Termination—Terminology

1. **Dissolution** is the commencement of the winding up process.
2. **Winding up** is the process of settling partnership affairs.
3. **Termination** is the point at which all the partnership affairs are wound up.

C. Dissolution

1. **Causes of Dissolution**

   a. **Mandatory Dissolution**

      (1) A partnership is dissolved and its business must be wound up upon the occurrence of any of the following events [RUPA § 801]:

      (a) in a partnership at will, the partnership receives notice from a partner (other than a partner who is dissociated by any means other than by the partner's express will to withdraw) of that partner's express will to withdraw as a partner;

      (b) in a partnership for a definite term or particular undertaking:

      EXAMPLE: A partnership is formed based on an agreement to continue until its lease term expires, or until all of the lots that the partnership is developing are sold, or, if an agreement states that all obligations would be paid from profits, until the profits are sufficient to pay the debts.

      1) within 90 days after a partner's dissociation by death, bankruptcy or insolvency, incapacity, distribution of all of a trust or estate that is a partner of such trust or estate's entire transferable interest in the partnership, or termination of a partner that is not an individual, partnership, corporation, trust, or estate, it is the express will of at least half of the remaining partners to wind up the partnership business; or

      2) the expiration of the term or completion of the undertaking;

      (c) an event agreed to in the partnership agreement resulting in the winding up of the partnership; or

      (d) an event that makes it unlawful for all, or substantially all, of the business of the partnership to be continued, except when there is a cure of illegality within 90 days after notice of the event to the partnership, which is effective retroactively to the date of the event for purposes of this section.

      EXAMPLE: If partners are residents of different nations that go to war with one another, commercial relations would be illegal and the partnership would be dissolved.

b. **Permissive Dissolution**

(1) A partnership can be dissolved at any time by unanimous consent, regardless of any duration specified in the partnership agreement [RUPA § 801(2)(ii)].

(2) A partnership can also be dissolved:

(a) on application by a partner, by a judicial determination stating that [RUPA § 801(5)]:

1) the economic purpose of the partnership is likely to be unreasonably frustrated;

2) another partner has engaged in conduct relating to the partnership business that makes it not reasonably practicable to carry on business in partnership with that partner; or

3) it is not otherwise reasonably practicable to carry on the partnership business in conformity with the partnership agreement; or

(b) on application by a transferee of a partner's transferable interest, by a judicial determination stating that it is equitable to wind up the partnership business [RUPA § 801(6)]:

1) after the expiration of the term of completion of the undertaking, if the partnership was for a definite term or particular undertaking at the time of the transfer or entry of the charging order that gave rise to the transfer; or

2) at any time, if the partnership was a partnership at will at the time of the transfer or entry of the charging order that gave rise to the transfer.

2. **Continuance after Dissolution**

a. A partnership continues after dissolution only for the purpose of winding up the business. The partnership is terminated when the winding up of its business is complete [RUPA § 802(a)].

b. Following dissolution and before winding up, all the partners, including any dissociating partner (except those that have wrongfully dissociated), may waive the right to have the partnership's business wound up and the partnership terminated [RUPA § 802(b)].

c. Upon a decision to waive the right to wind up the business and terminate the partnership [Id.]:

(1) the partnership resumes carrying on its business as if dissolution had never occurred, and any liability incurred by the partnership or a partner after dissolution and before the waiver is determined as if dissolution had never occurred; and

(2) the rights of a third party accruing by virtue of a partner's act to bind the partnership after dissolution, or arising out of conduct in reliance on the dissolution before the third party knew or received notice of the waiver, will not be adversely affected.

3. **Effect of Dissolution on Authority of Partner**
   a. **As to Third Parties**
      (1) A partnership is bound by a partner's act after dissolution that [RUPA § 804]:
         (a) is appropriate for winding up the partnership business; or
         (b) would have bound the partnership before dissolution, if the other party did not have notice of the dissolution.
      (2) The RUPA allows a partner who has not wrongfully dissociated to file a statement of dissolution with the appropriate state agency stating the name of the partnership and that the partnership has dissolved and is winding up its business [RUPA § 805(a)].
         (a) Such a filing cancels any statement of authority previously filed [RUPA § 805(b)].
      (3) A person not a partner is deemed to have notice of the dissolution and limitation on the partners' authority 90 days after the statement of dissolution has been filed [RUPA § 805(c)].
   b. **As to Co-Partners**
      (1) After dissolution, a partner is liable to the other partners for his share of any partnership liability incurred following dissolution [RUPA § 806(a)].
      (2) A partner who knows of the dissolution, and incurs a partnership liability by an act that is not appropriate for winding up the partnership business, is liable to the partnership for any damage caused to the partnership arising from the liability [RUPA § 806(b)].

D. **Winding Up**
   1. **Right to Wind Up**
      a. Generally, all the partners who have not wrongfully dissociated may participate in winding up the partnership's affairs [RUPA § 803(a)].
      b. The legal representative of the last surviving partner ultimately has the right to wind up [RUPA § 803(b)].
      c. Any partner, his legal representative, or his assignee, upon cause shown, may seek from a court judicial supervision of the winding up [RUPA § 803(a)].
   2. **Powers and Duties in Winding Up**
      a. A partner winding up a partnership may [RUPA § 803(c)]:
         (1) preserve the partnership business or property as a going concern for a reasonable time;
         (2) prosecute and defend actions and proceedings (whether civil, criminal, or administrative);
         (3) settle and close the partnership's business;
         (4) dispose of and transfer the partnership's property;
         (5) discharge the partnership's liabilities;

(6)   distribute the assets of the partnership;

(7)   settle disputes by mediation or arbitration; and

(8)   perform other necessary acts.

> **EXAMPLE:** A cake bakery, in winding up, can fill all orders, sell inventory and equipment, collect amounts due, and pay amounts due, but cannot take on new business.

E.   Distribution of Assets

1.   Order of Distribution

a.   In winding up the business, the assets of the partnership (including any contributions from the partners necessary to pay partnership obligations to creditors and to partners) must be applied in the following manner [RUPA § 807(a)]:

(1)   the assets must first be applied to discharge obligations owing to creditors, including, to the extent permitted by law, partners who are creditors; and

(2)   any surplus must be applied to pay in cash the net amount distributable to partners in accordance with their distribution rights [RUPA § 807].

(a)   Under prior versions of the RUPA, a distinction was made between inside and outside creditors. The assets were distributed to repay liabilities in the following order:

1)   to creditors other than partners;

2)   to partners who are creditors;

3)   to partners in respect of capital; and

4)   to partners in respect of profits.

b.   Although partners may vary these rules by agreement, they cannot change the creditors' priorities or their own liabilities to the partnership's creditors.

2.   Settlement of Accounts

a.   Each partner is entitled to a settlement of all partnership accounts upon winding up the partnership business [RUPA § 807(b)].

b.   Profits and losses that result from the liquidation of the partnership assets must be credited and charged to the partners' accounts, and the partnership must then make a distribution to each partner in an amount equal to the excess of the credits over the charges in such partner's account [Id.].

c.   A partner must contribute to the partnership any excess of charges over the credits in the partner's account (excluding charges attributable to obligations for which the partner is not personally liable) [Id.].

3.   Contribution

a.   Liabilities are satisfied first out of partnership property; if this is insufficient, the partners must contribute the amount necessary to satisfy the liabilities.

b. If a partner fails to contribute the full amount required, all of the other partners must contribute the additional amount necessary to satisfy the partnership obligations for which they are personally liable [RUPA 807(c)].

(1) Such contributions must be made in the same proportion as those in which the partners share partnership losses [Id.].

c. Any partner who pays more than his share can recover his contribution from the other partners to the extent that the amount exceeds his share [Id.].

d. The estate of a deceased partner is liable for the partner's obligation to contribute to the partnership [RUPA § 807(e)].

e. Following settlement, a partner must contribute (again, in proportion to the amount in which partners share partnership losses) an amount necessary to satisfy partnership obligations that were not known at the time of settlement and for which the partner is personally liable [RUPA § 807(d)].

VI. LIMITED LIABILITY PARTNERSHIPS

A. In General

1. A **limited liability partnership** ("LLP") is a general partnership that is authorized by a state statute and complies therewith to adopt limited liability for its general partners.

2. When a general partnership registers as an LLP, all the partners gain protection from liability for obligations of the partnership and of other partners, although they remain liable for their own negligence and the negligence of those they supervise.

> **NOTE** ▶ In other words, LLPs are general partnerships for all purposes except liability.

B. Formation

1. The name of a registered limited liability partnership must contain the words "Registered Limited Liability Partnership" or "Limited Liability Partnership," or the abbreviations "L.L.P.," "LLP," "R.L.L.P.," or "RLLP."

   EXAMPLE: The law firm of Proctor & Peters must refer to itself as Proctor & Peters LLP in all communications. If it does not, it may lose the liability shield.

2. In order to become a limited liability partnership, a partnership (other than a general partnership) must file a registration with the secretary of state executed by one or more partners and including the name of the partnership, the address of its principal office, the name and address of an agent for service of process, a brief statement of the business in which the partnership engages, and any other relevant information. A fee must also be paid.

   a. While a general partnership can become an LLP, limited partnerships cannot (although they can become an LLLP).

3. The filed statement provides notice that the partnership is a registered limited liability partnership.

4. A general partnership may convert to a registered limited liability partnership by a vote of the partners with a majority of the interests in the current profits of the general partnership. Upon conversion, the debts, obligations, liabilities, and penalties of the general partnership continue as the debts, obligations, liabilities, and penalties of the LLP.

C. Rights, Duties, and Obligations of Partners

1. Partners in an LLP have the same fiduciary duties as partners in a general partnership.

D. Liabilities

1. Partners in an LLP are not personally liable for the obligations of the LLP, whether arising from tort, contract, or otherwise, and are personally liable only for their own wrongful acts.

2. An LLP must ensure that it can meet its obligations for any liability taken on by providing security on any claims against it. Although stated separately for acts, errors, or omissions arising from the practice of accountancy, law, or architecture, an LLP must do one or more of the following:

a. provide insurance;

b. maintain an escrow account or similar interests as security for payment of liabilities;

c. have each partner guarantee payments; or

d. confirm that the LLP's net worth is above a specified amount.

3. A new partner is not personally liable for LLP obligations incurred before the person's admission as a partner.

E. Distributions

1. An LLP may not make a distribution if, after the distribution, it would not be able to pay its debts, or if the LLP's total assets would be less than the sum of its total liabilities and the amount the LLP would need if it were dissolved to satisfy superior rights of certain partners.

F. Dissolution

1. Dissolution of an LLP occurs in the same manner as for general partnerships under the RUPA.

NOTE ▶ Do not confuse an LLP with a limited partnership.

VII. LIMITED PARTNERSHIPS

A. In General

1. There are several versions of the Uniform Limited Partnership Act. The following section is based on the rules under the Uniform Limited Partnership Act of 2001 ("ULPA"). Some references will be made to the 1916 version ("1916 Act"), 1976 version ("1976 Act"), and 1976 version with amendments in 1985 ("1985 Act"). Most states still follow the 1976 Act or 1985 Act. Approximately 13 states have adopted the 2001 version so far.

B. Creation of Limited Partnerships

1. A **limited partnership** consists of:

   a. **general partners**, who manage the business and are personally liable without limitation for partnership obligations; and

   b. **limited partners**, who contribute capital and share in profits, but take no part in the control or management of the business, and whose liability is limited to their contributions.

2. A limited partnership must have at least one general partner and at least one limited partner.

3. A limited partnership's principal advantages are that it provides limited liability for the limited partners (as in a corporation) and direct deduction of expenses or losses against their other income by all partners (as in a general partnership).

4. **Formation**

   a. A limited partnership is formed by filing with the secretary of state a certificate of limited partnership, which must state [ULPA § 201]:

      (1) the name of the limited partnership;

      (2) the address of the designated office and name and address of the initial agent for service of process;

      (3) the name and address of each general partner;

      (4) whether the limited partnership is a limited liability limited partnership; and

      (5) any additional information otherwise required upon merger or conversion.

   b. The certificate of limited partnership must be signed by all general partners listed in the certificate [ULPA § 204(a)].

   c. Only the general partners have a duty to amend the certificate and have potential liability for false statements on which a third party relies [ULPA §§ 202, 208].

   d. The name of a limited partnership must contain the words "limited partnership" or the abbreviations "LP" or "L.P."

5. **Limited Liability Limited Partnerships**

   a. A limited liability limited partnership ("LLLP") is limited partnership whose certificate of limited partnership states that it is a limited liability limited partnership. In an LLLP, general partners, as well as limited partners, have limited liability.

    b.   The name of an LLLP must contain the words "limited liability limited partnership" or the abbreviations "LLLP" or "L.L.L.P." [ULPA § 108(c)].

C. Doing Business

1. A limited partnership may carry on any business that a general partnership is allowed to carry on—i.e., for any lawful purpose [ULPA § 104].

2. A limited partnership must continuously maintain an office and a resident agent for the service of process in the state where it is organized [ULPA § 114].

3. The limited partnership must maintain and make available for inspection and copying by any partner during business hours [ULPA § 111]:

    a.   a current list of the names and addresses of all partners;

    b.   copies of the certificate of limited partnership and the partnership agreement with any amendments thereto; and

    c.   copies of all income tax returns and financial statements for the immediately preceding three years.

4. Except as provided in the partnership agreement, a partner may lend money to and transact other business with the limited partnership, and has the same rights as a general creditor in the case of an unsecured loan [ULPA § 112].

D. Contributions

1. Under the ULPA, a limited partner may contribute cash, property, services, or a promissory note [ULPA § 501].

    a.   Under the original 1916 Act, a limited partner was not allowed to contribute services [1916 Act § 4].

2. A partner's obligation to contribute is not excused by the partner's death, disability, or other inability to perform personally [ULPA § 502(a)].

3. If the partner fails to contribute property or services, he must pay the cash value of property or services at the option of the partnership, unless the partnership certificate provides otherwise [ULPA § 502(b)].

    a.   The obligation of a partner to make a contribution (or to return money or other property paid or distributed in violation of the ULPA) may be compromised only by consent of all partners [ULPA § 502(c)].

    b.   However, a creditor of a limited partnership that extends credit or otherwise acts in reliance on an obligation by a partner to make a contribution, without notice of any compromise by all partners, may enforce the original obligation [ULPA § 502(c)].

E. Disclosure Requirements

1. Due to the different rights, liabilities, and powers conferred upon general and limited partners within a limited partnership, certain disclosure requirements are necessary to allow for the identification and differentiation of such parties.

2. As noted above, a limited partnership must be formed specifically as such by filing a certificate with the secretary of state to indicate level of membership and limitations of liability.

3. Such documentation must then be made available to the public for inspection.

F. Limited Partners

    1. **Liabilities and Limitations**

        a. **Use of Limited Partner's Name**

            (1) The name of the limited partnership may contain the name of any partner [ULPA § 108(a)].

                (a) Under pre-2001 versions of the ULPA, the use of a limited partner's name was a prohibited use except in unusual circumstances, and a limited partner who knowingly permitted his name to be used was liable to creditors who extended credit to the partnership without actual knowledge that the limited partner was not a general partner.

        b. **Control of Business**

            (1) A limited partner is not personally liable for partnership obligations beyond his contribution solely by reason of being a limited partner, even if he participates in the management and control of the limited partnership [ULPA § 303].

                (a) Under pre-2001 versions of the ULPA, a limited partner could become personally liable for partnership obligations if he participated in the control of the business.

                    1) In the 1916 version, what constituted control was not defined.

                    2) The 1976, and later the 1985, versions of the ULPA added a safe harbor list of activities that did not constitute participating in control and limited liability to those who reasonably believed the limited partner was a general partner.

        c. **Mistaken Status**

            (1) A person who erroneously, but in good faith, believes himself to be a limited partner is not liable as a general partner if, on learning of his mistake, he [ULPA § 306(a)]:

                (a) causes an amended certificate of limited partnership to be executed and filed; and

                (b) withdraws from future participation as an owner in the enterprise.

            (2) He is liable as a general partner, however, to any third party who has transacted business with the enterprise prior to his withdrawal and filing of the amendment, if the third party believed in good faith that he was a general partner [ULPA § 306(b)].

    2. **Judicial Proceedings**

        a. A limited partner is a proper party to proceedings by or against a limited partnership only if the object is to enforce his right or liability.

      b.   The creditors of a limited partner may obtain a charging order against his interest, and to the extent of the charge will have only the rights of a transferee of the partnership interest [ULPA § 703].

   3. **Rights and Powers**

      a. **Control of Limited Partnership**

         (1) A limited partner does not have the right or power to act for or bind the limited partnership [ULPA § 302].

      b. **Right to Information**

         (1) A limited partner has the right to inspect and copy the required partnership records and tax returns, and to obtain from the general partners true and full information as to the financial condition and state of the business of the partnership, and such other information as is just and reasonable, if the limited partner seeks the information for a purpose reasonably related to the partner's interest as a limited partner [ULPA § 304].

      c. **New Limited Partners**

         (1) A person becomes a limited partner [ULPA § 301]:

            (a) as provided in the partnership agreement;

            (b) as the result of a conversion or merger; or

            (c) with the consent of all the partners.

   4. **Fiduciary Duties**

      a. A limited partner does not have any fiduciary duty to the limited partnership, or to any partner, solely because he is a limited partner [ULPA § 305(a)].

      b. A limited partner must discharge the duties of the partnership and the other partners under the ULPA and under the partnership agreement, and exercise any rights consistent with the obligation of good faith and fair dealing [ULPA § 305(b)].

         (1) This obligation is not violated merely because the limited partner's conduct furthers his own interest [ULPA § 305(c)].

G. General Partners

   1. A general partner in a limited partnership has most of the same rights and powers, and is subject to the same restrictions and liabilities, as a partner in a general partnership.

   2. A person becomes a general partner [ULPA § 401]:

      a. as provided in the partnership agreement;

      b. by the consent of the limited partners following the dissociation of a limited partnership's last general partner in order to prevent dissolution of the partnership;

      c. as a result of a conversion or merger; or

      d. with the consent of all the partners.

   3. A person may be both a general partner and a limited partner simultaneously, with the rights, powers, and restrictions of a general partner, but, with respect to his contribution, the rights of a limited partner [ULPA § 113].

4. Each general manager has equal rights in the management and conduct of the limited partnership's activities, and any matter relating to the limited partnership's activities may be decided by a majority of the general partners [ULPA § 406(a)].

5. The consent of all partners is required to [ULPA § 406(b)]:

   a. amend the partnership agreement;

   b. amend the certificate of limited partnership (including adding or deleting a statement that the limited partnership is an LLLP); and

   c. sell, lease, exchange, or otherwise dispose of all, or substantially all, of the limited partnership's property other than in the usual and regular course of the limited partnership's activities.

H. Transfer of Partnership Interests

1. A partnership interest is personal property, and is generally transferable [ULPA §§ 701, 702].

2. A transfer does not dissolve a limited partnership, but a transferee is entitled only to receive the distributions to which his transferor would have been entitled [ULPA §§ 702(a)(2), (a)(3)].

3. A transferee, including a transferee of a general partner, may become a limited partner if, and to the extent that:

   a. the transferor gives him that right in accordance with the certificate; or

   b. absent such authority, all other partners consent.

4. A transferee who becomes a limited partner has all the rights and powers, and is subject to all the restrictions and liabilities, of a limited partner, but he is not liable for obligations of his transferor that were unknown to him at the time he became a partner and that could not have been ascertained from the certificate [ULPA § 702(g)].

5. A transferor is not released from liability for any knowing false statement in the certificate, or from liability for promised contributions [ULPA § 702(d)].

6. **Executors, Administrators, and Creditors**

   a. The legal representative of a deceased or incompetent partner may exercise all of that partner's rights, including the power to make a transferee a limited partner [ULPA § 704].

   b. A judgment creditor of a partner can obtain a charging order against a partner's interest, and to that extent will be a transferee of the interest [ULPA § 703].

I. Distributions and Dissociation

1. **Distributions**

   a. Distributions of assets are allocated among the parties on the basis of the value of each partner's contribution [ULPA § 503].

   b. A partner does not have a right to any distribution before the dissolution and winding up of the limited partnership unless the limited partnership decides to make an interim distribution [ULPA § 504].

    c.   A partner has no right to receive a distribution upon dissociation [ULPA § 505].

    d.   Regardless of the nature of his contribution, a partner has no right to receive his distribution in any form other than cash [ULPA § 506].

    e.   A partner entitled to receive a distribution has the status of a creditor of the limited partnership [ULPA § 507].

    f.   A partner may not receive a distribution if, after the distribution [ULPA § 508]:

       (1)   the limited partnership would not be able to pay its debts as they become due in the ordinary course of the limited partnership's activities; or

       (2)   the limited partnership's total assets would be less than the sum of its total liabilities plus the amount needed if the limited partnership were dissolved, wound up, and terminated at the time of the distribution, to satisfy, the preferential rights upon dissolution, winding up, and termination of partners whose rights are superior to those of persons receiving the distribution.

    g.   A general partner who consents to an improper distribution is personally liable to the limited partnership for the amount of the distribution that exceeds the amount that could have been distributed without the violation if in doing so he breached his duties of care and loyalty [ULPA § 509].

2. Dissociation

a. Dissociation of Limited Partner

       (1)   A person does not have a right to dissociate as a limited partner before the termination of the limited partnership [ULPA § 601(a)].

          (a)   In prior versions of the ULPA, a limited partner was permitted to withdraw upon not less than six months' prior written notice.

       (2)   A person is dissociated from a limited partnership as a limited partner upon the occurrence of any of the following [ULPA § 601(b)]:

          (a)   notice of the person's express will to withdraw as a limited partner, or upon a later date specified by that partner;

          (b)   an event agreed to in the partnership agreement;

          (c)   the person's expulsion as a limited partner pursuant to the partnership agreement;

          (d)   the person's expulsion as a limited partner by unanimous consent of the other partners if:

             1)   it is unlawful to carry on the limited partnership's activities with the person as a limited partner;

             2)   there has been a transfer of all of the person's transferable interest in the limited partnership, or a court order charging the person's interest;

             3)   the limited partner is a corporation and is subject to dissolution, suspension of its right to do business, and revocation of its charter, if not cured within 90 days of the event; or

        4)   the limited partner is a limited liability company or partnership that has been dissolved or its business wound up;

   (e) upon application of the limited partnership, the person's expulsion as a limited partner by judicial order because:

        1)   the person engaged in wrongful conduct that adversely and materially affected the limited partnership's activities;

        2)   the person willfully or persistently committed a material breach of the partnership agreement or of the obligation of good faith and fair dealing; or

        3)   the person engaged in conduct relating to the limited partnership's activities that makes it not reasonably practicable to carry on activities with that person as limited partner;

   (f) the person's death;

   (g) if the person is a trust or trustee, or an estate or representative of an estate, distribution of the trust or estate's transferable interest;

   (h) termination of a limited partner that is not an individual, partnership, limited liability company, corporation, trust, or estate; or

   (i) the limited partnership's participation in a conversion or merger if the limited partnership:

        1)   is not the converted or surviving entity; or

        2)   is the converted or surviving entity but, as a result of the conversion or merger, the person ceases to be a limited partner.

  (3) **Effect of Dissociation**

   (a) Upon dissociation, the limited partner has no further rights in the limited partnership, but dissociation as a limited partner does not in itself discharge the person from any obligation to the limited partnership or to the other partners that the person incurred while a limited partner [ULPA § 602].

   (b) The dissociated limited partner's obligation of good faith and fair dealing as a limited partner continues only as to matters arising and events occurring before dissociation [ULPA § 602(a)(2)].

  b. **Dissociation of General Partner**

  (1) A person is dissociated as a general partner upon the occurrence of any of the following events, most of which are the same as for the dissociation of a limited partner [ULPA § 603]:

   (a) notice of the person's express will to withdraw as a general partner, or on a later date specified by that partner;

   (b) an event agreed to in the partnership agreement;

   (c) the person's expulsion as a general partner pursuant to the partnership agreement;

    (d)   the person's expulsion as a general partner by unanimous consent of the other partners if:

       1)   it is unlawful to carry on the limited partnership's activities with the person as a general partner;

       2)   there has been a transfer of all of the person's transferable interest in the limited partnership or a court order charging the person's interest;

       3)   the person is a corporation and is subject to dissolution, suspension of its right to do business, and revocation of its charter, if not cured within 90 days of the event; or

       4)   the general partner is a limited liability company or partnership that has been dissolved or its business wound up;

    (e)   upon the application of the limited partnership, the person's expulsion as a general partner by judicial order because:

       1)   the person engaged in wrongful conduct that adversely and materially affected the limited partnership's activities;

       2)   the person willfully or persistently committed a material breach of the partnership agreement or of the obligation of good faith and fair dealing; or

       3)   the person engaged in conduct relating to the limited partnership's activities that makes it not reasonably practicable to carry on activities with that person as general partner;

    (f)   the person becoming a debtor in bankruptcy, execution of an assignment for the benefit of creditors, seeking, consenting to, or acquiescing in the appointment of a trustee, receiver, or liquidator of the person or of all or substantially all of the person's property, or failure to cure such appointment within 90 days;

    (g)   in the case of an individual, the person's death, the appointment of a guardian or conservator for the person, or a judicial determination that the person has otherwise become incapable of performing his duties as a general partner under the partnership agreement;

    (h)   if the person is a trust or trustee, or an estate or representative of an estate, distribution of the trust or estate's transferable interest;

    (i)   termination of a general partner that is not an individual, partnership, limited liability company, corporation, trust, or estate; or

    (j)   the limited partnership's participation in a conversion or merger if the limited partnership:

       1)   is not the converted or surviving entity; or

       2)   is the converted or surviving entity but, as a result of the conversion or merger, the person ceases to be a general partner.

  (2)   A person may also dissociate as a general partner at any time, rightfully or wrongfully, by express will [ULPA § 604].

        (3) **Wrongful Dissociation**

           (a) A dissociation is wrongful if:

              1) it is in breach of an express provision of the partnership agreement; or

              2) it occurs before the termination of the limited partnership, and:

                  a) the person withdraws as a general partner by express will;

                  b) the person is expelled as a general partner by judicial determination;

                  c) the person is dissociated as a general partner by becoming a debtor in bankruptcy; or

                  d) in the case of a person who is not an individual, trust, or estate, the person is expelled or otherwise dissociated as a general partner because the limited partnership was willfully dissolved or terminated.

        (4) **Effect of Dissociation**

           (a) Upon dissociation, the general partner's right to participate in management and conduct of the partnership's activities terminates, but obligations incurred while a general partner do not necessarily terminate [ULPA § 605].

           (b) A dissociated general partner binds the limited partnership [ULPA § 606(a)]:

              1) by any act that would have bound the limited partnership before dissociation; and

              2) if, at the time of the transaction, less than two years has passed since dissociation, and the other party does not have notice of the dissociation and reasonably believes that the person is a general partner.

           (c) If the dissociated general partner's act binds the limited partnership, the dissociated general partner is liable [ULPA § 606(b)]:

              1) to the limited partnership for any damage caused to the limited partnership as a result of the obligation incurred; and

              2) if a general partner or other person dissociated as a general partner is liable for the obligation, to the general partner or other person for any damage caused to the general partner or other person arising from the liability.

  J. **Dissolution**

    1. **Events of Dissolution**

       a. A limited partnership is dissolved [ULPA § 801]:

          (1) upon the occurrence of the events specified in the certificate; or

(2) upon the written consent of all general partners and limited partners owning a majority of the rights to receive distributions as limited partners at the time the consent is to be effective.

b. Dissolution will also occur automatically after the dissociation of a person as a general partner [Id.]:

(1) if there is at least one remaining general partner, consent to dissolve the limited partnership is given within 90 days after the dissociation by partners owning a majority of distribution rights at the time of consent; or

(2) if there are no remaining general partners, 90 days after the dissociation (unless before the end of the 90-day period):

(a) the limited partners owning a majority of distribution rights as limited partners consent to continue the activities of the limited partnership and admit at least one general partner; and

(b) at least one person is admitted as a general partner.

c. Dissolution will also occur automatically 90 days after the dissociation of the last limited partners, unless the limited partnership admits at least one limited partner before the 90-day period ends [Id.].

d. On application by a partner, a court may decree dissolution whenever it is not reasonably practicable to carry on the business in conformity with the partnership agreement [ULPA § 802].

2. **Power of General Partner to Bind Partnership after Dissolution**

a. A limited partnership is bound by a general partner's act after dissolution that [ULPA § 804]:

(1) is appropriate for winding up the limited partnership's activities; or

(2) would have bound the limited partnership before dissolution if, at the time of the transaction, the other party did not have notice of the dissolution.

K. Winding Up

1. Upon dissolution, the general partners who have not wrongfully dissolved the partnership (or, if none, then the limited partners) may wind up partnership affairs.

2. If it is not reasonably practicable to carry on the activities of the limited partnership in conformity with the partnership agreement, winding up by a court may be obtained [ULPA § 802].

3. A limited partnership continues after dissolution only for the purpose of winding up its activities [ULPA § 803].

4. In winding up, the limited partnership [ULPA § 803(b)]:

a. may amend its certificate of limited partnership to state that it is dissolved, preserve the limited partnership business or property as a going concern for a reasonable time, prosecute and defend actions and proceedings (whether civil, criminal, or administrative), transfer the limited partnership's property, settle disputes by mediation or arbitration, file a statement of termination, and perform other necessary acts; and

    b.   must discharge the limited partnership's liabilities, settle and close the limited partnership's activities, and marshal and distribute the limited partnership's assets.

5.   **Priority of Liabilities upon Dissolution**

    a.   In winding up a limited partnership's activities, the assets of the limited partnership, including contributions required upon winding up, must be applied in the following order [ULPA § 812]:

        (1)   first, the assets must be applied to satisfy obligations to creditors, including partners that are creditors; and

            (a)   Under the 1916 Act, creditors other than partners (outside creditors) had priority over creditors who were partners (inside creditors).

        (2)   second, any surplus remaining must be paid in cash as a distribution.

            (a)   under the 1916 Act, general partners were entitled to distributions only after all liabilities to limited partners had been satisfied [1916 Act § 23].

    b.   If the limited partnership's assets are insufficient to satisfy all of its obligations upon winding up, each person who was a general partner when the obligation was incurred and was not otherwise released from the obligation must contribute to the limited partnership in proportion to his right to receive distribution at the time the obligation was incurred [ULPA § 812(c)(1)].

    c.   If a person does not contribute the amount required, the other general partners required to make a payment must contribute the additional amount needed in proportion to their right to receive distributions at the time the obligation was incurred [ULPA § 812(c)(2)].

Secured Transactions

TABLE OF CONTENTS

I. INTRODUCTION

A. General Principles

1. A **security interest** arises when a party (the **debtor**) uses certain property as collateral to secure repayment of funds to another party (the **secured party**).

2. By using the property as collateral, if the debtor defaults on repayment of the funds, the creditor may take possession of the collateral and apply the collateral to the balance owed.

3. The creditor's interest in the collateral is called a **security interest**.

   EXAMPLE: Alice wants to buy a car but does not have enough money to do so. She gets a loan from Bank to buy the car and gives Bank an interest in the car as collateral. Bank's interest in the car is a security interest. This creates a secured transaction. If Alice defaults on her loan from Bank, Bank can take possession of the car and sell it. Alice is the debtor; Bank is the secured party.

NOTE ▶ Unless otherwise stated, citations in this outline are to the relevant sections of the Uniform Commercial Code.

B. Guarantor

1. A **guarantor** (or **surety**) is a person who promises to pay the obligation of the debtor only if the debtor defaults.

   a. A surety is liable only to the extent of the terms of the surety agreement.

2. A **guaranty** is a promise to answer for the debt, default, or miscarriage of another person.

3. A **continuing guaranty** is a guaranty relating to a future liability of the principal, under successive transactions, which either continues the guarantor's liability or from time to time renews it after it has been satisfied.

4. A guaranty executed contemporaneously with the principal obligations does not require separate consideration; a guaranty not executed contemporaneously with the principal obligation does require separate and distinct consideration.

   a. If a surety makes a promise to perform at the same time that the creditor performs or promises to perform, the creditor's promise will serve as consideration for the surety's promise, because the creditor has incurred a detriment in exchange for the surety's promise.

   b. If a gratuitous surety does not make her promise until after the creditor has performed or made an absolute promise to perform, there is no consideration to support the surety's promise because of the preexisting legal duty rule (the creditor has not incurred any new detriment in exchange for the surety's).

II. APPLICATION OF ARTICLE 9 OF THE UNIFORM COMMERCIAL CODE

A. When Applicable

1. The Code applies to [UCC § 9-109(a)]:

   a. any transaction, regardless of its form, that creates a security interest in personal property or fixtures by contract;

   EXAMPLE: Ben wants to buy a stove for $500 from Ed's Appliance Emporium. Ben and Ed's Appliance Emporium agree that Ben will pay $100 as a down payment and the remaining $400 over six months. Ben will take the stove home, but Ed's Appliance Emporium intends to retain title to the stove. This transaction creates a security interest.

   b. agricultural liens;

   (1) An **agricultural lien** is an interest in farm products that secures payment for goods or services furnished, or rent paid, in connection with a farming operation, created in favor of a person who furnishes such goods in the ordinary course of its business or leased real property to a debtor, and the secured party need not possess the personal property [§ 9-102(a)(5)].

   c. sales of accounts receivable, chattel paper, negotiable instruments, promissory notes, and payment intangibles;

   EXAMPLE: Clothing Manufacturer needs money to manufacture its fall fashion line. To get the money, Clothing Manufacturer sells $1,000,000 worth of payments due from department stores (accounts receivable) to Finance Co. This sale of accounts is governed by Article 9. Finance Co. must comply with Article 9 in order for its rights in the accounts receivable to be recognized by third parties.

   d. consignments; and

   (1) A **consignment** is a transaction in which a person delivers goods to a merchant for the purpose of sale; the merchant deals in goods of that kind; the aggregate value of each delivery is $1,000 or more; the goods are not consumer goods; and the transaction does not create a security interest that secures an obligation [§ 9-102(a)(20)].

   e. certain lease-purchase agreements.

   (1) A transaction creates a security interest, even if called a lease, if the consideration for the right to possession and use of the goods is an obligation for the term of the lease not subject to termination by the lessee, and [§§ 1-201(b)(35), 1-203]:

   (a) the original lease term is equal to or greater than the remaining economic life of the goods;

   (b) the lessee is required to renew the lease for the remaining economic life of the goods or is bound to purchase the goods;

       (c)   the lessee has an option to renew the lease for the remaining economic life of the goods for no (or nominal) additional consideration at the end of the lease; or

       (d)   the lessee has an option to purchase the goods for no (or nominal) additional consideration at the end of the lease.

   (2)   The substance of the transaction controls, not the label given to it by the parties. The retention or reservation of title by a seller of goods notwithstanding shipment or delivery to the buyer under Section 2-401 is limited in effect to a reservation of a "security interest" [UCC 1-201(b)(35)].

B. When Not Applicable

1.   UCC Article 9 is not applicable to [§§ 9-109(c)-(d)]:

   a.   landlord's liens;

   b.   a lien, other than an agricultural lien, given by statute or other rule of law for services or materials;

   c.   assignment of a claim for wages, salary, or other compensation of an employee;

   d.   a sale of accounts, chattel paper, payment intangibles, or promissory notes as part of a sale of the business out of which they arose;

   e.   assignment of accounts, chattel paper, payment intangibles, or promissory notes which is for the purpose of collection only;

   f.   assignment of a right to payment under a contract to an assignee that is also required to perform under the contract;

   g.   assignment of a single account, payment intangible, or promissory note to an assignee in full or partial satisfaction of a preexisting indebtedness;

   h.   a transfer of an interest in, or an assignment of, a claim under an insurance policy, other than with respect to a health insurance receivable owed to a provider;

   i.   assignment of a right represented by a judgment, other than one taken on a right to payment that was collateral;

   j.   a right of recoupment or set-off;

   k.   an interest in or lien on real property, including a lease or rents thereunder;

   l.   assignment of a claim arising in tort, other than a commercial tort claim;

   m.   assignment of a deposit account in a consumer transaction;

   n.   security interests governed by state or foreign law; or

   o.   security interests to the extent preempted by federal law.

III. TYPES OF COLLATERAL

A. **Categories of Collateral**

1. The Code provides for certain broad types of collateral and then breaks each down into more specific categories. The collateral in any given secured transaction must fit into one, and only one, of these categories.

2. Different rules governing enforcement, perfection of the security interest, and priorities often depend upon the category into which the collateral falls.

3. **Goods**

   a. **Goods** include all things that are movable at the time the security interest attaches. This generally includes fixtures and computer programs embedded in goods, if the program is associated with the goods so that it is customarily considered part of the goods or if an owner of the goods has a right to use the program in connection with the goods [§ 9-102(a)(44)].

   b. The term goods does not include accounts, chattel paper, commercial tort claims, deposit accounts, documents, general intangibles, instruments, investment property, letter-of-credit rights, letters of credit, money, a computer program embedded in goods that consist solely of the medium in which the program is embedded, or oil, gas, or other minerals before extraction [Id.].

   c. Goods are further broken down into several categories depending on in what capacity and how the debtor primarily uses them:

      (1) consumer goods;

         (a) **Consumer goods** are those "used or bought for use primarily for personal, family or household purposes" [§ 9-102(a)(23)].

      (2) inventory;

         (a) **Inventory** is goods, other than farm products, that [§ 9-102(a)(48)]:

            1) are leased by a person as lessor;

            2) are held for sale or lease or to be furnished under a contract of service;

            3) are furnished under a contract of service; or

            4) consist of raw materials, work in process, or materials used or consumed in business.

         (b) Inventory includes timber to be cut, because this is excluded from the definition of farm products.

      (3) farm products; and

         (a) **Farm products** generally means "goods, other than standing timber, with respect to which the debtor is engaged in a farming operation," including crops, livestock, products of crops or livestock in their unmanufactured state, aquatic goods produced in aquacultural operations, and supplies used or produced in a farming operation [§ 9-102(a)(34)].

(4) equipment.

    (a) **Equipment** is a catchall category, defined merely as goods "other than inventory, farm products, or consumer goods" [§ 9-102(a)(33)].

        1) This term usually refers to goods that are used or bought for use primarily in a business (e.g., machinery used in farming operations or manufacturing, tools of a mechanic or repairman, delivery trucks).

        2) The fact that the debtor periodically sells and replaces his equipment does not convert it to inventory.

        3) A debtor may use the same goods in more than one capacity, but it is the primary use that determines the characterization.

        EXAMPLE: A washing machine in the debtor's household is consumer goods, in the debtor's appliance store for resale is inventory, and in the debtor's automatic laundry is equipment.

d. In addition to pigeonholing the goods in one of the above categories, it is important to determine if any of the goods are, or will become, fixtures (parts of real estate) or accessions (identifiable parts of larger whole goods). These possibilities arise most often with consumer goods and equipment.

    (1) **Fixtures** are goods that become so related to particular real estate that an interest in those goods arises under real property law [§ 9-102(a)(41)].

        (a) Ordinary building materials (e.g., nails or wood), when incorporated into an improvement on land, are regarded by the Code as inseparable from the structure itself.

        (b) The Article 9 priority rules are inapplicable to this situation, and the secured party must look to other remedies [§ 9-334(a)].

            1) A security interest in fixtures is generally subordinate to a conflicting interest in the related real estate by one other than the debtor [§ 9-334(c)].

    (2) **Accessions** are goods that are physically united with other goods in such a manner that the identity of the original goods is not lost [§ 9-102(a)(1)].

        (a) A security interest may be created in an accession and continues in collateral which becomes an accession.

        (b) If a security interest is perfected when the collateral becomes an accession, the security interest remains perfected [§ 9-335(b)].

e. **Commingled goods** are goods that are physically united with other goods in such a way that their identity is lost in a product or mass [§ 9-336(a)]. The term includes goods whose identity is lost through manufacturing or production (e.g., flour that has become part of baked goods) and through mere mixing with other goods from which they cannot be distinguished (e.g., ball bearings).

(1) A security interest does not exist in specific goods that have become commingled [§ 9-336(b)].

(2) However, a security interest may attach to a product or mass that results when goods become commingled [Id.].

(3) If a security interest in collateral is perfected before the collateral becomes commingled goods, the security interest that attaches to the commingled product or mass is perfected [§ 9-336(d)].

4. **Tangible Intangibles**

a. Certain intangibles, such as contractual obligations to hold or deliver goods or to pay money, and ownership in goods or business entities, are commonly reduced to tangible or written form. The intangibles are transferred by transferring the writing.

b. Tangible intangibles may be categorized as:

(1) instruments;

(a) **Instruments**, as defined in Article 9, means negotiable instruments, i.e., drafts and notes as defined in Article 3 or any writing that evidences a right to the payment of a monetary obligation but is not itself a security agreement or lease [§ 9-102(a)(47)].

(b) The writing must be "of a type that, in the ordinary course of business, is transferred by delivery with any necessary endorsement or assignment" [Id.].

(c) It does not include investment securities, such as stocks and bonds as defined in Article 8, letters of credit, or writings that evidence a right to payment arising out of the use of a credit or charge card [Id.].

(2) documents; or

(a) **Documents** are documents of title, which include [§§ 1-201(b)(16), 9-102(a)(30)]:

1) bills of lading;

2) dock warrants and receipts;

3) warehouse receipts or orders for the delivery of goods; and

4) any other document that, in the regular course of business or financing, is treated as adequately evidencing that the person in possession of it is entitled to receive, hold, and dispose of the document and the goods it covers.

(b) In order to be a document of title, a document must purport to be issued by, or addressed to, a bailee and purport to cover goods in the bailee's possession that are either identified or are fungible portions of an identified mass [§ 1-201(b)(16)].

(c) Unlike instruments, which represent intangibles with no other tangible form (e.g., obligations to pay money or representing corporate ownership), documents of title "cover" or represent ownership in tangible goods.

    1)   It is those goods, or the property interests in them, in which the secured party is really interested.

    2)   Thus, interests may be created and protected with reference to the documents, the goods, or both.

(d)   Mere receipts for goods, such as dock warrants looking to later issue a bill of lading, are not documents of title.

(3)   chattel paper.

    (a)   **Chattel paper** means a record or records evidencing both a monetary obligation and a security interest in, or a lease of, specific goods [§ 9-102(a)(11)].

    (b)   If the transaction is evidenced by records that include an instrument or series of instruments, the group of records taken together constitutes chattel paper [Id.].

    (c)   Security agreements, such as conditional sales contracts or chattel mortgages, are chattel paper.

        1)   Instruments such as notes accompanying them are also chattel paper, although if transferred separately, they are instruments.

        EXAMPLE: Car Dealer sells a car to Consumer. Consumer signs a promissory note for $20,000 and a security agreement granting Car Dealer a security interest in the car. This package of note and security agreement, when used by Car Dealer as collateral for a loan to Consumer, is chattel paper.

    (d)   The Official Comment to section 9-102 discusses the new forms of chattel paper covered under Revised Article 9 (2001), including monetary obligations in computer software and electronic chattel paper.

        1)   The comment notes that traditional, written chattel paper is included in the definition of tangible chattel paper, while **electronic chattel paper** is chattel paper that is stored in an electronic medium instead of in tangible form [§§ 9-102(a)(31), 9-102, cmt. 5b].

        2)   The term **electronic medium** should be construed literally to include electrical, digital, magnetic, optical, electromagnetic, or any other current or similar emerging technologies [Id.].

        3)   The comment also notes that one of the monetary obligations included within the definition of chattel paper is an amount that has been "advanced by the secured party or lessor to enable the debtor or lessee to acquire or obtain financing for a license of the software used in the goods" [Id.].

5. **Intangible Intangibles**

   a. Many intangibles, such as monetary obligations or literary rights, while possibly evidenced by writings, are treated as intangibles. The writings take on no commercial significance of their own, i.e., they are not indispensable.

   b. Such intangibles include:

      (1) accounts;

         (a) **Accounts** are rights to "payment of a monetary obligation, whether or not earned by performance," generally for property that has been transferred or otherwise disposed of, for services, or arising out of the use of a credit or charge card [§ 9-102(a)(2)].

         (b) The term accounts includes health care insurance receivables, but does not include [Id.]:

            1) rights to payment evidenced by chattel paper or an instrument;

            2) commercial tort claims;

            3) deposit accounts;

            4) investment property;

            5) letter-of-credit rights or letters of credit; or

            6) rights to payment for money or funds advanced or sold, other than rights arising out of the use of a credit or charge card.

         (c) A **deposit account** means a demand, time, savings, passbook, or similar account maintained with a bank. The term does not include investment property or accounts evidenced by an instrument [§ 9-102(a)(29)].

      (2) commercial tort claims; and

         (a) A **commercial tort claim** is a claim arising in tort where the plaintiff is an organization, or where the plaintiff is an individual but the claim arose in the course of the plaintiff's business or profession and it does not include damages arising from personal injury or death [§ 9-102(a)(13)].

      (3) general intangibles.

         (a) A **general intangible** is intangible collateral that fails to fit into any other category. It includes things (choses) in action, payment intangibles, and software [§ 9-102(a)(42)].

         (b) A **payment intangible** is a general intangible under which the account debtor's principal obligation is a monetary obligation [§ 9-102(a)(61)].

6. **Investment Property**

   a. **Investment property** includes certificated and uncertificated securities, securities accounts, and entitlements, as defined in Article 8 [§ 9-102(a)(49)].

   b. It also includes commodity contracts and commodity accounts [Id.].

B. Proceeds

1. Collateral subject to a security interest may also be in the form of proceeds of the disposition of other collateral.

2. Proceeds include [§ 9-102(a)(64)]:

   a. whatever is acquired upon the sale, lease, license, exchange, or other disposition of collateral;

   b. whatever is collected on, or distributed on account of, collateral;

   c. rights arising out of collateral;

   d. to the extent of the value of collateral, claims arising out of the loss, nonconformity, or interference of rights in, or damage to, the collateral; or

   e. to the extent of the value of collateral and to the extent payable to the debtor or the secured party, insurance on the collateral.

3. There are two kinds of proceeds: cash proceeds (i.e., money, checks, deposit accounts and the like) and noncash proceeds, which includes all other proceeds [§§ 9-102(a)(9), (58)].

IV. THE SECURITY INTEREST

A. In General

1. A security interest is created by a written security agreement or by the secured party's taking possession, delivery, or control of the collateral with the intent to secure a debt, plus attachment of the security interest to the collateral.

B. Security Agreement

1. A **security agreement** is an agreement that creates or provides for a security interest in certain collateral [§ 9-102(a)(73)].

2. The security interest must be in writing and:

   a. contain a granting clause, i.e., state that it is creating a security interest;

      (1) The granting clause need not be formal and can be in a different document.

      (2) A **financing statement** is the document that is filed to give notice of the security interest—to perfect the security interest.

         (a) Cases have uniformly held that a financing statement is not sufficient as a security agreement unless the financing statement itself, or some other writing, contains a "granting clause," indicating that the debtor intends to give a security interest to the secured party [In re Mann, 318 F. Supp. 32 (W.D. Va. 1970), In re Montagne, 417 B.R. 214 (Br. D. Vt. 2009)].

   b. contain a description of the collateral [§ 9-203(b)]; and

      (1) A description is sufficient, whether or not it is specific, if it reasonably identifies what is described [§ 9-108(a)].

   c. be authenticated by the debtor.

      (1) **Authentication** means either signing a written document or (to include electronic transmissions) executing or otherwise adopting a symbol, or encrypting or similarly processing a record in whole or in part, with the present intent of the authenticating person to identify the person and adopt or accept a record [§ 9-102(a)(7)].

C. Possession

1. A written security agreement is necessary for the creation of a security interest unless the secured party has possession of the collateral.

2. Where the secured party has possession, all that is needed is an agreement, which can be oral, that the secured party is to have a security interest [§ 9-203(b)(3)(B), cmt. 4].

   a. Such security interests are frequently referred to as **pledges**.

   b. The Code's definition of agreement includes not just language, but "implication from other circumstances" [§ 1-201(b)(3)].

3. Possession may also give rise to perfection of the security interest.

4. The secured party is obligated to use reasonable care in the custody and preservation of collateral in the secured party's possession or control [§ 9-207(a)].

D. Control

1. With respect to certain types of collateral, such as investment property, the concept of control takes the place of possession.

2. Thus, the security agreement may be evidenced by control if the collateral is deposit accounts, electronic chattel paper, investment property, or letter-of-credit rights, and the secured party has control of the collateral [§ 9-203(b)(3)(D)].

3. Control may also give rise to perfection of the security interest. The requirements for control of different types of collateral are discussed infra, in the discussion of perfection by control.

4. The secured party is obligated to use reasonable care in the custody and preservation of collateral in the secured party's possession or control [§ 9-207(a)].

E. Validity

1. A security agreement is generally effective between the parties, against purchasers of the collateral, and against creditors [§ 9-201(a)].

2. Title to the collateral may be held by the secured party or the debtor without affecting the rights or duties of either party, except when the collateral is [§ 9-202]:

   a. a consignment or sale of accounts;

   b. chattel paper;

   c. a payment intangible; or

   d. a promissory note.

V. ATTACHMENT

A. Introduction

1. **Attachment** is the process by which the security interest is created. A security interest is created by a contract between the debtor and the secured party. Once the security interest has attached, the secured party has all of the enforcement rights provided by Article 9, including the right to repossess the collateral upon the debtor's default.

B. Security Interest

1. The security interest attaches when the following elements exist simultaneously [§ 9-203(b)]:

   a. the secured party gives value;

   EXAMPLE: Chris borrows $10,000 from Bank to purchase a snowmobile. Bank hands Chris the $10,000 check. Bank has given value.

   b. the debtor has rights in the collateral or the power to transfer rights in the collateral to a secured party; and

   EXAMPLE: Chris goes to Dan's Sports and buys a snowmobile. Chris has rights in the collateral.

   c. the debtor has authenticated a security agreement that sufficiently describes the collateral.

   EXAMPLE: Chris and Bank enter into an agreement under which Chris grants Bank a security interest in his snowmobile as collateral for the $10,000 loan. Chris signs the security agreement. Chris has authenticated a security agreement that sufficiently describes the collateral.

   NOTE ▶ Remember that the security agreement may be evidenced by possession or control.

   (1) A description of collateral is sufficient if it reasonably identifies what is described [§ 9-108(a)].

   (2) A description of collateral is deemed sufficient if it describes the collateral by UCC type.

   (3) However, a description by type is not sufficient if the collateral is consumer goods and the transaction is a consumer transaction. A more specific description is required in this case [§ 9-108(e)].

   (4) A supergeneric description (e.g., "all the debtor's personal property") is not sufficient in a security agreement [§ 9-108(c)].

2. **After-Acquired Collateral**

   a. In general, **after-acquired collateral** is collateral that the debtor acquires or comes into ownership of after the security agreement has been signed.

   b. A security agreement may provide for an interest in after-acquired collateral [§ 9-204(a)].

EXAMPLE: "Debtor grants to Secured Party a security interest in all of Debtor's equipment now owned or hereafter acquired." Equipment that the debtor acquires after the security agreement is signed will be covered by the secured party's security interest because there is an after-acquired property clause.

c. Inventory, by its nature, is constantly depleted and replenished. Therefore, a security agreement specifying an interest in inventory will create an interest in after-acquired collateral, notwithstanding the fact that there is no explicit after-acquired property clause. The same rule applies to accounts receivable.

d. A security agreement cannot provide that it covers after-acquired consumer goods, unless the debtor acquires rights in the consumer goods within 10 days of the secured party giving value [§ 9-204(b)(1)].

EXAMPLE: Bank makes a loan to Consumer. Consumer signs a security agreement that covers "all of Consumer's furniture, now owned or hereafter acquired." This agreement will be ineffective to cover the after-acquired furniture.

EXAMPLE: The BetterBuy electronics store offers financing through its BetterBuy Charge Card. The Card is a secured card, so BetterBuy retains a security interest in each item bought with the card. BetterBuy's security interest can reach after-acquired electronics because the debtor/cardholder will acquire the consumer goods at the same time that the secured party gives value.

e. A security agreement cannot provide that it covers an after-acquired commercial tort claim [§ 9-204(b)(2)].

3. **Future Advances**

a. A future advance clause generally indicates that the collateral secures future debt.

b. A security agreement may also provide that collateral secures future advances [§ 9-204(c)]. For instance, a security agreement may secure all advances under a revolving credit agreement, such that no additional security agreement is needed to secure the future advances.

4. A security interest in collateral automatically extends to identifiable proceeds of the collateral [§§ 9-203(f), 9-315(a)(2)].

EXAMPLE: Bank has a security interest in Chris's snowmobile. Chris trades his snowmobile to Frank. Frank gives Chris his boat in exchange for the snowmobile. Bank has a security interest in the boat.

EXAMPLE: Finance Company has a security interest in BetterBuy's accounts receivable. BetterBuy's customers pay their accounts with checks. Finance Company has a security interest in the checks.

5. A secured party's security interest in collateral will continue regardless of a sale, lease, or other disposition of the collateral, unless the secured party authorized disposition of the property free of the security interest [§ 9-315(a)(1)].

NOTE A secured party may end up with a security interest in both the original collateral and the identifiable proceeds of the collateral.

VI. PURCHASE-MONEY SECURITY INTEREST

A. In General

1. A security interest in goods is a **purchase-money security interest** (**PMSI**) if it pertains to goods that are purchase-money collateral [§ 9-103].

    a. **Purchase-money collateral** means goods or software securing a purchase-money obligation that a debtor incurs to purchase the goods [§ 9-103(a)(1)].

    b. A debtor incurs a **purchase-money obligation** if the obligation is incurred [§ 9-103(a)(2)]:

       (1) as all or part of the price of the collateral (as when a seller finances the purchase); or

       (2) for value given to enable the debtor to acquire rights in, or the use of, the collateral, if the value is in fact so used (as when a third party, such as a bank, finances the purchase).

B. PMSI in Goods

1. Thus, a security interest in goods is a PMSI [§ 9-103(b)]:

    a. to the extent the goods are given as collateral for an obligation the debtor incurred for the purchase of the goods and actually used to purchase the goods;

    b. if the security interest is in inventory that is or was purchase-money collateral, also to the extent that the security interest secures a purchase-money obligation incurred with respect to other inventory in which the secured party holds or held a PMSI; and

    c. also to the extent that the security interest secures a purchase-money obligation incurred with respect to software in which the secured party holds or held a PMSI.

       EXAMPLE: John borrows $500 from his parents to buy a new stove, on the condition that the stove will be used as collateral to secure the loan. John uses the money to buy the stove and gives his parents a security interest in the stove. This will be a PMSI.

       EXAMPLE: John wants to buy a $500 stove from Ed's Appliance Emporium, but does not have $500 in cash. John pays $100 in cash and signs a promissory note to Ed's Appliance Emporium for the remaining $400. John grants Ed's Appliance Emporium a security interest in the stove to secure the repayment of the $400. This will be a PMSI.

C. PMSI in Software

1. A security interest in software is a PMSI to the extent that the security interest also secures a purchase-money obligation incurred with respect to goods (e.g., a computer) in which the secured party holds or held a PMSI, if [§ 9-103(c)]:

    a. the debtor acquired its interest in the software in an integrated transaction in which it acquired an interest in the goods; and

b. the debtor acquired its interest in the software for the principal purpose of using the software in the goods.

D. PMSI in Inventory

1. A consignor's security interest in goods that are the subject of a consignment is a PMSI in inventory [§ 9-103(d)].

E. Dual Status Rule

1. A PMSI does not lose its status as such, even if [§ 9-103(f)]:

   a. the purchase-money collateral also secures an obligation that is not a purchase-money obligation;

   b. collateral that is not purchase-money collateral also secures the purchase-money obligation; or

   c. the purchase-money obligation has been renewed, refinanced, consolidated, or restructured.

> **NOTE** PMSI status is important to the perfection and priority of security interests.

VII. PERFECTION

A. Definition

1. **Perfection** is the process by which the secured party gives notice to the entire world of its security interest. Perfection is necessary for priority purposes.

2. A security interest is perfected if it has attached and if all of the requirements for perfection have been met. If the requirements are met before attachment, then upon attachment, the security interest is perfected [§ 9-308(a)].

B. Law Governing Perfection and Priority

1. Generally, the law governing perfection of a security interest is the law of the jurisdiction where the debtor is located [§ 9-301(1)].

   a. A debtor's location is determined as follows [§ 9-307]:

      (1) an individual debtor is located at the individual's principal residence;

      (2) a debtor that is an organization is located at:

         (a) the debtor's place of business, if it has only one place of business; or

         (b) the debtor's chief executive office, if it has more than one place of business;

      (3) a registered organization organized under state law is located in the state of organization; and

         (a) A **registered organization** is an organization organized under the law of a single state or of the U.S., and as to which the state or the federal government must maintain a public record of the organization [§ 9-102(a)(70)].

      (4) a registered organization organized under federal law is located:

         (a) in the state that U.S. law designates, if applicable;

         (b) in the state that the registered organization designates, if it is authorized to designate a location; or

         (c) if neither of the above applies, in the District of Columbia.

         EXAMPLE: ABC Partners is a general partnership organized under Missouri law. It has two offices—one in E. St. Louis, Illinois, and one in St. Louis, Missouri. All of the bills are sent to the St. Louis office and the letterhead shows the St. Louis office as the primary office. Bank must perfect its security interest in ABC Partners' equipment by filing a financing statement in the Missouri Secretary of State's office.

2. **Possessory Security Interest in Collateral**

   a. Where collateral is located in a jurisdiction, the local law of that jurisdiction will govern perfection, the effect of perfection or nonperfection, and the priority of a possessory security interest in that collateral [§ 9-301(2)].

3. **Security Interest in Fixture and Timber-to-Be-Cut**

   a. While negotiable documents, goods, instruments, money, or tangible chattel papers are located in a jurisdiction, the local law of that jurisdiction will govern perfection of a security interest in a fixture or timber-to-be-cut, the effect of perfection or nonperfection, and the priority of a nonpossessory security interest in the collateral [§ 9-301(3)].

4. **Agricultural Liens**

   a. While farm products are located in a jurisdiction, the local law of that jurisdiction governs perfection, the effect of perfection or nonperfection, and the priority of an agricultural lien on the farm products [§ 9-302].

5. **Goods Covered by a Certificate of Title**

   a. The local law of the jurisdiction that issued the most recent certificate of title over the goods will govern perfection, the effect of perfection or nonperfection, and the priority of a security interest in goods covered by the certificate of title [§ 9-303(c)].

6. **Security Interests in Deposit Accounts**

   a. The local law of a bank's jurisdiction governs perfection, the effect of perfection or nonperfection, and the priority of a security interest in a deposit account maintained with that bank [§ 9-304(a)].

   b. Absent an agreement between the bank and the debtor or customer, or identification of an office in an account statement, the bank's jurisdiction is the one in which the chief executive office is located [§ 9-304(b)].

7. **Security Interests in Investment Property**

   a. The local law of the jurisdiction in which the debtor is located will govern perfection by filing and automatic perfection by a securities or commodities intermediary [§ 9-305(c)].

   b. For a certificated security, the local law of the jurisdiction in which the security certificate is located will govern perfection, the effect of perfection or nonperfection, and the priority of a security interest in the certificated security [§ 9-305(a)(1)].

   c. For an uncertificated security, the local law of the issuer's jurisdiction (i.e., where the issuer is organized) will govern perfection, the effect of perfection or nonperfection, and the priority of a security interest in the uncertificated security [§ 9-305(a)(2)].

   d. For a security entitlement or securities account, the local law of the securities intermediary's jurisdiction (absent agreement, where the chief executive office is located) will govern perfection, the effect of perfection or nonperfection, and the priority of a security interest in the entitlement or account [§ 9-305(a)(3)].

   e. For a commodity contract or commodity account, the local law of the commodity intermediary's jurisdiction (absent agreement, where the chief executive office is located) will govern perfection, the effect of perfection or nonperfection, and the priority of a security interest in the contract or account [§§ 9-305(a)(4), (b)].

C. Methods of Perfection

1. A secured party perfects its security interest by filing or taking possession or control of the collateral.

2. **Filing**

   a. Filing a financing statement in a public office is the most common way to perfect a security interest.

   b. Generally, filing can be done [§ 9-501]:

      (1) usually in the secretary of state's office;

      (2) in limited circumstances (when the collateral consists of fixtures), in the office of the county clerk (land records) in the county where the land to which the collateral is attached is located; or

      (3) if the secured party is perfecting by filing a financing statement, the security interest is perfected only if the financing statement is filed in the correct office in the correct state.

         (a) According to section 9-301(1), the law governing perfection of a security interest is the law of the jurisdiction where the debtor is located, except that where collateral is located in a jurisdiction, the law of that jurisdiction will govern perfection and priority of a possessory security interest in that collateral.

   c. Filing is not effective for the following types of collateral [§ 9-312(b)]:

      (1) a deposit account, which may be perfected only by control;

      (2) a letter-of-credit right, which may be perfected only by control; and

      (3) money, which may be perfected only by possession.

> **NOTE** Filing a financing statement is not required for perfection when the security interest is in property subject to another law (such as a statute or treaty of the United States, or a certificate-of-title statute) [§ 9-311(a)]. Instead, compliance with the other applicable law's perfection requirements is equivalent to filing a financing statement under Article 9 [§ 9-311(b)]. However, if the collateral subject to a certificate-of-title statute is inventory, the normal Code rules will apply with regard to perfection [§ 9-311(d)].

3. **Possession**

   a. A secured party may also perfect a security interest by taking possession of the collateral [§ 9-313(a)].

   b. Taking possession of the collateral is possible only when the collateral is tangible.

   c. Perfection by possession only applies to the following types of collateral [§ 9-313(a)]:

      (1) negotiable documents;

      (2) goods;

      (3) instruments;

      (4) money; or

      (5) tangible chattel paper.

    d.   Perfection by possession is not permitted for the following types of collateral [§ 9-313, cmt. 2]:

        (1)   accounts;

        (2)   commercial tort claims;

        (3)   deposit accounts;

        (4)   investment property;

        (5)   letter-of-credit rights;

        (6)   letters of credit; and

        (7)   oil, gas, or other minerals before extraction.

    e.   If such collateral is in possession of a person other than the debtor, the secured party, or a lessee of the collateral from the debtor in the ordinary course of the debtor's business, a secured party takes possession of the collateral when [§ 9-313(c)]:

        (1)   the person in possession authenticates a record acknowledging that it holds possession of the collateral for the secured party's benefit; or

        (2)   the person takes possession after authenticating a record acknowledging that it will hold possession of collateral for the secured party's benefit.

    f.   A security interest in money is perfected only by the secured party's taking possession [§ 9-312(b)(3)]. Such perfection is effective only when, and for as long as, the secured party has possession.

    g.   **Duty of Care**

        (1)   A secured party who has taken possession of collateral must use reasonable care in its custody and preservation [§ 9-207].

            (a)   Reasonable expenses incurred in the custody and preservation of the collateral may be charged to the debtor.

            (b)   The risk of accidental loss is on the debtor.

            (c)   The secured party must keep the collateral identifiable, unless it is fungible collateral, which may be commingled.

            (d)   The secured party may use the collateral to preserve its value, as permitted by a court order, or (except in the case of consumer goods) as agreed to by the debtor.

            (e)   The secured party may hold as additional security any proceeds (other than money) received from the collateral, must apply any money received from the collateral to reduce the obligation or remit those funds to the debtor, and may create a security interest in the collateral.

4.   **Control**

    a.   A security interest may also be perfected by taking control of the collateral [§ 9-314(a)].

    b.   Taking control of the collateral applies only to [§§ 9-314(a)-(c)]:

        (1)   investment securities [see §§ 9-106, 8-106];

            (a)   A person has control of a certificated security in bearer form if he has possession of the security.

(b) A person has control of a certificated security in registered form if he has possession of the security and the certificate is indorsed to the purchaser or registered in the name of the purchaser.

(c) A person has control of an uncertificated security if he has possession of the security or the issuer agrees that it will comply with instructions from that person.

(2) letter-of-credit rights [§ 9-107];

    (a) A secured party has control of a letter-of-credit right to the extent of any right to payment or performance by the issuer if the issuer has consented to an assignment of proceeds of the letter of credit.

(3) deposit accounts; and

    (a) A secured party has control of a deposit account if [§ 9-104]:

        1) the secured party is the bank with which the deposit account is maintained;

           a) This is a form of automatic perfection. All creditors of the debtor are on notice that the bank with which the debtor's deposit account is maintained may assert a claim against that deposit account.

           b) Under this prong, the secured party has control even if the debtor retains the right to direct the disposition of funds from the deposit account [§ 9-104(b)].

        2) the debtor, secured party, and bank have agreed in an authenticated record that the bank will follow the secured party's instructions directing the disposition of the funds in the deposit account without further consent by the debtor; or

        3) the secured party becomes the bank's customer with respect to the deposit account.

(4) electronic chattel paper [§ 9-105].

    (a) A secured party has control of electronic chattel paper if the records comprising the chattel paper are created, stored, and assigned so that [§ 9-105]:

        1) a single authoritative copy that is unique, identifiable, and unalterable exists;

        2) the authoritative copy identifies the secured party as the assignee of the records;

        3) the authoritative copy is communicated to and maintained by the secured party;

        4) copies that add or change an identified assignee of the authoritative copy can be made only with the participation of the secured party;

        5) copies are readily identifiable as copies; and

        6) any revision of the authoritative copy is readily identifiable as an authorized or unauthorized revision.

c. **Time of Perfection by Control**

(1) A security interest in deposit accounts, electronic chattel paper, letter-of-credit rights, or electronic documents is perfected by control when the secured party obtains control, and remains perfected by control only while the secured party retains control [§ 9-314(b)].

(2) A security interest in investment property is perfected from the time the secured party obtains control, and remains perfected until [§ 9-314(c)]:

(a) the secured party does not have control; and

(b) one of the following occurs:

1) for a certificated security, the debtor acquires possession of the certificate;

2) for an uncertificated security, the issuer registers the debtor as the registered owner; or

3) for a security entitlement, the debtor becomes the entitlement holder.

d. **Duties When No Outstanding Secured Obligation**

(1) When a secured party has control of collateral for which there is no outstanding secured obligation, the secured party must, within 10 days of demand by the debtor [§ 9-208]:

(a) if the secured party has control of a deposit account:

1) send an authenticated statement releasing the bank that maintains a deposit account from further obligation to comply with the secured party's instructions (if an agreement was the basis for control); or

2) pay or transfer to the debtor the balance in a deposit account maintained with the secured party (if the secured party is now the bank's customer—i.e., the party's name is on the account);

(b) if the secured party (other than a buyer) has control of electronic chattel paper, communicate the authoritative copy of electronic chattel paper to the debtor or a designated custodian;

(c) if the secured party has control of a security entitlement or a commodity contract, send to the securities or commodity intermediary of any investment properties held as collateral an authenticated record that releases the intermediary from compliance with further instructions from the secured party; and

(d) if the secured party has control of a letter-of-credit right, send to each person with an unfulfilled obligation to pay or deliver proceeds of the letter of credit to the secured party an authenticated release from any further obligation to pay.

5. **Automatic Perfection**

a. There are limited instances in which perfection is automatic [§ 9-309].

b. **Automatic Permanent Perfection**

    (1)   If the security interest is a purchase-money security interest in consumer goods, perfection is automatic as soon as the security interest attaches and remains effective permanently (excluding motor vehicles and fixtures) [§ 9-309(1)].

        (a) The secured party need neither file nor have possession to have a perfected purchase-money security interest in consumer goods.

        (b) Automatic perfection of a PMSI in consumer goods does not apply to property subject to a certificate of title statute (other than inventory) or fixtures, even if they are consumer goods [§§ 9-309(1), 9-311].

    (2)   Automatic perfection also occurs in other situations, including [§§ 9-309, 9-206(c)]:

        (a) the assignment of accounts or payment intangibles that does not, by itself or in conjunction with other assignments to the same assignee, transfer a significant part of the assignor's outstanding accounts or payment intangibles;

        (b) the sale of a payment intangible or promissory note;

        (c) a security interest created by assigning a health care insurance receivable to the provider of the health care goods or services;

        (d) a security interest arising in the delivery of a financial asset;

        (e) a security interest in investment property created by a broker or securities intermediary or in a commodity contract or commodity account created by a commodity intermediary;

        (f) a security interest arising in the delivery of a financial asset if the security or other financial asset is transferred by delivery in the ordinary course of business and under an agreement between persons in the business of dealing with such assets, and the agreement calls for delivery against payment;

        (g) an assignment for the benefit of all creditors of the transferor and subsequent transfers by the assignee;

        (h) a security interest created by an assignment of a beneficial interest in a decedent's estate; and

        (i) a sale by an individual of an account that is a right to payment of winnings in a lottery or other game of chance.

c. **Automatic Temporary Perfection**

    (1) **Proceeds**

        (a) A security interest attaches to any identifiable proceeds of collateral upon disposition of the collateral [§ 9-315(a)].

        (b) A perfected security interest in proceeds is provided by the Code automatically when the security interest in the original collateral is perfected, unless the security agreement specifically provides that proceeds are not covered [§ 9-315(c)].

(c) This automatic perfection for proceeds continues for only 20 days after attachment (i.e., receipt of the proceeds by the debtor) unless [§ 9-315(d)]:

1) a filed financing statement covers the original collateral, the proceeds are collateral in which a security interest may be perfected by filing in the office in which the financing statement has been filed, and the proceeds are not acquired with cash proceeds;

EXAMPLE: Tire Company makes truck tires. Bank has a security interest in the tires, which are correctly described in Bank's financing statement as inventory. Tire Company sells tires to Auto Supply Store, which promises to pay for the tires 60 days after it receives them. Auto Supply Store's promise to pay creates an account receivable. Because Bank can perfect in both inventory and accounts by filing a financing statement in the secretary of state's office, Bank remains perfected in the accounts, even though the financing statement says that it covers "inventory."

2) the proceeds are identifiable cash proceeds; or

3) the security interest in proceeds is otherwise perfected when the security interest attaches to the proceeds or within 20 days thereafter.

(2) Other situations where Article 9 provides for temporary automatic perfection of a security interest include:

(a) an interest in certificated securities, negotiable documents, or instruments for 20 days after attachment of the security interest to the extent that it arises for new value given under an authenticated security agreement [§ 9-312(e)];

1) In this instance, there has been no filing and the collateral is in the debtor's possession [§ 9-312, cmt. 8].

(b) an interest in certificated securities or instruments, after the secured party has initially become perfected by possession of such collateral, for 20 days after the secured party delivers them back to the debtor for the purpose of ultimate sale or exchange, or presentation, collection, enforcement, renewal, or registration of transfer [§9-312(g)]; and

(c) an interest in negotiable documents or goods in possession of a bailee, other than one that has issued a negotiable document for the goods, and after such documents or goods have been initially placed with the bailee for purposes of perfecting a security interest, for 20 days if the secured party makes available to the debtor the goods or documents representing the goods for the purpose of ultimate sale or exchange, or loading, unloading, storing, shipping, transshipping, manufacturing, processing, or otherwise dealing with them in a manner preliminary to their sale or exchange [§ 9-312(f)].

1) This section affords the possibility of 20-day perfection in negotiable documents and goods in the possession of a bailee but not covered by a negotiable document [§ 9-312, cmt. 9].

d. **Purchase-Money Security Interests**

(1) Perfection generally takes place at the moment of filing or of possession; however, the Code provides what is equivalent to a limited 20-day grace period where the security interest is a purchase-money security interest [§ 9-317(e)].

(a) If the financing statement is filed within 20 days after the debtor receives delivery of the collateral, perfection relates back to the date the security interest attached upon the debtor's receipt of the collateral.

(b) This relation back is good against only intervening buyers, lessees, and lien creditors.

(2) In a sense, there is also a 20-day grace period in connection with the priority given by section 9-324(a), which provides that a purchase-money security interest in collateral other than inventory prevails over all other security interests, provided that it is perfected within 20 days of the time possession is given to the debtor.

EXAMPLE: If a store gives a purchase-money security interest to the B Bank on a cash register that it is purchasing, and the bank files it within 20 days of the time the store obtains possession of the register, then the bank's security interest would be perfected as to those who obtained a lien or who purchased the equipment between the time that the store got possession and the filing. The security interest of the B Bank would also prevail over intervening security interests, so long as the B Bank perfected within 20 days.

6. **Multiple Methods of Perfection**

a. If a security interest is perfected by one method and later perfected by another method without an intermediate period of being unperfected, the security interest is perfected continuously [§ 9-308(c)].

7. A security interest in certificated securities, negotiable documents, or instruments is perfected without filing or possession for a period of 20 days from the time it attaches, to the extent that it arises for new value given under an authenticated security agreement [§ 9-312(e)].

VIII. FINANCING STATEMENT

A. **Notice Filing**

1. The Code adopts the system of **notice filing**, which essentially requires a filing that provides notice that a person may have a security interest in the collateral indicated. The security agreement itself need not be filed; instead, the financing statement is filed [§ 9-502, cmt. 2].

B. **Necessary Information**

1. A financing statement must include [§ 9-502(a)]:

    a. the name of the debtor;

        (1) If the debtor is a registered organization, the statement must provide the name of the debtor indicated on the public record of the debtor's jurisdiction of organization that shows the debtor to have been organized [§ 9-503(a)(1)].

        (2) If the debtor is a decedent's estate, the financing statement must provide the name of the decedent and indicate that the debtor is an estate [§ 9-503(a)(2)].

        (3) If the debtor is a trust or trustee, the financing statement must provide the name of the trust, or if none is specified, the name of the settlor(s), and indicate that the debtor is a trust or trustee [§ 9-503(a)(3)].

        (4) In all other cases, if the debtor has a name, the individual or organizational name must be provided, and if the debtor does not have a name, the statement must provide the names of the partners, members, associates, or other persons comprising the debtor [§ 9-503(a)(4)].

    b. the name of the secured party or the secured party's representative; and

    c. a description of the collateral covered by the financing statement.

        (1) A financing statement sufficiently describes the collateral it covers if it provides [§ 9-504]:

            (a) a description of the collateral that reasonably identifies what is described; or

                1) The description may be by specific listing, category, type of collateral defined in the Uniform Commercial Code, quantity, or in any other way such that the identity of the collateral is objectively determinable [§ 9-108(b)].

            (b) an indication that the financing statement covers all assets or all personal property.

                1) Note that this rule differs from that for security agreements. A supergeneric collateral description in a financing statement is sufficient.

        (2) If the financing statement includes collateral related to real property, such as minerals, timber-to-be-cut, or fixtures, the real

property to which the collateral is related must also be described [§ 9-502(b)(3)].

    (a) The description must be sufficient to give constructive notice if used in a mortgage.

  (3) A financing statement will perfect interests in after-acquired property and future advances as long as the indication of collateral in the statement is sufficiently broad to cover the after-acquired property and/or future advances, even if they are not mentioned specifically [§ 9-502, cmt. 2].

C. Authorization of Financing Statement

1. A financing statement must be authorized by the debtor [§ 9-509(a)].

2. A security agreement is authorization for the financing statement whether it says so or not [§ 9-509(b)].

D. Special Rules for Fixtures

1. As noted above, **fixtures** are goods that are so related to real property that an interest in them passes under real estate law [§ 9-102(a)(41)].

  a. Therefore, in order to be a fixture, the item must be:

    (1) attached to the real estate;

    (2) adapted to the use of the real estate; and

    (3) intended to be a permanent attachment to the real estate.

      EXAMPLE: Kit buys a chandelier from Bowery Lighting. The chandelier is installed in her living room. Removing it would cause some damage to the ceiling. The chandelier is a fixture. If Bowery Lighting wants priority over Kit's mortgage creditor, Bowery Lighting will have to file a fixture filing.

  b. A fixture filing must [§ 9-502(b)]:

    (1) contain all of the information required in a financing statement by Section 9-502(a);

    (2) indicate that it covers fixtures;

    (3) indicate that it is to be filed in the real property records;

    (4) provide a description of the real property to which the fixture is related; and

    (5) if the debtor does not have an interest of record in the real property, provide the name of the record owner.

E. Acceptance and Effectiveness of Financing Statement

1. An ineffective financing statement does not perfect a security interest.

2. **Rightful Rejection**

  a. A filing office must refuse to accept a financing statement, and therefore filing will not occur, if [§§ 9-516(b), 9-520(a)]:

    (1) the record is not communicated by an authorized method;

   (2) the amount that is tendered is not equal to or greater than the sum of the applicable filing fee plus recording tax, if any, based on the representation of indebtedness required for the tax;

   (3) for an initial statement, the debtor's name is not provided;

   (4) for an amendment, the statement does not identify the initial financing statement or identifies an initial financing statement whose effectiveness has lapsed;

   (5) for real property, the statement does not provide a sufficient description of the real property;

   (6) there is a secured party of record, and the secured party's name or address is omitted;

   (7) the debtor's address and status as an individual or organization are not provided; or

   (8) the financing statement indicates that the debtor is an organization and the statement does not provide the type or jurisdiction of the organization or an organizational identification number.

  b. A filing office may only refuse to accept a financing statement for one of the reasons set forth above [§ 9-520(a)].

3. Wrongful Rejection

  a. If a statement is filed with the filing fee, but the filing office refuses to accept it for a reason not enumerated above, the financing statement is still effective as a filing except as against a purchaser of the collateral that gives value in reasonable reliance upon the absence of the record from the files [§ 9-516(d)].

4. Effectiveness Despite Correct Rejection

  a. A filed financing statement that provides the names of the debtor and the secured party and sufficiently describes the collateral is effective, even if the filing office must refuse to accept it because of one of the circumstances indicated under "Rightful Rejection," supra [§ 9-520(c)].

   (1) However, if the financing statement provides an incorrect address for the debtor or incorrect information about the debtor's organizational status, then [§§ 9-520(c), 9-338]:

    (a) a conflicting perfected security interest in the collateral will have priority to the extent that the holder of the conflicting interest gives value in reasonable reliance upon the incorrect information; and

    (b) a purchaser (other than a secured party) will take free of the security interest to the extent that the purchaser reasonably relies upon the incorrect information in giving value and, for tangible chattel paper, tangible documents, goods, instruments, or a security certificate, receives delivery of the collateral.

5. Authorization

  a. If a financing statement is not authorized by the debtor, it is ineffective [§ 9-509(a)].

6. **Errors or Omissions in Financing Statement**

a. A financing statement containing minor errors will still be effective if it substantially satisfies the requirements, unless the errors make the financing statement seriously misleading [§ 9-506(a)].

    (1) Failure to sufficiently provide the name of the debtor is seriously misleading [§ 9-506(b)].

    (2) However, if a search of the records of the filing office under the debtor's correct name, using the office's standard search logic, would disclose a financing statement that fails sufficiently to provide the name of the debtor, the financing statement is not seriously misleading [§ 9-506(c)].

    EXAMPLE: A financing statement for which John Quincy Adams is the debtor is filed, with the debtor's name listed as "John Q. Adams." So long as a search for "John Quincy Adams" would disclose a financing statement for "John Q. Adams," this will not be seriously misleading.

F. **Time of Filing**

1. A financing statement may be filed before a security agreement is made or a security interest otherwise attaches [§ 9-502(d)]. This is important to priority.

2. Note that the date of filing will be the date on which the secured party has complied with the filing requirements by presenting the statement for filing and tendering the filing fee, or the date on which the filing office accepts the statement, even though the officer receiving the statement does not stamp the document as "received" until a later date [§§ 9-516, 9-517].

G. **Changes That Can Affect the Effectiveness of a Financing Statement**

1. A filed financing statement remains effective even if the collateral is sold, exchanged, leased, or otherwise disposed of, and in which a security interest continues, even if the secured party knows of or consents to the disposition [§ 9-507(a)].

2. If the information in the financing statement becomes seriously misleading only after the financing statement is filed, the financing statement will remain effective unless the debtor changes its name or the original collateral is exchanged for proceeds [§§ 9-507(b)-(c)].

a. If a debtor changes his name, resulting in a financing statement that is seriously misleading, the financing statement will only be effective to perfect security interests in collateral acquired within four months of the name change, unless an amendment to the financing statement correcting this is filed within four months of the name change [§ 9-507(c)].

    EXAMPLE: After a long marketing study, We Stink Corp. decides to change its name to A Bed of Roses Corp. Before the name change, We Stink Corp. had borrowed $1,000,000 from Bank, secured by its inventory. Bank properly perfected its interest by filing a financing statement in the secretary of state's office. The name change became effective on March 1, 2008. Bank will remain perfected in all inventory that A Bed of Roses Corp. receives until

June 30, 2008. If Bank files an amendment before June 30, 2008, it will be continuously perfected in all of A Bed of Roses Corp.'s inventory.

3. **Debtor's Change of Address**

   a. A financing statement can also become ineffective if the debtor moves [§ 9-316].

   b. **Perfection Governed by Law of Debtor's Location**

      (1) A security interest perfected pursuant to the law of the jurisdiction where the debtor is located will remain perfected until the earliest of [§ 9-316(a)]:

         (a) the time perfection would have ceased under the law of that jurisdiction;

         (b) the expiration of four months after the debtor moves to another jurisdiction; or

         (c) the expiration of one year after the collateral is transferred to a new debtor in another jurisdiction.

      (2) Thus, if the debtor moves to another state, the secured party must file a new financing statement in the new state within four months of the debtor's move [§ 9-316(a)].

      (3) If the secured party does so, it is continuously perfected, and its priority will relate back to the date it filed in the debtor's original state [§§ 9-316(a)-(b)].

      (4) If the secured party does not file in the debtor's new state within four months of the debtor's move, the secured party becomes unperfected in all of the collateral covered by the financing statement and is deemed never to have been perfected as against a purchaser for value [§ 9-316(b)].

   c. **Possessory Security Interest**

      (1) A possessory security interest in collateral, which is governed by the local law of the jurisdiction in which the collateral is located [§ 9-301(2)], remains continuously perfected if [§ 9-316(c)]:

         (a) the collateral is located in one jurisdiction and subject to a security interest perfected under that jurisdiction's law;

         (b) the collateral is later brought into another jurisdiction; and

         (c) the security interest is then perfected under the law of the other jurisdiction.

   d. **Certificate of Title Goods**

      (1) A security interest in goods covered by a certificate of title—e.g., a motor vehicle—which is already perfected under the law of one state at the time the goods become covered by a certificate of title from another state will remain perfected until the security interest would have become unperfected under the law of the first state if no certificate of title had been issued from the second state [§ 9-316(d)].

   (2) However, a security interest in such goods will become unperfected against a purchaser for value, and will be deemed never to have been perfected as against such a purchaser, if the perfection requirements are not satisfied before the earlier of [§ 9-316(e)]:

    (a) the time when the security interest would have become unperfected under the law of the first state if no certificate of title had been issued by the second state; or

    (b) the expiration of four months after the goods became covered by the certificate of title.

  e. **Deposit Accounts, Letter-of-Credit Rights, Investment Property**

   (1) A security interest in deposit accounts, letter-of-credit rights, or investment property that is perfected under the law of the state of the bank, issuer, or securities or commodity intermediary, as applicable, remains perfected until the earlier of [§ 9-316(f)]:

    (a) the time the security interest would have become unperfected under the law of that jurisdiction; or

    (b) the expiration of four months after a change of the applicable jurisdiction to another jurisdiction.

H. Period of Effectiveness of Filed Financing Statement

 1. A filed financing statement is effective for five years after the date of filing [§ 9-515(a)].

  a. However, an initial financing statement that is filed in connection with a public finance transaction or manufactured home transaction, and that so states, is effective for a period of 30 years after the date of filing [§ 9-515(b)].

  b. A financing statement for a transmitting utility is effective until a termination statement is filed [§ 9-515(f)].

  c. A record of a mortgage that is effective as a financing statement filed as a fixture filing remains effective until the mortgage is released or satisfied or it otherwise terminates as to the real property [§ 9-515(g)].

 2. If the financing statement expires without a continuation statement being filed, the financing statement will lapse. Upon lapse, the filing statement becomes ineffective and any security interest that was perfected by the filing statement becomes unperfected [§ 9-515(c)].

 3. A **continuation statement** must be filed within six months before the expiration of the five-year period [§ 9-515(d)].

  a. A continuation statement extends the effectiveness of the original filing statement for another five-year term from the date that the financing statement would have become ineffective absent the filing of the continuation statement [§ 9-515(e)].

  b. Continuation statements may be filed repeatedly to extend the effectiveness of the financing statement.

4. A **termination statement** must be filed in two situations: consumer goods, and nonconsumer goods.

    a. **Consumer Goods**

        (1) A secured party must file a termination statement if the financing statement covers consumer goods and [§ 9-513(a)]:

            (a) there is no outstanding obligation and no commitment to make an advance, incur an obligation, or otherwise give value; or

            (b) the debtor did not authorize the filing of the initial financing statement.

        (2) The termination statement must be filed [§ 9-513(b)]:

            (a) within one month after there is no outstanding obligation and no commitment to make an advance, incur an obligation, or otherwise give value; or

            (b) if earlier, within 20 days after the secured party receives an authenticated demand from a debtor.

    b. **Nonconsumer Goods**

        (1) If a debtor makes an authenticated demand, the secured party must send the debtor a termination statement or file it in the filing office within 20 days, if [§ 9-513(c)]:

            (a) there is no outstanding obligation and no commitment to make an advance, incur an obligation, or otherwise give value;

                1) This does not apply if the collateral is accounts or chattel papers that have been sold, or goods that are the subject of a consignment.

            (b) the financing statement covers accounts or chattel papers that have been sold but as to which the account debtor or other person obligated has discharged its obligation;

            (c) the financing statement covers goods that were the subject of a consignment to the debtor but are not in the debtor's possession; or

            (d) the debtor did not authorize the filing of the initial financing statement.

I. **Assignment of Power to Amend**

    1. A secured party may designate in a financing statement an assignment of the power to amend the financing statement to a third party, or amend a financing statement to reflect such an assignment [§ 9-514].

IX. PRIORITIES

A. **General Rule: First-in-Time, First-in-Right**

1. The general rule regarding priority under Article 9 is "first-in-time, first-in-right."

    a. **Unperfected Security Interest**

        (1) Among unperfected security interests, the first security interest to attach will prevail [§ 9-322(a)(3)].

    b. **Perfected Over Unperfected**

        (1) A perfected security interest will prevail over an unperfected security interest [§ 9-322(a)(2)].

    c. **Two Perfected Interests**

        (1) Between two perfected security interests, the security interest with the earliest time of filing or perfection, whichever is earlier, which has continued without interruption, will prevail [§ 9-322(a)(1)].

        EXCEPTION: When the collateral is an instrument or chattel paper, the secured party who perfects by taking possession will have priority over the secured party who perfects by filing [§ 9-330].

B. **Second-in-Time, First-in-Right**

1. A perfected PMSI in goods (and its identifiable proceeds) will prevail over a conflicting security interest if the PMSI is perfected when the debtor receives possession of the collateral or within 20 days thereafter [§ 9-324(a)].

2. In other words, if the requirements of section 9-324 are met, the holder of a PMSI has a second-in-time, first-in-right priority.

    a. **Inventory**

        (1) However, when the collateral is inventory, the purchase-money secured party has to take additional steps to acquire priority over the first-in-time secured party.

        (2) The purchase-money secured party will have priority over a conflicting security interest in the same inventory, chattel paper or an instrument constituting proceeds of the inventory (and proceeds of the chattel paper), and identifiable cash proceeds of the inventory that are received on or before the delivery of the inventory to a buyer if [§§ 9-324(b)-(c)]:

            (a) the PMSI is perfected when the debtor receives possession of the inventory; and

            (b) if the holder of the conflicting security interest filed a financing statement covering the same inventory before the PMSI was perfected by filing or (if temporarily perfected without filing or possession) before the beginning of the 20-day period:

                1) the purchase-money secured party sends an authenticated notification to the holder of the conflicting security interest, stating that it has or expects to obtain a PMSI in the inventory and describing the inventory; and

        2) the holder of the conflicting security interest receives the notification within five years before the debtor takes possession of the inventory.

   b. **Software**

     (1) A perfected PMSI in software (and its identifiable proceeds) will prevail over a conflicting security interest if the PMSI in the goods in which the software was acquired for use has priority in the goods and their proceeds [§ 9-324(f)].

   c. **Consignments**

     (1) As noted above, a consignor's interest in consigned goods is a PMSI in inventory [§ 9-103(d)]. The second-in-time, first-in-right rule will apply to a consignor's PMSI if the consignor complies with the additional rules applicable to inventory, supra [see § 9-324, cmt. 7].

3. **Conflicting PMSIs**

   a. If more than one security interest qualifies for PMSI priority in the same collateral, then [§ 9-324(g), cmt. 13]:

     (1) a PMSI securing the price of the collateral (i.e., created in favor of the seller) prevails over a PMSI that secures a loan; and

     (2) in all other cases, the first-in-time, first-in-right rule applies.

C. Priority by Control

1. A security interest in a deposit account, investment property, or letter-of-credit right held by a secured party having control of the account or investment property has priority over a security interest held by a secured party that does not have control [§§ 9-327–329].

D. Contests with Lien Creditors

1. The first-in-time, first-in-right rule applies to priority contests between lien creditors and secured parties.

   a. Therefore, a secured party will have priority over a lien creditor if the secured party [§ 9-317(a)]:

     (1) perfects before the lien creditor's interest arises; or

     (2) files a financing statement and evidences a security agreement (by authentication, possession, or control) before the lien creditor's interest arises.

   b. A **lien creditor** is [§ 9-102(a)(52)]:

     (1) a creditor that has acquired an interest in the property by attachment, levy, or the like;

     (2) an assignee for the benefit of creditors;

     (3) a trustee in bankruptcy; or

     (4) a receiver in equity.

2. **Possessory Lien**

   a. A **possessory lien** is an interest, other than a security interest or agricultural lien, that [§ 9-333(a)]:

      (1) secures payment or performance of an obligation for services or materials furnished with respect to goods by a person in the ordinary course of business;

      (2) is created by statute or rule of law in favor of the person; and

      (3) its effectiveness depends on the person's possession of the goods.

   b. A possessory lien on goods has priority over a security interest in the goods unless the statute creating the lien provides otherwise [§ 9-333(b)].

3. **Special Rule for PMSIs**

   a. If the PMSI is perfected within 20 days after the debtor receives the collateral, the PMSI will take priority over an intervening lien creditor whose rights arise between the time the security interest attaches and the time of filing [§ 9-317(e)].

      EXAMPLE: On May 1, Green Delivery Service bought five mountain bikes from City Bike. Green Delivery Service paid a $500 down payment and gave City Bike a $2,000 promissory note for the remaining purchase price. Green Delivery Service signed a security agreement giving City Bike a security interest in the bikes to secure repayment of the note and received the bikes on May 3. On May 10, the sheriff seized the bikes pursuant to a writ from Bank, because Green Delivery Service had defaulted on an unsecured note to Bank. City Bike perfected its security interest in the bikes by filing a financing statement on May 15. Because City Bike has a PMSI and perfected its interest within 20 days after Green Delivery Service took possession of the bikes, City Bike has priority over Bank.

E. **Accessions**

   1. As noted above, an **accession** refers to goods that are physically united with other goods in such a manner that the identity of the original goods is not lost [§ 9-102(a)(1)].

   2. A security interest created in collateral that becomes an accession will continue [§ 9-335(a)].

   3. If such a security interest is perfected when the collateral becomes an accession, it remains perfected [Id.].

   4. The priority of a security interest in an accession is determined in the same manner as in any other collateral, except that a security interest in an accession is subordinate to a security interest in the whole that is perfected by compliance with the requirements of a certificate of title statute (e.g., a motor vehicle) [§§ 9-335(c)-(d)].

   5. After default, a secured party may remove an accession from other goods if the security interest in the accession has priority over the claims of every person having an interest in the whole [§ 9-335(e)].

a. However, the secured party must reimburse the owner or any others with a security interest in the whole or the other goods (other than the debtor) for any damage done as a result of the removal of the accession [§ 9-335(f)].

b. The secured party need not reimburse the owner or others with a security interest for any diminution in value of the whole or the other goods [Id.].

F. Commingled Goods

1. **Commingled goods** are goods that are physically united with other goods in such a manner that their identity is lost [§ 9-336(a)].

2. A security interest does not exist *per se* in commingled goods, but attaches to the product that results when goods become commingled goods [§§ 9-336(b)-(c)].

3. If the security interest in collateral is perfected before the collateral becomes commingled, the interest attached to the product is also perfected [§ 9-336(d)].

4. A security interest in collateral that is perfected before the collateral becomes commingled goods has priority over a security interest that is unperfected at the time the collateral becomes commingled goods [§ 9-336(f)(1)].

5. Multiple perfected security interests in commingled goods will rank equally in proportion to the value of the collateral at the time it became commingled goods [§ 9-336(f)(2)].

G. Goods Covered by Certificate of Title

1. If, while a security interest in goods is perfected by any method under the law of one jurisdiction, another jurisdiction issues a certificate of title that does not evidence that the goods are subject to the security interest [§ 9-337]:

a. a buyer for value who is not in the business of selling goods of that kind will have priority over the secured party if he receives delivery after the certificate is issued and without knowledge of the security interest; and

b. the security interest will be subordinate to a conflicting interest in the goods that attaches and is perfected after issuance of the certificate and without the conflicting secured party's knowledge of the security interest.

H. Security Interests Arising under Article 2 or 2A

1. Security interests that may arise in a buyer or seller, or lessor or lessee, under Article 2 or 2A are subordinate to a conflicting security interest until the debtor obtains possession of the goods [§ 9-110].

2. In addition, until the debtor obtains possession of the goods [Id.]:

a. filing is not required to perfect the security interest; and

b. the secured party's rights after default are governed by Article 2 or 2A (as applicable).

I.   Buyers versus Secured Parties

1.   Generally, a security interest survives a sale of the collateral [§ 9-315(a)].

2.   However, there are several exceptions to this rule:

    a.   **Consent**

        (1)   A security interest will not continue when the secured party authorizes the sale free of the security interest [§ 9-315(a)(1)].

    b.   **Buyer in the Ordinary Course**

        (1)   A buyer in the ordinary course of business, other than a person buying farm products from a person engaged in farming operations, takes free of a security interest created by the seller, even if the security interest is perfected and the buyer knows of its existence [§ 9-320(a)].

            (a)   A buyer in the ordinary course of business is a person who [§ 1-201(b)(9)]:

                1)   buys goods in good faith;

                2)   buys without knowledge that the sale violates the rights of another person in the goods; and

                3)   buys in the ordinary course from a person in the business of selling goods of that kind.

        (2)   Reading the definition of BIOCB in § 1-201 together with the rule of law in § 9-320(a) results in the following [§ 9-320 cmt. 3]:

            (a)   If the buyer merely knows that a security interest covers the goods, then the buyer takes free of the security interest.

            (b)   If the buyer knows that a security interest covers the goods and that the sale violates a term in an agreement with the secured party, then the buyer takes subject to the security agreement.

            EXAMPLE: BetterBuy financed its entire inventory of HDTVs with a loan from Bank. Bank properly perfected its security interest in the HDTVs. Marco buys an HDTV from BetterBuy, unaware that the sale violates a term in BetterBuy's agreement with Bank. Marco takes the HDTV free from Bank's security interest. Therefore, if BetterBuy does not pay Bank, Bank cannot recover the HDTV from Marco.

NOTE ▸ A licensee in the ordinary course of business also takes its rights under a nonexclusive license free of a perfected security interest in the general intangible created by the licensor, even if the licensee knows of its existence. Similarly, a lessee in the ordinary course of business also takes its leasehold interest free of a perfected security interest in the goods created by the lessor, even if the lessee knows of its existence [§§ 9-321(b)-(c)].

    c.   **Buyer of Consumer Goods**

        (1)   A buyer of consumer goods, where the sale qualifies as a

consumer-to-consumer or garage sale exception, takes free of a security interest (even if perfected) [§ 9-320(b)].

 (a) This exception applies only when a person buys goods from a person who used or bought the goods for use primarily for personal, family, or household use [§ 9-320(b)]:

  1) without knowledge of the security interest;

  2) for value;

  3) primarily for the buyer's personal, family, or household purposes; and

  4) before the filing of a financing statement covering the goods.

 (b) Remember that a PMSI in consumer goods can be perfected without filing a financing statement.

> **EXAMPLE:** Marco buys an HDTV from BetterBuy. BetterBuy takes back a note and security agreement for the purchase price. Because this is a PMSI, BetterBuy does not file a financing statement. Marco wants to upgrade to a better TV, so Marco sells the HDTV to Nikki at a garage sale. Nikki takes the HDTV free of BetterBuy's security interest; therefore, if Marco defaults on his obligation to BetterBuy, BetterBuy cannot recover the HDTV from Nikki.

 d. **Buyer of Chattel Paper**

 (1) A buyer of chattel paper has priority over a security interest in the chattel paper that is claimed merely as proceeds of inventory subject to a security interest if [§ 9-330(a)]:

  (a) the buyer buys in good faith and in the ordinary course of business;

  (b) the buyer gives value and takes possession or control of the chattel paper; and

  (c) the chattel paper does not indicate that it has been assigned to another party.

 (2) A buyer of chattel paper has priority over any other security interest in the chattel paper if he gives new value and takes possession or obtains control in good faith, in the ordinary course of business, and without knowing that the purchase violates the rights of the secured party [§ 9-330(b)].

 (3) A buyer who has priority in chattel paper also has priority in the proceeds of the chattel paper if the buyer would have had priority under the general priority rules, or if the proceeds consist of the specific goods covered by the chattel paper or cash proceeds of the specific goods, even if the buyer's security interest in the proceeds is unperfected [§ 9-330(c)].

 e. **Buyer of an Instrument**

 (1) A buyer of an instrument has priority over a security interest in

the instrument perfected by a method other than possession if the purchaser gives value and takes possession of the instrument in good faith and without knowledge that the purchase violates the rights of the secured party [§ 9-330(d)].

    (a) If an instrument indicates that it has been assigned to an identified secured party other than the purchaser, a purchaser of the instrument has knowledge that the purchase violates the rights of the secured party [§ 9-330(f)].

f. **Buyer Who Takes Delivery**

    (1) A lessee of goods or a buyer, other than a secured party, of tangible chattel paper, documents, goods, instruments, or a security certificate has priority over a secured party if the buyer or lessee [§§ 9-317(b)-(c)]:

        (a) gives value; and

        (b) receives delivery of the collateral without knowledge of the security interest before it is perfected.

    (2) A buyer or licensee, other than a secured party, of accounts, electronic chattel paper, electronic documents, general intangibles, or investment property other than a certificated security has priority over a secured party if the buyer or licensee [§ 9-322(d)]:

        (a) gives value;

        (b) without knowledge of the security interest; and

        (c) before it is perfected.

J. Future Advances

1. **Competing Secured Parties**

    a. Generally, a secured party takes subject to all advances secured by a competing security interest having priority under the first-in-time, first-in-right rule (under which the security interest with the earliest time of filing or perfection, whichever is earlier, which has continued without interruption, will prevail) [§§ 9-322(a)(1), 9-323, cmt. 3].

    b. However, when a security interest is perfected only automatically or temporarily, and the advance is not made pursuant to a commitment entered into while the security interest was perfected by another method, the advance will have priority from the date it is made [§§ 9-323(a), 9-323, cmt. 3].

    c. Note that this priority rule does not apply to sales of accounts, chattel paper, payment intangibles, promissory notes, or consignments [§ 9-323(b)].

2. **Lienholders**

    a. A secured party's previously perfected security interest in collateral and all future advances made pursuant to that interest have priority over a lienholder whose interest attaches after the initial security interest was perfected.

3. **Buyer or Lessee of Goods Not in the Ordinary Course**

   a. A buyer or lessee of goods not in the ordinary course has priority over a secured party if it secures advances made after the earlier of [§§ 9-323(c), (e)]:

      (1) the time the secured party acquires knowledge of the buyer's purchase or the lease; or

      (2) 45 days after the purchase or the lease contract becomes enforceable (as applicable).

   b. However, the buyer/lessee will not have priority if the advance is made pursuant to a commitment entered into without knowledge of the buyer's purchase or the lease and before the expiration of the 45-day period [§§ 9-323(d), (f)].

K. **Holder in Due Course**

   1. A holder in due course of a negotiable instrument, a holder to which a negotiable document of title has been duly negotiated, or a protected purchaser of a security will take priority over an earlier perfected security interest [§ 9-331(a)].

L. **Transferee of Money or Funds from Deposit Account**

   1. A transferee of money or funds from a deposit account will take the money or funds free of a security interest unless the transferee acts in collusion with the debtor in violating the rights of the secured party [§§ 9-332(a)-(b)].

M. **Proceeds**

   1. The time of filing or perfection as to a security interest in collateral is also the time of filing or perfection as to a security interest in proceeds [§ 9-322(b)(1)].

   2. A security interest in collateral that has priority over a conflicting security interest in a deposit account, investment property, a letter-of-credit right, chattel paper, negotiable documents, or an instrument (i.e., collateral in which the secured party achieves priority by control) also has priority over a conflicting security interest in proceeds of the collateral if [§ 9-322(c)(2)]:

      a. the security interest in proceeds is perfected;

      b. the proceeds are cash proceeds or of the same type as the collateral; and

      c. in the case of proceeds that are proceeds of proceeds, all intervening proceeds are cash proceeds, proceeds of the same type as the collateral, or an account relating to the collateral.

   3. However, if a security interest in chattel paper, deposit accounts, negotiable documents, instruments, investment property, or letter-of-credit rights is perfected by a method other than filing, conflicting perfected security interests in proceeds of the collateral rank according to priority in time of filing [§ 9-322(d)].

      a. This rule only applies if the proceeds are not cash proceeds, chattel paper, negotiable documents, instruments, investment property, or letter-of-credit rights [§ 9-322(e)].

N. Special Rules for Fixtures

1. When the collateral consists of a fixture, the creditor with a security interest in the fixture will want priority over the creditor who holds the mortgage on the real property to which the fixture is attached. Generally, the only way that such a creditor can obtain priority over the mortgagee is by filing a fixture filing [§ 9-334].

2. The general priority rule is first-in-time, first-in-right. Therefore, if the mortgage is recorded before the security interest in the fixture is perfected by a fixture filing, then the party holding the mortgage has priority.

   a. **Exceptions**

      (1) **PMSI in Fixture**

         (a) However, if the security interest in the fixture is a PMSI, then second-in-time, first-in-right priority applies, so long as the security interest is perfected by a fixture filing before the goods become fixtures or within 20 days thereafter [§ 9-334(d)].

         (b) **Exception to PMSI Exception**

            1) An exception to this rule is the construction mortgage rule. A mortgage is a **construction mortgage** to the extent that it secures an obligation incurred for the construction of an improvement on land [§ 9-334(h)].

            2) A fixture PMSI is subordinate to a construction mortgage if a record of the mortgage is recorded before the goods become fixtures and the goods become fixtures before the completion of the construction [Id.].

      (2) **Fixtures That Are Readily Removable**

         (a) A perfected security interest in fixtures—if the interest was perfected before the goods became fixtures—will have priority over a conflicting real property interest if the fixtures are readily removable [§ 9-334(e)(2)]:

            1) factory or office machines;

            2) equipment not primarily used in the operation of the real property; or

            3) replacements of domestic appliances that are consumer goods.

      (3) **Lien on Real Property**

         (a) A perfected security interest in fixtures will have priority over a conflicting real property interest that is a lien obtained after the security interest was perfected (by any method) [§ 9-334(e)(3)].

      (4) **Consent**

         (a) A security interest in fixtures—whether or not perfected—will have priority over a conflicting real property interest if the encumbrancer or owner has consented in an authenticated record, or the debtor has the right to remove the goods as against the encumbrancer or owner [§ 9-334(f)].

3. A secured party with priority over a mortgagee has the right to remove the fixture from the real property upon the debtor's default, but must reimburse any encumbrancer or owner of the property (other than the debtor) for the cost of repair of any physical injury caused by the removal. The secured party need not reimburse for any diminution in value resulting from the removal of the fixture [§§ 9-604(c)-(d)].

4. **Crops**

   a. A perfected security interest in crops growing on real property has priority over a conflicting interest of an encumbrancer or owner of the real property if the debtor has an interest of record or is in possession of the real property [§ 9-334(i)].

PRIORITIES Which Interest Prevails?				
vs.	Unperfected Security Interest	Perfected Security Interest	Perfected PMSI[1]	Lien Creditor
Unperfected Security Interest	first to attach	perfected security interest	perfected PMSI	lien creditor[2]
Perfected Security Interest		earliest to file or perfect, continued w/o interruption[3]	perfected PMSI[4]	first to perfect
Perfected PMSI			earliest to file or perfect, continued w/o interruption	perfected PMSI
Lien Creditor				first to perfect

[1] Assumes perfection within 20 days after debtor receives possession of the collateral. Otherwise, the PMSI is treated as an ordinary secured creditor for priority purposes.

[2] A lien creditor is perfected by definition.

[3] Except for collateral that is an instrument or chattel paper, in which case perfection by possession trumps perfection by filing.

[4] Except for collateral that is inventory, in which case the purchase-money secured party must take additional steps to acquire priority over the first-in-time secured party.

X. DEFAULT

A. In General

1. Generally, a **default** occurs whenever the debtor fails to tender an obligation when due. Thus, if a debtor fails to meet an installment payment, there is a default.

2. The parties may agree that other acts (e.g., taking the collateral out of the state) constitute a default.

B. Rights upon Default

1. Upon default, a secured party may reduce a claim to judgment, foreclose, or otherwise enforce the claim [§ 9-601(a)].

2. The secured party's rights after default are cumulative and may be exercised simultaneously [§ 9-601(c)].

3. A secured party in possession or control of collateral has the rights and duties as before the default [§ 9-601(b)].

4. A creditor must first seek payment from the debtor before approaching a guarantor.

5. A secured party has the right to repossess tangible collateral if it can do so without a breach of the peace [§§ 9-609(a)-(b)].

   a. Article 9 does not define breach of the peace. However, an act that is likely to lead to violence will be considered to breach the peace.

   EXAMPLE: Bank hires Repo, Inc., to repossess the inventory of Sam's Shoes. The Repo, Inc. employee responsible for the repossession takes a gun with him to Sam's Shoes and shows the gun when he requests entry to Sam's Shoes. Bank's repossession will likely be held to breach the peace.

   b. An entry into a home to repossess collateral will always be considered a breach of the peace.

6. If the secured party cannot obtain the collateral without a breach of the peace, the secured party will be required to bring an action for replevin. A court will issue a writ of replevin, under which the sheriff can seize the property for the secured party.

C. Payment to Secured Party

1. If the collateral consists of accounts receivable, instruments, or chattel paper, the secured party may, upon the debtor's default, notify the person obligated on the collateral to make payment to the secured party [§§ 9-607(a), 9-102(a)(3)].

   a. The notification must [§ 9-406]:

      (1) be authenticated by the secured party or the debtor; and

      (2) reasonably identify the rights assigned.

EXAMPLE: Charlie's Cuisine, a catering company, borrowed $50,000 from Finance Company, secured by its accounts receivable. State University owes Charlie's Cuisine $50,000 for catering the inauguration festivities for State University's new President. If Charlie's Cuisine defaults on the loan, Finance Company can notify State University to make payment to Finance Company. After such notification, State University can discharge its obligation only by paying Finance Company. State University has the right to request proof of the security interest from Finance Company. If Finance Company does not send such proof, State University can continue to pay Charlie's Cuisine.

D. Debtor's Right to Redeem

1. The debtor has a right to redeem the collateral by tendering to the secured party the amount of the obligation, including interest, together with reasonable expenses and attorney's fees caused by the default (unless the debtor has agreed otherwise in writing after default) [§§ 9-623(a)-(b)].

2. However, redemption must be effected before [§ 9-623(c)]:

   a. the collateral has been collected;

   b. the secured party has disposed of the collateral or has entered into a contract for its disposition; or

   c. the secured party has accepted the collateral in full or partial satisfaction of the obligation.

3. **Waiver**

   a. A debtor may waive his right to redeem the collateral by an agreement entered into, and authenticated after, the default [§ 9-624(c)]. The agreement of waiver may not be made in advance of the default or at the inception of the secured transaction.

   b. However, a debtor may not waive the right to redeem in a consumer goods transaction [Id.].

E. Disposition after Default

1. After default and repossession, a secured party may sell, license, or otherwise dispose of any or all of the collateral in its present condition, or following any commercially reasonable preparation or processing [§ 9-610(a)].

2. All aspects of disposition must be commercially reasonable, including the method, time, place, and other terms. Disposal may occur by public or private sale [§ 9-610(b)].

   a. A public disposition is one at which the price is determined after the public has had a meaningful opportunity for competitive bidding [§ 9-610, cmt. 7].

   b. **Whether Sale Is Commercially Reasonable**

      (1) A sale is considered commercially reasonable if it is made [§ 9-627(b)]:

         (a) in the usual manner on any recognized market;

(b) at the price current in any recognized market at the time of the sale; or

(c) otherwise in conformity with reasonable commercial practices among dealers in the type of property that was sold.

(2) A collection, enforcement, sale, or acceptance is commercially reasonable if it has been approved [§ 9-627(c)]:

(a) in a judicial proceeding;

(b) by a *bona fide* creditors' committee;

(c) by a representative of creditors; or

(d) by an assignee for the benefit of creditors.

(3) The fact that a greater amount could have been obtained by a sale, collection, enforcement, or acceptance at a different time or in a different method from that selected by the secured party is not, in and of itself, sufficient to preclude the secured party from establishing that the sale or other conduct was commercially reasonable [§ 9-627(a)].

3. **Notification**

a. Before disposing of collateral, the secured party must send to the debtor and any secondary obligor a reasonable authenticated notification of disposition [§§ 9-611(b)-(c)].

b. This requirement does not apply to collateral that is perishable, that may decline quickly in value, or that is of a type customarily sold on a recognized market [§ 9-611(d)].

(1) **Recognized market** is a very narrow term and refers only to a market with standard price quotes, such as a stock market.

c. Note that a debtor may waive the right to notification of the sale by an agreement entered into, and authenticated after, default [§ 9-624(a)].

d. **Nonconsumer Transaction—Additional Recipients**

(1) In a nonconsumer transaction, the notification must also be sent to [§ 9-611(c)(3)]:

(a) any other person from which the secured party had received an authenticated notification of a claim of an interest in the collateral;

(b) any other secured party or lienholder that, 10 days before the notification is sent or waived by the debtor, held a security interest perfected by filing a financing statement that identified the collateral, was indexed under the debtor's name as of that date, and was filed in the correct office; and

(c) any other secured party that, 10 days before the notification is sent or waived by the debtor, held a perfected security interest where filing was not required for perfection.

e. **Timeliness**

(1) Whether a notice is sent within a reasonable time, and as such, is a reasonable authenticated notification of disposition, is a question of fact [§ 9-612(a)].

(2) A notice of disposition sent after default and 10 days or more before the earliest time of disposition is deemed sent within a reasonable time [§ 9-612(b)].

NOTE Notice is an element of commercial reasonableness. Therefore, if no notice is sent, or if the notice is not sent within a reasonable time before disposition, the sale may be considered commercially unreasonable.

f. **Contents**

(1) The notification need not be phrased in a particular way [§§ 9-613(4), 9-614(2)].

(2) **Nonconsumer Transaction**

(a) In a nonconsumer transaction, the notification must include [§ 9-613(1)]:

1) a description of the debtor and secured party;

2) a description of the collateral;

3) the method of intended disposition;

4) a statement that the debtor is entitled to an accounting of all unpaid indebtedness; and

5) the time and place of a public disposition or the time after which the collateral will be sold in a private disposition.

(b) The notification will be sufficient if all of the above information is provided, even though the notification includes other information or minor errors, as long as the errors are not seriously misleading [§ 9-613(3)].

(3) **Consumer Goods Transaction**

(a) In a consumer goods transaction, the notice must additionally include [§ 9-614(1)]:

1) a description of any liability for a deficiency;

2) a telephone number the debtor can call to obtain the amount required to redeem the collateral; and

3) a telephone number or mailing address from which additional information is available.

(b) A notification in the form provided by the Code is sufficient even if it includes additional information at the end of the form or errors in information not required by the rule, unless the error is misleading with regard to rights under Article 9 [§§ 9-614(4)-(5)].

(c) If the notification is not in the form provided by the Code, then other law will determine the effect of including additional information not required by the rule [§ 9-614(6)].

4. **Effect of Sale**

a. A sale of collateral generally transfers to a transferee for value all of the debtor's rights in the collateral and discharges the security interest and any subordinate security interests or liens [§ 9-617(a)].

b. This is true as long as the transferee acts in good faith, even if the secured party fails to comply with the rules governing sales and dispositions [§ 9-617(b)].

c. A transferee who acts in bad faith takes subject to the debtor's rights in the collateral and the security interests in the collateral [§ 9-617(c)].

F. Strict Foreclosure

1. A secured party may also acquire the debtor's interest in the collateral without the need for a sale by conducting a full or partial strict foreclosure [§ 9-620, cmt. 2].

2. A secured party may accept the collateral in full or partial satisfaction of the debt if [§§ 9-620(a), (c)-(d), 9-621]:

   a. the debtor consents by:

      (1) agreeing to the terms of the acceptance in a record authenticated after default; or

      (2) for full strict foreclosure, failing to send an authenticated notice of objection to the secured party within 20 days of receiving the secured party's proposal to accept the collateral in full satisfaction of the debt;

   b. the secured party sends a notice of proposal to accept the collateral in full or partial satisfaction of the debt to:

      (1) any person who has sent the secured party an authenticated notice of a claim of interest in the collateral before the debtor consents;

      (2) any other secured party who, at least 10 days before the debtor consents, held a perfected security interest in the collateral by filing a financing statement or by compliance with another law, as applicable; and

      (3) any other person other than the debtor who holds a subordinate interest in the collateral;

   c. the secured party does not receive an authenticated notice of objection within 20 days after sending the notification; and

   d. if the collateral is consumer goods, it is not in the debtor's possession when the debtor consents.

3. **Mandatory Disposition of Consumer Goods**

   a. A secured party that has taken possession of collateral must dispose of the collateral within 90 days after taking possession, or within a longer period agreed to in writing by the debtor and all secondary obligors after default, if [§§ 9-620(e)-(f)]:

      (1) 60% of the cash price has been paid in the case of a PMSI in consumer goods; or

      (2) 60% of the principal amount of the obligation secured has been paid in the case of a non-PMSI in consumer goods.

NOTE ▶ Although a debtor generally may not waive the consent and notice requirements relating to strict foreclosure, a debtor may waive the right to require mandatory disposition of consumer goods by entering into and authenticating an agreement to that effect after default [§§ 9-602(10), 9-624(b)].

4. **No Partial Satisfaction in Consumer Transaction**

   a. In a consumer transaction, a secured party may not accept collateral in partial satisfaction of the debt (i.e., partial strict foreclosure is not permitted) [§ 9-620(g)].

5. **Effect of Acceptance of the Collateral**

   a. A secured party's acceptance of collateral in full or partial satisfaction of the debt [§ 9-622(a)]:

      (1) discharges the obligation to the extent of the debtor's consent;

      (2) transfers to the secured party all of a debtor's rights in the collateral;

      (3) discharges the debt and any subordinate security interest or other subordinate lien; and

      (4) terminates any other subordinate interest.

   b. If the secured party accepts collateral in satisfaction of the debt, subordinate interests will be discharged or terminated even if the secured party does not fully comply with the requirements for strict foreclosure [§ 9-622(b)].

6. **Proceeds of Collection, Enforcement, or Disposition**

   a. The cash proceeds of collection, enforcement, or disposition shall be applied as follows [§§ 9-608, 9-615]:

      (1) the reasonable expenses of collection and enforcement, or retaking, holding, preparing for disposition, processing, and disposing of the collateral, and reasonable legal fees and expenses incurred by the secured party;

         (a) Costs of sale are always paid first [§ 9-615, cmt. 2].

      (2) the satisfaction of obligations secured by the security interest under which the collection, enforcement, or disposition is made; and

      (3) the satisfaction of obligations secured by any subordinate security interest in, or other subordinate lien on the collateral, if the secured party has received an authenticated demand before disposal.

   b. The secured party must pay to the debtor any surplus, or the debtor shall be liable for any deficiency following sale, unless the underlying transaction is a sale of accounts, chattel paper, payment intangibles, or promissory notes [§§ 9-615(d)-(e), 9-608(a)(4), (b)].

   c. **Deficiency**

      (1) If the collateral does not bring enough at sale or collection to pay all outstanding obligations, the secured party is entitled to a judgment for the deficiency (except where the underlying transaction is a sale of accounts, chattel paper, payment intangibles, or promissory notes) [§§ 9-608(a)(4), 9-615(d)-(e)].

         (a) The **deficiency** is the difference between the amount owed on the debt and the proceeds received at sale.

         EXAMPLE: Charlie's Cuisine borrowed $5,000 from Bank, secured by one of its ovens. Charlie's Cuisine defaulted, owing Bank $4,500. Bank sold the oven in a commercially reasonable sale and recovered $3,500. Bank is entitled to a deficiency judgment for $1,000.

(2) **Commercially Unreasonable Sale**

   (a) If the sale is conducted in a commercially unreasonable manner, however, the deficiency can be reduced according to the **rebuttable presumption rule** [§ 9-626].

   (b) If the debtor places the commercial reasonableness of the sale in issue, and the secured party fails to prove that the sale was commercially reasonable, then the deficiency will be reduced to the difference between [§ 9-626(3)]:

      1) the outstanding amount of the loan; and

      2) the greater of:

         a) the actual proceeds of the sale; or

         b) the amount that the collateral would have sold for in a commercially reasonable sale.

   (c) For the purpose of this calculation, the amount that the collateral would have sold for in a commercially reasonable sale is presumed to be the outstanding amount of the debt; thus the deficiency would be $0. The secured party can rebut the presumption with evidence that the collateral is worth less than the outstanding amount of the debt [§ 9-626(4)].

   EXAMPLE: If Bank in the above example had failed to give notice of the sale, the sale would be considered commercially unreasonable. In the commercially unreasonable sale, Bank recovered $2,500. If Bank cannot prove that the oven is worth less than $4,500, the deficiency judgment will be $0.

d. **Debtor's Remedies**

   (1) A debtor may seek any lost surplus caused by the secured party's violation of Article 9, even if the debtor's deficiency is eliminated or reduced [§§ 9-625(c)-(d)].

      (a) If the collateral is consumer goods, a debtor may recover at least the amount of the credit service charge plus 10% of the principal amount of the obligation or the time-price differential plus 10% of the cash price [§ 9-625(c)(2)].

   (2) In the alternative, the debtor may seek any actual damages caused by the secured party's actions (e.g., lost profits) [§ 9-625(b)].

   (3) However, a debtor whose deficiency is eliminated or reduced may not recover actual damages [§ 9-625(d)].

e. **Calculation of Surplus or Deficiency if Purchaser is Secured Party**

   (1) If the transferee in the sale is the secured party, a person related to the secured party, or a secondary obligor, and the amount of proceeds of the sale is significantly below the range of proceeds that a sale to a disinterested third party would have

brought, then the amount of proceeds used to calculate the surplus or deficiency is the amount that would have been realized in a sale to a disinterested third party [§ 9-615(f)].

f. **Explanation of Calculation of Surplus or Deficiency**

(1) An **explanation** is a writing that [§ 9-616(a)(1)]:

(a) states the amount of the surplus or deficiency;

(b) provides an explanation of how the secured party calculated the surplus or deficiency;

(c) states, if applicable, that future debits, credits, charges, including additional credit service charges or interest, rebates, and expenses may affect the amount of the surplus or deficiency; and

(d) provides a telephone number or mailing address from which additional information concerning the transaction is available.

(2) In a consumer goods transaction in which the debtor is entitled to a surplus or is liable for a deficiency, the secured party must [§ 9-616(b)]:

(a) send an explanation to the debtor after the disposition:

1) before or when the secured party accounts to the debtor and pays any surplus or first makes written demand after the disposition for payment of the deficiency; and

2) within 14 days after receipt of a request from the debtor; or

(b) in the case of a consumer obligor who is liable for a deficiency, within 14 days after receipt of a request, send to the consumer obligor a record waiving the secured party's right to a deficiency.

Trusts

TABLE OF CONTENTS

I. INTRODUCTION

A. Overview

1. A **trust** is a fiduciary relationship where one party holds legal title to property for the benefit of another [Restatement (Third) of Trusts § 2].

2. Trusts are created when someone (the grantor, settlor, donor, or testator) transfers legal title to property to a trustee, who administers the trust in accordance with the settlor's wishes for the benefit of the beneficiaries.

3. The essence of a trust is a division of the legal and equitable (or beneficial) ownership of property.

4. Trusts are very flexible devices that give settlors the ability to tailor their gratuitous transfers to the demands of a particular situation.

5. Trusts are particularly useful when transferring property to minors, incapacitated beneficiaries, or charities, and can play an important role in tax planning and the maintenance of family wealth through the generations.

B. Sources of Law

1. As with wills and estates, the law of trusts developed from the common law.

2. Most states have subsequently enacted statutes governing the administration of trusts.

3. The Uniform Probate Code ("UPC") has been less influential regarding trusts than it has been regarding wills.

4. As a result, in 2000 the National Conference of Commissioners on Uniform State Laws approved a Uniform Trust Code ("UTC") to provide a comprehensive codification of trust law for those states that have not addressed these issues comprehensively.

5. The Restatement (Third) of Trusts is also an important interpretive aid and gap-filler to supplement the uniform codes.

   a. The Restatement is the primary secondary source cited by courts and commentators.

6. Although federal estate- and gift-tax considerations are very important to trust drafting, the tax rules do not affect the validity of trusts.

7. Pension trusts that qualify for tax benefits are regulated by ERISA, a federal law that sets minimum standards for many pension and health plans offered by private employers.

C. Types of Trusts

1. The UTC applies to trusts which fall within one of two categories, depending upon how they are created [UTC § 102]:

   a. **express trusts**, which arise from the intention of the property owner; and

      (1) There are two types of express trusts:

         (a) **private express trusts**, which comprise most of the trusts established by individuals [Restatement (Third) of Trusts § 2]; and

        (b) **charitable trusts**, which resemble private express trusts but have some significant, distinguishing characteristics [Restatement (Third) of Trusts § 28].

  b.   **implied trusts**, which arise by operation of law in certain circumstances.

    (1)   There are two types of implied trusts:

        (a) **resulting trusts**, which place property in the hands of rightful owners when circumstances require it, even though there has not been any wrongdoing on anyone's part [Restatement (Third) of Trusts §§ 7-9]; and

        (b) **constructive trusts**, which deprive a wrongdoer from retaining improperly obtained property [Restatement (Third) of Trusts § 18].

           1)   Constructive trusts are usually erected to remedy fraud or unjust enrichment.

    (2)   Implied trusts are equitable remedies.

II. CREATING EXPRESS TRUSTS

A. Parties to a Trust

1. Every trust has three parties, though these parties need not be three different people [Restatement (Third) of Trusts § 3].

2. **Settlor**

   a. The property owner who creates the trust is called the **settlor**, **grantor**, or **testator**. The settlor creates the trust by transferring assets to a trustee with manifest intent to create a trust relationship [UTC § 103(15); Restatement (Third) of Trusts § 3, cmt. a].

   b. A trust created during the settlor's lifetime is called an *inter vivos* trust [Restatement (Third) of Trusts § 10(b)]. A trust created in a settlor's will is called a **testamentary trust** [Restatement (Third) of Trusts § 10(a)].

      (1) The settlor of an *inter vivos* trust can also serve as trustee and may be one of the trust's beneficiaries [Restatement (Third) of Trusts § 3, cmt. c].

   c. The settlor must deliver title to the trust assets to the trustee.

      (1) When the settlor also serves as trustee, the trust is created by declaration of trust [Restatement (Third) of Trusts § 10(c)].

         (a) The declaration can be oral unless the trust assets include real property, in which case the Statute of Frauds requires that it be written [Restatement (Third) of Trusts §§ 20, 22].

         (b) In some states, titled assets (i.e., assets whose ownership is reflected in a written document, such as a title, deed, or stock certificate) must be retitled in the name of the settlor as trustee in order for the trust to be valid.

      (2) When the settlor names a third-party trustee, trust assets must be actually transferred to the trustee. A mere recital of transfer in a written instrument is insufficient.

3. **Trustee**

   a. The **trustee** is the legal owner of trust property, who holds it for the benefit of the beneficiaries [Restatement (Third) of Trusts § 3, cmt. c]. Legal title to, and responsibility for, the management of the trust property resides in the trustee.

   b. A trustee can also be the settlor and may be a beneficiary [Id.]. Central to a trustee's position, however, is that he owes duties to someone other than himself.

      (1) There must always be a beneficiary in existence that can enforce the trust against the trustee. The sole trustee may be one of several beneficiaries, but the trustee may not be the sole beneficiary; rather, there must be at least one additional beneficiary [Restatement (Third) of Trusts § 3, cmt. d].

      (2) If the trustee beneficiary has a co-trustee, then the trustee beneficiary can enforce the trust against his co-trustee and the trust is valid.

c. A trust must have a trustee, but failure to designate or appoint a qualified trustee will not necessarily cause the trust to fail [Restatement (Third) of Trusts § 31].

    (1) Generally, the court will appoint a trustee if no trustee is designated, or if the designated trustee:

        (a) is incompetent;

        (b) fails to survive the settlor; or

        (c) otherwise fails to qualify.

    (2) If the settlor's selection of the trustee was obviously "personal" and exclusive in nature, the trust might fail if the specifically designated person refuses to accept the trusteeship.

d. **Capacity**

    (1) A trustee must have the mental capacity to administer the trust [Restatement (Third) of Trusts § 32]. He cannot be a minor or a mentally incompetent person [Restatement (Third) of Trusts § 32, cmt. c].

        (a) In some jurisdictions, a noncitizen or convicted felon may be barred from serving as a trustee.

    (2) Under modern law, corporations are allowed to be trustees [Restatement (Third) of Trusts § 33].

        (a) Many states, however, have statutes prohibiting corporations from engaging in trust activities, unless the corporate entity is incorporated under the laws of the particular jurisdiction.

        (b) Corporate trustees may be subject to reporting requirements under federal banking law.

e. Because the trustee is the legal owner (titleholder) to the trust property but not the beneficial owner, he has the legal authority to act toward the property as an owner would, but cannot spend it for his own benefit (unless specifically authorized to do so) or act in ways that are inconsistent with the provisions of the trust.

f. **Duties of a Trustee**

    (1) A trustee must be given some active duties to direct him with respect to the trust property in order for the trust to be valid [Restatement (Third) of Trusts § 6(1)].

        (a) If the trustee does not have active duties, the trust is considered **passive** or "dry," and title to the trust assets will pass directly to the beneficiaries [Restatement (Third) of Trusts § 6(2)].

    (2) The trustee is a fiduciary and duties of the trustee vary by trust.

        (a) Duties commonly assigned by statute or legally implied include the obligations to [Restatement (Third) of Trusts § 6, cmt. d]:

            1) preserve property;

            2) make trust property productive;

            3) invest prudently;

            4) administer the trust pursuant to the settlor's directions;

        5)   keep accurate accounts;

        6)   segregate trust assets; and

        7)   exercise fairness with respect to all beneficiaries, regardless of the nature of their interests.

g. Acceptance or Disclaimer

    (a)   An individual or corporation named as trustee has the opportunity to accept or decline the position [UTC § 701]. Acceptance may be indicated by words or conduct, but merely protecting property temporarily is usually not sufficient [Restatement (Third) of Trusts § 35, cmt. b].

    (b)   Silence and inaction by a named trustee is usually treated as a disclaimer of the position. In some jurisdictions, however, a trustee must promptly disclaim the role in order to avoid its obligations.

    (c)   Once accepted, the trustee's acceptance ordinarily relates back to inception of the trust relationship.

h. Co-Trustees

    (1)   Where two or more persons have been named as co-trustees, they are ordinarily considered joint tenants.

    (2)   Co-trustees who are unable to reach a unanimous decision may act by majority decision [UTC § 703(a)].

    (3)   If a vacancy occurs in a co-trusteeship, the remaining co-trustees may act for the trust [UTC § 703(b)].

    (4)   If a co-trustee is unavailable to perform duties because of absence, illness, disqualification under other law, or other temporary incapacity and prompt action is necessary to achieve the purposes of the trust or to avoid injury to the trust property, the remaining co-trustee or a majority of the remaining co-trustees may act for the trust [UTC § 703(d)].

    (5)   A trustee who does not join in an action of another trustee is not liable for the action [UTC § 703(f)].

        (a)   A dissenting trustee who joins in an action at the direction of the majority of the trustees and who notified any co-trustee of the dissent at or before the time of the action is not liable for the action unless the action is a serious breach of trust [UTC § 703(h)].

i. Compensation

    (1)   Trustees are usually compensated for their efforts. Most states have a statutory fee schedule that can be used as a default.

j. Removal and Resignation

    (1)   A trustee may be removed involuntarily from his position in accordance with the terms of the trust or for cause by a proper court [Restatement (Third) of Trusts § 37].

    (2)   A trustee may resign at any time by providing written notice to the settlor (if living), any co-trustee(s), and the income beneficiaries of the trust [Restatement (Third) of Trusts § 36].

     k.   Legal title to the trust property vests automatically in the beneficiaries when the trust terminates. The trustee ceases to have legal authority to exert control over the property beyond what is necessary to wind up the affairs of the trust.

  4. **Beneficiary**

     a. **Beneficiaries** are the equitable owners of the trust property [Restatement (Third) of Trusts § 42, cmt. a].

     b. A beneficiary is a person that [UTC § 103(3)]:

       (1) has a present or future beneficial interest in a trust, vested or contingent; or

       (2) in a capacity other than that of trustee, holds a power of appointment over trust property.

     c. Trusts often create multiple, concurrent, or successive beneficial interests.

     d. Beneficiaries have the right to enforce the terms of the trust [Restatement (Third) of Trusts § 48, cmt. a].

       (1) Beneficiaries can hold trustees personally liable for breach of their duties.

       (2) Beneficiaries can recover wrongfully transferred property from gratuitous transferees.

     e. A beneficiary must have the ability to enforce terms of the trust.

       (1) Minors and other legally incompetent beneficiaries can sue to enforce a trust through a guardian *ad litem* [UTC § 303; Restatement (Third) of Trusts §§ 43, cmt. a; 65, cmt. b].

     f. A trust can be validly created even if the beneficiaries do not know about it and have not accepted their interests.

B. General Effects of Trust Creation

  1. Once a trust has been created, the settlor no longer owns the assets because they have been transferred into the trust.

  2. The trustee has legal title to the assets and is obligated to adhere to the terms of the trust with respect to the preservation, enhancement, and distribution of the trust property to the beneficiaries [Restatement (Third) of Trusts § 42, cmt. a].

  3. The beneficiaries are the beneficial owners of the trust assets, but cannot ordinarily affect or alter the dispositive or administrative provisions of the trust [Id.].

C. Elements Necessary to Create a Trust

  1. A valid trust requires [UTC § 402]:

     a. that a settlor, with the requisite capacity, expresses a present intent to create a trust (i.e., to create the trust now, not some time in the future) [Restatement (Third) of Trusts § 13];

       (1) The settlor's intention is determined from the language used, his relationship with the parties involved, and any other appropriate circumstances.

(2) No particular words (e.g., "trust") or actions are necessary to manifest the settlor's intention to create a trust [Restatement (Third) of Trusts § 13, cmts. b-c].

(a) Conversely, use of the words "trust" or "trustee" do not automatically create a trust [Restatement (Third) of Trusts § 13, cmt. b].

EXAMPLE: X conveys "Blackacre to Y, to hold and manage for Alice, Carole, and Ted." Even though X has not used words like "trust" or "trustee," this conveyance probably would be found to have created a trust relationship. Y is the trustee, holding Blackacre (the trust property) in trust for Alice, Carole, and Ted (the beneficiaries).

(3) Oral declarations of trusts are allowed under the Restatement.

(4) Where the settlor "suggests" or expresses only a "hope" (known as precatory language) that the property being transferred be used for the benefit of another, the requisite intent to create a trust is usually deemed to be lacking [Restatement (Third) of Trusts § 13, cmt. d].

(a) In certain contexts, however, precatory language has been interpreted as evidencing an intention to create a trust. For example, courts are likely to find an intent to create a trust, despite precatory language, where the recipient of the property stood in a preexisting fiduciary relationship with the settlor, or the instructions to the recipient concerning the settlor's intentions with regard to use of trust property are detailed and specific.

EXAMPLE: X gives $10,000 to his friend Paul. At the time of the gift, X tells Paul that he "hopes" the latter will use the money for his daughter Pam's college education. This grant would probably be viewed as a gift to Paul. Thus, Paul could use the $10,000 in any manner he chose.

EXAMPLE: X gives $100,000 to A, her accountant. She advises A that she hopes he will use the income to pay $1,000 a month to X's widowed sister, W, until such time as W remarries. The rest of the income is to be used for the support of X's son in some "sensible" career, other than practicing law. Under these circumstances, although X uses precatory (as opposed to mandatory) language, X probably intends to create a trust.

EXAMPLE: X conveys "Blackacre to Z, with the expectation that Z will use the income for Ann's support and maintenance." While the language might be precatory, if X had previously assisted in Ann's support, a court might find that a trust relationship existed.

(5) Where a purported settlor gratuitously promises to create a trust at some future point in time, the present intention to create a trust is lacking [Restatement (Third) of Trusts § 10, cmt. g].

EXAMPLE: T writes a letter to Y, in which he states, "I'm going to establish a trust for you as soon as I see my attorney." T's statement shows merely an unenforceable intention to create a trust in favor of Y at some future time.

(6) If the settlor purports to create a trust but designates certain prerequisites (e.g., delivery of the trust property, description of the beneficiaries, etc.) to be completed in the future, no "present" trust intent exists [Restatement (Third) of Trusts § 13, cmt. a].

    (a) However, if the settlor re-manifests the intent when the missing element is furnished, the trust is effective as of the later date.

        EXAMPLE: T transfers $500,000 "to Joe, as trustee, for such persons as I shall name at a later time." No express trust has been formed at this time. Without beneficiaries, there cannot be a trust. That does not mean that Joe gets to keep the money; a resulting trust will be imposed in favor of T. However, if T later hands Joe a paper that states, "The beneficiaries of the trust are Ann and Sally," a trust probably has been created as of the later date. T's intent to establish a trust at the later time is shown by the writing that he handed to Joe.

(7) The words or conduct manifesting a present trust intent do not have to be communicated to the beneficiary. However, the failure to inform anyone of the trust arguably shows that the settlor lacked the present intent to create a trust relationship [Restatement (Third) of Trusts § 13, cmt. c].

    EXAMPLE: T executes a deed to Blackacre, naming himself "as trustee for A and B." T then inserts the deed into an envelope, which he puts in his desk drawer. Under these facts, it could be contended that a trust relationship has been created. On the other hand, T's failure to record the deed or inform the beneficiaries about the trust might suggest that T lacked the requisite present trust intent. Thus, the outcome of this issue must be resolved by the fact finder.

(8) A transfer "in trust" with no specification of the trust's terms will not create a trust [Restatement (Third) of Trusts § 4].

    EXAMPLE: T executes a deed to Blackacre, naming "C as trustee for A and B." No additional terms are provided. A trust relationship has not been created principally because the settlor did not impose any active duties on the trustee. C does not know what she is to do with the trust property; it is unclear whether she should pay the income from Blackacre to A, B, or both, and whether she should distribute Blackacre to B upon A's death. This trust would be considered passive or dry, and title would pass directly to A and B. Note that because T has transferred full title (legal title to C and equitable title to A and B), T has totally divested himself of ownership, and there is no basis for creating a resulting trust in T's favor.

b. delivery of specific trust property [Restatement (Third) of Trusts § 2, cmt. i];

    (1) A trust cannot exist without property (the trust *res*, *corpus*, or principal) that is the subject of the trust relationship. Once created, the trustee owes fiduciary obligations to the beneficiaries with respect to the specified trust assets [Restatement (Third) of Trusts § 2, cmt. b].

    (2) A settlor may use several methods to place title to the trust *res* in the trustee, including the following [Restatement (Third) of Trusts § 10]:

        (a) the settlor can make an *inter vivos* transfer of title to the trustee sometimes called a deed of trust;

        (b) the settlor can orally or in writing declare himself the trustee over particular property standing in his name (a declaration of trust);

        (c) the settlor can, in a valid will, direct the executor to distribute property to a trustee (i.e., a testamentary trust); or

        (d) a settlor can enter into an enforceable contract with another person who thereby becomes obligated to transfer property to a trustee for the purpose of establishing a trust.

    (3) Whichever method of creation is used, no trust can be established until the trustee has legal title to the trust *res*.

    (4) In general, any identifiable property right that is transferable and capable of ownership may constitute a trust *res* [Restatement (Third) of Trusts § 40].

        (a) Property interests that can serve as a trust *res* include:

            1) vested possessory interests;

            2) contingent, nonpossessory, future interests;

            3) contract rights; and

            4) equitable interests in another trust.

            EXAMPLE: A life insurance policy taken out on a person who is still alive may fund a trust even though the date when the income from the policy will physically be available is undetermined.

    (5) As a general matter, the following interests may not be used as the *res* of a trust [Restatement (Third) of Trusts § 41]:

        (a) the mere expectancy that a person has in the prospective estate at death of a living person as his heir or under a will;

            1) There is, however, a limited exception for a contracted-for trust.

        (b) expectations of future earnings that are unsupported by an enforceable contract; and

        (c) debts or obligations owed by the trustees.

EXAMPLE: X properly executes a deed that conveys, "Blackacre to Belle for life, remainder to Z in trust for Mary and John." Although the *res* is not a present possessory interest, the vested future interest conveyed to Z nevertheless is an effective trust *res*. Z, the trustee, has present duties (e.g., to verify that Belle refrains from dissipating or causing permanent damage to Blackacre during her life estate).

EXAMPLE: X declares a trust of all "future profits from stock trading." This attempted trust will fail for lack of a trust *res*.

(6) Generally, the settlor must be capable of conveying to the trustee the property that is to serve as the trust *res*.

(7) The trust *res* must be capable of being identified [Restatement (Third) of Trusts § 40, cmt. e].

    (a) A description such as "most of the money in my bank account at ABC Bank" would be too indefinite to constitute a valid trust *res*. A promise to pay a beneficiary "$200 a month for five years" would also be invalid unless the settlor specified the assets to be used to generate or make the payments [Restatement (Third) of Trusts § 40, cmt. b].

    (b) A gift of an undivided fractional interest in specific property ("one-half of the land that I presently own") usually is adequate. The trustee becomes a tenant in common with the other owner [Id.].

c. an ascertainable beneficiary [Restatement (Third) of Trusts § 44];

(1) Except with respect to charitable trusts, a trust must have definite or ascertainable beneficiaries whose interests will vest or fail within a period of time dictated by the Rule Against Perpetuities [Restatement (Third) of Trusts § 44].

(2) Any natural or artificial person may be a beneficiary, as long as he can legally own property [Restatement (Third) of Trusts § 43].

    (a) The trust beneficiaries must be [Restatement (Third) of Trusts § 49, cmt. b]:

        1) presently ascertainable (either specifically named or capable of being determined without undue difficulty); or

        2) ascertainable at a future time (within the Rule Against Perpetuities) when their interests are to vest.

    (b) The beneficiaries of a trust may be a designated class of persons if [Restatement (Third) of Trusts § 45]:

        1) the class is sufficiently definite; and

        2) all of its members are ascertainable within the period of time prescribed by the Rule Against Perpetuities.

    (c) The members of a class usually are determined at the time when their interests are to vest, rather than when the trust was created [Restatement (Third) of Trusts § 44, cmt. a].

EXAMPLE: If X creates a trust to benefit Y for life, and then to Y's children, "Y's children" are determined as of Y's death (rather than when X created the trust).

(d) There must be some reasonably objective basis for determining the members of the class.

1) A trust whose beneficiaries are a class comprised of "X's children" is clearly permissible [Restatement (Third) of Trusts § 44, cmt. b].

2) A trust established by T for "all of my friends," without naming these persons or otherwise providing a formula through which they can reasonably be identified, would be impermissibly vague.

3) Where a class of beneficiaries is described as the settlor's "family," "relatives," "relations," or "kindred," courts often treat the vague language as evidencing an intent to create a trust for the benefit of the settlor's heirs, determined by the state's rules of intestate succession [Restatement (Third) of Trusts § 45, cmt. e].

4) The trustee is often empowered to [Restatement (Third) of Trusts § 49, cmt. c(1)]:

a) select from members of a class for distribution from the trust *res*; or

b) determine the amount of each recipient's distribution.

5) The class within which the trustee is to make his selection must be sufficiently definite [Restatement (Third) of Trusts § 45, cmt. c].

a) Thus, a trust established for five of the settlor's "friends" should fail (even if the settlor was obviously fond of the persons subsequently chosen by the trustee), because a group denominated as "friends" is arguably too indefinite.

i) If the settlor had identified the friends in the trust instrument, then the trust would have been valid.

(e) Beneficial interests in a trust (including class gifts) must comply with the Rule Against Perpetuities, unless the settlor established a qualified perpetual trust [Restatement (Third) of Trusts § 44].

(f) A minor or legally incompetent person may be a beneficiary. Any claims that they might have against the trustee can be asserted by legal guardians appointed to act on their behalf [Restatement (Third) of Trusts § 49, cmt. c(2)].

(g) Under modern rules, unincorporated associations may stand as trust beneficiaries [Restatement (Third) of Trusts § 43, cmt. d]. However, if the settlor indicates that the support of such an organization is to be ongoing indefinitely, the trust may fail under the Rule Against Perpetuities.

EXAMPLE: Susan establishes a trust for the benefit of her book group, the Reading Rebels. If she indicates that the group should be funded for "all perpetuity," the trust will fail, inasmuch as it will be unclear as to whether the interest will vest within 21 years of Susan's life (or even that of the other book club members).

(h) The fact that one is incidentally benefited in the context of a trust relationship does not result in that person being a beneficiary of the trust [Restatement (Third) of Trusts § 48].

EXAMPLE: X creates a trust, pursuant to which Y, as trustee, is instructed to purchase Cadillacs for X's children. X's children, not Cadillac dealers in the area, are the beneficiaries. If Y fails to perform the terms of the trust, local Cadillac dealers could not compel him to do so.

(i) The rule regarding definite and ascertainable beneficiaries does not apply to charitable trusts [UTC § 402(a)(3)(A); Restatement (Third) of Trusts § 28].

d. active duties imposed on the trustee [Restatement (Third) of Trusts § 6];

e. a proper trust purpose; and

(1) Trusts may be created for virtually any purpose, except for one that [UTC § 404; Restatement (Third) of Trusts § 29]:

(a) is illegal;

(b) violates rules relating to perpetuities; or

(c) is contrary to public policy.

1) A trust provision that encourages a beneficiary to refrain from marrying or to obtain a divorce is invalid (except that restraints upon remarriage by the settlor's spouse are ordinarily upheld) [Restatement (Third) of Trusts § 29, cmt. j].

2) A trust condition that terminates a beneficiary's interest if he subsequently becomes divorced is usually valid [Id.].

EXAMPLE: T deeds Blackacre to X, as trustee, to distribute the income to Sonny (T's son) for life, and then to deliver the real property to the Red Cross at Sonny's death. However, the trust instrument also provides that Sonny's income interest is extinguished if he ever marries. The condition subsequent pertaining to marriage most probably is invalid, and Sony will receive the trust income.

EXAMPLE: T deeds Blackacre to X, as trustee, to distribute the income to W (T's wife) for her life, and then to deliver the remainder of the trust property to the Red Cross at W's death. However, the trust instrument provides that if W remarries after T's death, her income interest is extinguished. This provision is probably effective.

(2) In some jurisdictions, a trust that orders the destruction of property at any point will be declared invalid.

(3) Whenever possible, courts attempt to merely delete an objectionable provision and retain the balance of the trust [Restatement (Third) of Trusts § 29, cmt. e].

    (a) However, where this result would frustrate the settlor's overall purposes, the entire trust is invalidated.

f. a trustee [Restatement (Third) of Trusts § 2, cmt. g].

D. Creation of Express *Inter Vivos* Trusts

1. Legal title to the trust *res* must be transferred to the trustee of the trust. Where the trust *res* is real property, transfer is effectuated by:

a. execution of a deed conveying title to the trustee; and

b. delivery of that document to the trustee (or his agent).

2. Where the trust *res* is personal property, transfer may be made by:

a. physical delivery (i.e., delivering actual possession of the item);

b. symbolic delivery (i.e., delivery to the trustee or his agent of an object that represents or gives access to the property, such as delivering the key to a car with the intention of transferring ownership of the car itself); or

c. constructive delivery (i.e., executing a deed, gift, or instrument of title in favor of the trustee and delivering that document to the trustee or his agent).

3. A settlor may create a trust by [UTC § 401]:

a. transfer of property to another person as trustee during the settlor's lifetime or by will or other disposition taking effect upon the settlor's death;

b. declaration by the owner of property that the owner holds identifiable property as trustee; or

c. exercise of a power of appointment in favor of a trustee.

4. The settlor, in effect, continues to hold legal title to the property as trustee, while transferring equitable title to the beneficiaries.

5. The settlor may also manifest an intent to create a trust by:

a. declaring himself trustee; and

b. earmarking particular assets as the trust *res*.

EXAMPLE: The settlor's marking an envelope "held for B" with the requisite intent would probably constitute a sufficient declaration of trust. The envelope's contents would be the trust *res*.

EXAMPLE: T declares that he is putting 20 head of cattle from his herd into a trust for B. However, T fails to separate or otherwise designate which animals are subject to the trust and continues to treat all of his cattle in a similar manner. No effective transfer has occurred. However, a gift of a fractional interest in a known number of items of a particular asset is valid. Thus, T's declaration that he holds 20 percent of his stamp collection in trust for B would probably be upheld. Under these circumstances, T, as trustee, would hold the stamp collection in a tenancy in common with the settlor, individually.

6. **Statute of Frauds**

    a. *Inter vivos* transfers of personal property to a trust are generally not subject to the Statute of Frauds [Restatement (Third) of Trusts § 22, cmt. a].

        (1) A few jurisdictions, however, have extended the Statute of Frauds writing requirement to trusts of personal property.

        (2) In a small number of states, there is or appears to be no Statute of Frauds requirement that *inter vivos* trusts, even trusts of land, be created or proved in writing.

    b. Where an *inter vivos* conveyance of an interest in real property is made, the requirements of the Statute of Frauds must be met, or the trust is not enforceable against the trustee [Restatement (Third) of Trusts § 22(1)].

        (1) The Statute of Frauds requires that a trust of real property be evidenced by a writing that is signed by the party to be charged (i.e., the party who, at the time of the transfer, had the power to create a trust upon that property) [Restatement (Third) of Trusts § 22(2)].

            EXAMPLE: T deeds Blackacre to himself, "as trustee, for X and Y." Because the conveyance is memorialized in a signed writing (i.e., the deed), the trust complies with the Statute of Frauds.

            EXAMPLE: T orally advises several people that he is holding Blackacre in trust for X and Y. Because the purported change in the legal title of Blackacre from T personally to T as trustee of a trust in favor of X and Y is not memorialized in a signed writing, T could repudiate the purported trust if X or Y sought to enforce it.

        (2) Failure to comply with the Statute of Frauds does not preclude voluntary performance of the trust by a willing trustee; notwithstanding the Statute of Frauds, an oral trust involving real property may be performed by the trustee [Restatement (Third) of Trusts § 22, cmt. b].

            (a) If the trustee voluntarily chooses to carry out the terms of the trust or to execute a writing sufficient under the Statute of Frauds, no one (e.g., the trustee's creditors) has standing to contest the trust.

        (3) When the trustee permits the alleged beneficiary to be in possession of the land, and the beneficiary makes substantial improvements to the property or otherwise relies upon the trust to his substantial detriment, lack of compliance with the Statute of Frauds can be overcome under the equitable part performance doctrine.

        (4) Where a trustee's own actions clearly and objectively indicate a trust relationship despite title standing in his name (personally), a trustee may be equitably estopped from denying the existence of the trust.

(5) Courts may use a constructive trust (an equitable device that is not subject to the Statute of Frauds) either to enforce an oral trust or to prevent unjust enrichment of the purported trustee.

EXAMPLE: O conveys land to X upon an oral trust to pay the income to A for life and transfer the property upon A's death to B. Because the Statute of Frauds prevents enforcement of the oral trust, some courts would permit X to retain the land as an outright owner. Other courts, however, would utilize a constructive trust either for the benefit of O or O's heirs or for the benefit of A and B. The constructive trust prevents the unjust enrichment of X.

(6) If a *bona fide* purchaser acquires trust property while it stands in the trustee's name (without any reference to the trust relationship), the beneficiary's rights in the asset are extinguished.

(a) The acquisition of property by a *bona fide* purchaser cuts off any hidden equities in that asset. In this situation, the sole recourse of the beneficiaries is against the trustee for breach of his fiduciary duties (presuming the beneficiaries can prove the existence of an enforceable trust).

c. In some states, specific formalities to create a trust (e.g., notarization) are required by statute.

E. Testamentary Trusts

1. A **testamentary trust** is created by the testator's will [Restatement (Third) of Trusts § 17].

a. Its essential terms are described in or incorporated by reference into a valid will. The "present intent" element is satisfied, because a will "speaks as of the testator's death" and the settlor intended that the trust take effect at that time.

2. A **secret trust** situation arises where property is devised to another without reference in the will to the fact that the devisee promised the settlor-decedent, or expressly or impliedly agreed, to hold the property received under the will in trust for another [Restatement (Third) of Trusts § 18(a)].

a. A secret trust also arises where a decedent refrains from making a will based upon promises by his intestate heirs to hold the estate in trust for specific beneficiaries at his death [Restatement (Third) of Trusts § 18(b)].

b. If the devisees/trustees refuse to perform the secret trust, extrinsic evidence is admissible to prove its existence [Restatement (Third) of Trusts § 18, cmt. e].

c. In most states, a constructive trust may be imposed upon the secret trust *res* in favor of the beneficiaries.

EXAMPLE: In his will, T leaves "$50,000 to X." After T dies, Mel claims that X had promised to hold the money in trust for Mel. In most states, Mel can introduce extrinsic evidence of X's alleged promise to T. If Mel proves the secret trust, a constructive trust will be imposed upon

X's devise in Mel's favor. In a minority of jurisdictions, if a secret trust is proven, the devise is held in a constructive trust for T's estate. The rationale of these cases is that enforcement of a "secret" trust is inconsistent with the Statute of Wills because it permits extrinsic evidence to contradict the provisions of a will or codicil (i.e., to prevent unjust enrichment, X must be divested of the property, but the asset need not be given to Mel to remedy the wrongdoing).

EXAMPLE: T advises Sonny, T's only child, that he wants Sonny to hold property passing to Sonny under intestacy principles in trust for T's elderly sister. Sonny does not expressly promise to do so, but acknowledges T's request by responding, "Understood." If, when T dies intestate, Sonny refuses to hold his intestate share in trust for T's sister, the latter may succeed in imposing a constructive trust upon the property in her favor.

3. Where a testator indicates in his will that property is being devised to a trustee "in trust," but fails to identify the beneficiaries, a **semisecret trust** results [Restatement (Third) of Trusts § 18, cmt. a].

   a. In a majority of jurisdictions, semisecret trusts are void. The trustee holds the property in a resulting trust for the settlor's estate.

   b. In a minority of jurisdictions, assuming the terms of the trust can be proven, a constructive trust can be imposed upon the property for the benefit of the beneficiaries if the trustee refuses to perform the trust.

   EXAMPLE: T's will contains a provision that states, "I devise Blackacre, in trust, to Bill, as trustee." The terms of the trust and the beneficiaries are not stated in the will or in any documents incorporated by reference into the will. In a majority of jurisdictions, the trust fails and Blackacre passes via the residuary clause of T's will (or, if there is no residuary provision, under intestacy principles).

4. Wills frequently contain **pour-over provisions** that direct the transfer of the decedent's property into a trust established either by the testator during his lifetime or by another person [Restatement (Third) of Trusts § 19].

   a. Words outside a will generally cannot be given testamentary effect. Thus, a typical pour-over provision, which pours assets into a trust that is named but not fully described by or created in the will, risks running afoul of this rule.

   b. In order to pour assets into such a trust under the traditional rules of wills, a court must find that one of two doctrines applies.

      (1) In jurisdictions that have adopted the **incorporation by reference doctrine**, pour-over provisions are valid if in existence when a will is executed, and may be incorporated by reference if the will manifests this intention and describes the writing sufficiently to permit its identification, with further technical requirements sometimes imposed by the law of a given jurisdiction [Restatement (Third) of Trusts § 19, cmt. b; Rest. § 17, cmt. c].

         (a) If the trust is amended after execution of the will, the probate assets will be disposed of according to the original trust provisions or, if this is inconsistent with the testator's intent, will pass through the residuary clause or via intestacy.

    (2)   Pour-over provisions may also be valid under the **facts of independent significance doctrine** if the trust has assets in it prior to the testator's death.

        (a)   There is no requirement that a fact (or entity) be one existing at the time of the execution of the will [Restatement (Third) of Trusts § 19, cmt. b].

        (b)   Under this doctrine, the pour-over assets will go to the trust in its current version at the time the will takes effect.

   c.   Frustration with doctrinal obstacles to pour-over gifts led every state to adopt the Uniform Testamentary Additions to Trusts Act ("UTATA"), first promulgated in 1960 and significantly amended in 1991 [Restatement (Third) of Trusts § 19, cmt. a(4)].

    (1)   The UTATA makes it possible to craft valid pour over wills in a much wider variety of circumstances.

    (2)   Under the UTATA, a will can devise assets to a trust that is established during the testator's lifetime or established at his death by the devise itself, as long as the terms of the trust are set forth in a written instrument, other than a will, executed before, concurrently with, or after execution of the will [Id.].

    (3)   The trust need not have any *res* prior to the testator's death, and the probate assets pour into the trust to which they are devised, as amended.

F.   Trusts Arising by Contract

   1.   A person can create a trust by entering into an enforceable contact with someone who, by virtue of the agreement, is obligated to:

    a.   become a trustee of certain property that he owns; or

    b.   transfer title to property to another person as trustee.

   2.   If the promisor fails to perform his obligations, the promisee or beneficiaries can often compel specific performance.

EXAMPLE: Bill promises to give Harry his antique car in exchange for Harry's promise to convey Blackacre, in trust, to George, pursuant to a trust arrangement whereby Bill and Bill's wife, Mary, would receive the income from that property for their lives. If Bill transfers the car to Harry, but Harry fails to create the trust, Bill and Mary might be able to obtain an order compelling Harry to carry out the trust arrangement.

   3.   When the promisor fails to perform his obligation to establish a trust because he does not own the asset that is to serve as the trust *res*, a trust relationship automatically arises when the asset is subsequently acquired by the promisor.

G. Totten Trusts

1. When a person opens a bank account in his own name as trustee for other parties, it is often unclear as to whether he intends to create a trust relationship pertaining to the deposited funds and subject himself to the fiduciary duties of a trustee.

   a. If he executes a trust instrument pertaining to the deposit, or otherwise indicates he is creating a formal trust relationship (e.g., delivering the passbook to the beneficiary, making accountings, etc.), an *inter vivos* trust arises.

   b. If, however, the depositor's intention was merely tentative (i.e., he intended the beneficiaries to have no rights in the account until he died), in most jurisdictions the arrangement is viewed as a Totten trust [Restatement (Third) of Trusts § 26].

      (1) A **Totten trust** is a hybrid creation of the courts that melds both will and trust characteristics [In re Totten, 71 N.E. 748 (N.Y. 1904)].

      (2) Totten trusts are created like trusts and do not have to comply with the formalities of a will. However, Totten trusts are similar to wills in that [Id.]:

         (a) they are revocable by the depositor at any time;

         (b) the beneficiary has no interest in the account until the depositor dies;

         (c) the beneficiary must survive the depositor to receive the account;

         (d) the depositor owes no fiduciary duties to the beneficiary; and

         (e) the deposit is subject to the claims of the depositor's creditors.

      (3) The withdrawal or transfer of all funds from the Totten trust account will act as a complete and permanent revocation of the trust [Restatement (Third) of Trusts § 26, cmt. c].

H. Supplemental Needs Trust

1. A **supplemental needs trust** is a specially designed trust that permits a person with a severe disability to collect a limited income from a trust without sacrificing eligibility for Medicaid or other forms of governmental assistance.

2. Most states have a statute enabling this specific trust and specifying certain rules that must be followed.

I. Honorary Trusts

1. An **honorary trust** is one that does not qualify as a charitable trust, but lacks definite beneficiaries [Restatement (Third) of Trusts § 47, cmt. a].

2. A trust may be created to provide for the care of an animal alive during the settlor's lifetime [UTC § 408]. The trust terminates upon the death of the animal or, if the trust was created to provide for the care of more than one animal alive during the settlor's lifetime, upon the death of the last surviving animal [Id.].

   a. If enforceable in a particular jurisdiction, such trusts may also be used to provide for the care of a gravesite [Restatement (Third) of Trusts § 47, cmt. d(2)].

3. Trusts of this type would ordinarily violate both the rules of trust creation (for lack of a definite beneficiary) and the Rule Against Perpetuities (for lack of any limit on their duration) [UTC § 409].

a. Courts and legislatures, however, have permitted such honorary trusts to stand, with the trustee bearing only a moral or honorary obligation to follow the terms of the trust [Id.; Restatement (Third) of Trusts § 47].

J. Rule Against Perpetuities

1. As a general proposition, private trusts cannot last forever [Restatement (Third) of Trusts § 44].

2. The **Rule Against Perpetuities** (the "Rule" or "RAP") serves as the primary limit on the duration of trusts and states that "no interest is good unless it must vest, if at all, not later than 21 years after some life in being at the creation of the interest."

a. "No interest is good" means that any contingent interest that does not conform to the Rule is void *ab initio*. All vested interests are valid under the Rule, even if subject to partial or total divestment.

b. "Must vest" means that the contingent interest must become a vested interest (or fail) within the period of the Rule.

(1) The time for vesting is generally calculated from the time the creating instrument takes effect. In the case of a will, it is the date of the testator's death. In the case of an irrevocable trust, it is the date the trust is created. In the case of a revocable trust, it is the date of the testator's death.

EXAMPLE: If A establishes a trust for B and C (who are born and ascertainable) to pay for their college education, the Rule is satisfied, because they will go to college, if at all, within the period of the Rule.

c. "If at all" means that if the contingent interest is absolutely certain to either "vest" or "fail" entirely within the period of the Rule, it is valid.

d. "Not later than 21 years after some life in being" includes within the period lives in being, provided they are not so numerous as to prevent practical determination of the time when the last one dies, plus 21 years, plus such actual periods of gestation as come within the proper purpose of the Rule. Any person in being at the time the interest is created can serve as a "measuring life."

(1) Under the Rule, lives in being must be human lives, not the lives of animals or corporations.

(2) The lives in being must precede, not follow, the 21 years.

(3) Every human being is conclusively presumed capable of having children during his or her lifetime.

(4) The lives in the measuring group or class must not be so numerous or so situated that the survivor cannot be practically determined by the ordinary evidentiary processes (e.g., if the lives in being were all the persons now living in the state of California, or in Great Britain, the interest would be void).

e. "At the creation of the interest" means that, in the ordinary case, the period of the Rule begins when the creating instrument (e.g., trust or will) takes effect.

3. The Rule is directed entirely against remoteness of vesting (i.e., the sole test being whether the interest vests (or fails) within the period of the Rule) [Restatement (Third) of Trusts § 49, cmt. b].

   a. If the interest may possibly vest beyond the maximum period permitted by the Rule, it is void.

   b. The Rule's ultimate purpose is to prevent the clogging of titles beyond reasonable limits in time by contingent interests and to keep land freely alienable in the marketplaces.

4. Interests subject to the Rule Against Perpetuities include:

   a. contingent remainders;

   b. executory interests;

   c. options to purchase land not incident to a lease;

   d. powers of appointment;

   e. class gifts; and

   f. rights of first refusal.

5. Interests not subject to the Rule Against Perpetuities include:

   a. present possessory interests;

   b. reversions;

   c. vested remainders (whether or not subject to partial or complete divestment);

   d. possibilities of reverter;

   e. powers of termination;

   f. charitable trusts;

   g. resulting trusts; and

   h. constructive trusts.

6. Most jurisdictions have modified the common law Rule Against Perpetuities in some way.

   a. One reform adopted by some states has been the "wait-and-see" or "second-look" doctrine for contingent future interests. Under this doctrine, the court's determination of whether the Rule has been violated depends upon what actually happened rather than what might have happened.

   b. Many states have adopted the Uniform Statutory Rule Against Perpetuities, which codifies the "wait-and-see" rule [UPC § 2-903].

   c. In a jurisdiction with a "wait-and-see" statute, the court simply waits out the perpetuities period to see whether the future interests will vest.

      (1) Under this type of statute, the interest will be invalidated only if it has actually not vested after the death of all lives in being plus 21 years.

   d. In jurisdictions with *cy pres* statutes, courts look to the grantor's intent and attempt to meet the grantor's wishes as closely as possible by altering the grant slightly to fit the Rule [UTC § 413; Restatement (Third) of Trusts § 67].

e. In some states, interests that would be invalid in certain circumstances are deemed valid by "patch-up" statute.

f. Statutes with alternative perpetuities periods still require initial certainty, but they use another—usually longer—specified period to give future interests a chance to vest.

7. Where the settlor's intent as to the identity of the beneficiaries of a trust is subject to more than one meaning, an interpretation that avoids application of the RAP is ordinarily preferred [Restatement (Third) of Trusts § 67, cmt. b].

EXAMPLE: X conveys funds to Y, "in trust, for the maintenance and support of team members of the New York Yankees." Whether X intended a gift to the Yankees as constituted at the time of the transfer to the trustee, or to whoever might subsequently become members of that group, is determined by the settlor's intent. However, the former interpretation avoids invalidation of the entire trust under the RAP and would, therefore, be preferred.

III. THE TRUSTEE'S POWERS AND RESPONSIBILITIES

A. **Sources of the Trustee's Powers**

   1. A trustee's powers are [Restatement (Third) of Trusts § 85]:

      a. derived from the trust instrument (either expressly or by implication); and

         (1) In addition to exercising those powers that are specifically delegated to the trustee in the trust instrument, the trustee is also authorized to undertake acts that are, by implication, necessary or convenient to accomplish the trust's purposes.

         (2) If a trustee is unclear as to whether or not contemplated action is permitted under a trust instrument, clarifying instructions may be obtained from a proper court.

      b. granted by statute or implied in law as necessary or appropriate to accomplish the trust's purposes.

         (1) Unless expressly precluded by the trust instrument, a trustee has the power, *inter alia,* to:

            (a) settle or abandon trust claims [Restatement (Third) of Trusts § 85, cmt. f];

            (b) exercise all rights and powers of a competent, unmarried individual with respect to individually owned property [Restatement (Third) of Trusts § 86(1)];

            (c) borrow money [Restatement (Third) of Trusts § 85, cmt. d];

            (d) sell or lease trust assets [Restatement (Third) of Trusts § 85, cmt. c];

            (e) to apportion the trust income; and

            (f) incur reasonable expenses, including the purchase of insurance, that are necessary to maintain trust property [Restatement (Third) of Trusts § 88].

         (2) The trustee has no implied power to invade trust principal for a beneficiary who has merely the right to receive income from the trust.

            (a) In some jurisdictions, however, trustees are specifically granted an invasion power for the benefit of income beneficiaries.

         (3) Under the Third Restatement view, the trustee does not have an implied right to mortgage, pledge, or otherwise encumber trust property.

   2. A trustee's actions pertaining to matters within his discretion are not subject to attack unless he has abused his discretion in undertaking the conduct in question [Restatement (Third) of Trusts § 77].

      a. The trustee's exercise of discretion is ordinarily reviewed under an objective standard (i.e., he must act reasonably under the circumstances).

      b. Where the trustee is given sole or absolute discretion under the trust instrument, his actions are reviewed under a good-faith standard (i.e., they are not improper unless undertaken in bad faith).

B. Duty of Loyalty and Good Faith

1. A trustee owes a duty of utmost loyalty and good faith to the beneficiaries in carrying out his obligations under the trust [UTC § 801].

2. A trustee is [UTC § 802]:

   a. prohibited from self-dealing in any manner (even if done in good faith) with trust assets; and

      (1) Examples of prohibited self-dealing include the trustee or persons under his control:

         (a) buying assets from or selling assets to the trust (even if the sales are for fair market value or occur at a public auction); or

         (b) borrowing money from or loaning money to the trust.

      (2) The trustee is not absolutely prohibited from entering into transactions with beneficiaries of the trust he is administering. However, he is viewed as having a fiduciary relationship with these beneficiaries, and he must therefore disclose all pertinent facts known by him with respect to the transaction. Additionally, the transaction must be "fair" when viewed objectively [UTC § 802(d)].

   b. ordinarily precluded from obtaining any personal benefit other than the agreed-upon or statutory fees as a consequence of his position [UTC § 709(a)].

      (1) A trustee is permitted to receive reasonable compensation from services rendered to the trust beyond those normally required of a trustee, provided that those services are necessary and an extension of his ordinary trust duties [UTC § 708(a)].

         (a) The UTC does not take a specific position on whether dual fees may be charged when a trustee hires its own law firm to represent the trust. The trend, however, is to authorize dual compensation as long as the overall fees are reasonable [UTC § 708, cmt.].

         (b) The Restatement view is that trustees who are also insurance agents or stockbrokers are precluded from receiving their usual commissions for services involving trust property. However, attorney-trustees and real estate-trustees rendering legal services on behalf of the trust have been able to recover when the courts have accepted the rationale that these services were a necessary extension of the trustee's ordinary trust duties [Restatement (Third) of Trusts § 38, cmt. d].

      (2) The trustee cannot obtain any personal benefit from a third party with respect to dealings involving the trust estate. Thus, obtaining a personal commission, bonus, finder's fee, or other benefit for placing trust business with others is strictly prohibited.

      EXAMPLE: The XYZ Bank, to attract new depositors, offers free television sets to anyone procuring a certificate of deposit of $5,000 or more. T, a trustee, deposits $5,000 into the XYZ Bank and personally receives the advertised television set. T would be obliged to deliver the item, or its fair market value, to the trust.

3. The trustee is precluded from permitting himself to be in an apparent conflict of interest with respect to the trust and third parties [UTC § 802(b)].

   a. A corporate or bank trustee should not purchase its own shares or deposit trust funds into an account at its institution. There is even a question as to whether a corporate or bank trustee can retain its own shares when they are already part of the trust estate, or must promptly sell that stock and repurchase different assets [Restatement (Third) of Trusts § 78, cmt. e(2)].

4. The trustee is ordinarily expected to segregate trust assets from his own assets, and earmark or otherwise identify trust property [UTC § 810(b)].

   a. Corporate fiduciaries are, however, generally permitted to utilize pooled or common trust funds (i.e., funds in which the assets of various trusts are combined, in order to make more diversified and desirable investments).

5. The trust instrument may expressly permit specified acts of self-dealing. For example, the trustee may be authorized to lend money to, or purchase assets from, the trust. Even in these instances, however, the trustee must act in good faith and with the "utmost fairness" in transactions involving trust property.

6. Any profits earned by the trustee as a result of self-interested transactions belong solely to the trust [UTC § 802(d)]. Conversely, any losses become debts to the beneficiaries.

C. Affirmative Duties with Respect to Trust Assets

1. In administering a trust, the trustee may incur only costs that are reasonable in relation to the trust property, the purposes of the trust, and the skills of the trustee [UTC § 805].

2. A trustee has an affirmative duty to preserve and enhance trust property [UTC § 809; Restatement (Third) of Trusts § 76].

   a. This duty includes considering the best interests of all life beneficiaries and remaindermen (i.e., the trustee must consider both the investment's ability to produce a reasonable rate of income and the safety of the principal).

      (1) **Definitions:**

         (a) **Principal:** The principal of a trust is the amount originally received, plus capital gains and less debts, expenses, and capital losses. Also known as the trust corpus.

         (b) **Income:** The income is the interest, receipts, dividends, and other income earned by the principal.

      (2) Income and principal are often distributed separately to different beneficiaries. A state will have enacted its own principal-and-income accounting legislation that trustees are to follow. [Restatement (Third) of Agency § 110].

      (3) The Uniform Principal and Income Act specifies the distribution of receipts between trust principal and income.

         (a) Rents and cash dividends received are allocated to trust income, and then are distributed to trust's income beneficiary

(b) Sales proceeds and stock dividends are allocated to principal of trust.

(c) Ordinary expenses incurred in connection with the preservation of trust property, including ordinary repairs, are allocated to income. Ordinary repairs are repairs required by day-to-day wear and tear. Extraordinary repairs, repairs that are beyond the usual or customary kind, are allocated to the principal [Unif. Principal and Income Act § 501].

(d) The default rules may be preempted by the terms of the trust. There are different implications depending on how clear the testator is: E.g. "allocate all capital gains to the income account" versus "T is authorized to exercise its discretion in matters of principal-and-income accounting." So receipts (rents, dividends) may be allocated differently depending on the terms of the trust and the specific state statute involved, if any.

b. The trustee's actions must be examined under an objective standard of care. He must exercise that degree of care, skill, and prudence with respect to trust assets as would a reasonably prudent businessperson with respect to his own affairs and property [Restatement (Third) of Trusts § 77(2)].

(1) Where a trustee possesses superior business expertise or is a professional fiduciary (e.g., a trust company or bank), a higher standard is applied [UTC § 806]. He will be held to the care, skill, and prudence of an individual or entity possessing those capabilities [Restatement (Third) of Trusts § 77(3)].

c. The duty of care incumbent upon a trustee includes the obligation to take reasonable steps to protect and preserve the trust estate. Examples of this include [Restatement (Third) of Trusts § 76]:

(1) obtaining necessary insurance;

(2) satisfying trust obligations as they become due;

(3) maintaining trust assets to prevent untimely deterioration and ensure that no one is injured on the premises;

(4) defending the trust when subjected to legal attack by creditors of the settlor; and

(5) preventing trust property from being stolen or otherwise appropriated.

d. The trustee is obliged to attempt to utilize trust property in a productive manner; subject, at all times, to the obligation to be prudent (i.e., invest only in a conservative manner) [UTC § 804]. Thus, land should be leased and personal property utilized, if possible, to produce income for the trust. Where cash is a trust asset, it should be invested, consistent with the trust's overall liquidity needs.

(1) Almost all jurisdictions follow the **prudent investor rule**. The vast majority of states have enacted legislation codifying the prudent investor principles, most by enacting the Uniform Prudent Investor Act, which was promulgated in 1994 to offer a ready

means of codifying the Restatement principles. The remaining states have comparable, modernized statutes.

(a) Under this doctrine, a trustee is permitted to invest trust assets as would a prudent investor, considering both the interests of life beneficiaries and remaindermen (i.e., the trustee must consider both the investment's ability to produce a reasonable rate of income and the safety of the principal) [Id.].

(b) Under this standard, the trustee must also seek to diversify the investments, so that all of the trust's "eggs are not placed in one basket" [Restatement (Third) of Trusts § 90, cmt. g].

(2) The following types of investments are generally appropriate for trust assets [Restatement (Third) of Trusts § 90, cmts. l-n]:

(a) government and highly rated corporate bonds;

(b) first-trust deed mortgages (assuming they are adequately secured); and

1) The prudent investor standard, however, recognizes no simple rule of thumb concerning the percentage of an asset's value that may be advanced under a first mortgage, and no arbitrary prohibition against investing in junior mortgages. Ordinarily, although first mortgages have advantages over second mortgages in the reduction of risk, the latter offer the compensating prospect of higher return [Restatement (Third) of Trusts § 90, cmt. n].

(c) blue-chip common and preferred stock.

(3) A majority of courts permit investment in mutual funds, provided the investment objectives are consistent with trust investments [Restatement (Third) of Trusts § 90, cmt. m].

(4) Impermissible investments often include unsecured loans, "penny" stocks, and commodities futures.

(a) Earlier court decisions tended to disapprove equity positions in real property as trust investments. Although real estate ownership involves special risks, investment in land is not prohibited under the flexible principles of the prudent investor rule. Diversified real estate holdings have tended to offer, with less apparent volatility, returns comparable to those of a diversified portfolio of marketable securities. Despite the potential advantages of investing in real estate, however, it would not be prudent for a trustee to disregard the complexities, burdens, and special risks associated with a decision to commit a portion of the trust estate to such investments. Thus, a trustee has the usual fiduciary duty to make with care, skill, and caution an analysis of the role the property is to play and an analysis of the risk-reward tradeoffs involved [Restatement (Third) of Trusts § 90, cmt. o].

3. Unless expressly instructed otherwise by the trust instrument, a trustee must generally seek to dispose of wasting (most frequently, mines, oil wells, etc.) or nonproductive (i.e., vacant land) assets expeditiously and for a reasonably fair price. The trustee must recognize that special sensitivity and attention are required in selecting shares of suitable real estate investment pools and in dealing with the competence and delegation issues that are virtually inherent in holding real estate directly as a part of the trust *corpus* [Id.].

4. The trustee has the duty to maintain a clear, accurate accounting with respect to all transactions that he enters into on behalf of the trust [UTC § 810(a); Restatement (Third) of Trusts § 83].

5. In deciding whether to undertake, or refrain from undertaking, action for or on behalf of the trust, the trustee may seek the advice of professionals [Restatement (Third) of Trusts § 77, cmt. b(2)].

   a. A trustee may not ordinarily delegate discretionary functions [Restatement (Third) of Trusts § 80, cmt. c].

      (1) A trustee may (and if he lacks the necessary background to make a reasonably competent decision, must) delegate investment functions, provided he uses reasonable care, skill, and caution in [UTC § 807(a)]:

         (a) selecting the investment agent;

         (b) establishing the scope and terms of the delegation, consistent with the purposes and terms of the trust; and

         (c) periodically reviewing the agent's actions in order to monitor the agent's performance and compliance with the terms of the delegation.

   b. A trustee is permitted to delegate purely ministerial duties (i.e., painting a structure, collecting rent, etc.) and minor discretionary functions (exclusive of substantive investment decisions) to the extent that a reasonably prudent trustee would employ others to assist him in similar circumstances [Restatement (Third) of Trusts § 80, cmt. e].

      (1) In performing a delegated function, an agent owes a duty to the trust to exercise reasonable care to comply with the terms of the delegation [UTC § 807(b)]. A trustee is not liable to the beneficiaries or to the trust for an action of the agent to whom the function was delegated [UTC § 807(c)].

D. Trustee's Liability

1. A trustee stands in a fiduciary relationship with respect to the beneficiaries of the trust [Restatement (Third) of Trusts § 86, cmt. b]. Thus, when duties owed to the beneficiaries have been breached, any questions of liability are typically resolved against the trustee [UTC § 1001(a)].

   a. Only the beneficiaries (or their guardians *ad litem*) can commence an action against the trustee for breach of the duties that are owed to them.

   b. The settlor, except where he is also a beneficiary, ceases to have any interest in the trust once delivery of the trust *res* has occurred.

2. Where a trustee breaches his duty of loyalty, the beneficiaries have several potential actions and remedies [Id.].

   a. To remedy a breach of trust that has occurred or may occur, the court may [UTC § 1001(b)]:

     (1) compel the trustee to perform the trustee's duties;

     (2) enjoin the trustee from committing a breach of trust;

     (3) compel the trustee to redress a breach of trust by paying money, restoring property, or other means;

     (4) order a trustee to account;

     (5) appoint a special fiduciary to take possession of the trust property and administer the trust;

     (6) suspend the trustee;

     (7) remove the trustee;

     (8) reduce or deny compensation to the trustee;

     (9) void an act of the trustee, impose a lien or a constructive trust on trust property, or trace trust property wrongfully disposed of and recover the property or its proceeds; or

     (10) order any other appropriate relief.

   b. Where the trustee has utilized trust funds for his own purposes, the court may:

     (1) compel the trustee to convey to the trust any property that he obtained with those funds; or

     (2) recover any profits made by the trustee with those monies.

     EXAMPLE: T, the trustee of a trust, uses $5,000 of trust funds to personally acquire title to particular land. If the land subsequently increases in value, the beneficiaries are entitled to have a constructive trust in their favor imposed upon the real property. Thus, the entire benefit resulting from this transaction will accrue to the beneficiaries of the trust.

   c. A trustee is accountable to an affected beneficiary for any profit made by the trustee arising from the administration of the trust, even absent a breach of trust [UTC § 1003(a)].

     EXAMPLE: T, the trustee of a trust, combines $5,000 of trust funds with $5,000 of his own monies to purchase an antique car, personally taking title to this asset. The automobile appreciates in value to $15,000. The beneficiaries can compel T to sell the vehicle and return $10,000 (the initial $5,000 plus the entire $5,000 of appreciation) to the trust.

   d. Where property removed from the trust has been dissipated or can no longer be identified, the trustee is liable for:

     (1) its value; and

     (2) any interest that could have been earned on those funds.

   e. Because a trustee's breach of the duty of loyalty is ordinarily intentional (rather than as a consequence of negligence or inadvertence), punitive damages may be recoverable. The deliberate breach of one's fiduciary duties is arguably conduct that should be discouraged.

  f. A trustee's breach of the duty of loyalty may serve as a basis for removing him from his trusteeship [UTC § 706(b)].

3. Absent a breach of trust, a trustee is not liable to a beneficiary for a loss or depreciation in the value of trust property or for not having made a profit [UTC § 1003(b)].

4. The trustee is liable, however, to the beneficiaries for any damages or losses resulting from:

  a. improper investments; or

  b. his failure to take reasonable steps to make trust assets productive.

   (1) Where a trustee makes an imprudent investment that results in a loss, he cannot offset these losses against profits made from other improper transactions, except where the losses and gains are attributable to a single transaction or one substantially related to the breach of the trustee's duties.

    EXAMPLE: T, a trustee, makes two concurrent investments that violate the "prudent investor" rule. In the first, T purchases $50,000 worth of ABC Company stock (a corporate entity whose securities are not highly rated and have not paid dividends in recent years). In the second, T purchases land for speculation. The first investment is unsuccessful, and the stock is presently worth only $25,000. The second investment, however, realizes appreciation of $50,000. T cannot offset the $25,000 loss against the $50,000 gain. T is liable to the beneficiaries for the $25,000 stock loss, while the real property remains an asset of the trust.

    EXAMPLE: T, as trustee, uses $10,000 of trust assets to purchase 100 acres of rural land for the trust as a speculative investment. A few years later, 10 acres of this land is condemned to build a freeway. The governmental entity pays the trust $35,000 for the 10 acres, and the remaining 90 acres are now worth $5,000 each. Although the trustee breached his duty of care in making a speculative investment, a court would most likely view this as a single breach. Inasmuch as the improper investment was a profitable one, the beneficiaries would probably ratify it.

5. The trustee is liable to the beneficiaries for lost interest or other income that would have been earned in the absence of the failure to perform his duties.

EXAMPLE: T creates a trust for B, naming X as trustee and transferring $100,000 in cash and 1,000 shares of ABC company stock to the trust. The trust instrument prohibits the sale of ABC stock except under certain specified, limited circumstances. Despite the directive in the trust instrument, and without any other justification, X sells the ABC stock for $500,000 (its fair market value at that time). X then utilizes these proceeds, plus the original $100,000, and places the entire sum in a safe deposit box. When X's actions become known, 1,000 shares of ABC stock are worth $1,000,000. Under these circumstances, the beneficiary, B, can hold X liable for the income and interest that would have been earned if the trustee had not breached his duty, (i.e., the full appreciation on the ABC stock that was wrongfully sold, including any dividends paid in the interim, plus interest on the $100,000 at the rate of interest that would have probably been earned if X had properly invested it).

6. A trustee ordinarily has no liability for breaches of duty by the trustee whom he succeeds, except where the successor-trustee:

   a. knew or should have become aware of the prior trustee's breach and failed to undertake appropriate action to minimize its effects or to pursue the appropriate remedies on behalf of the beneficiaries; or

   b. was negligent in failing to obtain a complete accounting and delivery of trust property from the preceding trustee.

7. Where the trustee has transferred trust property (or identifiable proceeds from trust assets) to persons who are not *bona fide* purchasers, the beneficiaries can often have a constructive trust imposed upon it.

8. Where an action has been brought against the trustee by the beneficiaries, the former may assert equitable and legal defenses against the latter [UTC § 1001(b)].

   a. Occasionally, the trust instrument expressly authorizes the trustee to undertake certain actions that would otherwise be improper.

   b. In these specified instances, the trustee's acts are not deemed wrongful or in breach of the trust, as long as he acts within the scope of the instrument's authorization.

9. An exculpatory clause is a provision in the trust instrument that relieves the trustee of liability for potentially wrongful acts (e.g., "the trustee shall not be liable for negligence or errors of judgment with respect to his activities involving the trust estate").

   a. When the trustee's conduct falls within the purview of this clause, he is ordinarily relieved of liability (i.e., a trustee's acts are generally not wrongful or in breach of the trust) as long as they are within the scope of the instrument's authorization.

      (1) Thus, the trustee incurs no liability in these circumstances unless his acts would violate the state's public policy.

   b. An exculpatory clause is ineffective to the extent that it purports to relieve the trustee of liability for acts of bad faith and intentional misconduct, recklessness, or gross negligence [UTC § 1008(a)].

      (1) Permitting its application in these situations is viewed as violating public policy.

   c. An exculpatory term drafted or caused to be drafted by the trustee is invalid as an abuse of a fiduciary or confidential relationship unless the trustee proves that the **exculpatory** term is fair under the circumstances and that its existence and contents were adequately communicated to the settler [UTC § 1008(b)].

   d. Exculpatory clauses are narrowly construed by the courts.

      (1) A provision relieving the trustee from liability for "errors in judgment" would probably be construed as applying only to mistakes

in judgment, rather than providing him with a defense where he failed to exercise any judgment at all.

e. Where a beneficiary has full knowledge of the material facts and expressly approves of the complained-of action by the trustee, he may:

(1) be deemed to have waived the trustee's breach; or

(2) be estopped from asserting an action.

E. Removal and Resignation of Trustees

1. The settlor, a co-trustee, or a beneficiary may request the court to remove a trustee, or a trustee may be removed by the court on its own initiative [UTC § 706(a)].

2. A court may remove a trustee if [UTC § 706(b)]:

a. the trustee has committed a serious breach of trust;

b. lack of cooperation among co-trustees substantially impairs the administration of the trust;

c. because of unfitness, unwillingness, or persistent failure of the trustee to administer the trust effectively, the court determines that removal of the trustee best serves the interests of the beneficiaries; or

d. there has been a substantial change of circumstances or removal is requested by all of the qualified beneficiaries, the court finds that removal of the trustee best serves the interests of all of the beneficiaries and is not inconsistent with a material purpose of the trust, and a suitable co-trustee or successor trustee is available.

3. Courts are more reluctant to remove a trustee who was designated by the settlor than a person who was judicially appointed to their position [UTC § 706, cmt.].

4. Once a trustee has accepted the appointment to his position, he can resign at any time by giving notice to the co-trustee(s), if any, or to the successor trustee, or to all of the income-beneficiaries [Restatement (Third) of Trusts § 36, cmt. a].

a. When a co-trustee resigns, the remaining trustee shall continue to act with all of the rights, powers, and duties of a trustee [UTC § 704].

b. If one or more co-trustees remain in office, a vacancy in a trusteeship need not be filled. However, a vacancy in a trusteeship must be filled if the trust has no remaining trustee [UTC § 704(b)].

F. Trustee's Liability to Third Parties

1. Although the trustee is performing trust duties, he may incur personal liability to those with whom he interacts on behalf of the trust [UTC § 1012]. In certain situations, the trustee can obtain indemnification from the trust to the extent of his personal liability.

2. A trustee may, however, obtain reimbursement from the trust where he was not personally at fault [Restatement (Third) of Trusts § 38, cmt. b]. For example, a trustee is entitled to be indemnified by the trust where:

a. the tort was a normal incident to an activity in which the trustee was properly engaged on behalf of the trust;

b. the tort is based on strict liability; or

c. liability is based upon *respondeat superior* principles, and the trustee did not make an improper delegation of discretionary functions to the agent or violate his duty to exercise reasonable care in the selection and supervision of the agent.

EXAMPLE: T is the trustee of a trust. His trust responsibilities include the operation of a bank. Thomas, one of T's employees, embezzles $20,000 from a depositor's account. Ordinarily, T is entitled to reimbursement from the trust for the amount he is obligated to repay the depositor (i.e., T did not personally cause the loss). However, if T failed to exercise reasonable care in hiring Thomas or supervising Thomas's activities, T would not be entitled to reimbursement from the trust.

EXAMPLE: T is the trustee of a trust. His trust responsibilities include the operation of a newspaper. If T is successfully sued for defamation as a consequence of an article published in the newspaper, he could obtain reimbursement from the trust. The tort involved in this instance is a normal occurrence incidental to operating and publishing a newspaper.

3. Except as otherwise provided in the contract, a trustee is not personally liable on a contract properly entered into in the trustee's fiduciary capacity in the course of administering the trust if the trustee in the contract disclosed the fiduciary capacity [UTC § 1010(a)].

a. A claim based on a contract entered into by a trustee in the trustee's fiduciary capacity, on an obligation arising from ownership or control of trust property or on a tort committed in the course of administering a trust, may be asserted in a judicial proceeding against the trustee in the trustee's fiduciary capacity, whether or not the trustee is personally liable for the claim [UTC § 1010(c)].

b. The trustee has an implied right of reimbursement and indemnification against the trust where the contract was for the benefit of the trust and within his authority [Restatement (Third) of Trusts § 38].

c. Where a right of reimbursement exists, the trustee can pay any contractual obligation (including reasonable attorneys' fees) directly from trust assets [Restatement (Third) of Trusts § 38, cmt. d].

d. A trustee is personally liable for torts committed in the course of administering a trust, or for obligations arising from ownership or control of trust property, including liability for violation of environmental law, only if the trustee is personally at fault [UTC § 1010(b)].

e. Where the trustee is personally liable but has a right of reimbursement from the trust, creditors can proceed against trust assets only after their efforts to obtain payment from the trustee have been exhausted.

f. Where the contract was not a proper one, the trustee (personally) is generally the only party liable under it, even if he purported to limit liability.

IV. ALIENABILITY OF TRUST BENEFICIARIES' INTERESTS AND CREDITORS' RIGHTS

A. **Beneficiaries' Interests**

1. In the absence of a restrictive provision to the contrary, a trust beneficiary may freely assign (gratuitously or for consideration) his right to receive income or principal from a trust [Restatement (Third) of Trusts § 51].

   a. Where the trust estate is composed of an interest in land (including leasehold interests), the Statute of Frauds is applicable.

   (1) Thus, an assignment of this type of interest by the beneficiary may typically be evidenced by a writing that is signed by the beneficiary. In the absence of a written memorandum, the assignment may be unenforceable.

   (2) In some states, a writing is required for a transfer of the beneficiary's interest in a trust of land only; in some, a writing is required for the transfer of a beneficial interest in any trust. In others, no writing is required, even in a trust of land [Restatement (Third) of Trusts § 53, cmt. a].

   b. Except where expressly required by the trust instrument, notice to the trustee is not necessary for an assignment by the beneficiary to be effective [Restatement (Third) of Trusts § 52, cmt. a]. However, the trustee ordinarily has no liability to an assignee for refusing to honor a purported assignment if:

   (1) there is no writing evidencing the assignment; and

   (2) the beneficiary contends that no assignment has been made.

   c. Unless the trust agreement provides for a gift-over in case of the beneficiary's death (i.e., the beneficiary only has a life estate), a beneficiary's interest in a trust can be devised by will or pass pursuant to intestacy principles.

   d. Where a beneficiary makes multiple assignments of his interest in a trust, the first in time, first in right rule will usually apply [Restatement (Third) of Trusts § 54].

   (1) Where an earlier transferee neglects to inform the trustee of the assignment and a subsequent assignee pays consideration to the assigning beneficiary for the assignment after inquiring of the trustee as to the existence of any previous assignments and receiving a negative response, the latter assignee is often given priority.

   EXAMPLE: T creates a trust with Art as trustee. Mary and Sal are the beneficiaries, who receive the income from the trust until they attain the age of 35, at which point the principal is to be distributed to them in equal shares. Sal assigns his interest to Gus. Subsequently, however, Sal assigns the same interest to Peter. Ordinarily, once an interest is assigned, the assignor no longer has anything additional to convey. If, however, Gus neglected to inform Art of the assignment, and Peter loaned money to Sal upon the basis of the assignment and Art's statement that Sal's interest had not previously been assigned, Peter might be given priority.

2. In the absence of a restrictive provision in the trust instrument to the contrary, creditors can ordinarily attach and foreclose upon a beneficiary's interest in a trust [Restatement (Third) of Trusts § 56].

    a. If this occurs, the trustee must deliver the beneficiary's interest to the successful purchaser (to the extent of the beneficiary's obligation) at the foreclosure sale.

B. Support, Discretionary, and Spendthrift Trusts

1. Where a beneficiary's interest in a trust is restricted by a valid discretionary, support, or spendthrift provision, he cannot assign that interest [Restatement (Third) of Trusts § 58(1)].

2. **Support Provision**

    a. A **support provision** is one in which the trustee is directed to provide only so much income and/or principal of the trust as is necessary for the latter's support and for no other purpose.

        (1) A typical support provision is "for the beneficiary's health, education, maintenance, and support."

    b. A support provision is not merely an expression of the settlor's motive for creating the trust, but actually limits the beneficiary's interest to amounts necessary for his support [Restatement (Third) of Trusts § 50, cmts. d(2)–(3)].

        (1) Any trust property in excess of what is necessary for the beneficiary's support must be distributed as otherwise provided for in the trust instrument.

    c. Where a support provision exists, a beneficiary cannot transfer his interest in the trust, and creditors cannot ordinarily attach a beneficiary's interest in a support trust.

3. **Discretionary Trust**

    a. A **discretionary trust** interest is one in which payment to the beneficiary (even for a stated purpose) is to be made, if at all, at the trustee's absolute discretion [Restatement (Third) of Trusts § 50].

        (1) The hallmark of a discretionary provision is the trustee's ability to prevent a beneficiary from receiving anything under the trust, if the trustee believes it is appropriate to do so.

        (2) Where a discretionary provision exists independent of a support clause, the beneficiary can assign his interest in the trust. However, an assignee's right is of no marketable value unless and until the trustee determines that a distribution to the beneficiary is to be made.

        (3) In jurisdictions without mandatory spendthrift statutes, creditors may attach a beneficiary's interest in a discretionary trust. However, that interest has no marketable value until the trustee determines that a

contribution to the beneficiary should be made and a creditor cannot compel a trustee of a discretionary trust to pay him.

   (a) In some states, the creditor can obtain a "cutoff" order, which directs the trustee to pay the creditor before paying the beneficiary. Such an order has the effect of depriving the beneficiary of trust income, though it does not necessarily ensure that the creditor is ever paid.

   (4) If the trustee makes a distribution to the beneficiary after being notified of an assignment by the beneficiary or attachment by a creditor, he is liable to the assignee or creditor for the amount of that distribution.

4. **Spendthrift Provision**

   a. A **spendthrift provision** is one that precludes [UTC § 103(16); Restatement (Third) of Trusts § 58]:

      (1) a beneficiary from voluntarily transferring his interest in the trust; and

      (2) creditors from reaching that interest.

   b. No specific language is necessary to accomplish this result.

   c. Whether the settlor intended to create a spendthrift trust is a factual issue, determined from all of the circumstances.

      (1) In some states, a spendthrift provision is implied into all income interests unless affirmatively rejected in the trust instrument.

   d. Where, despite a valid spendthrift provision, the beneficiary attempts to voluntarily assign his interest, the trustee may (if he chooses to do so) comply with the transferee's demand, unless the beneficiary has expressly notified the trustee to disregard the assignment.

   e. Where the spendthrift provision prevents alienation by the beneficiary and attachment by creditors, creditors cannot ordinarily reach the beneficiary's interest directly [Restatement (Third) of Trusts § 58, cmt. d(2)].

      (1) Once there has been a distribution from the spendthrift trust to the beneficiary, however, creditors have the right to reach that distribution [Id.].

   f. Spendthrift provisions that limit only the beneficiary's right of alienation are valid. In this situation, creditors of the beneficiary are not prevented from reaching his interest in the trust.

      (1) Spendthrift provisions sometimes apply only to income interests in trusts. They can also be used, however, to limit the alienability of remainders.

C. **Limitations upon the Enforceability of Spendthrift, Support, and Discretionary Trusts**

   1. In certain situations, creditors of a beneficiary can reach the beneficiary's interest in a trust despite a valid support, discretionary, or spendthrift clause.

   2. Once the trustee has actually made a distribution to the beneficiary, the beneficiary's creditors can attach that property through the same means

that are applicable to any debt or owned assets [Restatement (Third) of Trusts § 58, cmt. d(2)].

3. The UTC provides that even if a trust contains a spendthrift provision, a creditor of a beneficiary may reach a mandatory distribution of income or principal if the trustee has not made the distribution to the beneficiary within a reasonable time after the designated distribution date [UTC § 506].

4. Outside of a few states and offshore locations, a settlor is not permitted to insulate his own property from creditors by means of spendthrift, support, or discretionary provisions.

   a. Where a person creates a trust, or furnishes consideration to another person to establish a trust, in which he is a beneficiary, his creditors can reach the maximum portion of the trust that could have been distributed to him despite a valid support, discretionary, or spendthrift provision.

      EXAMPLE: T and X enter into an agreement. T conveys Blackacre to X. In return, X establishes a spendthrift trust for $200,000. The trust instrument provides that T will receive the income for life, and that the principal will pass to the persons designated in T's will. Creditors of T can invade the trust that was established by X to satisfy obligations owed to them by T.

5. In most states, a beneficiary's interest in a trust is subject to the claims of spouses, ex-spouses, and children for alimony or support, notwithstanding a spendthrift clause [Restatement (Third) of Trusts § 59(a)].

   a. In most jurisdictions, persons or entities that furnish necessities of life (i.e., food, clothing, emergency medical attention, etc.) to a beneficiary are entitled to reimbursement from the trust despite a valid support or spendthrift clause [Restatement (Third) of Trusts § 59(b)].

      EXAMPLE: Mickey, the beneficiary under a discretionary spendthrift trust, was taken care of at a state hospital for the mentally ill. In most states, the state is permitted to reach Mickey's interest in the trust to obtain reimbursement for the services and supplies provided to him while he was a patient at the hospital.

   b. The Restatement provides that a beneficiary's interest, even though protected by a spendthrift provision, is subject to the claims of creditors who "preserve the beneficial interest" of that beneficiary [Restatement (Third) of Trusts § 59, cmt. d].

      EXAMPLE: An attorney who, on behalf of the beneficiary of a spendthrift trust, performs services that protect or preserve the trust interest of that otherwise impecunious beneficiary will be able to collect his fees from the beneficiary's interest in the trust.

6. A trust can be invaded by the United States or a state governmental entity to satisfy tax claims against a beneficiary [Restatement (Third) of Trusts § 59, cmt. a(1)].

7. In some jurisdictions, creditors are permitted to reach that part of income not needed for the beneficiary's support or exceeding a certain fixed amount (e.g., $10,000).

   a. In some jurisdictions, creditors can reach some percentage of the income from a spendthrift trust.

   b. In some jurisdictions, tort creditors can reach spendthrift trust income.

D. **Rights of the Settlor's Creditors**

1. Any beneficial interest (e.g., a life estate or reversion) retained by the settlor in a trust is subject to the claims of his creditors.

2. Where the settlor creates a trust in favor of others, as a consequence of which he is or will be rendered insolvent (i.e., his liabilities exceed his assets or he will be unable to pay his debts as they become due) or for the purpose of hindering or defrauding his creditors, the creditors can reach the trust *res* to satisfy their claims against the settlor.

3. In most jurisdictions, the fact that an *inter vivos* trust is revocable by the settlor does not permit his creditors to attach the trust's assets to satisfy their claims against him (unless the trust also constitutes a fraudulent conveyance). Nevertheless, if the settlor is placed into bankruptcy, the court may exercise his power of revocation.

EXAMPLE: T creates a trust, making himself the trustee and conveying Blackacre to the trust. The income is to be distributed to Joe and Jan for life, and the principal to their children. Assuming T is not rendered insolvent by the transfer of Blackacre to the trust, if he subsequently incurs obligations that he cannot pay, T's creditors cannot invade the trust *corpus* to satisfy his obligations to them. If T declares, or is forced into, bankruptcy and he has not previously renounced his power of revocation, the trustee-in-bankruptcy may exercise this power, causing title to Blackacre to be returned to T, and thereby subject that realty to the claims of T's creditors.

V. MODIFICATION OR TERMINATION OF TRUSTS

A. Termination by Settlor

1. Unless the terms of a trust expressly provide that the trust is irrevocable, the settlor may revoke or amend a trust created after the effective date of the adoption of the UTC [UTC § 602(a)].

    a. Effective dates vary by jurisdiction.

2. Under common law, the irrevocability of a trust is presumed unless the right of revocation is reserved.

    a. The common law is applicable for the majority of trusts, including those created before the effective date of the UTC or where the UTC has not been adopted.

3. A revocable *inter vivos* trust may be revoked by the settlor [UTC § 602(c)]:

    a. by substantially complying with the method specified in a trust instrument; or

    b. if no method is specified, by:

        (1) executing a later will or codicil that expressly refers to the trust or specifically devises property that would otherwise have passed according to the terms of the trust; or

        (2) any other method manifesting clear and convincing evidence of the settlor's intent.

4. If the terms of the trust reserve to the settlor a power to revoke or amend the trust exclusively by a particular procedure, the settlor can exercise the power only by substantial compliance with the method prescribed. If the terms of the trust do not make that method exclusive, the settlor's power can be exercised either in the specified manner or in any way that provides clear and convincing evidence of the settlor's intention to do so [Restatement (Third) of Trusts § 63, cmt. i].

5. A settlor may terminate an irrevocable trust only with the consent of all the beneficiaries.

B. Termination of a Trust by Merger

1. If a sole trustee becomes the only beneficiary (i.e., he becomes the holder of all of the beneficial interests of the trust), the trust ceases to exist and he (personally) becomes the owner of the trust assets [UTC § 402; Restatement (Third) of Trusts § 69, cmt. b].

    EXAMPLE: T creates an *inter vivos* trust of which she is the sole trustee. The beneficiaries are herself, X, and Y as joint tenants with right of survivorship. X and Y are killed in a common accident. Inasmuch as T has become the sole trustee and beneficiary, the trust is terminated and T owns the trust property outright (that is, free of the trust).

    EXAMPLE: T creates a trust with himself as trustee. The income is to be paid to T and his wife during their lives, and the principal passes to T's children at his death. If T's wife dies, the trust continues to exist, because additional beneficiaries (T's children) are still alive. The fact that T's children hold only a future interest in the trust is not significant.

C. Termination by Operation of Law

1. A trust is terminated by operation of law where:

   a. accomplishment of the material purposes of the trust have become illegal, impossible, or impractical [Restatement (Third) of Trusts § 67];

   b. the trust *res* has been consumed, destroyed, or lost; or

   c. the trust's purposes have been fully accomplished [Restatement (Third) of Trusts § 61].

D. Administrative Deviations

1. Where exact compliance with the administrative provisions of the trust would, as a result of unforeseen circumstances, frustrate or substantially impair a material purpose sought to be accomplished by the trust, the court, on petition of the trustee, may allow deviation from those administrative provisions as necessary to accomplish the settlor's purposes.

2. The **administrative deviance doctrine** may not, however, be used to change the beneficial interests in the trust.

   EXAMPLE: T creates a trust under which Blackacre (which used to be his farm) is the main asset. The trust instrument states that the farm is not to be sold, and that the income is to be distributed to Sue and Jeffrey. Nevertheless, if farming in that locale becomes unprofitable, the trustee may be able to obtain a court order permitting the sale of the land rather than have the property depreciate in value to the point where it is virtually worthless.

E. Termination by Beneficiaries after Settlor's Death

1. After the settlor has died, courts are reluctant to terminate an active trust if that would interfere with the settlor's intent.

2. The rule of Claflin v. Claflin [20 N.E. 454 (Mass. 1889)] is that after the settlor's death, the trust will not be terminated before the period specified by the settlor has expired and the purposes of the trust have been accomplished, even though all of the beneficiaries approve of such termination.

   a. A material purpose of the trust may be to require the trustee to hold and manage the trust property until the beneficiary reaches an age beyond 21, such as 25 or 30.

   b. If the trust is a spendthrift or discretionary trust, courts are likely to find that the settlor's purpose of protecting the beneficiary continues, and the trust cannot be terminated by consent.

3. However, where no material purpose of the settlor remains, the court may allow termination upon the request of the beneficiaries if all have vested interests, are before the court to grant approval, and are of legal age and not under guardianship.

a. If the trust creates the possibility of interests in unborn beneficiaries, the trust may be impossible to terminate unless a statute permits the appointment of a guardian *ad litem* for an unconceived child.

4. **With Consent of the Trustee**

a. While the trustee alone has no power to terminate the trust unless such power was expressly granted, the trustee and beneficiaries acting together can effect a termination without court order by a conveyance of legal title from the trustee to the beneficiaries, or by another conveyance which merges legal and equitable title and automatically terminates the trust [Restatement (Third) of Trusts § 69].

b. However, if by the terms of the trust or by statute a valid restraint is imposed upon the transfer by the beneficiary of his interest, a conveyance of his interest by the beneficiary to the trustee is ineffective to terminate the trust.

F. Natural Expiration

1. Where the trust was to be in operation for a specified number of years, or until the occurrence of a prescribed event, and that period of time has elapsed or the incident has occurred, the trust ordinarily terminates in accordance with the instrument's terms [Restatement (Third) of Trusts § 61].

G. Modern Trends

1. The Restatement and the UTC both urge that courts have greater authority to grant requests for modification or termination of trusts [Restatement (Third) of Trusts § 62, cmt. b].

2. In addition, courts have shown increasing willingness to permit modification or termination in order to achieve tax advantages for beneficiaries [Restatement (Third) of Trusts § 62, cmt. c].

VI. TRUSTS ARISING BY OPERATION OF LAW—IMPLIED TRUSTS

A. In General

1. Trusts that arise by operation of law or that are used by courts as a remedy are not trusts in the legal sense of the word. The trustee of a resulting or constructive trust has no active duties other than to transfer title to the assets to the appropriate party.

B. Resulting Trusts

1. There are two circumstances in which resulting trusts arise:

a. when an express trust makes an incomplete disposition of assets or fails after property has been conveyed to the trustee [Restatement (Third) of Trusts § 8]; and

(1) Where an express trust partially or completely fails, or is terminated by operation of law, and there is no alternative disposition for the trust's assets, a resulting trust ordinarily arises. Typical situations are where [Restatement (Third) of Trusts § 8, cmt. b]:

(a) the trust has no beneficiaries (e.g., none were ever named, they have died, they cannot be located or identified, or they disclaim their trust interests);

(b) no provision has been made for a portion of the trust *res;*

(c) where a trust designated for a specific purpose is invalid, insufficient, or excessive;

(d) the trust purpose was never described or is unclear; or

(e) carrying out the material purposes of the trust has become impractical or illegal.

EXAMPLE: T conveys Blackacre to Y, as trustee, with instructions to hold the land in trust for beneficiaries that T will name later. However, T fails to name any beneficiaries prior to his death. At T's death, Y holds Blackacre in a resulting trust for the residuary devisees of T's will, or if T's will did not contain a residuary clause or T died intestate, for T's heirs.

EXAMPLE: T transfers $100,000 to X, as trustee, to use the income from this amount to support Elmer (T's brother). If T fails to designate how the principal should be utilized after Elmer dies, at Elmer's death the remainder is held by X in a resulting trust for T's estate.

EXAMPLE: T's will leaves $50,000 in trust to support the activities of the local Boy's Club. However, the Boy's Club has insufficient other resources and is obliged to close. If the *cy pres* doctrine is not applicable, the principal and unexpended interest are held in a resulting trust for T's estate.

EXAMPLE: T transfers $1 million to X, as trustee, to build a small playground for children on a parcel of land that T had previously conveyed to the city. Assuming the *cy pres* doctrine is not applicable, if it takes only a portion of this sum to complete the playground, X would hold the balance in a resulting trust for T (or, if T has died, his estate).

EXAMPLE: T, in his will, devises $500,000 to X, as trustee, to pay the income to Z until she reaches 35 years of age, and then to distribute the principal to her if she is then living. If Z fails to reach 35, and no alternative disposition has been provided for in the trust, X holds the principal in a resulting trust for T's estate.

b. purchase-money trusts [Restatement (Third) of Trusts § 9].

  (1) If a party pays (or obligates himself to pay) the original purchase price of property, but directs that title to the asset be placed in another's name, then, unless the payor and grantee stand in a certain, close familial relationship, there is a rebuttable presumption that the grantee holds the property in a resulting trust for the payor [Restatement (Third) of Trusts § 7, cmt. c].

    (a) Where the payor is the spouse, descendant, or other natural object of the bounty of the person in whose name title is taken, there is a rebuttable presumption that a gift was intended [Restatement (Third) of Trusts § 9(2)].

    (b) Generally, other familial relationships have not been deemed to raise a presumption of gift.

    EXAMPLE: Where a brother provides the purchase money and directs title to be taken in the name of his sister, there is a rebuttable presumption that the grantee holds title to the property in trust for her brother.

    (c) Some courts are divided on which presumption applies when a spouse is the payor and directs that title be taken in the other spouse's name.

      1) The emerging view under these circumstances is to presume that an outright gift was intended [Id.].

  (2) Some jurisdictions have abolished the purchase-money resulting trust by statute.

  EXAMPLE: T pays Owner $50,000 for Greenacre, but directs that Josh be named as grantee upon the deed. Assuming T and Josh do not stand in a close familial relationship, there is a rebuttable presumption that Josh holds Greenacre in a resulting trust for T.

  (3) Purchase-money resulting trusts also arise where [Restatement (Third) of Trusts § 9, cmt. d]:

    (a) one or more persons provide all or part of the purchase money for property; and

    (b) title is taken in the name of another, or in the names of the payors in shares different from the proportions in which the purchase money was provided.

(4) In such cases, there is a rebuttable presumption that the takers of title, unless standing in a certain, close familial relationship with the payor, hold the property in trust for the payor and in conformity with the share of purchase money each contributed.

EXAMPLE: T and X each contribute $25,000 toward the purchase of Greenacre, but the owner of the parcel is instructed to designate X as the sole grantee in the deed. Inasmuch as T paid one-half of the purchase price, there is a rebuttable presumption that X owns an undivided one-half interest in the land and holds the balance in a resulting trust for T. Thus, X, individually, and X as resulting trustee for T, are tenants in common.

EXAMPLE: T pays $50,000 to Owner for Blackacre and directs that title be taken in Al's name. If T claimed that Al held Blackacre in a resulting trust for him (T), Al could rebut the presumption by showing that he (Al) had borrowed the money from T, and directed T to pay the proceeds from the loan to Owner. In this situation, while Al is liable to T for repayment of the loan, he would not be obliged to convey Blackacre to T. No resulting trust occurs, because the funds used to purchase the land actually belonged to Al (i.e., he acquired ownership of the funds by borrowing them from T). Under these circumstances, T might have an equitable lien against Blackacre for the amount of his loan to Al.

2. As a general matter, the trustee of a resulting trust has the same duties and obligations as other trustees. Primary among his responsibilities, however, are to:

a. convey the trust *res* back to the settlor (or his estate) or payor (where a purchase-money trust is involved); and

b. account for any income traceable to the trust from the time that it arose.

C. Constructive Trusts

1. A **constructive trust** is an equitable remedy whereby a trust is erected on the holder of specific property to redress wrongdoing or prevent unjust enrichment [Restatement (Third) of Trusts § 18].

a. It is typically imposed when property has been wrongfully obtained (e.g., acquired by fraud or undue influence) or the beneficiary has killed the decedent (if a slayer statute does not apply) [Id.].

2. The purpose of a constructive trust is to oblige the holder of property to divest himself of it and transfer it to the person entitled to that asset [Restatement (Third) of Trusts § 18, cmt. a].

EXAMPLE: X orally promises T that if T will convey Blackacre to him, he will hold it in trust for Darryl until Darryl reaches 30 years of age. Subsequently, X refuses to transfer the land to Darryl. If it can be shown that X never intended to convey Blackacre to Darryl (i.e., that X had made a fraudulent promise), a court may impose a constructive trust upon the land in favor of Darryl.

3. The Statute of Frauds does not apply to resulting or constructive trusts [Restatement (Third) of Trusts § 7, cmt. g].

VII. CHARITABLE TRUSTS

A. Distinguishing Characteristics

1. Charitable trusts have certain characteristics that distinguish them from express, private trusts [UTC § 405].

2. Four significant aspects of a charitable trust are its charitable purpose, indefinite beneficiaries, exemption from the Rule Against Perpetuities, and use of the *cy pres* doctrine [Restatement (Third) of Trusts § 28, cmts. a-d].

B. Charitable Purpose

1. The trust must have a charitable purpose.

2. The major categories of charitable purposes are [UTC § 405(a)]:

   a. the relief of poverty;

   b. the advancement of education;

   c. the advancement of religion;

   d. the promotion of health;

   e. the performance of governmental and municipal purposes (e.g., maintenance of parks); and

   f. other purposes beneficial to the community.

3. A charitable purpose can be broad, as long as the trustee is constrained to use the trust exclusively for that objective.

   a. A trust established simply for charity is permissible, but courts have sometimes refused to sustain trusts established for the attainment of benevolent, philanthropic, liberal, or worthy purposes (although the modern trend is to construe these terms as synonymous with charity whenever possible, inasmuch as courts favor charitable gifts).

4. The objective of a charitable trust must be to benefit the public; but the subjective motive of the settlor for establishing the trust may be selfish in nature [Restatement (Third) of Trusts § 28, cmt. a].

   EXAMPLE: A settlor may create a valid charitable trust for the advancement of education even though the predominant reason for this action is to reduce his taxes, gain favorable notices, or achieve some similar personal objective.

5. The terms of a charitable trust must facilitate the valid charitable purpose.

   EXAMPLE: A trust that directs payments to be made directly to elementary school children at Christmas and Easter breaks "to be used by such child in the furtherance of his or her obtainment of an education" is not valid as a charitable trust because its structure does not support the alleged purpose. The form of payment (cash), the timing of payments (at holiday breaks), and the lack of any device for ensuring the funds are used for education suggest that the settlor's true intent was to bestow happiness on schoolchildren rather than to promote education.

6. A settlor cannot restrict benefits of a charitable trust to a small group of people (like friends or relatives), even if the benefits are payable only for

otherwise charitable purposes like education or health [Restatement (Third) of Trusts § 28, cmt. a(1)].

EXAMPLE: A trust to pay for the education of the settlor's kin is invalid as a charitable trust. However, a trust to pay for the education of students interested in physics, with a preference for qualified applicants who are related to the settlor, would be valid in many jurisdictions.

C. Indefinite Beneficiaries

1. The beneficiaries must be indefinite [Restatement (Third) of Trusts § 28, cmt. c].

2. The fact that there are a limited number of persons actually receiving funds does not cause a charitable trust to fail if the recipients are to be chosen from a sufficiently large and indefinite group.

   EXAMPLE: A trust to provide college scholarships for up to five needy children whose fathers were killed while on law-enforcement duty would be valid. Although it might be conceivable to ascertain all children eligible for such a scholarship, the difficulty inherent in this task means the class is sufficiently "indefinite."

3. **Enforcement by Beneficiaries**

   a. Potential beneficiaries of a charitable trust have no standing to sue for enforcement of its terms unless they comprise a small group of beneficiaries with a special interest in the trust [Id.].

   b. The attorney general in most states, as representative of the community, has the authority and duty to sue to enforce charitable trusts operating in their state [Id.].

   c. The settlor can also sue to enforce a charitable trust that he created [UTC § 405(c)].

D. Perpetual Existence

1. Charitable trusts may have a perpetual existence (i.e., the Rule Against Perpetuities has limited application to charitable trusts) [Restatement (Third) of Trusts § 28, cmt. d].

   a. Although a charitable trust may be of perpetual duration, where the charitable trust is preceded by a noncharitable estate, the charitable interest must vest within the period of time prescribed by the RAP [Restatement (Third) of Trusts § 29, cmt. g(2)].

2. A **mixed trust** has both charitable and private purposes [Restatement (Third) of Trusts § 28, cmt. e].

   a. The characteristics of charitable and private trusts are mutually exclusive in that:

      (1) a charitable trust must have indefinite beneficiaries; and

      (2) a private trust must have ascertainable beneficiaries.

   b. A trust that has both charitable and private purposes will fail unless the private and public purposes can be segregated (either proportionally or at different points in time) into separate trusts [Id.].

EXAMPLE: T creates a trust pursuant to which X, the trustee, is to distribute the income to A for life, and thereafter to use the income to purchase reference books for the local public library. The latter purpose is charitable, because it represents a gift for the advancement of education. The trust is valid. While there are both private and charitable purposes, the periods of time during which each is operative are distinct. There are actually two trusts, a private trust of a life estate, followed by a charitable trust of the remainder.

EXAMPLE: T creates a testamentary trust, under the terms of which the trustee is to use the income of the trust "for the support of settlor's wife and children, or for the maintenance of Central Park." The trust will fail in its entirety. As a whole, it neither qualifies as a private nor charitable trust. Furthermore, there is no objective standard by which the trust might be divided into two distinct components, so that each could separately qualify as a valid trust.

EXAMPLE: T creates a trust designating "X as trustee, to use the income as president of Elks Lodge #57 and support veterans of the U.S. armed forces." The trust could be viewed as having mixed purposes: supporting Elks Lodge #57, which constitutes a private purpose, and supporting U.S. armed forces veterans, which is a charitable purpose. If this is the situation, the entire trust fails. However, the gift can arguably be bifurcated into two separate trusts (one for Elks Lodge #57, and the other for veterans of the U.S. armed forces). Alternatively, it could be contended that the trust is entirely charitable in nature, if the "and" is construed as meaning "for." Under this interpretation, the words "president of Elks Lodge #57" are viewed as merely assisting in the identification of X (rather than constituting a distinct trust purpose).

E. *Cy Pres* Doctrine

1. If the settlor's exact charitable purpose cannot be carried out, the court may direct the application of the trust property to another charitable purpose that approximates the settlor's intention [Restatement (Third) of Trusts § 67].

    a. This doctrine, which permits courts to draw on their general equitable powers over trusts, is necessary to meet contingencies that arise over time.

2. *Cy pres* may be applied where:

    a. the settlor's specific charitable purpose with respect to a valid charitable trust becomes impossible, impracticable, or illegal to carry out; and

    b. the settlor had, in addition to this specific charitable purpose, a general charitable intent (i.e., the settlor's specific charitable purpose was not intended to be exclusive).

3. If these requirements have been met, the court may modify the trust to allow the trustee to carry out a substantially similar charitable purpose.

4. Generally, the court will infer from the making of a charitable trust that the settlor had a general charitable intent. However, where the trust instrument

makes clear that the settlor would have preferred the trust to terminate rather than to be used in another manner, the *cy pres* doctrine cannot be utilized [Restatement (Third) of Trusts § 67, cmt. b].

    a.   If the settlor has provided for a "gift-over" in the event that the charitable purpose cannot be accomplished, this is ordinarily viewed as an indication that the settlor lacked a general charitable intent.

> **NOTE** ▶ In the typical gift-over situation, unless the transfer is to another charitable trust, the gift often violates the Rule Against Perpetuities.

    5.   Language in a trust instrument that the trust *res* is to be used only for the stated charitable purpose is not dispositive on the question of whether the settlor had a general charitable intent.

        a.   While such language indicates that the settlor intended the trust to be used only for the specific charitable purpose while possible to accomplish it, it does not necessarily show that the settlor would have preferred the trust to terminate, rather than be used for a similar charitable purpose if the original charitable purpose was no longer possible to accomplish.

        EXAMPLE: T creates a charitable trust to support medical research to develop a cure for a rare disease that primarily afflicts children. If a complete cure for that malady is later discovered, under the *cy pres* doctrine, the trustee could be instructed to carry out the trust for a different disease that has a disproportionately high impact upon children.

        EXAMPLE: T creates a charitable trust to support medical research to develop a cure for a certain disease that primarily afflicts children. T established this trust because one of his daughters had died of this disease. If a complete cure for this malady is later discovered, the *cy pres* doctrine would not be applied if the court determines that T was interested only in mitigating the effects of the particular disease that took his child's life. Consequently, any remaining assets in the trust would be held by the trustee in a resulting trust for T's estate.

    6.   The *cy pres* doctrine can be used only to modify an already valid, existing charitable trust. This doctrine cannot be used to turn a private trust into a charitable trust or to reform an invalid trust.

    7.   *Cy pres* is not applicable when the trust instrument specifies an alternative charitable beneficiary [Id.].

F.   Termination

    1.   If a charitable trust cannot be performed as intended and the requirements for *cy pres* are not met, the trust terminates and a resulting trust in favor of the settlor's estate arises [Restatement (Third) of Trusts § 8, cmt. g].

VIII. FUTURE INTERESTS

A. **In General**

1. Reversions, remainders, executory interests, life estates, and estates for years, and the rules applicable to them are discussed at length in the Real Property outline.

B. **Powers of Appointment**

1. A **power of appointment** is a power created by the **donor** of property which enables another individual (the **donee** of the power) to designate transferees of the property and the shares they are to receive. The donor may limit the donee's power by specifying in what manner or upon what conditions the power may be exercised.

    EXAMPLE: The donee may be given the right to exercise the power during the donee's lifetime, or may only be able to exercise the power in a will. The donee may be given the power to designate anyone in the world, including the donee's estate, or may be limited to choosing among individuals selected by the donor.

2. A **power of attorney** qualifies as a power of appointment.

3. Powers of appointment are commonly used in trusts and wills because of the flexibility that they provide in an estate plan.

    EXAMPLE: H, a married man with young children, may wish to ensure that his wife and children are effectively provided for upon his death, but he may wish to give his wife (W) the flexibility to determine how much money is spent on each child. He might choose either a testamentary trust or a will that gives W (the donee) the power to choose how much of his estate should be distributed to each child at the time of W's death. H, therefore, might leave his entire estate "to W for life, and at her death to such of our children as she shall appoint by will." Because it is possible that W will fail to exercise her power of appointment in her will, H's will may further provide "If W fails to make such an appointment, then to our children in equal shares." In this typical example, H is the donor, W the donee, and the children the objects of the power, or appointees. The property to be disposed of by appointment is the subject matter of the power, and the provision for disposition if the power is not exercised is the gift in default of appointment.

4. Powers of appointment are classified in several ways, including on the basis of the manner in which they may be exercised (by *inter vivos* deed, will, or by either deed or will) and the permissible objects (appointees) specified.

5. Where the donee of the power may appoint to anyone, including the donee or the donee's estate, the donee is said to have a **general power**.

    a. A general power exercisable by *inter vivos* deed is considered the equivalent of outright ownership of the property.

    b. The power to convey only by will is, of course, somewhat more restrictive.

6. Under a **special power**, the donee is limited by the donor's selection of the ultimate takers.

   a. Thus, the donor may give the power to appoint certain property to "such one or more of my children as the donee may believe are in need," or "to such of my descendants as the donee may select," or "to such of the following charities as the donee may believe most deserving."

   b. The examples above with H and W involve special powers of appointment.

C. Exercise of Power

1. Powers of appointment may be classified not only as general or special, but also by the time at which the power may be exercised.

   a. A power exercisable only by will is a **testamentary power**.

   b. A power which may be exercised at any time by deed is a presently exercisable (or *inter vivos*) **power**.

2. The power must be exercised in the manner specified by the donor. Thus, a testamentary power which the donee purports to exercise by *inter vivos* conveyance will be ineffective.

3. In the absence of restrictions by the donor, the donee effectively exercises the power whenever the donee's intent to exercise the power is evident.

4. The donee may not delegate to others a power of appointment, but may circumvent this restriction by exercising the general power to create a partial estate (e.g., a life estate) and creating in a new donee a power of appointment to take effect when the partial estate has terminated.

5. **Exercise by Residuary Clause in Donee's Will**

   a. A power of appointment which permits the donee of the power to exercise that power in the donee's will may be exercised by a general devise of all the donee's property.

   b. Testamentary power of appointment gives the appointee, in his will, power to designate who receives what share of trust assets, and can be limited to a group selected by the donor of power.

   c. Absent a specific reference requirement, a power of appointment is exercised if the general residuary clause is coupled with a blanket exercise clause.

      (1) A blanket exercise clause exercises a power of appointment if it contains language that encompasses all property over which a testator has a power of appointment.

      (2) If the donor requires a donee to specifically name the instrument that created the power of appointment, it must be done for the power to be properly exercised.

   d. In a minority of states, a standard residuary clause adequately expresses the testator's intent to exercise the power of appointment, although the testator did not expressly mention powers of appointment in the will.

6. **Exercise in Favor of Fiduciary**

   a. Unless specifically allowed by the will, trust document, or other writing appointing a fiduciary, the fiduciary may not exercise a power of appointment in favor of himself, his estate, creditors, or creditors of the his estate.

7. **Exercise of Special Powers**

   a. The donee of a special power must exercise it in compliance with the expressed intention of the donor.

   b. If the instrument creating the special power enables the donee to distribute the subject matter to any one or more of the designated objects (appointees), the power is called **exclusive**.

   c. If the donee is required to distribute at least part of the subject matter to each object, it is a **nonexclusive** power. With a nonexclusive power, the donee determines the amount that each object, or appointee, will receive, but the donee may not refuse to distribute some part of the subject matter to each object. An extremely small share could be challenged by the object as an "illusory" exercise of the donee's power.

   d. The donee of a special power of appointment can only exercise in favor of objects designated by the donor of power, excluding the donee, donee's creditors, and donee's estate as permissible objects.

   e. If the donee can appoint trust assets outright, he can also create more limited interests unless the donor stated otherwise.

      (1) Donees can appoint property in trust for objects of power.

D. Release of Power

1. A donee may release, or destroy, a power of appointment in most circumstances.

2. This differs from failure to exercise a power in that a donee who releases a power takes action to effect the release.

3. A donee often releases a power for tax reasons, but may also do so to transfer the subject matter in a manner not necessarily intended by the testator.

   EXAMPLE: A donee of a special testamentary power can transfer property during the donee's lifetime to the person named as the taker in default, by releasing the power.

4. A release of the power, which is normally made by written *inter vivos* instrument, is distinguishable from a disclaimer, or renunciation, where the proposed donee refuses to accept the power.

E. Creditors' Rights

1. Creditors of the donee may seek to reach the assets of the power of appointment.

2. Creditors will be unsuccessful in attempting to reach the subject matter of special power, because the donee serves in a capacity analogous to that of a trustee.

3. If the donee exercises the general power of appointment, creditors will be able to reach the assets.

   a. The result is the same as if a person creates a protective trust for the settlor's own benefit.

F. Rule Against Perpetuities Applied to Powers of Appointment

1. All special powers of appointment and general testamentary powers are subject to the Rule Against Perpetuities.

2. A special power of appointment and a general testamentary power, since they both relate back to the time of the creation of the power, are void if the power is capable of being exercised beyond the period of perpetuities.

Wills

TABLE OF CONTENTS

I. INTRODUCTION

A. Governing Law

1. The law governing wills and intestate succession developed from the common law and has largely been codified in the statutes of the 50 states, the District of Columbia, and the territories.

2. Where the law has not been codified in statute, those states have typically adopted the Uniform Probate Code ("UPC"), either in whole or in part.

    a. Another important source is the Restatement (Third) of Property: Wills and Other Donative Transfers ("Restatement (Third) of Prop.: Wills").

B. Definitions

1. A deceased person is known in the law of estates as a **decedent**.

2. A decedent's **estate** is the real and personal property the decedent leaves at death [UPC § 1-201(13)].

    a. A decedent's **personal property** passes according to the law of the decedent's domicile at the time of his death.

    b. A decedent's **real property** passes according to the law of the state where it is located.

3. A person who dies without a will dies **intestate**; one who dies leaving a will dies **testate**.

4. The process of distributing intestate property is often referred to as **estate administration**; the process of proving a will is technically referred to as **probate**.

    a. Nowadays, however, the terms are used somewhat interchangeably.

5. **Issue** includes all lineal descendants from an ancestor in any degree, e.g., children, grandchildren, etc. [UPC § 1-201(24)].

6. **Heirs** means persons, including the surviving spouse and the state, who are entitled under the statutes of intestate succession to the property of a decedent [UPC § 1-201(20)].

7. A **devise** (to a **devisee**) means a testamentary disposition of real or personal property [UPC § 1-201(10)].

II. INTESTATE DISTRIBUTION

A. In General

1. A person who dies without a will dies intestate; his estate is an **intestate estate** [UPC § 2-101].

2. Property of the estate that, for some reason, does not pass under a will passes according to the intestacy laws, which are called "the laws of descent and distribution."

3. **Testacy proceeding** means a proceeding to establish a will or determine intestacy [UPC § 1-201(52)].

    a. Intestacy is **total** if the person who dies either does not make a will or makes a will that is totally invalid.

    b. Intestacy is **partial** when the testator makes a will, but part of the property in the estate does not pass under the will.

    > **EXAMPLE:** A leaves an estate (after expenses, debts, and taxes) of $1,000. His will states only that C, D, and E are each to receive $300, and does not specify what is to be done with any excess property. The $100 not distributed under the will passes by intestacy and will be distributed according to the laws of descent and distribution.

B. Statutory Provisions

1. **Spouse Survives**

    a. The entire estate goes to the surviving spouse if [UPC § 2-102(1)]:

        (1) no descendant or parent of the decedent survives the decedent; or

        (2) all of the decedent's surviving descendants are also descendants of the surviving spouse and there is no other descendant of the surviving spouse who survives the decedent.

    b. In some instances (e.g., divorce or annulment), a spouse is disqualified from taking pursuant to the laws of intestacy [UPC § 2-802].

    c. A decree of separation that does not terminate the status of a married couple is not a divorce for purposes of this section [UPC § 2-802(a)].

    d. Although some state statutes bar the surviving spouse for desertion or adultery, the UPC requires some definitive legal act to bar the surviving spouse. Normally, this is divorce [UPC § 2-802, cmt.].

    e. If there is no surviving descendant of the decedent but he is survived by a parent or parents, the first $300,000 plus three-fourths of the balance of the intestate estate goes to the surviving spouse [UPC § 2-102(2)].

        (1) The remainder of the property goes to the surviving parent, or if both parents survive, in equal shares to each.

    f. If there are surviving descendants of the decedent, all of whom are issue of the surviving spouse, and the surviving spouse has one or more surviving descendants who are not descendants of the decedent, the first $225,000 plus one-half of the balance of the intestate estate goes to the surviving spouse [UPC § 2-102(3)].

    (1)   The remaining portion of the estate is divided among the descendants.

  g.   If there are surviving descendants of the decedent, one or more of whom are not issue of the surviving spouse, the first $150,000 plus one-half of the intestate estate goes to the surviving spouse [UPC § 2-102(4)].

    (1)   The remaining portion of the estate is divided among the descendants.

2. No Surviving Spouse or Spouse Not Entitled to Take

  a.   Any part of the intestate estate not passing to a decedent's surviving spouse under Section 2-102, or the entire intestate estate if there is no surviving spouse (or the surviving spouse is not entitled to take), passes in the following order to the individuals who survive the decedent [UPC § 2-103]:

    (1)   to the decedent's descendants by representation;

        (a)   If a decedent's intestate estate passes **by representation** (or *per capita)* to the decedent's descendants, the estate is divided into as many equal shares as there are [UPC § 2-106(b)]:

            1)   surviving descendants in the generation nearest to the decedent that contains one or more surviving descendants; and

            2)   deceased descendants in the same generation who left surviving descendants, if any.

        (b)   Each surviving descendant in the nearest generation is allocated one share. The remaining shares, if any, are combined and then divided in the same manner among the surviving descendants of the deceased descendants as if the surviving descendants who were allocated a share and their surviving descendants had predeceased the decedent [UPC § 2-106(b)].

           <u>EXAMPLE:</u> T has three children: A, B, and C. B and C predecease T, but A survives. A has three children: 1, 2, and 3. B had one child, X. C had two children, Y and Z. T is thus survived by one child and three grandchildren. The estate is divided first by thirds, and A takes a third. 1, 2, and 3 take nothing, because A survived T. X, Y, and Z are treated equally under the rules of representation, so B and C's shares will be combined into one share totaling two-thirds of T's estate, and X, Y, and Z will split that evenly, with each taking a 2/9th share of the estate.

           <u>EXAMPLE:</u> If X's children, A and B, predecease him, but A's children, E, F, and G, and B's children, C and D, survive, the grandchildren take *per capita,* each getting a one-fifth share. When persons are entitled to take *per capita,* each takes in his own right (not by representation from the parent) and shares equally in the estate.

    (2)   if there is no surviving descendant, to the decedent's parents equally if both survive, or to the surviving parent if only one survives;

        (a)   A parent can be barred from inheriting from or through a child if the child died before reaching 18 years of age and there is clear and convincing evidence that immediately before the child's death, the parental rights of the parent could have been terminated on the basis of nonsupport, abandonment, abuse, neglect, or other actions or inactions of the parent toward the child [UPC § 2-114(a)(2)].

(3) if there is no surviving descendant or parent, to the descendants of the decedent's parents or either of them by representation;

(4) if there is no surviving descendant, parent, or descendant of parent, but the decedent is survived on both the paternal and maternal sides by one or more grandparents or descendants of grandparents:

(a) half to the decedent's paternal grandparents equally if both survive; to the surviving paternal grandparent if only one survives; or to the descendants of the decedent's paternal grandparents or either of them if both are deceased, the descendants taking by representation; and

(b) half to the decedent's maternal grandparents equally if both survive; to the surviving maternal grandparent if only one survives; or to the descendants of the decedent's maternal grandparents or either of them if both are deceased, the descendants taking by representation; and

(5) if there is no surviving descendant, parent, or descendant of a parent, but the decedent is survived by one or more grandparents or descendants of grandparents on the paternal but not the maternal side, or on the maternal but not the paternal side, to the decedent's relatives on the side with one or more surviving members in the manner described in subsection (4).

b. In some instances, the courts will look to priority of distribution by looking at the degree of consanguinity, but this is the minority rule.

3. **Limitations on Inheritance by Relations Beyond Grandparents**

a. If there is no taker by a descendant of the grandparents, but the decedent has [UPC § 2-103(b)]:

(1) one deceased spouse who has one or more descendants who survive the decedent, the estate passes to that spouse's descendants by representation; or

(2) more than one deceased spouse who has one or more descendants who survive the decedent, an equal share of the estate passes to each set of descendants by representation.

4. **Escheat**

a. If there is no spouse or other person entitled to inherit under the statute, the property **escheats** (passes) to the state [UPC § 2-105].

5. **Heir Must Survive Decedent by 120 Hours**

a. An individual who fails to survive the decedent cannot take as an heir or a devisee [Restatement (Third) of Prop.: Wills § 1.2].

b. If the time of death of the decedent or the heir, or both, cannot be determined so as to establish that the decedent survived the heir by

120 hours, the otherwise heir will be deemed to have failed to survive the 120-hour period [UPC § 2-702(a)].

    (1)   An individual born before a decedent's death who fails to survive the decedent by 120 hours is deemed to have predeceased the decedent [UPC § 2-104(a)(1)].

c.   The UPC further adds a clear and convincing evidence standard of proof. Thus, a person who cannot be established by clear and convincing evidence to have survived the decedent by 120 hours is deemed to have predeceased the decedent.

    (1)   By resolving doubtful questions of survival by 120 hours in favor of non-survival, the clear-and-convincing-evidence standard of proof is designed to further the decedent's presumed intention of passing property only to persons who can personally benefit from it [Restatement (Third) of Prop.: Wills § 1.2, cmt. d].

d.   Under the UPC, the 120-hour requirement of survival applies not only to probate transfers, but also to certain non-probate transfers taking effect at death, such as life insurance and joint tenancies [Id.].

e.   This requirement does not apply if its application would cause the estate to escheat to the state [UPC § 2-104(b)].

EXAMPLE: A and his spouse, B, die together in a car crash. Witnesses report that B survived A by two hours. B is treated as having predeceased A for purposes of succession, despite sufficient evidence of B's chronological survival.

C. Special Problems of Intestate Distribution

1.   There are several special categories of children who are treated somewhat differently in inheritance law from the natural-born children of married parents born in the lifetimes of both partners.

a.   The definition of **child** includes one entitled to take from a parent who dies intestate, but excludes a stepchild, foster child, grandchild, or any more remote descendant [UPC § 1-201(5)].

2.   **Adopted Children**

a.   **Adoptee** is defined in the UPC as an individual who is adopted [UPC § 2-115]. The term is not limited to an individual who is adopted as a minor, but includes an individual who is adopted as an adult [UPC § 2-119, cmt.].

b.   The UPC follows a **transplantation theory** with regard to adopted children. That is, an adopted child loses any relationship with his natural parents and is treated as the natural-born child of the adoptive parents, so that such child can inherit from and through his adoptive parents and their kindred, and the latter can inherit from and through the adopted child [UPC § 2-119(a)].

    (1)   Thus, a parent-child relationship exists between an adoptee and the adoptee's adoptive parent or parents [UPC § 2-118]. If the adoptee dies intestate, his property is distributed among those persons who would have been kindred if he had actually been born to the adopting parents.

c. If the natural parent remarries and consents to the adoption of his child by his new spouse, the right of the adopted child to inherit from both of his natural parents is not affected. A parent-child relationship exists between an individual who is adopted by the spouse of either natural parent and [UPC § 2-119(b)]:

   (1) the genetic parent whose spouse adopted the individual; and

   (2) the other genetic parent, but only for the purpose of the right of the adoptee or a descendant of the adoptee to inherit from or through the other genetic parent.

   EXAMPLE: Following her divorce, M gets custody of her child, A, and then subsequently remarries. If the stepfather now adopts the child with M's consent, A will not be cut off from either natural parent, and can inherit from M as well as his natural father.

d. A parent-child relationship exists between both genetic parents and an individual who is adopted by a relative of a genetic parent, or by the spouse or surviving spouse of a relative of a genetic parent, but only for the purpose of the right of the adoptee or a descendant of the adoptee to inherit from or through either genetic parent [UPC § 2-119(c)].

e. A parent-child relationship exists between both genetic parents and an individual who is adopted after the death of both genetic parents, but only for the purpose of the right of the adoptee or a descendant of the adoptee to inherit through either genetic parent [UPC § 2-119(d)].

f. Most intestacy statutes, including the UPC, treat an adopted child as a full member of the child's adoptive family [UPC § 2.5, cmt. d].

   (1) Thus, if a class gift is made by any instrument to persons described as the adoptive family's children, issue, descendants, etc., the adopted child takes as a member of the class in the same way as a natural child, unless the testator expresses a contrary intention.

3. **Stepchildren**

   a. Stepchildren have no inheritance rights unless they are adopted, or unless they can prove adoption by estoppel.

   b. **Adoption by estoppel** can be shown if there is an attempt to adopt that does not occur because of a technical defect, or if the stepparent contracts with the natural parents to adopt the child, but for some reason does not.

   EXAMPLE: David filed papers to adopt his stepson Kevin, but died unexpectedly before the adoption became legal. Kevin would still be able to inherit from David.

   c. In this latter case, stepparents cannot rely on the doctrine of adoption by estoppel in an attempt to inherit from their stepchildren, thus taking advantage of their own failure to carry out the contract.

4. **Half-Blood Relatives**

   a. Half-blood relatives are siblings of the decedent by only one of his parents; their representatives take equally with relatives of the whole blood and their representatives [UPC § 2-107].

   EXAMPLE: If the decedent is survived by a brother who shares the same mother and father, and by a half brother who only shares the same mother, both brothers are on an equal footing for inheritance purposes.

5. **Nonmarital Children**

   a. A child born out of wedlock is considered the child of his mother and her kindred for purposes of intestate inheritance.

   b. Inheritance by an illegitimate child from his natural father has been the subject of recent litigation and legislative action. For purposes of descent, a child born out of wedlock is considered to be the child of his father when the identity of the father is determined in any one of the following ways:

      (1) the parents marry each other;

      (2) during the lifetime of the child, the father openly holds out the child to be his and receives the child into his home, or openly holds the child out to be his and provides support for the child; or

      (3) there is clear and convincing evidence that the man was the father of the child; this may include a prior court determination of paternity.

   c. Paternity may be established by any reliable scientific method, including DNA analysis [Restatement (Third) of Prop.: Wills § 2.5, cmt. b].

   d. A father who has refused to acknowledge paternity should be barred from inheriting from or through the child [Restatement (Third) of Prop.: Wills § 2.5, cmt. m]. The parent's ancestors and collateral relatives should also be barred from inheriting through the parent from the child [Id.].

6. **Posthumous Children**

   a. Persons conceived before the decedent's death, but born alive thereafter, take as if they were born in his lifetime. An individual in gestation at a decedent's death is deemed to be living at the decedent's death if the individual lives 120 hours after birth. If it is not established by clear and convincing evidence that an individual in gestation at the decedent's death lived 120 hours after birth, it is deemed that the individual failed to survive for the required period [UPC § 2-104(a)(2)].

   b. Nowadays, problems may arise with children who are the product of *in vitro* fertilization; for example, they may exist as fertilized embryos before the death of the decedent, but they may not be born until several years after the decedent's death, long after the requisite time period. Traditional law rejects claims by or on behalf of children *en ventre sa Frigidaire*.

      (1) Under the UPC, if an individual is a parent of a gestational or assisted-reproduction child who is conceived after the individual's

death, the child is treated as in gestation at the individual's death if the child is [UPC §§ 2-121(h), 2-120(k)]:

(a) *in utero* not later than 36 months after the individual's death; or

(b) born not later than 45 months after the individual's death.

D. Advancements

1. If a person dies intestate as to all or any part of his estate, property that he gave to an heir in his lifetime is treated as an advancement against the estate only if [UPC § 2-109(a)]:

   a. declared in a contemporaneous writing by the decedent or acknowledged in writing by the heir as an advancement; or

   b. the decedent's contemporaneous writing or the heir's written acknowledgement indicate that the gift is to be taken into account in computing the division and distribution of the decedent's intestate estate.

2. The property advanced is valued as of the earlier of the time the heir came into possession or enjoyment of the property or the time of the decedent's death [UPC § 2-109(b)].

3. If the recipient of the property fails to survive the decedent, the property is not taken into account in computing the division and distribution of the decedent's intestate estate unless the decedent's contemporaneous writing provides otherwise [UPC § 2-109(c)].

III. EXECUTION OF ORDINARY WILLS

A. In General

1. A **will** is a document executed by a testator that takes effect on the death of the testator.
2. Usually, a will disposes of a person's property, but need not actually do so in order to constitute a valid will.
3. A will may also include any codicil and testamentary instrument that [UPC § 1-201(57)]:
   a. appoints an executor;
   b. nominates a guardian;
   c. revokes or revises another will; or
   d. expressly excludes or limits the rights of an individual or class to succeed to property of the decedent passing by intestate succession.

B. Capacity to Execute a Will

1. **Age**
   a. To execute a valid will, a person must be 18 years of age or older [UPC § 2-501].
   b. A will executed by a person under 18 years of age is invalid even if he was older than 18 when he died.

2. **Mental Capacity**
   a. In addition to meeting the age requirement, a testator must be of sound mind in order to make a valid will [Id.].
   b. Generally speaking, **of sound mind** means that the testator, at the time the will is executed, must have the ability to understand [Restatement (Third) of Prop.: Wills § 8.1(b)]:
      (1) the nature, condition, and extent of his property;
      (2) the nature of the disposition that he is making of his property; and
      (3) the names of and his relationship to the natural objects of his bounty.
   c. The fact that a testator may be eccentric or may have unusual opinions or behavior does not necessarily render him mentally incapable of making a will.

      EXAMPLE: X lived in a filthy house and liked to scare his neighbors by holding his breath. He was, however, aware of his property and left a will clearly indicating what he wanted to do with it. In other words, he met the mental capacity standard.

   d. The crucial period during which the executor must have testamentary capacity for the will to be valid is the time of its execution.
      (1) A person who is mentally incapacitated part of the time, but who has lucid intervals during which he meets the standard for mental capacity, can, in the absence of an adjudication or statute that has contrary effect, make a valid will or a valid *inter vivos*

donative transfer, provided such will or transfer is made during a lucid interval [Restatement (Third) of Prop.: Wills § 8.1, cmt. m].

(2) The condition of the testator's mind before or after that time will not invalidate the will, except insofar as such may be evidence of the condition of his mind at the time of execution.

C. Formal Requirements of Wills

1. A valid will must be [UPC § 2-502(a)]:

   a. in writing;

      (1) Any reasonably permanent record is sufficient [UPC § 2-502, cmt.].

         (a) The requirement of a writing does not mandate that the will be written on sheets of paper, but it does require a medium that allows the markings to be detected. A will, for example, scratched in the paint on the fender of a car would be in writing, but one "written" by waving a finger in the air would not be [Restatement (Third) of Prop.: Wills § 3.1, cmt. i].

      (2) Nuncupative (oral) wills have never been allowed by the UPC.

   b. signed by the testator or in the testator's name by some other individual in the testator's conscious presence and by the testator's direction; and

      (1) There is no requirement that the testator's signature be at the end of the will. Thus, if the testator writes his name in the body of the will and intends it to be his signature, the statute is satisfied [UPC § 2-502, cmt.].

      (2) Ideally, the testator signs the will by writing out his name in full. Signatures by mark, cross, nickname, or initials are sufficient [Id.].

         (a) Also sufficient are signatures indicating a term of relationship (such as "Dad," "Mom," or "Auntie"), abbreviation, a pet name, a first name, a last name, or pseudonym, or even by fingerprint or seal.

         (b) The name need not be spelled correctly, nor must it need be legible.

         (c) It may be made with the assistance of another, who guides the testator's hand. The crucial requirement is that it must be done with intent of adopting the document as the testator's will [Restatement (Third) of Prop.: Wills § 3.1, cmt. j].

      (3) There is no requirement that the testator publish the document as his will, that he request the witnesses to sign, or that the witnesses sign in the presence of the testator or of each other. In other words, a subscribing witness need not know that it is a will to which he subscribed. The testator may sign the will outside the presence of the witnesses, if he later acknowledges to the witnesses that the signature is his (or that his name was signed by another) or that the document is his will. An acknowledgment

need not be expressly stated, but can be inferred from the testator's conduct [UPC § 2-502, cmt.].

(a) A testator sometimes attempts to alter a will by marking it up, crossing out attested language, and inserting unattested substitute language [Restatement (Third) of Prop.: Wills § 4.3, cmt. d]. The purpose is usually to alter the disposition of property or the designation of persons.

(b) Under the **harmless error rule**, such an alteration will be validated if the proponent proves by clear and convincing evidence that the testator intended the alteration to constitute part of his will [Id.]:

1) In particular, although such interlineations are not executed in compliance with the formal requirements for executing or revoking a will, the writing may be treated as if it had been executed in compliance with the requirements if the proponent establishes that the decedent intended the writing to constitute [UPC § 2-503]:

a) the decedent's will;

b) a partial or complete revocation of the will;

c) an addition to or an alteration of the will; or

d) a partial or complete revival of his formerly revoked will or of a formerly revoked portion of the will.

2) The harmless error rule effectively prevents a great deal of unnecessary litigation because it eliminates disputes about technical lapses and limits the zone of dispute to the functional question of whether the instrument correctly expresses the testator's intent [UPC § 2-503, cmt.].

(c) When the will consists of several sheets of paper, the testator need not sign each page if the sheets compose one instrument connected in composition [Restatement (Third) of Prop.: Wills § 3.5, cmt. a]. No state requires each sheet of paper of a multiple-page will to be separately executed.

1) A will, whether on a single page or on multiple pages or composed of other kinds of writings, is a single document that needs to be executed only once. Each page or writing that makes up a will need not be independently executed.

2) What is required is that the pages or other writings that were intended to be part of the will were all present at the time of execution. Pages or other writings that were present at the time of execution but not intended to be part of the will are not part of the will [Restatement (Third) of Prop.: Wills § 3.5].

3) Quite commonly, the pages of a will are stapled or otherwise fastened together at the time of execution. This is not a requirement, however. In fact, no physical connection, not even by devices such as paper clips, is required [Restatement (Third) of Prop.: Wills § 3.5, cmt. a].

(4) If the testator is unable to sign his name for any reason, a will to which he makes his mark and to which his name is subscribed in his presence (before or after he makes his mark) will be valid.

(a) The testator need not sign the will himself. The UPC allows someone else to sign the testator's name for the testator, if the testator directed the other person to sign the testator's name and if the other person acted in the testator's presence [Restatement (Third) of Prop.: Wills § 3.1, cmt. n].

(b) If some other individual signs the testator's name in the testator's presence and by the testator's direction, the conscious presence test is codified under the UPC, where a signing is held to be sufficient if it was done in the testator's conscious presence (i.e., within the range of the testator's senses, such as hearing) [UPC § 2-502, cmt.]. The signing need not have occurred within the testator's line of sight [Id.].

c. either:

(1) signed by at least two individuals, each of whom signed within a reasonable time after the individual witnessed either the signing of the will or the testator's acknowledgement of that signature or acknowledgment of the will; or

(2) acknowledged by the testator before a notary public or other individual authorized by law to take acknowledgments.

(a) The UPC does not require the witnesses to sign in the presence of the testator or in the presence of each other. It requires the witnesses to "witness" the testator's act of signing the will or "witness" the testator's act of acknowledging either the signature or the will. The witnessing requirement means that the witnesses must observe the act. The requirement would not be satisfied by showing simply that the act took place in their line of vision [Restatement (Third) of Prop.: Wills § 3.1, cmt. p].

(b) The witnesses must sign as witnesses and must sign within a reasonable time after having witnessed the testator's act of signing or acknowledgment. There is, however, no requirement that the witnesses sign before the testator's death. In a particular case, the reasonable-time requirement could be satisfied even if the witnesses sign after the testator's death [UPC § 2-502, cmt.].

(c) The exact order of signing is not critical if the testator and the witnesses sign as part of a single (or continuous) transaction [Restatement (Third) of Prop.: Wills § 3.1, cmt. m].

(d) A will, whether or not it is properly witnessed, can also be acknowledged by the testator before a notary public or other individual authorized by law to take acknowledgments [UPC § 2-502, cmt.].

(e) An **attestation clause** consists of the subscription of the names of the witnesses to the will as a declaration that the testator's signature was made and acknowledged in their presence.

1) It is also a declaration that they bear witness to and certify facts required by law for a valid will.

2) An attestation clause is located immediately below the testator's signature and above the signature of the attesting witnesses [Restatement (Third) of Prop.: Wills § 3.1, cmt. q].

3) Although no state requires that a will contain an attestation clause as a prerequisite to validity, the use of one is desirable and lawyers routinely use them because they create a rebuttable presumption of the truth of the recitals contained in the clause [Id.]. In most states, the presumption is regarded as a presumption of fact. That means the presumption remains operative and is entitled to evidentiary weight notwithstanding the introduction of contrary evidence.

2. A fully effective will must also show the indispensable element of testamentary intent.

a. To be a will, the document must be executed with **testamentary intent**—that is, the decedent must intend the document to be a will or to become operative at the decedent's death [Restatement (Third) of Prop.: Wills § 3.1, cmt. g].

b. Whether the decedent executed a document with testamentary intent is a question of fact on which evidence of intention may be considered. A clear, unambiguous expression of testamentary intent in the document creates a strong (but not irrebuttable) presumption that the document was executed with testamentary intent. The presumption is rebuttable only by clear and convincing evidence. In the absence of a clear expression of testamentary intent in the document, testamentary intent can be inferred from the document or established by extrinsic evidence [Id.].

c. A signature provides evidence of finality, and serves to distinguish the final will from a preliminary draft, an incomplete document, or scribbled thoughts about how the will might take shape in the future [Restatement (Third) of Prop.: Wills § 3.1, cmt. j]. Thus, when the testator signs his name, he has the intent of adopting the document as his own.

d. If an instrument is in writing and signed by the decedent at the end, and if it is a legal declaration of his intention, which he wills to be performed after his death, it will be given effect as a will [UPC § 2-502].

(1) The testator's handwritten name in freestanding form at the end of the document unquestionably satisfies the signature requirement.

(2) The testator's handwritten name in freestanding form at any other place on the document raises an inference that the testator "signed" the document [Restatement (Third) of Prop.: Wills § 3.1, cmt. j].

e. Contestants of a will have the burden of establishing lack of testamentary intent or capacity, undue influence, fraud, duress, mistake, or revocation [UPC § 3-407].

D. Probate of Will

1. The **proving** of a will involves the process by which the testator's signature is established.

2. Once execution is proved, a presumption of testamentary capacity arises, and in the absence of a contest, the will is admitted to probate.

3. In a contested case in which the proper execution of a will is at issue, the following rules apply:

   a. If the will is witnessed but not notarized or self-proved, the testimony of at least one of the attesting witnesses is required to establish proper execution if the witness is within the state, competent, and able to testify. Proper execution may be established by other evidence, including an affidavit of an attesting witness. An attestation clause that is signed by the attesting witnesses creates a rebuttable presumption that the events recited in the clause occurred [UPC § 3-406(3)].

   b. If the will is notarized but not self-proved, there is a rebuttable presumption that the will satisfies the requirements for execution upon filing the will [UPC § 3-406(2)].

   c. **Self-Proving Will**

      (1) If the will is **self-proved**, the will satisfies the requirements for execution without the testimony of any attesting witness upon the filing of the will and the acknowledgment and affidavits annexed or attached to it, unless there is evidence of fraud or forgery affecting the acknowledgment or affidavit [UPC § 3-406(1)]. Thus, execution of a self-proving will avoids problems with hostile or unavailable witnesses.

      (2) A will may be made self-proved if it is simultaneously executed and attested by acknowledgment of the testator and affidavits of the attesting witnesses, each made before an officer authorized to administer oaths and evidenced by the officer's certificate, under official seal [UPC § 2-504(a)].

      (3) A will may also be made self-proved at any time after its execution by acknowledgment of the testator and affidavits of the attesting witnesses, each made before an officer authorized to administer oaths and evidenced by the officer's certificate, under official seal [UPC § 2-504(b)].

E. Qualifications of Witnesses

1. Generally, a witness is competent if he has the ability to observe the testator affix his signature, coupled with the ability to comprehend the nature of his act [UPC § 2-505].

   a. A witness is competent to prove the signature of the testator if he has ever seen the testator write.

   b. A person may even be a competent witness if he himself signed the will on behalf of the testator.

2. Mental incompetency, whether from mental deficiency, extreme intoxication, or the influence of drugs, remains a grounds of disqualification as a witness. Today in almost all states the conviction of a crime no longer renders a person an incompetent witness to a will [Restatement (Third) of Prop.: Wills § 3.1, cmt. o].

3. A few states specifically provide by statute a minimum age, such as 18, for attesting witnesses. More commonly, however, no age is specified in the statute. If no age is specified in the statute, a minor is a valid witness, unless the minor was not old enough to observe, remember, and relate the facts occurring at the execution ceremony [Id.].

4. A subscribing witness may give testimony that is relevant and material on any issue as to the genuineness of a will, as may any other competent witness.

5. The signing of a will by an interested witness does not invalidate the will or any provision of it.

   a. Such witnesses may testify even if they are beneficiaries; their interest in the outcome affects only their credibility.

   EXAMPLE: A sister's interest in her brother's estate would not preclude her from testifying as subscribing witness to her brother's will, nor would her interest alone discredit her testimony.

6. Subsequent incompetency of a witness does not invalidate a will.

IV. SPECIAL WILLS, CODICILS, AND WILL PROVISIONS

A. Types of Wills

1. **Holographic Wills**

   a. A **holographic will** is one written by the testator entirely in his own handwriting [UPC § 2-502(b)]. It must be signed by the testator at the end. There need be no witnesses. The only requirement is that the signature and the material portions of the document be in the testator's handwriting [UPC § 2-502, cmt.].

   b. Intent that a document constitute the testator's will can be established by extrinsic evidence, including, for holographic wills, portions of the document that are not in the testator's handwriting [UPC § 2-502(c)].

   EXAMPLE: A handwritten note or letter signed by the testator may qualify as a holographic will as long as it is found to have the requisite testamentary intent. An improperly witnessed printed form will that the testator has filled in, cannot, however, be saved as a holograph.

      (1) Inasmuch as subscribing witnesses are not required for a will signed by the testator, there are no requirements that witnesses subscribe a holographic will.

      (2) The will may be sufficiently proven by the testimony of two witnesses who are familiar with the testator's handwriting.

2. **Conditional Wills**

   a. In a **conditional will**, a testator may choose to make a particular gift, or a will, conditional on the occurrence or non-occurrence of a specific event.

   b. The condition or contingency must be clear on the face of the will and must comply with the formal requirements for a will.

   c. The conditional character of the will depends on the intention of the testator as expressed in the will itself. Furthermore, most states require that the condition be an event independent from the making of the will.

   d. Because the effect of determining a will or gift to be invalid is that the property will pass in whole or in part by intestacy, and because courts prefer that property pass by will, courts generally do not favor conditional wills. Thus, such conditions are construed narrowly.

      (1) Most courts, when faced with a questionable provision, will hold that it is not a condition, but rather merely a statement of the testator's motive for making a will.

   e. Extrinsic evidence will not be allowed to make a facially valid will conditional.

   f. Conditional wills are permitted in most states by statute or common law.

   g. The type of language that has been found to create a conditional or contingent will includes the following: "should I die before March 1, 1982" or "in case of my death on my trip away from home" or "in case I do not return."

     h.   On the other hand, the words "if I never see you again" have been interpreted as an explanation for making a will, and proof that the testator and his son saw each other frequently did not establish a failure of a condition precedent.

B. Codicils

    1.   A **codicil** is an instrument that is executed subsequent to a will by which the will is altered, explained, added to, subtracted from, or confirmed by way of republication [UPC § 2-507]. It must be executed with the same formalities as a will.

    2.   A reference to a will includes all codicils [UPC § 1-201(57)].

    3.   When a codicil to a will is executed, the will and all prior codicils are said to be "republished" as of the date of the codicil. That is, they are treated as if they were re-executed as of the day of the execution of the codicil [Restatement (Third) of Prop.: Wills § 3.4].

        EXAMPLE: A executes a will in September 2003, at which point he has two children. He executes a codicil in April 2006, by which point he has a third child, unnamed in either the will or the codicil. Because the codicil republished the original will as of the date of the codicil, the left-out third child could not claim to be after-born and will be deemed intentionally disinherited.

    4.   A validly executed codicil cures any defects in the execution of the original will.

C. Validity of Execution of Foreign Wills

    1.   A will is validly executed if executed in compliance with Sections 2-502 or 2-503 (relating to form and execution of a will), in compliance with the law at the time of execution of the place where the will is executed, or of the law of the place where at the time of execution, or at the time of his death, the testator is domiciled, has a place of abode, or is a national [UPC § 2-506].

D. Classification of Testamentary Distributions

    1.   A **specific bequest** or **specific devise** is a gift by will of a specific article or other real or personal property, which is identified and distinguished from all other things of the same kind, and is satisfied only by delivery of the particular thing (e.g., "my property known as 3 Baltimore Avenue, Florida").

        a.   The use of possessive words (e.g., "my") indicates that a specific legacy was intended.

    2.   A **general legacy** is one payable out of the general assets of the decedent's estate and not in any way separated or distinguished from other things of like kind.

    3.   A bequest or devise is classified as **demonstrative** when it is a bequest of a certain sum to be paid out of a particular fund.

        a.   Such dispositions often provide that certain property is to be sold and the proceeds used to pay the distributee.

b. If the fund is not in existence at the testator's death or if it is insufficient, the legatee will be entitled to satisfaction out of the general estate.

EXAMPLE: "100 shares of ABC stock to B," or "$100 to A." Note that the 100 shares of stock are not a specific devise of "my 100 shares of ABC stock"—the executor could buy any 100 shares of ABC stock (assuming it is publicly traded) and satisfy the legacy.

4. There is a presumption in favor of general legacies and against specific legacies.

V. LIMITATIONS ON TESTAMENTARY DISPOSITIONS

A. **Spouse's Elective Share**

1. State laws regulating the distribution of a decedent's property generally put restrictions on the decedent's ability to reduce his spouse's share in his estate below a statutorily specified minimum percentage of the property deemed subject to election.

2. A surviving spouse has the right to decline to take under the will or pursuant to the intestacy statute, and instead may choose to take an **elective share** amount equal to 50% of the value of the marital-property portion of the augmented estate [UPC § 2-202(a)].

   a. The right of election may be exercised only by a surviving spouse who is living when the petition for the elective share is filed in the court [UPC § 2-212(a)].

   b. If the election is not exercised by the surviving spouse personally, it may be exercised on the surviving spouse's behalf by his conservator, guardian, or agent under the authority of a power of attorney [Id.]. In any case, the surviving spouse must be alive when the election is made [UPC § 2-212, cmt.].

3. If the election is exercised on behalf of a surviving spouse who is an incapacitated person, that portion of the elective share, payable from the decedent's net probate estate and non-probate transfers to others, must be placed in a statutory custodial trust for the benefit and support of the surviving spouse [UPC § 2-212(b)].

   a. An election on behalf of a surviving spouse by an agent under a durable power of attorney is presumed to be on behalf of a surviving spouse who is an incapacitated person [Id.].

   b. For purposes of the custodial trust established by this subsection [Id.]:

      (1) the electing guardian, conservator, or agent is the custodial trustee;

      (2) the surviving spouse is the beneficiary; and

      (3) the custodial trust is deemed to have been created by the decedent by written transfer that takes effect at the decedent's death and that directs the custodial trustee to administer the custodial trust as for an incapacitated beneficiary.

4. The right, if any, of the surviving spouse of a decedent who dies domiciled outside the state to take an elective share in property in this state is governed by the law of the decedent's domicile at death [UPC § 2-202(d)].

5. **Procedure for Election**

   a. The court in the county of the decedent's domicile is responsible for the determination of all matters concerning a spouse's election, including the interests and liabilities of the spouse and others with respect to all property subject to election, disclaimer, release, or conveyance [UPC § 2-211].

   b. The surviving spouse must make his election by filing in the court and mailing or delivering to the personal representative, if any, a petition for the elective share within nine months after the date of the decedent's death, or within six months after the probate of the decedent's will, whichever limitation later expires [UPC § 2-211(a)].

   c. The surviving spouse must give notice of the time and place set for hearing to persons interested in the estate and to the distributees and recipients of portions of the augmented estate whose interests will be adversely affected by the taking of the elective share [Id.].

   d. Within nine months after the decedent's death, the surviving spouse may petition the court for an extension of time for making an election [UPC § 2-211(b)]. If, within nine months, the spouse gives notice of the petition to all persons interested in the decedent's non-probate transfers to others, the court may extend the time for election [Id.].

6. **Property Subject to Election**

   a. The surviving spouse of a decedent who dies domiciled in this state has a right to take an elective share amount equal to 50% of the value of the marital property portion of the augmented estate [UPC § 2-202(a)].

   b. The **augmented estate** consists of the sum of all property, whether real or personal, movable or immovable, tangible or intangible, and wherever situated, that constitutes [UPC § 2-203(a)]:

     (1) the decedent's net probate estate;

     (2) the decedent's non-probate transfers to persons other than the surviving spouse;

     (3) the decedent's non-probate transfers to the surviving spouse; and

     (4) the value of the surviving spouse's net assets at the decedent's death, plus the surviving spouse's non-probate transfers to others.

   c. Under the Uniform Probate Code, the amount of the surviving spouse's elective share is calculated by applying a specified percentage to the augmented estate. The percentage increases with the length of the marriage until it reaches a maximum of 50%, which is the percentage applicable to a marriage that has lasted 15 years or longer [Restatement (Third) of Prop.: Wills § 9.2(a); UPC § 2-203(b)].

   d. In satisfying the amount of the elective share, the decedent's probate and non-probate transfers to the surviving spouse and the marital portion of the surviving spouse's assets are applied first. If these amounts equal or exceed the amount of the elective share, the surviving spouse is not entitled to any additional amount. If the amount of the elective share is not satisfied from these items, the decedent's probate and non-probate transfers to others are proportionately liable to satisfy the balance [Restatement (Third) of Prop.: Wills § 9.2(c)].

   e. The principal feature of the elective share under the UPC that distinguishes it from other elective share statutes is that it seeks to implement the economic-partnership theory of marriage by equalizing marital assets at death [Restatement (Third) of Prop.: Wills § 9.2, cmt. b].

     (1) Thus, the statute constructs a system that separates the marital assets from the nonmarital assets for both the decedent and the

surviving spouse. In order to achieve the objective of assuring that the surviving spouse obtains a fully equal share of the marital assets, marital assets of both spouses that were placed in certain will substitute or other non-probate transfer form are counted as part of the augmented estate [Id.].

    f.   The UPC also provides for an amount of a **supplemental elective share**, a special feature for small estates that is designed to bring the surviving spouse's assets up to at least $75,000, or as close to that figure as the value of the assets permits [UPC § 2-202(b)].

        (1)   This feature is based on a support theory, not on the partnership theory of marriage [Restatement (Third) of Prop.: Wills § 9.2, cmt. g].

7. Property Not Subject to Election

    a.   Any transfer that was supported by adequate and full consideration in money or money's worth, as well as any transfer that was made with the written consent or joinder of the surviving spouse, is excluded from the augmented estate [UPC § 2-208(a)].

    b.   The right of election of a surviving spouse may be waived, wholly or partially, before or after marriage, by a written contract, agreement, or waiver signed by the surviving spouse [UPC § 2-213].

    c.   The surviving spouse may withdraw his demand for an elective share at any time before entry of a final determination by the court [UPC § 2-211(c)].

    d.   Prenuptial agreements wherein each party waives all rights, including the right to elect against the will of the other, will be upheld if there was full financial disclosure and the agreement is essentially equitable [UPC § 2-213, cmt.][In re Estate of Geyer, 516 Pa. 492 (1987)].

        (1)   Under the Uniform Probate Code, a unilateral waiver in a premarital agreement signed only by the surviving spouse is enforceable [UPC § 2-213(a)].

B. Children Not Mentioned in the Will

1. Omitted Heirs—Children Living at Time of Execution of Will

    a.   Under the UPC, a testator can disinherit a child intentionally. There is no forced or elective share for children as there is for a spouse [UPC § 2-302(b)(1)].

    b.   **Omitted heirs** are children of the testator, living at the time of the execution of the testator's last will, who are neither mentioned nor provided for in the will and would have inherited from the testator had he died intestate.

    c.   The UPC allows disinheritance of these heirs by the testator, but disinheritance must be by express language or necessary implication of the will [UPC § 2-302(b)].

2. Children Born after Execution of the Will—Statutory Protection

    a.   If the testator fails to provide in his will for a child born or adopted after making his will, unless it appears from the will that the failure was intentional, the UPC protects such child from unintentional disinheritance [UPC § 2-302(a)].

b. Under the UPC, if a testator's will fails to provide for a child born or adopted after the execution of the will, the omitted after-born or after-adopted child receives a share in the net probate estate that depends on whether or not the testator had children living when the will was executed and, if so, whether the will made a devise to any of the then-living children.

(1) If the testator had no child living when the will was executed, an omitted after-born or after-adopted child receives an intestate share, unless the will devised all or substantially all of the estate to the other parent of the omitted child and that other parent survives the testator and is entitled to take under the will. In satisfying the child's intestate share, devises abate as provided under the ordinary rules of abatement for the payment of claims.

(2) If the testator had one or more children living when the will was executed, and the will made a devise to one or more of the then-living children, an omitted after-born or after-adopted child is entitled to share in the portion of the testator's estate devised to the testator's then-living children as if the child had been given an equal share of that portion of the estate.

(a) To the extent feasible, the interest granted an omitted after-born or after-adopted child is to be of the same character, whether equitable or legal, present or future, as that devised to the testator's then-living children.

(b) Devises to the testator's then-living children abate ratably. In abating the devises of the then-living children, the court is directed to preserve to the maximum extent possible the character of the testamentary plan adopted by the testator.

(3) The UPC does not grant a share to an after-born or after-adopted child if the testator had one or more children living when the will was executed, but the will did not make a devise to any of the then-living children.

c. A class gift, by nature, includes after-born or after-adopted members of the specified class, because class terms permit an increase of class members. If the testator's will contains a class gift in favor of his children or descendants, any child who is born or adopted after the execution of the will is provided for in the will, and thus does not receive an additional share under an omitted child statute [Restatement (Third) of Prop.: Wills § 9.6, cmt. f].

3. **Special Applications**

a. Nonmarital after-born children are entitled to take under this statute from their mother's estate, and from their father's estate if the father and mother of the child marry, the father holds the child out to be his during his lifetime, or if there is clear and convincing evidence of paternity.

b. If a valid codicil is executed after the birth of the after-born child, the entire will is republished as of that date. Thus, the statute does not apply, and the child is not entitled to an intestate share.

4. **Satisfaction of After-Born Child's Share**

   a. The after-born child may recover the share of the testator's estate to which he is entitled, either from the other children (if a provision was made for them) or from the testamentary beneficiaries (if no children were living at the time of execution), ratably, out of the portions of the estate passing to such persons under the will.

C. **Exemptions of Property for the Benefit of the Decedent's Family**

   1. The surviving spouse and minor children whom the decedent was obligated to support are entitled to a reasonable allowance in money out of the estate for their maintenance during the period of administration. This is called the **family allowance** [UPC § 2-404(a)].

      a. It may be paid as a lump sum or in periodic installments.

      b. The allowance is payable to the surviving spouse, if living, for the use of the surviving spouse and minor and dependent children, or otherwise to the children or persons having their care and custody.

      c. If a minor child or dependent child is not living with the surviving spouse, the allowance may be made partially to the child or his guardian or other person having responsibility for the child's care and custody and partially to the spouse, as their needs may appear.

      d. The personal representative may determine the family allowance in a lump sum not exceeding $27,000, or periodic installments not exceeding $2,250 per month, for one year [UPC § 2-405(a)].

   2. The family allowance is intended to provide the family with enough money to pay their expenses during the probate period.

   3. There is no statutory time limit for claiming the exemption, but the allowance may not continue for longer than one year if the estate is inadequate to discharge allowed claims [UPC § 2-404(a)].

   4. Note that if the spouse is alive, the right to claim the exemption is personal to him.

   5. Generally, the personal representative delivers the exempt items of personal property to the claiming party.

   6. The exemption may also be claimed, in whole or part, from real estate.

D. **Restrictions on Charitable Dispositions**

   1. Any rule that a charitable devise is invalid if it exceeds a certain proportion of the testator's estate or if it is contained in a will that was executed within a certain time before the testator's death is abolished [Restatement (Third) of Prop.: Wills § 9.7].

   2. Mortmain statutes were motivated primarily by a desire to protect the testator's family from disinheritance [Restatement (Third) of Prop.: Wills § 9.7, cmt. b].

   3. All of the mortmain statutes, however, have been repealed [Restatement (Third) of Prop.: Wills § 9.7, cmt. c]. There is now no restriction on charitable dispositions.

VI. INTERPRETATION OF WILLS

A. In General

1. Wills are always to be construed in accordance with the discernible will of the testator.

2. However, problems may arise in interpreting the will and intent of the testator.

B. Integration

1. Problems of **integration** arise when there is uncertainty as to precisely what papers and terms were intended to be part of the will at the time of its execution. Generally, this is not a problem because the pages of a will are ordinarily stapled together, or the writing of the will shows an internal coherence that carries from page to page.

2. However, if a question of integration does arise, the will proponent must show that the will offered for probate is actually the will that the testator intended to make, and that no insertions or removals of pages from the will have occurred.

C. Incorporation by Reference

1. The UPC recognizes the common law doctrine of **incorporation by reference**, which permits the inclusion by reference of unattested documents as part of a will if [UPC § 2-510]:

   a. the writing was in existence at the time of execution of the will;

   b. the language of the will manifests this intent; and

   c. the will describes the writing sufficiently to permit its identification.

   EXAMPLE: A decedent's will providing that it be carried out according to the terms of the will of the decedent's late husband adopted the provisions of the husband's will pursuant to the doctrine of incorporation by reference [Clark v. Dennison, 129 A. 94 (Pa. 1925)].

2. However, a paper not referred to in the will is not incorporated, even if it was in existence at the execution of the will.

3. Similarly, a devise not in the will cannot be made effective by a reference.

   EXAMPLE: When a will referred to and incorporated a diagram of various tracts of land with the word's "A.W.'s lot" written across one lot, this was held not to be a devise of the tract because there was no corresponding devise in the will itself [Houser v. Moore, 31 Pa. 346 (1858)].

4. This section codifies the common law doctrine of incorporation by reference, except the requirement that the will refer to the document as being in existence when the will was executed has been eliminated [UPC § 2-510, cmt.].

D. Facts of Independent Significance

1. Under the doctrine of **facts of independent significance**, a will may provide for the designation of a beneficiary or the amount of a disposition by reference to some future unattested act occurring after the execution of the will.

2. Thus, a will may dispose of property by reference to acts and events that have significance apart from their effect upon the dispositions made by the will, whether they occur before or after the execution of the will or before or after the testator's death. The execution or revocation of another individual's will is such an event [UPC § 2-512].

3. Such a provision can be valid only if the future act has some significance apart from the will.

   EXAMPLE: The actual property disposed under a bequest of "all my household furnishings" will be dependent on what kinds of property the testator dies owning. These are facts of independent—i.e., non-testamentary—significance. Alternatively, a bequest to "such persons as I have named in a paper to be found in my desk marked 'Last Instructions'" would require the application of the doctrine of incorporation by reference.

4. **Dispositions to *Inter Vivos* Trusts**

   a. A will may pour over into an existing *inter vivos* trust.

   b. A **pour-over devise** is a provision in a will that [Restatement (Third) of Prop.: Wills § 3.8(a)]:

      (1) adds property to an *inter vivos* trust; or

      (2) funds a trust that was not funded during the testator's lifetime, but whose terms are in a trust instrument that was executed during the testator's lifetime.

   c. Unless validated by statute, on the theory of incorporation by reference, or on the theory that an *inter vivos* trust has independent legal significance, a pour-over devise is invalid because the beneficial devisees are not identified in a document executed in compliance with the statutory formalities for a valid will [Restatement (Third) of Prop.: Wills § 3.8, cmt. a].

   d. Nearly all states have enacted legislation validating pour-over devises in specified circumstances. The Uniform Testamentary Additions to Trusts Act ("UTATA") was also promulgated in 1960, and subsequently revised in 1991 in accordance with the revisions to the UPC [UPC § 2-511, cmt.]. States that enact UPC Section 2-511 need not enact the UTATA.

      (1) Under the UPC, a devise to the trustee of an *inter vivos* trust is valid if the trust is identified in the testator's will and its terms are set forth in a written instrument, other than a will, executed before, concurrently with, or after the execution of the testator's will or in another individual's will if that other individual has predeceased the testator, regardless of the existence, size, or character of the *corpus* of the trust.

      (2) The trust itself need not be established during the testator's lifetime, but can be established by the pour-over devise.

      (3) The pour-over devise is not invalid because the trust is amendable or revocable, or because the trust was amended after the execution of the will or the testator's death [UPC § 2-511(a)].

        (a)   Unless the testator's will provides otherwise, however, a revocation or termination of the trust before the testator's death causes the devise to lapse [UPC § 2-511(c)].

    e.   Of the common law bases for validating pour-over devises, the doctrine of incorporation by reference is less satisfactory than independent significance. Incorporation by reference should be utilized only if no other theory is available [Restatement (Third) of Prop.: Wills § 3.8, cmt. c].

        (1)   In order for that doctrine to be applicable, the *inter vivos* trust instrument had to be in existence when the will was executed. If this requirement was met, some courts would still only incorporate the terms of an irrevocable trust [Id.].

        (2)   Other courts would incorporate the terms of a revocable and amendable trust, but not if the trust had been amended after the will was executed. Because the post-execution amendment could not be incorporated, the court was left with the choice of incorporating only the terms of the original trust or invalidating the devise altogether. The usual choice was to invalidate the devise altogether because incorporating the original terms of the trust, ignoring the amendment, would be intent-defeating [Id.].

    f.   The doctrine of independent significance provides a validating basis that is more satisfactory than incorporation by reference [Restatement (Third) of Prop.: Wills § 3.8, cmt. d].

        (1)   Under independent significance, the trust instrument does not have to be in existence when the will is executed, and post-execution amendments to the trust are given effect [Id.].

        (2)   The only requirement under the doctrine of independent significance is that the *inter vivos* trust must be more than nominally funded in order to give the trust document and any subsequent amendments independent significance [Id.].

    g.   Unless the will provides otherwise, the property so devised is not deemed to be held under a testamentary trust of the testator, but it becomes a part of the trust to which it is devised, and must be administered and disposed of in accordance with the provisions of the governing instrument establishing that trust and any amendments made before or after the testator's death [UPC § 2-511(b)].

E. Selected Statutory Rules of Interpretation

1. The legislature created a set of rules and definitions intended to clarify the meaning of some terms used in the law and in drafting wills.

2. In the absence of a contrary intent appearing therein, wills are to be construed as to real or personal estate in accordance with the following rules:

    a.   A will is to be construed so as to apply to all property that the testator owned at his death and all property acquired by the estate after the testator's death [UPC § 2-602].

          (1)   Thus, items such as bonuses awarded to an employee after his death will pass under his will [UPC § 2-602, cmt.].

     b.   The Rule in Shelley's Case is not applied under the UPC. A devise or bequest to a life tenant with remainder to his heirs, issue, or next of kin does not create fee title in the life tenant.

     c.   The Doctrine of Worthier Title is abolished as a rule of law and as a rule of construction. Language in a governing instrument describing the beneficiaries of a disposition as the transferor's heirs, heirs at law, next of kin, distributees, relatives, or family, or language of similar import, does not create or presumptively create a reversionary interest in the transferor [UPC § 2-710].

VII. STATUTORY PROVISIONS COVERING SPECIAL CIRCUMSTANCES

A. Disqualifications

1. **Slayer Act**

   a. Any person who participates, either as a principal, co-conspirator, or an accessory before the fact, in the willful and unlawful killing of any other person may not acquire any property or receive any benefit as a result of the death of the decedent.

   b. An individual who feloniously and intentionally kills the decedent forfeits all benefits with respect to the decedent's estate, including an intestate share, an elective share, an omitted spouse's or child's share, a homestead allowance, exempt property, and a family allowance. If the decedent died intestate, the decedent's intestate estate passes as if the killer disclaimed his intestate share [UPC § 2-803(b)].

   c. After all right to appeal has been exhausted, a judgment of conviction establishing criminal accountability for the felonious and intentional killing of the decedent conclusively establishes the convicted individual as the decedent's killer [UPC § 2-803(g)].

   (1) The findings of criminal proceedings do not, however, necessarily determine the issues involved in a civil proceeding [UPC § 2-803, cmt.]. The absence of a final judgment of conviction establishing a person as a slayer does not preclude the court in a civil proceeding from determining that a person is responsible for the felonious and intentional killing of the decedent [Restatement (Third) of Prop.: Wills § 8.4, cmt. e].

   d. The slayer rule does not apply if the killing was reckless, accidental, or negligent [Restatement (Third) of Prop.: Wills § 8.4, cmt. f].

   e. **Distribution of Property**

   (1) The slayer will be deemed to have predeceased the decedent as to property that would have passed from the decedent or his estate to the slayer under the statutes of descent and distribution or by statutory right of the surviving spouse [UPC § 2-803(b)].

   (2) Similarly, property that would have passed by devise or legacy from the decedent will be distributed as if the slayer predeceased the decedent [Id.].

   (3) The felonious and intentional killing of the decedent further severs the interests of the decedent and killer in property held by them at the time of the killing as joint tenants with the right of survivorship, transforming the interests of the decedent and killer into equal tenancies in common [UPC § 2-803(c)(2)].

   (4) The slayer rule also applies to cases in which the property probably would have gone to the slayer eventually. Thus, property in which the slayer held a reversion or vested remainder, which would have become a present possession on the decedent's

death, passes to the estate of the decedent. By interfering with the order of deaths, a slaying causes the victim to die before he would have died in the natural course of events. Accordingly, the slayer is not allowed to benefit from the victim's premature death, whether or not the victim was the donor [Restatement (Third) of Prop.: Wills § 8.4, cmt. c].

EXAMPLE: If the remainder beneficiary of a trust is responsible for the felonious and intentional killing of the income beneficiary, the slayer is denied the right to immediate possession of the *corpus*.

f. **Proceeds of Insurance**

(1) If the slayer is the beneficiary or assignee of a policy insuring the life of the decedent, or is the survivor of a joint life policy, the proceeds will be paid to the decedent's estate, or, if designated, to a contingent beneficiary, even if the contingent beneficiary is a relative of the slayer [UPC § 2-803; Restatement (Third) of Prop.: Wills § 8.4, cmt. k].

(2) If the decedent was a beneficiary or an assignee of a policy insuring the slayer's life, upon the slayer's death, the proceeds are paid to the estate of the decedent or the alternative beneficiary.

2. **Other Circumstances**

a. **Refusal to Support or Desertion**

(1) Although some statutes bar a surviving spouse for desertion or adultery, the UPC requires some definitive legal act in order to bar the surviving spouse. Normally, this is divorce. Thus, desertion or adultery would not be sufficient [UPC § 2-802, cmt.].

(2) A surviving spouse who would not be entitled to have a share of the decedent's intestate estate in accordance with this provision will have no right of election.

b. **Effect of Divorce and Remarriage upon Wills**

(1) An individual who is divorced from the decedent, or whose marriage to the decedent has been annulled, is not a surviving spouse unless, by virtue of a subsequent marriage, he is married to the decedent at the time of death [UPC § 2-802(a)].

(2) A decree of separation that does not terminate the status of a married couple does not constitute a divorce for purposes of this section [Id.].

(3) Similarly, a surviving spouse does not include an individual who, following an invalid decree or judgment of divorce or annulment obtained by the decedent, participates in a marriage ceremony with a third individual [UPC § 2-802(b)(2)].

c. **Birth or Adoption**

(1) If a testator fails to provide in his will for any of his children born or adopted after the execution of the will, the omitted after-born or after-adopted child may receive a share in the decedent's estate, as discussed above [UPC § 2-302(a)]:

    (2)   This rule will not apply, however, if [UPC § 2-302(b)]:

        (a) it appears from the will that the omission was intentional; or

        (b) the testator provided for the omitted after-born or after-adopted child by transfer outside the will and the intent that the transfer be in lieu of a testamentary provision is shown by the testator's statements or is reasonably inferred from the amount of the transfer or other evidence.

    (3)   If at the time of execution of the will the testator fails to provide in his will for a living child solely because he believes the child to be dead, that child is entitled to share in the estate as if the child were an omitted after-born or after-adopted child [UPC § 2-302(c)].

B. Simultaneous Death

1.   A simultaneous death occurs when two or more persons, one of whom is the beneficiary of the other, die under circumstances where there is insufficient evidence to determine which party survived the other (e.g., a common disaster such as a plane crash).

2.   Under the UPC, a person who cannot be established by clear and convincing evidence to have survived the decedent by 120 hours is deemed to have predeceased the decedent [UPC § 2-104(a)(1)].

    a.   Where the insured and the beneficiary of a life or accident insurance policy die simultaneously, the proceeds are distributed as if the insured had survived the beneficiary [Restatement (Third) of Prop.: Wills § 1.2, cmt. d].

3.   However, if a will contains language dealing explicitly with simultaneous deaths or deaths in a common disaster, and if such language is operable under the facts of the case, the requirement of survival by 120 hours does not apply [UPC § 2-702(d)].

4.   **Co-Owners with Rights of Survivorship**

    a.   A similar rule is provided in several situations concerning the simultaneous deaths of co-owners with rights of survivorship. Co-owners with right of survivorship includes joint tenants, tenants by the entireties, and other co-owners of property or accounts held under circumstances that entitle one or more to the whole of the property or account on the death of the other or others [UPC § 2-702(c)].

    b.   If it is not established by clear and convincing evidence that one of two co-owners with right of survivorship survived the other co-owner by 120 hours, one-half of the property passes as if one had survived by 120 hours and one-half as if the other had survived by 120 hours.

    c.   If there are more than two co-owners and it is not established by clear and convincing evidence that at least one of them survived the others by 120 hours, the property passes in the proportion that one bears to the whole number of co-owners.

        (1)   Thus, if there are three joint tenants, a one-third interest in the property will be distributed through each estate as if the owner of that estate had survived the other tenants.

C. Disclaimer of Property Interests

1. A person may **disclaim**, in whole or part, any interest in or power over property, including a power of appointment. A person may disclaim the interest or power even if its creator imposed a spendthrift provision or similar restriction on transfer or a restriction or limitation on the right to disclaim [UPC § 2-1105(a)].

2. The ability to disclaim interests is comprehensive; it does not matter whether the disclaimed interest is vested, either in interest or in possession [UPC § 2-1105, cmt.].

3. The statute was designed primarily to allow a distributee or beneficiary to avoid payment of estate and gift taxes on assets that he does not really need or want [UPC §§ 2-1105, cmt.; 2-1114].

4. In order to be effective, a disclaimer must [UPC § 2-1105(c)]:

    a. be in writing or other record;

    b. declare the disclaimer;

    c. describe the interest or power disclaimed;

    d. be signed by the disclaiming party; and

    e. be delivered or filed.

5. A disclaimer may be made on behalf of a decedent, a minor, or an incapacitated person by his personal representative, or in the case of an incapacitated person, by his attorney-in-fact, if properly authorized [UPC § 2-1108, cmt.].

6. The rules set forth in the UPC are designed so that anyone who has the duty to distribute the disclaimed interest will be notified of the disclaimer.

    a. Thus, a disclaimer of an interest in a decedent's estate must be delivered to the personal representative of the estate. If an interest in a third-party beneficiary contract is being disclaimed, the disclaimer must be delivered to the insurance company, employer, or other obligor and to the person who is entitled to the interest by reason of the disclaimer [UPC § 2-1112].

    b. On the other hand, a disclaimer must be filed in court only when there is no one person or entity to whom delivery can be made [UPC § 2-1112, cmt.].

7. If an instrument transferring an interest in or power over property subject to a disclaimer is required or permitted to be filed, recorded, or registered, the disclaimer may be so filed, recorded, or registered.

    a. Failure to file, record, or register the disclaimer does not affect its validity as between the disclaimant and persons to whom the property interest or power passes by reason of the disclaimer [UPC § 2-1115].

    b. This section permits the recordation of a disclaimer that is the subject of a recording system. While local practice may vary, disclaimants should realize that in order to establish the chain of title to real property, and to ward off creditors and *bona fide* purchasers, the disclaimer may have to be recorded. The UPC does not alter or modify the law governing notice [UPC § 2-1115, cmt.].

8. **Time for Disclaimer**

    a.   A disclaimer can be made at any time so long as [UPC § 2-1113]:

        (1)   the disclaimant is not barred by a written waiver of the right to disclaim;

        (2)   the disclaimant has not accepted the interest;

        (3)   the disclaimant has not voluntarily assigned, conveyed, encumbered, pledged, or transferred the interest; or

        (4)   a judicial sale of the interest has not occurred.

    b.   Although the UPC specifically rejects a time requirement for disclaimers, persons seeking to make tax qualified disclaimers will still have to conform to the time requirements set forth in the Internal Revenue Code [UPC § 2-1113, cmt.].

        (1)   Under the IRC, a disclaimer must be made 9 months after the later of [26 CFR 25.2518-2]

            (a) the date on which the transfer creating the interest in the disclaimant is made; or

            (b) the day on which the disclaimant turns 21.

    c.   Whether particular actions by the disclaimant amount to accepting the interest sought to be disclaimed will necessarily be determined by the courts [Id.]. An acceptance may be express, or inferred from actions such as taking possession or accepting delivery of the property, written waiver of the right to disclaim, or an assignment, conveyance, pledge, or transfer of the interest.

        (1)   To constitute a bar to disclaimer, prior acceptance must be affirmatively proved. Mere lapse of time, with or without the disclaimant's knowledge, is not an acceptance.

9. **Effect of Disclaimer**

    a.   A disclaimer relates back to the date of the death of the decedent [UPC § 2-1106(b)(1)]. It is binding upon the disclaimant and all persons claiming through or under him.

    b.   Unless the testator provided otherwise, the effect of a disclaimer is that the property passes as if the disclaiming party predeceased the decedent [Id.].

        (1)   Thus, the disclaimer will accelerate the possession of subsequent interests [UPC § 2-1106(b)(4)].

            EXAMPLE: If T left property to L for life and remainder to L's children, and L disclaimed, the remainder will be distributed to the children as though L had predeceased T. Even if there is a gift-over in case one of the remaindermen dies during the life estate, the remainder will be accelerated if the life tenant disclaims.

    c.   A contingent remainder will not be accelerated where there are prior successive interests.

        EXAMPLE: If T leaves property "to A for life, remainder to B and his heirs, but if B dies without issue, to A's heirs," A's disclaimer will not accelerate the interests of A's heirs, because B's interest precedes theirs.

    d.   If the disclaimed interest would pass to the disclaimant's estate had the disclaimant died before the time of distribution, the disclaimed interest instead passes by representation to the disclaimant's descendants who survive the time of distribution [UPC § 2-1106(b)(3)(D)].

        (1)   If no descendant of the disclaimant survives the time of distribution, the disclaimed interest passes to those persons, including the state but excluding the disclaimant, and in such shares as would succeed to the transferor's estate under the intestacy law. However, if the transferor's surviving spouse is living but is remarried at the time of distribution, the transferor is deemed to have died unmarried at the time of distribution [Id.].

10. **Other Statutes**

    a.   The UPC provisions regarding disclaimer do not abridge the right of any person to disclaim interests under another statute and do not affect the additional disclaimer requirements for inheritance tax or other statutory purposes [UPC § 2-1113, cmt.].

VIII. CHANGES IN PROPERTY AND BENEFICIARIES AFTER EXECUTION OF THE WILL

A. Ademption

1. **Ademption by Extinction**

    a. The property a person leaves in his will may not be the same property he owned when he executed his will.

    (1) This situation does not present a problem when the will disposes of "shares" of the estate, or speaks in terms of sums of money that can be satisfied by selling the estate's assets for cash or by direct distribution of property to the beneficiary.

    (2) However, if the will devises or bequeaths specific property, such as "Blackacre" or "my diamond wedding ring," the beneficiary will not be able to receive the property unless it is part of the estate at the time of the testator's death.

    b. A testamentary gift is **adeemed by extinction**—that is, it fails—when property specifically bequeathed or devised is not in the testator's estate at his death.

    c. The ademption may occur by an intentional act on the part of the testator (e.g., a sale or gift), or by an involuntary circumstance (e.g., fire or theft).

    d. Ademption occurs even if the property has been exchanged for other property.

    EXAMPLE: If the testator specifically devised Blackacre to X, and then exchanged Blackacre for Whiteacre prior to death, the devise of Blackacre would be said to be adeemed by extinction.

    e. Generally, a specific devise will be deemed to have adeemed if, at the testator's death, the testator no longer possesses an interest in the property devised and no contrary intention is set forth in the will [Restatement (Third) of Prop.: Wills § 5.2(c)].

    f. Note that the doctrine of ademption by extinction applies only to property specifically described by the testator in his will, not to general or demonstrative dispositions [Restatement (Third) of Prop.: Wills § 5.2, cmt. c].

    (1) For purposes of ademption, it is well established that there is a presumption against classifying a devise as specific. To rebut this presumption, the language creating the devise must unambiguously be in the form of a specific devise [Id.].

    g. When a will alludes to adeemed property, the will can still be probated, but it does not operate to pass the adeemed property.

    h. **Conveyance of an Incapacitated Person's Property**

    (1) Generally, the common law was that a would-be legatee or devisee had no interest in the proceeds of a sale or exchange of property subject to ademption.

    (2) However, if specifically devised property is sold or mortgaged by a conservator or agent acting by a durable power of attorney for an incapacitated principal, or a condemnation award,

insurance proceeds, or recovery for injury to the property is paid to a conservator or agent with a durable power of attorney, the devisee has the right to a general devise equal to the sale price, the unpaid loan amount, the condemnation award, the insurance proceeds, or the recovery [UPC § 2-606(b)].

i. **Non-Ademption—Balance**

(1) A specific devisee has a right to specifically devised property in the testator's estate at the testator's death and to [UPC § 2-606(a)]:

(a) any balance of the purchase price, together with any security agreement, owed by a purchaser at the testator's death by reason of a sale of the property;

(b) any amount due for the condemnation of the property and unpaid at the testator's death;

(c) any proceeds unpaid at the testator's death on fire or casualty insurance on or other recovery for injury to the property;

(d) any property owned by the testator at death and acquired as a result of foreclosure, or obtained in lieu of foreclosure, of the security interest for a specifically devised obligation;

(e) any real property or tangible personal property owned by the testator at death which the testator acquired as a replacement for specifically devised real property or tangible personal property; or

EXAMPLE: T's will devised to X "my 1995 Ford." After T executed his will, he sold the 2005 Ford and purchased and 2005 Chevy. Later, T sold the Chevy and bought a 2015 Dodge, which he owned until her death. Under this subsection, X takes the 2015 Dodge.

EXAMPLE: If T had sold his 1995 Ford (or any of the replacements) and used the proceeds to buy shares in a stock, which he owned at death, this subsection does not give X the shares in the stock. If T owned an automobile at death as a replacement for his 1995 Ford, however, X would be entitled to that automobile, even though it was bought with funds other than the proceeds of the sale of the 1995 Ford.

(f) if not covered by any of the above paragraphs, a devise equal to its value, as of the date of disposition of other specifically devised property disposed of during the testator's lifetime, but only to the extent that ademption would be inconsistent with the testator's plan of distribution or that the testator did not intend ademption of the devise.

(2) **Stock**

    (a) Dispositions of stock are often troublesome, because it is unclear whether the testator intended a general or a specific bequest.

    (b) If the will says, "My fifty (50) shares of Wood stock to Jimmy," the possessive pronoun makes this a specific disposition of the identified shares (i.e., those the testator owns); if he owns none at his death, the bequest is adeemed.

        1) On the other hand, if the will says, "Fifty (50) shares of Vladivos stock to Leonid," and the testator owned no such shares at his death, the court interprets this as a general bequest, and Leonid is entitled to the value of 50 shares of Vladivos stock as of the date of the testator's death.

    (c) UPC Section 2-605 controls the construction of will provisions bequeathing securities, unless a contrary intention is indicated by the will.

    (d) If a testator executes a will that devises securities, and the testator then owned securities that meet the description in the will, the devise includes additional securities owned by the testator at death to the extent the additional securities were acquired by the testator after the will was executed as a result of the testator's ownership of the described securities and are securities of any of the following types [UPC § 2-605(a)]:

        1) securities of the same organization acquired by reason of action initiated by the organization or any successor, related, or acquiring organization, excluding any acquired by exercise of purchase options;

        2) securities of another organization acquired as a result of a merger, consolidation, reorganization, or other distribution by the organization or any successor, related, or acquiring organization; or

        3) securities of the same organization acquired as a result of a plan of reinvestment.

    (e) Thus, the legatee is entitled to all of the stock dividends issued with respect to the bequeathed stock, and all the additional shares issued as the result of a stock split, both before and after testator's death.

    (f) Distributions in cash before death with respect to a described security are not part of the devise [UPC § 2-605(b)].

2. **Ademption by Satisfaction**

    a. An **ademption by satisfaction** is similar to the idea of an advancement; it occurs when a testator makes an *inter vivos* gift of property to a beneficiary of a general or residuary disposition with the intent that the provision of the will be thereby satisfied.

      b.   Property a testator gave in his lifetime to a person is treated as a satisfaction of a devise only if [UPC § 2-609(a)]:

         (1)   the will provides for deduction of the gift;

         (2)   the testator declared in a contemporaneous writing that the gift is in satisfaction of the devise or that its value is to be deducted from the value of the devise; or

         (3)   the devisee acknowledged in writing that the gift is in satisfaction of the devise or that its value is to be deducted from the value of the devise.

      c.   For purposes of partial satisfaction, property is valued as of the time the devisee came into possession or enjoyment of the property or at the testator's death, whichever occurs first [UPC § 2-609(b)].

      d.   If the devisee fails to survive the testator, the gift is treated as a full or partial satisfaction of the devise, as appropriate, unless the testator's contemporaneous writing provides otherwise [UPC § 2-609(c)].

B. Encumbered Property—No-Exoneration Rule

1.   At common law, a person to whom the testator specifically devised real estate was entitled to have any mortgage or lien outstanding on the property paid off out of the other assets of the estate, leaving his devise unencumbered.

      a.   The UPC abolishes the common law rule.

2.   Under the UPC, the beneficiary of a devise or bequest under a will is entitled only to the interest of the testator in the property—that is, he takes the property subject to any lien or mortgage outstanding at the testator's death; there is no exoneration [UPC § 2-607].

      a.   A **specific devise** passes subject to any mortgage interest existing at the date of death, without right of exoneration, regardless of a general directive in the will to pay debts [Id.].

3.   The personal representative of the estate is not liable for the satisfaction of the encumbrance out of the property of the estate. The UPC empowers the personal representative to pay an encumbrance under some circumstances [UPC § 3-814].

      a.   That section, however, makes it clear that such payment does not increase the right of the specific devisee.

      b.   In particular, the UPC provides that if any assets of the estate are encumbered by mortgage, pledge, lien, or other security interest, the personal representative may pay the encumbrance, convey, or transfer the assets to the creditor in satisfaction of his lien, if it appears to be for the best interest of the estate [Id.].

      c.   However, payment of an encumbrance does not increase the share of the distributee entitled to the encumbered assets unless the distributee is entitled to exoneration [Id.].

4. This no-exoneration rule applies to both real and personal property, and it applies whether the security interest was created by the testator or by a previous owner.

5. This general rule that liens will not be exonerated does not apply if the testator has provided, expressly or by necessary implication, that the lien on the property should be paid off.

   a. A general directive in the will for the payment of debts (e.g. "I request first that my executor pay all my just debts") does not qualify as such a provision.

   b. The beneficiary has the burden of showing that the testator intended the property to pass free of the encumbrance.

C. Abatement

1. If the assets of the testator's estate are insufficient, after payment of all claims against the estate, to satisfy all the bequests or devises, the beneficiaries' shares will **abate**, or be reduced.

   EXAMPLE: A leaves a will indicating that each of his two children is to receive $50,000. After payment of claims and taxes, only $30,000 is left in the estate for distribution. The original amounts going to each child have to be abated.

2. Abatement issues arise where a spouse elects against the will, a child not mentioned in the will makes a claim, or a spouse or minor child claims a family exemption.

3. Absent contrary directions in the will, the shares of distributees abate, without any preference or priority as between real and personal property, in the following order [UPC § 3-902(a)]:

   a. property not disposed of by the will;

   b. residuary devises;

   c. general devises; and

   d. specific devises.

      (1) Demonstrative legacies are deemed as specific bequests under the statute.

4. Abatement within each classification is in proportion to the amounts of property each of the beneficiaries would have received if full distribution of the property had been made in accordance with the terms of the will [UPC § 3-902].

D. Class Gifts

1. A **class gift** exists when the testator makes a gift to a number of persons as a group and the size of the group may increase or decrease in size; the share of each depends upon the ultimate number in the class.

   a. Traditionally, to qualify as a class, the group must be a natural group (e.g., children, nephews, nieces, etc.).

   b. Unless a contrary intention appears from the will, the court will not hold a group composed of persons of diverse relationships to the testator to be a class.

c. Generally, where there is a gift by will to several legatees who are named, and the gift is to be divided among them in equal shares, the gift is to them as individuals, even though the named individuals do, in fact, constitute a class and are described as a class.

EXAMPLE: A devise in a will "to my children, A, B, C, and D" will be treated as individual bequests to each of the four named children, rather than as a class gift.

2. **Construction of Class Terms**

a. In determining who is included within a class, the testator's intent controls; however, where this is unclear, the following statutory rules will apply.

b. A class gift that uses a term of relationship to identify the class members includes a child of assisted reproduction, a gestational child, and, except as otherwise provided, an adoptee and a child born to parents who are not married to each other, and their respective descendants if appropriate to the class, in accordance with the rules for intestate succession regarding parent-child relationships [UPC § 2-705(b)].

c. In construing a dispositive provision of a transferor who is not the genetic parent, however, a child is not considered the child of the genetic parent unless the genetic parent, a relative of the genetic parent, the spouse or surviving spouse of the genetic parent, or a relative of the genetic parent functioned as a parent of the child before the child reached 18 years of age [UPC § 2-705(e)].

d. Similarly, in construing a dispositive provision of a transferor who is not the adoptive parent, an adoptee is not considered the child of the adoptive parent unless [UPC § 2-705(f)]:

(1) the adoption took place before the adoptee reached 18 years of age;

(2) the adoptive parent was the adoptee's stepparent or foster parent; or

(3) the adoptive parent functioned as a parent of the adoptee before the adoptee reached 18 years of age.

e. Terms of relationship in a governing instrument that do not differentiate relationships by blood from those by marriage, such as those involving uncles, aunts, nieces, or nephews, are construed to exclude relatives by marriage, unless [UPC § 2-705(c)]:

(1) when the governing instrument was executed, the class was then and foreseeably would be empty; or

(2) the language or circumstances otherwise establish that relatives by marriage were intended to be included.

f. Terms of relationship in a governing instrument that do not differentiate relationships by the half blood from those by the whole blood are construed to include both types of relationships [UPC § 2-705(d)].

g. If a class gift in favor of "descendants," "issue," or "heirs of the body" does not specify the manner in which the property is to be distributed among the class members, the property is distributed among the class members who are living when the interest is to take effect in possession or enjoyment, in such shares as they would receive, under the applicable law of intestate succession, if the designated ancestor had then died intestate owning the subject matter of the class gift [UPC § 2-708].

3. **Closing of Class—Maximum Membership**

   a. If a class gift to a general group such as children, brothers, sisters, and the like is contained in a will, the following rules of construction are used to determine when the class closes—that is, when the maximum membership has been reached.

   b. Under the UPC, a **distribution date** is defined as the date when an immediate or postponed class gift takes effect in possession or enjoyment [UPC § 2-705, cmt.].

   c. Generally, the courts employ the **rule of convenience**—a person must be born before the period of distribution in order to share in a class gift.

      (1) A child *in utero* at a particular time is treated as living at that time if the child lives 120 hours after birth [UPC § 2-705(g)(1)].

      (2) If a child of assisted reproduction or a gestational child is conceived posthumously and the distribution date is the deceased parent's death, the child is treated as living on the distribution date if the child lives 120 hours after birth and was *in utero* not later than 36 months after the deceased parent's death or born not later than 45 months after the deceased parent's death [UPC § 2-705(g)(2)].

      (3) An individual who is in the process of being adopted when the class closes is treated as adopted when the class closes if the adoption is subsequently granted [UPC § 2-705(g)(3)].

   d. If the gift is an immediate gift, the class closes at the death of the testator. This is also the time set for distribution of an immediate gift.

   EXAMPLE: If T bequeaths $10,000 to the children of A, the class closes at T's death, and only those children of A living or born within the gestational period thereafter will take. Should A have no children that qualify, the general rule is that the closing will be postponed so that all of A's children born after T's death can be included; otherwise, the entire gift would fail.

   EXAMPLE: However, should the gift be *per capita*—i.e., "$1,000 to each child of A"—and no children were living at T's death, the entire gift must fail. The reason for this is simply a practical one; to let in all the children, as was done in the preceding situation, would delay distribution of T's entire estate.

   e. If the gift is postponed, ordinarily there will be no inconvenience involved in allowing the class to remain open until the time set for distribution. Thus, the closing is not at T's death but at the distribution date [UPC § 2-705, cmt.].

   EXAMPLE: If T devises property "to A for life, remainder equally to A's children," the time for closing the class is not at T's death, but at the time for distribution—namely, the death of A.

EXAMPLE: However, where the testator devises property "to the children of A, each child to receive his share upon attaining the age of 21," the class is closed when the first child reaches 21 years of age. This is necessary in order that his share may be determined and allotted at the time stated for its distribution.

(1) Where *per capita* gifts are concerned, even if the gift is postponed, the general view is that the class must close at the testator's death, whether or not there are members of the class in existence at that time.

4. **Vesting of Class Gifts—Minimum Membership**

a. Although a class may increase after the testator's death, absent a condition that members of a class must survive to a time subsequent to the testator's death, membership in a class will generally not decrease after the testator's death.

EXAMPLE: A leaves property "to B for life, remainder to the children of C." At A's death, C has three children, W, X, and Y. In-between A's death and B's death, W dies and C has another child, Z. At B's death, the property will be divided four ways, to X, Y, and Z, and to W's estate. This is because A's bequest did not state any condition of survivorship at B's death. Therefore, at A's death, the class could increase but not decrease.

5. A problem of construction may occur when the gift is to heirs or kin classified as surviving or then-living.

EXAMPLE: Assume that T devises property "to A for life, and on A's death, remainder to my then-living heirs." At T's death, his heirs are his two children, B and C. Before the death of A, B died and was survived by D. It would appear that B cannot take at the death of A, because he is not "then living." At common law, T's heirs are determined at the date of his death, and C would have taken all of the property inasmuch as he would be the only heir of T living at the death of A.

a. Similarly, under the UPC, a future interest is contingent on the beneficiary's surviving the distribution date [UPC § 2-707(b)].

b. Although some courts interpret the word "surviving" as merely requiring survival of the testator, the UPC interprets "surviving" as requiring survival of the life tenant. Thus, the UPC codifies the predominant common law and Restatement position that survival relates to the distribution date [UPC § 2-707, cmt.].

E. **Lapse**

1. Under the common law, a **lapse** occurs when a disposition fails because the beneficiary predeceases the testator.

a. Lapsed dispositions pass to the residuary estate, or if there is no residuary provision, by intestacy.

b. Lapse can generally be avoided by class gifts or by naming an alternative beneficiary.

2. **Anti-Lapse Statute**

   a.   The common law lapse doctrine applies, except where prevented by an anti-lapse statute [UPC § 2-603, cmt.].

   b.   Under this statute, if no alternative disposition of the property in question is made in the will, lapse will nonetheless be prevented in the following circumstances if a devisee fails to survive the testator and is a grandparent, a descendant of a grandparent, or a stepchild of either the testator or the donor of a power of appointment exercised by the testator's will [UPC § 2-603(b)]:

     (1)   if the devise is not in the form of a class gift and the deceased devisee leaves surviving descendants, a substitute gift is created in the devisee's surviving descendants;

        (a)   They take by representation the property to which the devisee would have been entitled had the devisee survived the testator.

     (2)   if the devise is in the form of a class gift, other than a devise to issue, descendants, heirs of the body, heirs, next to kin, relatives, or family, or a class described by language of similar import, a substitute gift is created in the surviving descendants of any deceased devisee; or

        (a)   The property to which the devisees would have been entitled had all of them survived the testator passes to the surviving devisees and the surviving descendants of the deceased devisees.

        (b)   Each surviving devisee takes the share to which he would have been entitled had the deceased devisees survived the testator.

        (c)   Each deceased devisee's surviving descendants who are substituted for the deceased devisee take by representation the share to which the deceased devisee would have been entitled had the deceased devisee survived the testator.

        (d)   A "deceased devisee" means a class member who failed to survive the testator and left one or more surviving descendants.

     (3)   in any other case, if the devise that is not part of the residuary estate fails or is void because the beneficiary fails to survive the testator, it is contrary to law, it is otherwise incapable of taking effect, it was revoked by the testator, it is not disposed of, or it is released or disclaimed by the beneficiary, the devise will be included in the residuary clause contained in the will.

        (a)   If a devise or gift fails as described above, and is included in the residuary clause in the will, it will pass to the other residuary devisees or legatees in proportion to their respective interests in the residue.

3. **Class Gifts**

   a.   A class gift exists when the testator makes a gift to a number of persons as a group, and the size of the group may either increase or decrease in the future.

    b.   A much-litigated question is whether mere words of survivorship—such as in a devise "to my daughter, A, if A survives me" or "to my surviving children"—automatically defeat the anti-lapse statute. The very fact that the question is litigated so frequently is itself proof that the use of mere words of survivorship is far from foolproof. The UPC expressly adopts the position that mere words of survivorship do not—by themselves, in the absence of additional evidence—lead to automatic defeat of the anti-lapse statute [UPC §§ 2-603(b)(3); 2-603, cmt.].

    c.   A person who would otherwise be a member of a class is not included if he died before the will was executed.

       (1)   However, if such a person dies after the execution of the will, but before the testator dies, the statute applies. In other words, there is a presumption that the testator intended the class to consist of the individuals who were alive on the date of the execution of his will [UPC § 2-603].

          EXAMPLE: T has three daughters, A, B, and C. A dies in 1977 leaving issue. T executes a will in 1978, leaving his entire estate "to my daughters." T dies in 1980. The disposition lapses with regard to A and A's issue will receive nothing. B and C will split the entire estate.

       (2)   However, though contrary to some decisions, it seems likely that the testator would want the descendants of a person included, for example, in a class term but dead when the will is made to be treated like the descendants of another member of the class who was alive at the time the will was executed but who dies before the testator. [UPC § 2-603, cmt].

          EXAMPLE: T has three daughters, A, B, and C. A dies in 1977, leaving issue. T executes a will in 1978, leaving his entire estate "to my daughters." B dies in 1979, leaving issue. T dies in 1980. While the courts may rule either way, the code indicates a preference that both A's and B's descendants would split the estate along with C *per stirpes* rather than having the gift lapse for A and split between B's issues and C *per stirpes*.

IX. REVOCATION AND REVIVAL OF WILLS

A. Methods of Revocation

1. Under the UPC, wills may be revoked by [UPC § 2-507(a)]:

    a. performing a revocatory act on the will, if the testator performed the act with the intent and purpose of revoking the will, or if another individual performed the act in the testator's conscious presence and by the testator's direction;

    (1) A **revocatory act on the will** includes burning, tearing, canceling, obliterating, or destroying the will or any part of it, whether or not the burn, tear, or cancellation touched any of the words on the will [UPC § 2-507(a)(2)].

    (a) An insignificant act, such as a small tear or burn is sufficient, as long as the evidence establishes that the testator performed the act with the intent to revoke [Restatement (Third) of Prop.: Wills § 4.1, cmt. g].

    (2) **Cancellation** encompasses acts such as crossing out or marking through the will or part of it or writing words on the will such as "canceled" or "null and void" [Id.].

    (a) Some courts have required words of cancellation to touch the words on the will.

    (b) The better approach, adopted by the UPC and the Restatement, is that words written on another document (rather than on the will itself) cannot serve as a revocation by cancellation. Words written on the will, whether they touch the words on the will or not, can be a revocation by cancellation. Thus, a revocatory act must be performed on the will. Performing the act on another document or on an unexecuted copy of the will is insufficient [Restatement (Third) of Prop.: Wills § 4.1, cmt. f].

    (3) By substantial authority, it is further held that removal of the testator's signature by drawing a line through it, erasing or obliterating it, tearing or cutting it out of the document, or removing the entire signature page constitutes a sufficient revocatory act to revoke the entire will [UPC § 2-507, cmt.].

    (4) If the testator does not perform the revocatory act, but directs another to perform the act, the act is a sufficient revocatory act if the other individual performs it in the testator's conscious presence. The act need not be performed in the testator's line of sight [Id.].

    EXAMPLE: A called her attorney, B, and told him to immediately destroy her will. He did so while she was on the line. The attempted revocation is invalid.

    (5) To effect a revocation, a revocatory act must be accompanied by revocatory intent. Determining whether a revocatory act was

accompanied by revocatory intent may involve exploration of extrinsic evidence, including the testator's statement as to intent [Id.].

(6) The UPC specifically permits partial revocation [Id.].

b. executing a subsequent will that revokes the previous will or part expressly or by inconsistency; or

(1) A will, duly executed and proved, that contains an express clause of revocation revokes all former wills.

(2) If a subsequent will does not expressly revoke a previous will, the execution of the subsequent will wholly revokes the previous will by inconsistency if the testator intended the subsequent will to replace, rather than supplement, the previous will [UPC § 2-507(b)].

(3) The testator is presumed to have intended a subsequent will to replace, rather than supplement, a previous will if the subsequent will makes a complete disposition of the testator's estate. If this presumption arises and is not rebutted by clear and convincing evidence, the previous will is revoked; only the subsequent will is operative on the testator's death [UPC § 2-507(c)].

(4) The testator is presumed to have intended a subsequent will to supplement, rather than replace, a previous will if the subsequent will does not make a complete disposition of the testator's estate. If this presumption arises and is not rebutted by clear and convincing evidence, the subsequent will revokes the previous will only to the extent the subsequent will is inconsistent with the previous will; each will is fully operative on the testator's death to the extent they are not inconsistent [UPC § 2-507(d)].

c. operation of law.

(1) If the testator is divorced after making a will, all provisions of the will in favor of or relating to the spouse so divorced become ineffective for all purposes, unless it is apparent in the will that the provisions were intended to survive the divorce [UPC § 2-804(b)].

(a) Even a provision conferring a power of appointment on the former spouse or on a relative of the former spouse, or nominating the former spouse or relative of the former spouse to serve in any fiduciary or representative capacity, including a personal representative, executor, trustee, conservator, agent, or guardian, is nullified by this section [UPC § 2-804(b)(1)].

(2) If a testator's surviving spouse married the testator after he executed his will, the surviving spouse is entitled to receive, as an intestate share, no less than the value of the share she would have received if the testator had died intestate. The surviving spouse's share comes from that portion of the testator's estate, if any, that is neither devised to a child of the testator who was born before the testator married the surviving spouse and who is not

a child of the surviving spouse nor is devised to a descendant of such a child, unless [UPC § 2-301(a)]:

(a) it appears from the will or other evidence that the will was made in contemplation of the testator's marriage to the surviving spouse;

(b) the will expresses the intention that it is to be effective notwithstanding any subsequent marriage; or

(c) the testator provided for the spouse by transfer outside the will, and the intent that the transfer be in lieu of a testamentary provision is shown by the testator's statements or is reasonably inferred from the amount of the transfer or other evidence.

(3) In satisfying the surviving spouse's share, devises made by the will to the surviving spouse, if any, are applied first, and other devises abate, other than a devise to a child of the testator who was born before the testator married the surviving spouse and who is not a child of the surviving spouse or a devise to a descendant of such a child [UPC § 2-301(b)].

B. Dependent Relative Revocation

1. Frequently, a testator revokes an old will with the intention that a newly executed will shall replace it [UPC § 2-507].

   a. If the new will is not made or is invalid, some jurisdictions will admit the revoked will to probate on the theory that the testator did not intend the revocation to occur unless the new will's provisions should take effect; that is, that the revocation occurred through a mistake of law or fact by the testator.

2. The doctrine of **dependent relative revocation** is the law of second best, i.e., its application does not produce the result the testator actually intended, but is designed to come as close as possible to that intent [UPC § 2-507, cmt.].

3. Dependent relative revocation has been applied only where there is:

   a. a defective execution of a subsequent will or codicil; or

   b. an intrinsic defect in a subsequent will or codicil.

4. The doctrine is not favored and is rarely applied by courts.

   a. If it is applied by the courts, it is used as a rule of testamentary construction, in aid of ascertaining the testator's intent.

5. A precondition to the application of dependent relative revocation is, or should be, good evidence of the testator's actual intention; without that, the court has no basis for determining which of several outcomes comes the closest to that actual intention [UPC § 2-507, cmt.].

6. Under the UPC, each court is free to apply its own doctrine of dependent relative revocation. The doctrine, however, is less often necessary under the revised provisions of UPC. Instead, when there is good evidence of the

testator's actual intention, the revised provisions of the UPC usually facilitate the effectuation of the result the testator actually intended [Id.].

a. If, for example, the testator revokes a second will for the purpose of reviving a former will, the evidence necessary to establish the testator's intent to revive the former will should be sufficient under Section 2-509 to effect a revival of the former will, making the application of dependent relative revocation as to the second will unnecessary.

b. If the testator revokes a will in conjunction with an effort to execute a new will, the evidence necessary to establish the testator's intention that the new will be valid should, in most cases, be sufficient under Section 2-503 to give effect to the new will, making the application of dependent relative revocation as to the old will unnecessary.

c. If the testator crosses out parts of a will or dispositive provision in conjunction with an effort to alter the will's terms, the evidence necessary to establish the testator's intention that the altered terms be valid should be sufficient under Section 2-503 to give effect to the will as altered, making dependent relative revocation as to the crossed-out parts unnecessary.

7. Where the revoking instrument is in itself valid and operative, but the subsequent disposition fails for some extrinsic reason (such as incapacity of the devisee to take), the revocation remains effective.

C. Revival of Revoked Wills

1. The UPC provides that if, after the making of a will, the testator executes a later will that expressly or impliedly revokes the earlier will, the revocation of that later will does not revive the earlier will. The previous will is revived only if it is evident from the circumstances of the revocation of the subsequent will or from the testator's contemporary or subsequent declarations that the testator intended the previous will to take effect as executed [UPC § 2-509(a)].

2. Alternatively, revival can be accomplished if, after the revocation of the later will, the earlier will is re-executed.

X. CONTRACTS TO MAKE A WILL AND JOINT OR MUTUAL WILLS

A. Contracts to Make a Will

1. The UPC will uphold as valid a contract to dispose of by will all or part of a person's property, whether real or personal.

   a. The contract must exhibit the general contractual requisites of consideration, contractual intent, and definiteness of terms.

2. A contract to make a will or devise, not to revoke a will or devise, or to die intestate may be established only by [UPC § 2-514]:

   a. provisions of the decedent's will stating material provisions of the contract;

   b. an express reference in the decedent's will to a contract and extrinsic evidence proving the terms of the contract; or

   c. a writing signed by the decedent evidencing the contract.

3. The Statute of Frauds requires that an agreement to will real estate be in writing.

   a. The Statute can be satisfied, however, if the promisee relies on an oral promise or contract to leave him certain real estate by will, if the will or another writing is connected with and supports the oral contract.

B. Joint or Mutual Wills

1. In many states, when two persons execute a single document as their joint will, this gives rise to a presumption that the parties had contracted not to revoke the will except by consent of both. Under the UPC, however, the execution of a joint will or mutual will does not create a presumption of a contract not to revoke the will [Id.].

2. Both joint and mutual wills are revocable by either party.

   a. However, contracts for the execution of irrevocable mutual wills (separate wills with reciprocal provisions) are valid and enforceable when properly proved.

3. If the agreement is valid and enforceable and the will is inconsistent, the probate of the will is unaffected; the contract affects distribution only and is enforceable by an action for breach.

XI. PROBATE OF WILLS

A. In General

1. **Probate** is the process by which a will is established as the valid last will of a decedent.

2. A **formal testacy proceeding** is litigation to determine whether a decedent left a valid will [UPC § 3-401].

3. Venue for the proceeding is [UPC § 3-201(a)]:

   a. in the county where the decedent had his domicile at the time of his death; or

   b. if the decedent was not domiciled in the state, in any county where property of the decedent was located at the time of his death.

B. Proof of Wills

1. **Burden of Proof**

   a. The burden of proving that a will was duly executed is always on the person offering the will for probate. Thus, proponents of a will have the burden of establishing *prima facie* proof of due execution in all cases [UPC § 3-407].

   b. Proof of a will requires that it be established that the signature appearing on the will is that of the testator. There is no requirement that the testator's signature be at the end of the will [UPC § 2-502, cmt.].

      EXAMPLE: If the testator writes his name in the body of the will and intends it to be his signature, the statute is satisfied.

   c. If the will is witnessed but not notarized or self-proved, the testimony of at least one of the attesting witnesses is required to establish proper execution if the witness is within the state, competent, and able to testify. Proper execution may be established by other evidence, including an affidavit of an attesting witness. An attestation clause that is signed by the attesting witnesses raises a rebuttable presumption that the events recited in the clause occurred [UPC § 3-406(3)].

   d. If the will is notarized but not self-proved, there is a rebuttable presumption that the will satisfies the requirements for execution upon filing the will [UPC § 3-406(2)].

2. **Self-Proving Affidavit**

   a. Most probate proceedings are uncontested. To avoid the inconvenience of calling witnesses and to simplify proof of wills in such cases, affidavits of witnesses may be filed in uncontested cases in lieu of their testimony.

   b. If the will is self-proved, the will satisfies the requirements for execution without the testimony of any attesting witness upon filing of the will, the acknowledgment, and affidavits, unless there is evidence of fraud or forgery affecting the acknowledgment or affidavit [UPC § 3-406(1)].

   c. The affidavits can be executed together with the will; they set forth facts sufficient to establish due execution of the will and the capacity of the testator [UPC § 2-504].

3. **Presumptions and Burden of Proof**

    a. Although proof of a will does not require any representation of testamentary capacity from the witnesses, upon proof of the testator's execution of the will, a presumption of testamentary capacity arises and the burden of proof shifts to the contestant to overcome the presumption by clear and compelling evidence [UPC § 3-407].

    b. Contestants of a will have the burden of establishing lack of testamentary intent or capacity, undue influence, fraud, duress, mistake, or revocation [Id.].

C. Proof of Lost Wills

1. If a will is traced to the testator's possession and cannot be found after death, the law presumes that the testator destroyed the will with intent to revoke it [Restatement (Third) of Prop.: Wills § 4.1, cmt. j].

2. This presumption may be overcome by the proponents of a lost will.

3. If a will cannot be located after death but the trier of fact finds that it was not revoked, the will is entitled to probate if its due execution and contents can be proved [Restatement (Third) of Prop.: Wills § 4.1, cmt. k].

4. If the original will is neither in the possession of the court nor accompanies the petition for formal probate of the will, and no authenticated copy of a will probated in another jurisdiction accompanies the petition, the petition must state the contents of the will and indicate that it is lost, destroyed, or otherwise unavailable [UPC § 3-402(a)].

    a. Commonly in such cases, the will is proved by evidence of a law-office or other copy, or from the drafter's notes and recollection. If its full contents cannot be proved, the will is entitled to probate to the extent that its contents can be proved [Restatement (Third) of Prop.: Wills § 4.1, cmt. k].

D. Appointments of Personal Representative

1. Persons who are not disqualified have priority for appointment as the estate's personal representative in the following order [UPC 3-203]:

    a. the person named as personal representative in a will;

    b. the surviving spouse of the decedent who is a devisee of the decedent;

    c. other devisees of the decedent;

    d. the surviving spouse of the decedent;

    e. other heirs of the decedent;

    f. 45 days after the death of the decedent, any creditor.

2. An objection to an appointment must be made in formal proceedings [Id.].

3. Persons under the age of 21 and persons whom the court finds unsuitable in formal proceedings are not qualified to serve as the personal representative [Id.].

XII. WILL CONTESTS

A. **In General**

1. In a **will contest**, a person interested in the distribution of the estate objects to the admission of the will to probate on the grounds that the will is invalid for some reason.

2. If the contesting party is successful in preventing the will from being admitted and there is no other will in effect, the estate will be distributed as if the creator of the will died intestate.

3. If a valid will that has not been revoked exists, the fact that another or later will was invalid will not prevent the valid will from being admitted to probate.

B. **Grounds for Contesting a Will**

1. The grounds for contest of a properly executed will are [UPC § 3-407]:

    a. lack of testamentary capacity;

    b. undue influence;

    c. mistake; and

    d. fraud.

2. **Lack of Testamentary Capacity**

    a. A testator must have testamentary capacity in order to make a valid will [UPC § 2-501].

    b. An adjudication of mental incompetence near the date of execution of the will does not necessarily prove the lack of testamentary capacity [Restatement (Third) of Prop.: Wills § 8.1, cmt. m].

        (1) In particular, an adjudication of mental incapacity to manage property does not conclusively establish that the individual subsequently lacked capacity to make, revoke, or amend a will or a revocable will substitute [Restatement (Third) of Prop.: Wills § 8.1, cmt. h].

            (a) Such an adjudication does, however, raise a rebuttable presumption that the protected person lacked the requisite capacity, shifting the burden of proof to the proponent to show that the person possessed the requisite capacity at the time of execution of the will [Id.].

        (2) A person who is mentally incapacitated part of the time but who has lucid intervals during which he meets the standard for mental capacity can make a valid will, provided such will is made during a lucid interval [Rest. 8.1, cmt. m].

            (a) However, a purported will by such a person is void, not voidable, if the person lacked the capacity necessary for making a will at the time of execution of the will [Restatement (Third) of Prop.: Wills § 8.1, cmt. h].

    c. Evidence that the decedent was incompetent in handling business affairs is insufficient to show lack of testamentary capacity; less capacity is needed to make a will than is needed to transact business.

EXAMPLE: A person may be under guardianship and legally incapable of entering into any contract or other lifetime dealing but may still be able to write a valid will, provided that he meets the mental capacity requirements.

d. An **insane delusion** is defined as a mere figment of the imagination or a belief that is so against the evidence and reason that it must be the product of derangement [Restatement (Third) of Prop.: Wills § 8.1, cmt. s].

EXAMPLE: A cut off his wife, B, from her statutory share in the belief that she was having an extramarital affair, despite the fact she had been living in isolation in a nursing home for five years.

  (1) A belief resulting from a process of reasoning from existing facts is not an insane delusion, even though the reasoning is imperfect or the conclusion illogical [Id.].

  (2) Mere eccentricity does not constitute an insane delusion [Id.]. Similarly, a suspicion with some basis in fact is not an insane delusion.

  (3) A person who suffers from an insane delusion is not necessarily deprived of capacity to make a donative transfer. A particular donative transfer is invalid, however, to the extent that it was the product of an insane delusion [Id.].

    (a) Thus, a will is invalid if the insane delusion caused the decedent to make his will in a manner entirely different from what he would have if the insane delusion did not exist.

  (4) Disinheriting a child or relative does not in itself invalidate a will, disclose a lack of testamentary capacity, or establish an insane delusion, even if the prejudice against the relative is an unexplained or violent dislike.

  (5) The burden of proving that the testator had sufficient mental capacity to make the will is on the proponent of the will [Restatement (Third) of Prop.: Wills § 8.1, cmt. h].

3. **Undue Influence**

a. The doctrine of **undue influence** protects against overreaching by a wrongdoer seeking to take unfair advantage of a donor who is susceptible to such wrongdoing on account of the donor's age, inexperience, dependence, physical or mental weakness, or other factor [Restatement (Third) of Prop.: Wills § 8.3, cmt. e].

b. Undue influence is sufficient to void a will if the wrongdoer exerted such influence over the donor that it overcame the donor's free will and caused the donor to make a donative transfer that the donor would not otherwise have made [Restatement (Third) of Prop.: Wills § 8.3(b)].

  (1) The alleged wrongdoer need not be present when the donative document was executed in order to exert undue influence [Restatement (Third) of Prop.: Wills § 8.3, cmt. e].

c. In order to show undue influence as grounds for refusing probate of a will, the party alleging undue influence must show that some influence or power subverted the intent of the testator at the time of execution of the will and that, except for such influence, the testator would not have executed this will [UPC § 3-407].

    (1)   Direct evidence of the wrongdoer's conduct and the donor's subservience is rarely available to establish the actual exertion of undue influence [Restatement (Third) of Prop.: Wills § 8.3, cmt. e].

    (2)   In the absence of direct evidence of undue influence, circumstantial evidence is sufficient to raise an inference of undue influence if the contestant proves that [Id.]:

        (a) the donor was susceptible to undue influence;

        (b) the alleged wrongdoer had an opportunity to exert undue influence;

        (c) the alleged wrongdoer had a disposition to exert undue influence; and

        (d) there was a result appearing to be the effect of the undue influence.

    d.   Ordinarily, only the donative transfer that was procured by undue influence is invalid. Thus, if a devise in a will was procured by undue influence, only that devise, not the entire will, is ordinarily invalid. The court may, however, hold the entire will invalid if it determines that complete invalidity would better carry out the testator's intent [Restatement (Third) of Prop.: Wills § 8.3, cmt. d].

    e.   A presumption of undue influence arises if the alleged wrongdoer was in a confidential relationship with the donor and there were suspicious circumstances surrounding the preparation, formulation, or execution of the will.

    (1)   The term **confidential relationship** embraces three sometimes distinct relationships [Restatement (Third) of Prop.: Wills § 8.3, cmt. g].

        (a) A **fiduciary relationship** is one in which the confidential relationship arises from a settled category of fiduciary obligation.

        (b) In demonstrating a **reliant relationship**, the contestant must establish that there was a relationship based on special trust and confidence, that the donor was accustomed to being guided by the judgment or advice of the alleged wrongdoer, or that the donor was justified in placing confidence in the belief that the alleged wrongdoer would act in the interest of the donor.

        (c) In establishing a **dominant-subservient relationship**, the contestant must show that the donor was subservient to the alleged wrongdoer's dominant influence.

    (2)   The presumption is strengthened if the beneficiary of the alleged wrongdoing was not a natural object of the testator's bounty [Restatement (Third) of Prop.: Wills § 8.3, cmt. f].

    (3)   The existence of a confidential relationship is not sufficient to raise a presumption of undue influence. There must also be suspicious circumstances surrounding the preparation, execution,

or formulation of the will raising an inference of an abuse of the confidential relationship between the alleged wrongdoer and the donor [Restatement (Third) of Prop.: Wills § 8.3, cmt. h].

    (a) In evaluating whether suspicious circumstances are present, all relevant factors may be considered, including [Id.]:

        1) the extent to which the donor was in a weakened condition physically, mentally, or both, and therefore susceptible to undue influence;

        2) the extent to which the alleged wrongdoer participated in the preparation or procurement of the will;

        3) whether the donor received independent advice from an attorney or from other competent and disinterested advisors in preparing the will;

        4) whether the will was prepared in secrecy or in haste;

        5) whether the donor's attitude toward others had changed by reason of his relationship with the alleged wrongdoer;

        6) whether there is a decided discrepancy between new and previous wills of the donor;

        7) whether there was a continuity of purpose running through former wills indicating a settled intent in the disposition of his property; and

        8) whether the disposition of the property is such that a reasonable person would regard it as unnatural, unjust, or unfair.

  (4) If these factors are shown by clear and convincing evidence, the burden of proof returns to the proponent of the will to show that the gift or bequest was not the product of undue influence [UPC § 3-407].

  (5) The presumption justifies a judgment for the contestant as a matter of law only if the proponent does not come forward with evidence to rebut the presumption [Restatement (Third) of Prop.: Wills § 8.3, cmt. f].

  f. A substantial devise by will to a person who is one of the witnesses to the execution of the will is itself a suspicious circumstance, and the devise might be challenged on grounds of undue influence [UPC § 2-505, cmt.].

  g. The fact that a parent does not leave property to his children without disclosing his reasons for disinheriting them does not require a finding of undue influence.

  h. A presumption of undue influence is raised, regardless of the mental condition of the testator, where an attorney drafts a will under which he is a beneficiary [Restatement (Third) of Prop.: Wills § 8.3, cmt. n].

4. **Mistake**

  a. An innocent or negligent misrepresentation regarding a material fact can lead the donor to make a donative transfer that the donor would not otherwise have made. In such a case, the donative transfer has been induced by mistake, and should be remedied accordingly [Restatement (Third) of Prop.: Wills § 8.3, cmt. k].

    (1)   Mistake may be distinguished from fraud by the lack of intent to deceive the testator.

b.   The following rules apply only to innocent mistakes that may have caused the testator to include certain provisions in his will, or that may have misled him as to the contents of his will.

c.   **Mistake in the inducement** is a mistake as to facts outside the will that induced the testator to dispose of his property in a certain manner.

    EXAMPLE: A mistake as to the value of one's property, a mistake as to the amount of loans and advancements made to the beneficiaries, or a mistake about whether the natural object of one's bounty is living or dead are all examples of mistakes in the inducement.

    (1)   Generally, provisions of a will cannot be set aside for mistakes in the inducement.

    (2)   The fact that the testator wished to divide his property equally among his children, but failed to achieve that effect because of a mistake on his part about the value of his property, is typically not, in the absence of fraud, incapacity, or undue influence, sufficient to set aside the provisions of the will.

    (3)   However, under the UPC, the court may reform the terms of a governing instrument, even if unambiguous, to conform the terms to the transferor's intention if it is proved by clear and convincing evidence that the transferor's intent and the terms of the governing instrument were affected by a mistake of fact or law, whether in expression or inducement [UPC § 2-805].

d.   **Mistake in the factum** relates to a mistake in the will itself.

    (1)   The general rule is that the court will not reform a will for mistake in the factum (e.g., an erroneous identification of a beneficiary). However, if the mistake goes to the testator's testamentary capacity, the will may be held invalid.

    EXAMPLE: If the testator signed a document believing the document was something other than a will (e.g., a contract to buy peanuts), the will may be held invalid for lack of testamentary capacity.

    (2)   In the alternative, the court may reform the terms of a will, even if unambiguous, to conform the terms to the transferor's intention if it is proved by clear and convincing evidence that the transferor's intent and the terms of the governing instrument were affected by a mistake of fact or law [Id.].

e.   The burden of proof of a mistake in a will is on the party alleging the mistake.

5.   **Fraud**

a.   **Fraud in the inducement** is established upon proof that a beneficiary made a knowingly false representation to the testator for the purpose of inducing the testator to draw a will in his favor, and that the testator made a different will than he would have made in the absence of the representation.

EXAMPLE: X induces Y to marry him by representing that he is single, when in fact X is already married. This is fraud in the inducement.

    b.   **Fraud in the execution** is fraud as to the very nature of an instrument or its contents.

        EXAMPLE: An attorney deceives a testator who is blind or hard of hearing as to the contents of a will.

    c.   In both of the above cases, the will, or the fraudulently induced part of it, will be denied probate.

        (1)   If fraud is alleged with respect to only a part of the will, the court may reject that part and admit the rest to probate. The legacy that is void due to fraud then falls into the residue, or if there is no residuary clause, passes by intestacy.

        (2)   If the entire will is tainted, all the property will pass by intestacy.

    d.   Where, however, there is a fraudulent interference with the revocation of a will, the probate court cannot refuse to probate a will that has not been revoked in the statutory form; and if there is a fraudulent interference with the making of a will, the probate court cannot make a will for the testator. In both of these situations, the appropriate remedy is a constructive trust.

    e.   The burden of proving fraud is on the party alleging fraud.

        (1)   To invalidate a will, a party must show that the contested will was the fruit of the fraud, i.e., that the dispositions in the will were brought about by intentional misrepresentation.

C. Ambiguity

    1.   An **ambiguity** in a donative document is an uncertainty in meaning that is revealed by the text or by extrinsic evidence other than direct evidence of intention contradicting the plain meaning of the text [Restatement (Third) of Prop.: Wills § 11.1].

    2.   Ambiguities are resolved by construing the text of the will in accordance with the donor's intention, to the extent that the donor's intention is established by a preponderance of the evidence [Restatement (Third) of Prop.: Wills § 11.2(a)].

    3.   Because the primary objective of construction is to give effect to the donor's intention, extrinsic evidence relevant to the donor's intention may be considered along with the text of the document in seeking to determine the donor's intention [Restatement (Third) of Prop.: Wills § 11.2, cmt. b].

    4.   Ambiguities in a will are either patent or latent.

    a.   **Patent ambiguities** appear on the face of the instrument [Restatement (Third) of Prop.: Wills § 11.1, cmt. b].

        EXAMPLE: Testator A purports to leave "one-thirdquarter of my estate" to each of threefour designated charities.

b. **Latent ambiguities** refer to ambiguities arising when language of the will, otherwise clear, is applied to the thing given or the person benefited under the will, and some extrinsic fact necessitates interpretation or choice among two or more possible meanings [Restatement (Third) of Prop.: Wills § 11.1, cmt. c].

EXAMPLE: Testator A leaves her estate to "my daughter B, who lives in New York." B, however, lives in Boston. A's daughter C, otherwise omitted from the will, lives in New York. Which daughter is A referring to?

(1) Where the ambiguity is latent, extrinsic evidence is admissible to resolve the ambiguity [Id.].

(a) Such evidence includes information relating to the circumstances surrounding the execution of the document. Information relating to the testator's circumstances at death must also be considered in order to determine the property available for distribution and the persons who are living at the testator's death or who survive the testator by a prescribed period of time [Id.].

(2) In the interpretation of a will, however, the testator's oral statement of his intentions is inadmissible to prove his intentions because the testamentary wishes of a testator must be in writing.

c. Once an ambiguity, patent or latent, is established, both direct and circumstantial evidence of the donor's intention may be considered in resolving the ambiguity in accordance with the donor's intention [Restatement (Third) of Prop.: Wills § 11.2, cmt. d].

D. **Standing to Object to Probate or Contest the Will**

1. A formal testacy proceeding is litigation to determine whether a decedent left a valid will [UPC § 3-401]. The validity of a probated will can be set aside only on an appeal from its probate.

2. The UPC allows an **interested person** to contest a will. The statute's definition of such a person, however, is rather vague [UPC §1-201(23)]. Thus, case law generally holds that standing to contest a will requires that the party have a pecuniary interest that is directly and adversely affected by a judgment of the validity of the will. The party contesting the will must stand to gain financially.

a. Persons who cannot take under the intestacy statute if the will is declared invalid have no standing to contest the will, unless they can show another will under which they would take or a contract to make a will in their favor.

3. Generally, no informal probate or formal testacy proceeding may be commenced more than three years after the decedent's death. However, a proceeding to contest an informally probated will, and to secure appointment of the person with legal priority for appointment in the event the contest is successful, may be commenced within the later of 12 months from the informal probate or three years from the decedent's death [UPC § 3-108(a)(3)].

E. **Restrictions on Testamentary Power**

1. In certain circumstances, apart from alienation of property away from a spouse contrary to elective share laws, courts will hold unenforceable efforts by the decedent to block potential will challenges or make benefits under a will subject to an intrusive condition.

2. *In Terrorem* **Clauses (No-Contest Clauses)**

    a. Generally, an *in terrorem* **clause** in a will attempts to disqualify anyone contesting the will from taking under it.

    b. Most states hold that the clause is ineffectual if the person affected had reasonable cause to contest the will.

    c. Under the UPC, a provision in a will purporting to penalize an interested person for contesting the will or instituting other proceedings relating to the estate is unenforceable if probable cause exists for instituting such proceedings [UPC § 2-517].

    d. An *in terrorem* clause will be enforceable if the will contest is unsuccessful and no probable cause existed.

3. **Provisions Restraining Marriage or Religion**

    a. Will provisions attempting to condition a bequest on a beneficiary's future behavior are often said to be attempted instances of **dead-hand control**. Courts will refuse to enforce these if they are found to be overly intrusive or disruptive to living persons contrary to public policy.

    b. If a testator's purpose in imposing a condition to a legacy is to induce a future separation or divorce of a married couple, the condition will be void as against public policy and the legacy will take effect.

    c. However, if the will merely provides for the contingency of divorce and does not express an intent to bring it about, then the provision may be held valid.

    d. A condition requiring adherence to a specific religion is void as against public policy.

F. **Universal Succession**

1. The Uniform Probate Code permits the heirs of an intestate or residuary devisees of a testator to accept the estate assets without administration by assuming responsibility for discharging those obligations that normally would be discharged by the personal representative [UPC § 3-312, cmt.].

2. The heirs of an intestate decedent or the residuary devisees under a will, excluding minors and incapacitated, protected, or unascertained persons, may become universal successors to the decedent's estate by assuming personal liability for taxes, debts of the decedent, claims against the decedent or the estate, and distributions due other heirs, devisees, and persons entitled to property of the decedent [UPC § 3-312].

3. Universal succession is favored because it helps to avoid will contests.

4. An application to become universal successors by the heirs of an intestate or the residuary devisees under a will must be signed and verified by each applicant [UPC § 3-313].

XIII. NON-TESTAMENTARY TRANSFERS

A. In General

1. Wills and intestacy only govern assets that pass through a decedent's probate estate. There are, however, a variety of ways to transmit property during life that will result in the recipient receiving title or possession at the transferor's death.

2. Oftentimes, heirs or will beneficiaries challenge the efficacy of these transfers with an eye toward making them a part of the probate estate, and thereby acquiring rights to them.

B. Gifts

1. **Gifts** are *inter vivos* transfers made during life that require donative intent, delivery, and acceptance by the donee.

    a. A transfer in which the donor does not relinquish dominion and control lacks present donative intent and can be attacked as a sham transaction that ought not to be given effect. If the challenge is successful, the subject of the gift will become an asset of the decedent's estate.

    b. Effective delivery is essential to the completion of a gift.

        (1) If the transfer of title involves an agent, the gift is completed only after the donor's agent has delivered the subject of the gift. Delivery to the donee's agent is effective to complete the gift.

    c. Usually acceptance by the donee is presumed, but it still must occur in order for the gift to be complete.

2. Completed gifts are irrevocable unless there has been some agreement to the contrary between the donor and donee. The existence of such an agreement could call into question:

    a. whether was there was present donative intent when the gift was made; and

    b. the underlying validity of the gift.

3. Transfers of real estate, including gifts, must be made by delivery of a properly executed deed.

    a. A deed that is signed by the grantor and attested to by two or more credible witnesses is not a will and cannot serve to transfer title at death. The deed must be delivered by the grantor or the grantor's agent during the grantor's life in order to convey title.

    b. A deed that creates a future interest in a grantee conveys title, but not possession, upon delivery.

4. A **gift *causa mortis*** is an *inter vivos* gift made with the understanding that the donee takes possession upon delivery, but does not acquire title unless the donor dies of a feared imminent threat of death.

    a. Gifts *causa mortis* require delivery and that the donor dies from an imminently feared death.

(1) The imminent fear must relate to some dangerous impending matter, not just a normal fear of death.

EXAMPLE: D gives X a clock and says that X can keep it if D dies as a result of his upcoming heart surgery. If D dies from complications of the surgery, X will keep the gift. If D recovers from the operation but dies in an accident on the way home from the hospital, X will have to return the clock to D's estate because D did not die from the thing he feared. If D survives the operation, he has the option of requesting the return of the clock from X (and X must comply with the request) or allowing X to keep the clock, which effectively makes a completed *inter vivos* gift at that time.

C. Joint Tenancy

1. As a general rule, surviving joint tenants become the full owners of the joint tenancy property because the deceased tenant's interest is deemed to disappear upon his death.

   a. When a grantor transfers property into joint tenancy with another person, there is a presumption that the grantor has made a gift to that person.

2. Unlike traditional joint tenancies, joint bank accounts are governed by the agreement the tenants make with the bank.

   a. Unless otherwise provided, joint account tenants have the right to withdraw the full amount of the funds on deposit without seeking permission from or accounting to the other tenant(s).

3. **Convenience accounts** usually are joint accounts in which all of the funds have been supplied by one tenant with the other tenant being put on the account to access funds on behalf of the contributing tenant.

   a. Convenience accounts do not give survivorship rights to the noncontributing tenant because there was no present donative intent to make a gift at the time the account was established.

   b. Because convenience accounts are usually joint accounts, the person (normally the deceased tenant's heir, will beneficiary, or a representative thereof) claiming a convenience account must overcome the presumption of gift raised by the creation of a joint tenancy.

D. Pay-on-Death Registrations

1. **Payable-on-death accounts** are bank accounts in which a person remains the owner during his life with complete control over the funds on deposit, and the funds in the account pass directly to a named beneficiary or beneficiaries at the owner's death.

   a. The beneficiary does not have any right, title, or interest in the account until the owner dies.

   b. The owner has the unfettered right to cancel the account, withdraw all or part of the funds, or change its beneficiary.

    c.   If there are two or more account owners, they are treated as joint tenants, and upon the death of one, the survivor(s) continue as the owner(s). The beneficiary does not take any interest in the account until all of the owners have died.

    d.   If there is more than one owner, any owner can cancel, fully or partially withdraw the funds from, or change the beneficiary of the account without the consent of the other owner(s).

    e.   If there is more than one beneficiary, the beneficiaries are tenants in common and not joint tenants.

2.   **Pay-on-death registrations** can be established for brokerage accounts.

    a.   These are called transfer-on-death ("TOD") security registrations.

    b.   The rules for TOD security registrations are the same as those for pay-on-death bank accounts.

    c.   Individual stock certificates can be registered in transfer-on-death form, with title to the stock passing directly to the named beneficiary or beneficiaries without passing through probate.

    <u>**EXAMPLE:**</u> T has a will that provides, "I give all the stock I own at my death to X." T has 500 shares of Apple stock that is endorsed with a TOD security registration in favor of B. The Apple stock will pass directly to B and not through the will to X.

E. Power of Attorney

1.   A **power of attorney** is a relationship wherein the principal appoints an agent to act on his behalf.

    a.   The power gives the agent the authority to deal with the principal's property and execute business transactions on behalf of the principal during the latter's life.

2.   An agent is a fiduciary. As such, the agent has a duty of loyalty and care to the principal.

    a.   An agent cannot self-deal with the principal's property.

    b.   There is a presumption of fraud attached to a transfer by a fiduciary for his own benefit.

3.   The agent has the obligation to maintain accurate records of the transactions executed on behalf of his principal.

4.   A power of attorney can become effective upon its creation, or at some future time chosen by the principal.

5.   Often a power of attorney will become effective upon the principal's loss of mental capacity or otherwise becoming disabled. Such a power is called a **springing power of attorney**.

6.   The agency can be either durable or nondurable.

    a.   **Nondurable** means that the agency terminates upon the principal's incompetence.

    b.   **Durable** powers continue even during the principal's incapacity.

7.   A power of attorney terminates upon the death of the principal.